Protestant Church Growth in Korea

Protestant
Church
GROWTH
in KOREA

Dr. John T. Kim

Essence PUBLISHING

Belleville, Ontario, Canada

Protestant Church Growth in Korea

ISBN: 1-896400-05-1

Essence Publishing is a Christian Book Publisher dedicated to furthering the work of Christ through the written word. For more information, write: 103B Cannifton Road, Belleville, ON, Canada K8N 4V2. Phone: 1-800-238-6376. Fax: (613) 962-3055. Email: essence@intranet.on.ca

Printed in Canada
by

Essence
PUBLISHING

TABLE OF CONTENTS

TABLES

ACKNOWLEDGMENTS

This book is based on my dissertation for the Doctor of Philosophy degree in Religion and Missiology at the Free University, Amsterdam in the Netherlands. I have re-written and re-organized it and incorporated new research. It was my privilege to specialize in post-graduate studies in Religion and Missiology at the Free University in Amsterdam, the Netherlands. I wish to take this opportunity to express my gratitude to the various persons and institutions that have contributed to the progress of my studies and the completion of this book.

First of all, I am grateful to the faculty of Free University, who enriched my knowledge with vision and inspiration in the field of the theology of mission. I am particularly indebted to Professor Anton Wessels, my mentor and promoter, who taught me the methods of research with his profound insight in the field of Missiology. His consecrated personal Christian life also deeply influenced me and has left a lasting impression. I wish also to thank my academic advisors for this dissertation; my co-promotor, Professor R. Fernhout, and referent, Professor H. M. Vroom, and also Dr. J. Gort and Dr. H.C. Stoffels, for their constructive advice, supervision and criticism regarding its content and structure. To them, I owe more than words can express.

I would like to thank many Christian friends and institutions. First of all, I am indebted to the Christian Reformed Church in North America, Home Missions, and Calvin Theological Seminary for providing the tangible support and assistance which enabled me to do post-graduate study; Dr. Peter Borgdorff of the Christian Reformed Church, the Rev. John Rozeboom, the Rev. Alfred Mulder, Dr. Duane VanderBrug, the Rev. Peter Holwerda of Home Missions, Professors James De Jong, Robert Recker, Richard De Ridder, Harold Dekker and the late John Kromminga of Calvin Theological Seminary.

I also thank the congregations of the Korean American Christian Reformed Church and Calvin Korean American Christian Reformed Church in California, and Ill-shim Presbyterian Church in Korea for their generous financial assistance, which made it possible for me to complete my study at the Free University. Especially I also would like to mention the encouragement and financial support of my brother, Rev. Yun-shin Kim in Korea, and my mother and brothers-in-law, Duck-Joo Cho and Chul-ho Cho in California.

For brotherly love and encouragement offered me during my stay in Baambrugge, the Netherlands, I express my sincere gratitude to my brothers and sisters in Christ, Dr. and Mrs. Bastiaan Van Elderen, Mrs. Donna Gort, the Rev. Peter Smilder and the congregation of Gereformeerde Kerken of Baambrugge, the Rev. Olsen and the congregation of the American Protestant Church of the Hague. By them I and my family have been exceptionally favored with an abundance of Christian fellowship, encouragement, stimulation and comfort. They have shown us their brotherly love and have given much more than friendship to make our stay in Amsterdam a very pleasant one. It is, indeed, difficult to make formal expression of appreciation to them. Especially I would like to thank Professor Walraven and Mr. Olof of Leiden University for their generous guidance and assistance of research work at the library of University of Leiden, Leiden, the Netherlands.

I would like to thank my friends, Dr. John W. Cooper, Rev. Wilbert M. Van Dyk, Rev. Lawrence Lunceford, Rev. Robert Meyering and Mr. Daniel Copeland, who read my manuscripts and made comments and corrected my English. My sincere thanks to my esteemed friends, Dr. Roger Greenway and Dr. Peter Borgdorff, for their kindness in writing the forword and preface. Special thanks go to professors Henry De Moor and Harry Boonstra, who helped me translate my English summary into Dutch smenvatting. I also thank Mr. Myung-kyun Shin and James Jonker who took care of the computer work and the basic layout of this book with precision.

Above all, many thanks should go to my late godly mother in Korea who brought me up in the knowledge of Christ and for her unceasing prayer support by daily early morning prayer until she went into glory. My deepest gratitude is extended to my wife Sue, and to my four children, Hannah, Joseph, Sarah and Rebecca, for their sacrifice, love and prayers.

John T. Kim
Grand Rapids, Michigan

FOREWORD

I first met Dr. John T. Kim in 1978 when we were both involved in the ministry of Home Missions for the Christian Reformed Church. From the very beginning of our relationship, I have appreciated his commitment to the Lord, to ministry, to the principles of church growth, and to the Christian Reformed Church.

Dr. Kim is well qualified to offer his perspective on the issues and practice of church growth. He has been a practitioner, he has "walked the talk," and he has been used by the Lord to plant several congregations. Dr. Kim's academic work has focused primarily on Korean church growth throughout the world and he continues to teach from that material in his responsibilities at Calvin Theological Seminary.

Together Dr. Kim and I have ministered in various places throughout North America, and on a preaching mission in Korea as well. He has become my ear and my voice among th Korean membership in the Christian Reformed Church. Without fail, Dr. Kim's gifts have been received with appreciation, and I thank the Lord for his contributions to me and to the whole church. It is my sincere prayer that the reader will likewise benefit from Dr. Kim's ministry.

Dr. Peter Borgdorff
Executive Director of Ministries
Christian Reformed Church
Grand Rapids, Michigan

PREFACE

Korean Protestants have become the recognized masters of the "high technology" of numerical church growth, and Christian leaders around the world want to know how they do it. This book provides some surprising answers. It examines how Korean churches have multiplied in a particular cultural setting and it offers insights into contextualization which growth-driven missionaries and church leaders everywhere should consider.

The fact that Korean models of evangelism and church development are being copied in lands far from Korean shores gives global significance to Dr. Kim's research and writing. Those who copy Korean methods should be aware of the cultural setting in which Korean churches flourish and the pros and cons of how Korean Protestants have appropriated and adapted to shamanistic traditions.

Without a doubt, the Spirit of God has done a mighty work of grace among Korean people, and to God be all the glory for this. Not only has God raised up strong churches in South Korea, he has used the overseas dispersion of Koreans to multiply Christian congregations in widely scattered parts of the world, including certain Muslim countries where churches are not normally permitted. The potential of the Korean dispersion for the evangelization of the nations is great. It is something that some of us are watching with great interest and much prayer.

In addition, Korean Christian missionaries, sent and supported by Korean churches, are now working in dozens of countries. Korean missionary efforts extend from Eastern Europe to Africa, Latin America and Asia. Through the influence of Korean missionaries many of the special features of Korean Christianity are making an impact on churches in other lands. This makes it all the more important for Christian leaders to understand the underlying spiritual dynamics that make Korean Protestantism what it is.

In this book, John T. Kim offers fresh insights into the shamanistic context in which Korean Christian faith developed and the influence that shamanism continues to exert on Korean Protestant churches. This is an extremely important study, both to Korean Christians in helping them recognize aspects of their faith and practice which call for biblical evaluation, and to non-Koreans seeking to explain the explosive growth of Korean Christianity.

Perhaps even more importantly, Dr. Kim's analysis of shamanism and its effect on the growth of Christianity among Koreans will be helpful to pastors, missionaries and church leaders working in places where some form of shamanism constitutes the religious and cultural background of the people. As one who has taught, evangelized and pastored in both southern Asia and Latin America, and who has visited churches and mission stations in various parts of Africa, I can personally affirm that parallels are numerous between Korean shamanism and traditional spiritism in other countries. The missionary and pastoral challenges represented by shamanism cannot be exaggerated.

Dr. Kim's analysis of various attempts by Korean scholars to contextualize Christianity helps the reader to understand the complexity of the issues, to appreciate the attempts to express the gospel authentically in Korean culture, and to be warned of the pitfalls of syncretism into which some have fallen. Kim's conclusions regarding proper ways to contextualize Christianity and the importance of submitting to the authoritative Scriptures, are carefully and clearly set forth.

Because it is based on honest research, the book may create a measure of controversy as it brings to the surface factors about Korean Protestantism that few people know about and that some may prefer to keep buried. Dr. Kim's research inescapably challenges Korean Protestant leaders to examine to what extent the churches' faith and practice are influenced by shamanistic traditions which, from the viewpoint of God's Word, need to be discarded.

Because shamanism has played a significant role in Korean Protestant church growth and the spiritual practices of millions of members, shamanism must be addressed theologically, missiologically and pastorally. We deal here with one of the mysteries of God's providence and the surprising means he uses to achieve his redemptive purposes. At the same time, he challenges his people to purge from their lives and churches all that displeases him

Dr. Roger S. Greenway
Calvin Theological Seminary

Chapter One

INTRODUCTION

PROSPECTUS

In recent years, Korea has become one of the countries to which the attention of the world has been drawn because of its remarkable economic growth and the phenomenon of Protestant church growth.[1] Though the Protestant church in Korea is only one hundred and ten years old, its growth is generally recognized as one of the most remarkable in the world. Korea, once known as "the hermit nation," gained fame from the expansion of Christianity, especially over the last two decades.[2] In 1984 the Korean Roman Catholic Church celebrated the bicentennial of the first missions in Korea with a visit by Pope John Paul II. In 1994 the Korean Protestant Church celebrated the one hundred-tenth anniversary of the arrival of the first official Protestant missionaries, Horace Underwood and Henry Appenzeller. In 1907 John R. Mott declared:

> During my recent visit in the Far East I found the deep conviction that if the present work on the part of the cooperating mission in Korea is adequately sustained and enlarged in the immediate future, Korea will be the first nation in the non-Christian world to become a Christian nation.[3]

The Korean Protestant community came close to doubling its size during each of three decades since 1940, from 370,000 in 1940 to 600,000 in 1950, 1,520,000 in 1960 to 3,240,000 in 1970.[4] In 1980 the Protestant Christian segment reached 23 percent of the population of South Korea, whereas in the 1950 census it was only 2 percent of the population. By the end of 1981 government statistics reported 4,760 churches in the capital, Seoul.[5] Sun-do Kim writes:

> This century has seen the most amazing church growth throughout the world. According to the Mission Advanced Research and Communication Center (MARC), there are than 55,000 new Christians converted each day,

and 1,400 new churches are established every week in the world. Korean churches are no exception. The Korean church is one of the fastest growing churches in the world today. For example, every day six new churches are planted and 1,400 more Christians are added in Korea.[6]

According to David Barrett, the Christian church in Korea has been growing by 6.6 percent a year since 1982, fully two-thirds through conversions rather than the birth rate. He projected that South Korea will be 42% Christian by the end of the century.[7] South Korea demonstrates one of the world's most dramatic Christian revivals. Many Korean Christians believe that Korea has become a *CHOSEN* nation (I Peter 2:9) today for God's purpose of evangelizing the world with the gospel in this generation. In fact, Korea during the *Yi* Chosen Dynasty (1392-1910) had been called the *CHOSEN* Dynasty. Patrick Johnstone writes:

> Praise God for the Korean Church - founded on sound indigenous principles, blessed with revival, refined by suffering and now becoming a significant missionary-sending body. The well-attended daily early-morning prayer meetings are a notable characteristic. As a result, over 20 churches are planted every day, and the gospel has penetrated every part of society. Pray that wealth, success and cultural acceptability may not stunt this growth or dampen the spiritual energies of Christians...The capital city, Seoul, is almost 40 percent Christian, with over 7,000 churches, and is also home to ten of the 20 largest congregations in the world. The largest congregation (Full Gospel Central Church), and the largest Presbyterian and Methodist congregation in the world are here. The largest theological seminaries in the world.[8]

According to *A Handbook of Korea,* by 1991 the Korean Christian population had already grown to more than 15 million [2,477,000 Roman Catholics and 12,571,000 Protestants], over 30 percent of the country's 45 million inhabitants, and this is the one of the highest percentages of Christians in any Asian country.[9] Recent government statistics indicate that nearly a fifth of the South Korean population is a member of one of the Protestant denominations.[10] Samuel H. Moffett, a retired veteran missionary in Korea and now at Princetion Theological Seminary, described the explosive church growth:

> When my father reached Seoul in 1890, there were between 10,000 and 17,000 Roman Catholics. Records for 1889 show only 74 communicant Protestants. Forty years later, when I was a boy in Korea in 1930, the number was 415,000 Christians, or 2 percent of the population. When I returned in 1955 there were 1,117,000, or about 5 percent. Today (1987) there are over 10 million Christians in Korea, or about 23 percent. Very roughly that would mean one Korean in a thousand was Christian in 1890, 1 in 50 in 1930, 1 in 20 in 1955, and 1 in 4 today.[11]

There is no simple answer as to why the church has grown so fast in Korea. However, we must seek to define the primary human factors influencing this wildfire spread of the gospel and rapid church growth. There have been many attempts made by missionary scholars and Korean church leaders to analyze various factors in the church and in Korean culture that have contributed to this rapid expansion. The rapid growth of the Protestant church in Korea has been the subject of study and analysis at least since T. Stanley Soltau wrote his classic work *Korea the Hermit Nation and Its Response to Christianity* (World Dominion Press, England, UK. 1932). In chapters 2 and 4, Soltau discusses the background to the explosive growth of the church. A more modern study by Roy E. Shearer, *Wildfire: Church Growth in Korea* (Grand Rapids, MI: Eerdmans Publishing Co.,1966), analyzes the regional and sub-cultural reasons for differential church growth in the peninsula. During the centennial celebrations of Protestant missions in 1984-1985, much emphasis was placed on the unusually high rate of increase in membership and institutional development in the Protestant churches during the last century.

Foreign mission scholars enumerate factors such as indigenous principles or the Nevius method,[12] the homogeneous character of Korean society,[13] the sociopolitical situation,[14] social work and evangelistic activities of missionaries,[15] the divisions of the church,[16] the Great Revival of 1907,[17] nationalism,[18] ministry through home cell groups,[19] the church's emphasis on healing ministry, and holistic evangelism.[20] James H. Grayson discusses four factors which created conditions which contributed to the rapid acceptance of the Protestant form of Christianity as follows:

1. The rejection at the end of the last century of the Confucian values of the *Chosen* Dynasty (1392-1910) by the younger, progressive elements of the social elite which in turn predisposed them to accept novel, non-traditional ideas.

2. The lack of any essential conflict between Christianity and the key values of Korean society, and the highlighting of parallels between Christianity and certain elements of the folk religion.

3. The early achievement of tolerance for the new religion by the elite, and the eventual close association of that religion with Korean nationalism during the Japanese colonial era (1910-1945).

4. The lack of any organized religious resistance to the advent of Protestant Christianity.[21]

Korean scholars also list numerous factors such as the concept of a high God,[22] the religious culture of the Korean people,[23] the evangelistic work of Korean Christians,[24] the sociopolitical situation,[25] the indigenization of the church,[26] church schisms,[27] and other contributing causes. Sung-bum Yun, the late president of the Methodist Seminary in Seoul, Korea, stated six major reasons for rapid church growth in Korea as follows:

1. Christianity was understood as a religion of plain men, the common people of society. It was contrasted with neighboring Japan where Christianity was received mostly by the military knight class.

2. Under the dominant Chinese culture, Christianity stressed the original Korean language which was invented by King *Sejong* and his royal scholars during the *Yi* dynasty. The Bibles and hymnals were printed in the Korean language so that the people of little education could read them. This vernacular language became the most effective medium in the spreading of the gospel.

3. The idea of heaven and hell of Christianity was a kin idea to the Buddhist idea of Paradise or Nirvana.

4. The social situation was also favorable to the propagation of the gospel. There were several attempts of an independence movement, but all of them failed tragically. Therefore, people shifted their thought to a long-range national movement, and people thronged to the church. Among the people there were outstanding national leaders who were later converted to Christianity.

5. Personal evangelism: mass evangelism was more often used and popular, but personal evangelism was the most characteristic Christian witness.

6. Finally, Korean Protestantism contributed to the modernization of Korea. The modernization impact was in many fields, such as in education, in medicine, in social work, and so forth.[28]

Most foreign scholars of mission have attributed Korean church growth to outside factors, whereas Korean scholars have attempted to discover the reasons for growth inside Korea. In addition to reexamining the factors just mentioned, the present study will concern itself in particular with an analysis of shamanistic belief and practice as a possible causal element in the growth of the church in Korea.[29] The question concerning the way in which the message of the gospel was brought by missionaries and Korean evangelists with specific sensitivity toward the particular shamanistic context and cultural forces in Korea and whether this partly explains the remarkable growth of the church there, has been posed many times by missiologists and church growth scholars in the USA. Roy E. Shearer, who studied Korean church growth extensively, writes:

Through the animistic religion, the people of Korea were also to accept and understand some important tenets of the Christian faith. They were prepared in a unique way by the Holy Spirit to receive Christianity...I have seen enough in this study and have had enough experience to realize that animism has a most important relationship to church growth in Korea... What is needed is a study of the dynamics of church growth, showing how Christianity wins or loses the power struggle with the animistic forces in Korea. Increased understanding is demanded if our presentation of the Gospel is to be successful. The continuing animism of the country people of Korea must be taken more seriously in the future.[30]

The Korean church won converts primarily in the purely animistic areas of Korea. Koreans are aware of supernatural power and have a fear of spirits. They worship their gods in order to make contact with them so that they may have blessings and prosperity. According to Byung-suh Kim, one of the particular characteristics of the Korean church which contributed to its explosive growth is a prevalent tendency of the Korean church itself is that it tends to be shamanistic, and that it accommodates indigenous belief system such as shamanistic faith in spirit worship, which are much inclined to seek blessings in material wealth, good health, and other forms of personal and financial well-being.[31] Donald McGavran states, "pure animism has great importance for church growth." According to Shearer, "the animism of Korea prepared the way to hearing and understanding this same gospel."[32] In 1954, The World Council of Churches Assembly in Evanston reported that large numbers of people had been converted to Christianity from responsive animistic and shamanistic societies, World Council of Churches Assembly, Evanston.[33]

What effect have factors rooted in shamanistic faith had on quantitative church growth in Korea? Is this remarkable growth comparable to the rapid spread of Christianity noted among animistic and shamanistic people elsewhere? What is needed in the Christian church of Korea today is theological reflection and a practical solution to the question of how the Protestant church should relate to its own religious, cultural environment. Ought it to view this environment as an important factor in continuing church growth? We will attempt to bring about a better understanding of the cultural forces in Korean society affecting the growth of the Protestant church. Our thesis is that these forces, particularly shamanism, even though largely ignored by early missiologists, contributed significantly to the growth of the Protestant church in Korea.[34] The Korean church needs to understand the dynamics of this relation between shamanistic faith and church growth, which may lead to reevaluation of shamanism and acceptance of it as the specific context of the church in Korea.

It should be remembered that the term "church growth," as used throughout this book, means primarily numerical church growth, though of course it also has a qualitative connotation pointing to growing maturity of the faith of church members. Numerical church growth and spiritual church growth are not mutually exclusive. A statement from a World Council of Churches-sponsored study on church growth says:

> Numerical expansion and quality of Christian life are not alternatives, but correlatives, inasmuch as each is vitally related with the other. Again and again, it has been shown that the spontaneous expansion of a church quickens its own spiritual life; on the other hand a church which is truly growing in grace thereby grows in concern for its missionary outreach.[35]

The Church Growth School has a particular insight into the methods of church growth and how they were applied in Korea. The Church Growth School came into existence in the 1950s. It took root in the mind and ministry of Donald McGavran while he was serving as a third-generation missionary to India over a period of thirty years. His first attempts at putting his ideas into writing date back to 1936. But the widespread diffusion of the movement began with the publication of *The Bridges of God* (New York, NY: Friendship, 1955), and *How Churches Grow* (New York, NY: Friendship, 1959). The founding of the Fuller Theological Seminary School of World Mission and Institute of Church Growth in Pasadena, Ca., in 1965, and the publication of his major work, *Understanding Church Growth*, in 1970, laid solid foundations for the development of the movement. The most formalized definition of Church Growth appears in the Constitution of the Academy for American Church Growth.

> Church growth is that science which investigates the planting, multiplication, function and health of Christian churches as they relate specifically to the effective implementation of God's commission to 'make disciples of all nations' (Matt.28:19-20).[36]

One should then ask the question: In what way does this theory shed light on what happened in Korea? The church growth school has studied the religious climate and structure of Korean society extensively. In reality church growth theory contributed to a numerical church growth in Korea through emphasis on evangelism and missionary work by all believers based on Matt. 28:19-20.[37] It should also be pointed out that the Korean word for church, *kyohoe,* refers collectively to all of the churches in Korea. Therefore, in this book the term "the church of

Korea" refers to the Korean Christian Church, that is, the combined Roman Catholic Church and Protestant churches. The singular term "church" refers to a specific congregation and a local church, while the plural form "churches" refers primarily to a sum of single congregations or denominations.

This book consists, thus, of seven chapters dealing with the causes of the remarkable growth of the Protestant churches in Korea and the question as to what the church should do to ensure growth in the future. In the remainder of this introduction we will give a short general survey of the geography, people and history of Korea. In the second chapter, the author deals with the different religions of Korea except for Christianity; shamanistic faith, *Taechongkyo*, Confucianism, Buddhism, Taoism, and *Chundokyo*. Because of the particular interest in the shamanistic factors, the author deals in the third chapter more specifically with the basic belief system of Korean Shamanism. In the fourth chapter, after making a brief reference to the role of the Roman Catholic mission, the author delineates the history of Protestant missions and the growth of the Protestant churches in Korea. This review will not conclude the Roman Catholic churches in Korea because of the limitation of the subject. Chapter five contains an analysis of both the external and internal factors contributing to church growth. In the sixth chapter the author examines the shamanistic component. In the including chapter the author will describe the past and present stances of the Protestant church vis-à-vis its own cultural and political context and offer a missiological evaluation of these attitudes. For chapters II, III, and VI, which deal mainly with the background of Korean religions and the history of Christian mission and church growth, the phenomenological analysis of shamanism and the rituals of shamanistic folk religion, Korean literature written by Korean scholars in this field has been used. Very little English literature was available on the history and structure of the belief system of Korean shamanism.

It should be added here that there are not enough reliable sources for numerical church growth in Korea. And it is difficult to get them. But the general feelings of remarkable growth can not be denied. The data used in this study have been collected from a number of sources. The statistics of numerical church growth in this book are largely based on secondary sources such as books, journals, newspapers and the annual official report of the Cultural Department of the Republic of Korea, and the various Christian Mission organizations in Korea. When inconsistencies occur in given statistics, the author points these out or attempts to indicate the more plausible alternative. The resources for this book are as follows. The library research was done in the US at Calvin Theological Seminary, Reformed Bible College, Grand Rapids; Fuller Theological Seminary, Pasadena; Claremont School of Theology, Claremont; The Korean Cultural Center, Los Angeles; in the Netherlands at the Free University of Amsterdam; Leiden University; Zendingshuis Library, Hendrik Kraemer Institute, Oegstgeest; in Germany at Tübingen University; in Seoul, Korea, *Yonsei* University, Korean Presbyterian Theological Seminary, Korean Methodist Theological Seminary, the Asian Center Theological and Mission Library, and the Korean Research Center.

THE GEOGRAPHICAL BACKGROUND OF KOREA

The Korea peninsula extends southward from northeastern China to some 125 miles off Japan at its southeastern tip.[38] Korea is a land of mountains and hills, and presents one of the rare mountainous countries in the world. A range of mountains extends along the East Coast, from north to south, from which lateral mountain ranges extend across the peninsula, becoming lower as they near the western seacoast. There are broad plains along the coasts and between the high mountain ranges, which means that only one-fifth of Korea is fertile and available for producing rice and other agricultural products.[39] About 70 percent of the land area consists of beautiful high mountains and uplands, so Koreans often call it the "land decorated with golden embroidery." The highest peak, Mt. *Paektu,* stands 9,003 feet [2,744 meters] high on the northern border facing Manchuria,[40] and the very picturesque mountain scenery exists in the Mt. *Kumgang,* or the Diamond Mountain area. Samuel Moffett writes,

> Korea will always be one of the most beautiful little countries. She has been called the Switzerland of Asia. Her own people call her 'the queen of ten thousand peaks and ten thousand islands and ten thousand waterfalls.' Korean Christians used to say that when God created the world in six days he must have spent the first five days creating the 'Diamond Mountain,' and then dashed off the rest of the world on the sixth day... Yes, Korea is still beautiful. [41]

Isabella Bird Bishop, a well known world traveler, describes the "Diamond Mountain" as "not much exceeded anywhere on earth."[42] Korea has a large number of rivers and streams considering the relatively small size of this land.[43] Because of its location in the East Asian monsoons, or seasonal winds belt, the climate of Korea is characterized by four distinct seasons and a variety of different weather types. The peninsula has hot and humid summers and long dry-cold winters. Spring and autumn are rather short, but very pleasant with many days of sunshine.

THE ETHNIC BACKGROUND OF KOREA

Little is known of the aboriginal inhabitants of Korea, and today there is still disagreement as to where they should be placed ethnologically. However, according to archaeological and linguistic studies, as well as legendary sources, tribes inhabiting the Altaic mountains about the third millennium B.C. started migrating eastward to Manchuria and Siberia. Ethnologically the Korean people are members of the Altaic race which includes the Turkish, Mongolian and Tugustic peoples. However, in recent years, archaeology indicates that Paleolithic people already inhabited the peninsula from as early as 50,000 B.C.[44] The people of Korea are homogeneous in race, language, history, culture, custom and even in social attitudes in general throughout their long history of 5,000 years. Koreans were one ethnic homogeneous people speaking one language with the same cultural background by the beginning of the Christian era, and in the seventh century A.D., they were politically unified for the first time by the *Shilla* Kingdom (57 B.C.-A.D. 935) and achieved a great cultural flowering.[45]

According to linguistic and ethnological sources the Korean language belongs to the Ural-Altaic language group, especially the Altaic language family.[46] The written language is a combination of Chinese characters and the Korean script, which is generally called "*Hangul.*" A phonetic alphabet, originally called "*Hunmin Jungoom*" [literally, "the right sounds to teach the people"] was invented about 1443 A.D. by a group of scholars by the commission of King *Sejong.* Two principles were applied in devising the forms of vowels and consonants: consonants symbolize the organs of speech and vowels symbolize heaven, earth and man - the three elements in the Oriental philosophical view of the universe. The Korean alphabet consists of 10 vowels and 14 consonants, which can be combined to form numerous syllabic groupings. The Korean alphabet was considered one of the most methodical writing systems in use in any language in the world.[47] In 1992 South Korea had a population of 43,663,000 and North Korea had about 22,627,000.[48]

THE POLITICAL HISTORY OF KOREA

The tradition of Korean history goes back to 2,333 B.C. when *Tangun*, a legendary king, established the first kingdom named *Chosen*, or the Land of the Morning Calm. According to tradition prince *Hwan-ung*, the son of Heaven's supreme deity, descended and married the bear-woman who wished to become a human and miraculously bore a son called *Tangun*. The legendary first king, *Tangun* founded the "country of God in the year 2333 B.C. with *Pyongyang* as its capital, and he and his descendants reigned in the land for more than a millennium.[49]

Korea's earliest recorded history began at about the time of the beginning of the Christian era. For the next seven hundred years Korea was divided into three small kingdoms (57 B.C-935 A.D) that waged continual war against one another. The three kingdoms were: *Koguryo* (37 B.C.-A.D.668) in the far north, *Paekche* (18 B.C.-A.D.660) in the southwest, *Shilla* (57 B.C.-A.D.935) in the southeast. In A.D.668 Korea was unified under the control of the *Shilla* kingdom. Since then it has been ruled by a single control authority and has maintained political independence and established a cultural and ethnic identity that laid the foundation of modern Korea. Korea introduced a metal culture for the first time in the fourth century B.C., and eight centuries later Buddhism and Chinese characters and the arts of Korean culture were diffused into Japan. For two and half centuries (668 A.D.- 935.A.D.) the unified *Shilla* kingdom achieved rapid development in diversified fields of culture. Its capital, the present day *Kyungju*, had a population of over one million. The unified *Shilla* kingdom came to an end in *Koryo* kingdom proclaimed a policy to recover the lost territory of *Koguryo* in Manchuria. Therefore, he named his kingdom *Koryo*, from which the modern name Korea is derived. The name of Korea is believed by some to be derived from the phrase "high mountains, sparkling streams." [50]

The founder of the *Koryo* kingdom adopted Buddhism as the state religion. In the first of his ten commandments, king *Taejo* declared that the *Koryo* kingdom had been founded with the help and guidance of the Buddha and that his successors should worship Buddha and defend his name. This played an important role in the culture, ideology, and way of life in Korea. During the kingdom's later years, it was severely weakened by the corruption of Buddhism and internal problems. The invasions and occupation of the Mongols, which lasted nearly a century, shattered and put an end to the *Koryo* kingdom.[51] The innovative era of Korean history dates from the beginning of the *Chosen* kingdom (1392-1910), which is known in the West by its dynastic name *Yi*. The early rulers of the *Yi* dynasty replaced Buddhism with Confucianism, which was probably introduced into Korea during the late fourth century. Confucian ethics and values came to dominate the social structure and behavior through the following centuries. Because of its location, Korea has many times become a battleground in the struggle for power in the area of East Asia. In the late 16th century, Korea experienced a seven-year war with Japan, having rejected the request of Japan to make way for its invasion of China. This conflict ended in 1598, leaving the peninsula devastated. G. T. Brown says: "Because of the ruthlessness of this invasion the minds of the Koreans were poisoned against all foreigners. From this time on Korea became the "Hermit Nation," determined to resist every attempt of the outside world to pry open her closed door.[52]

Several attempts were made by Western countries to enter Korea. The first trade treaty was made with Japan in 1876 and with the United States in 1882, and then other Western nations followed.[53] After defeating China in 1885 and Russia in 1905, Japan formally annexed Korea, and the *Chosen* kingdom fell in 1910. Korea lost not only its sociopolitical freedom but also its religious freedom to Japan for thirty-five years. In spite of persecution and suffering, the Koreans never lost their hope for independence. In 1919 a nationwide independence movement began to operate at the cost of thousands of lives. Independence was restored by the allies at the end of World War II in 1945.

Because of its geopolitical location surrounded by such powers as Russia, China and Japan, Korea has unfortunately always been a buffer state between these contending powers, and as a peninsula it has served as a land bridge over which continental cultural traits were transmitted to the Pacific area. Korea had been frequently called the "Balkan of the Orient" and its people have experienced many invasions, foreign military occupations, foreign rule: in 108 B.C. China conquered the northern half of Korea; in 1259 Mongol armies conquered; in 1592 Japan invaded; in 1630 Manchu armies conquered; in 1910 Japan took control; in 1945 Russian forces occupied northern Korea; and in 1948 after world War II U.S. forces occupied southern Korea.[54] In 1948 Korea was divided, however, with a communist North, the Democratic People's Republic of Korea, and a strongly anti-Communist South, the Republic of Korea. Two years later, on June 25, 1950, North Korean forces invaded South Korea and for three years the peninsula was ravaged by the tragic Korean War (1950-53). A truce was signed in July 1953, and since then Korea has been divided with very little tangible sign of permanent peace and reunification. Ki-baik Lee writes,

> The Korean War was one of the most tragic such episodes in the nation's history. The suffering that it caused was cruel beyond expression. South Korean casualties in the fighting alone are estimated at 150,000 dead, 200,000 missing, and 250,000 injured, while more than 100,000 civilians were abducted to North Korea and the number of war refugees reached several million. North Korean casualties were several times these figures.[55]

The political history of South Korea has been that of the struggle for democracy. This struggle has been carried out by the people of South Korea during the entire span of thirty-five years following the First Republic, which ended in 1960. The period from 1960 to the present is divided as follows: the Second Republic of 1960-61; the military junta rule of 1961-63; the Third Republic of 1963-1972; the Fourth Republic of 1972-79; the interim period of 1979-81; the Fifth Republic of 1981-88; the Sixth Republic of 1988-93. The last period was succeeded by that of the Seventh Republic, which began in February 1993. Rising from the ashes of the modern devastation which befell it, South Korea, with its population of 44 million, is a nation with a growing democracy in the political sector, growing expectations in the economic sector, increasing social equality, and an expanding cultural horizon. At this time, Korea remains divided into two states, each attempting to modernize and increase its economic power while endeavoring each in its own way to bring about the reunification of the partitioned land and people.

NOTES

[1]*Hankuk Ilbo* [*The Korea Daily News*] (April 11, 1982), p. 8; Paul and Bernice Schrotenboer, "Growth and Dangers in Korean Church," in: *The Banner* 118 (April 18, 1983), p. 6.

[2]Ted. W. Engstrom, *What in the World is God Doing?* (Waco, TX: Word Books, 1978), p. 160; Samuel Moffet, "The Church in Asia: Getting on the Charters," in: *Christianity Today,* 25 (October 2, 1981), p. 39; Lawrence E. Keyes, *The Last Age of Mission* (Pasadena, CA: William Carey Library, 1983), p. 84.

[3]Lord Cecil, *London Times,* in: George Paik, *History of Protestant Missions in Korea* (Pyongyang, Korea: Union Christian College Press, 1929), p. 360.

[4]See Neill L. Kennedy, "Troubled South Korea Manages a Very Big Bash for Missions," in: *Christianity Today* 24 (September 19, 1980), pp. 44,48.

[5]In 1983, 31 percent of the National Assembly of Korea was reported to be Protestant Christians, Joon G. Kim, *Asia Theological News* 9 (April-June, 1983).

[6]Sun-do Kim, "Church Growth in Korea," David J. Cho, ed. *The Third Force* (Seoul, Korea: East-West Center for Missions Research & Development, 1986), p. 183; Cf. Ho-jin Chun, *Hankuk Kyohoe Sungjang-kwa Kee Wonin* [*Korean Church Growth and Its Causes*], Jong Y. Lee, Nelson, *Kyohoe Sungjang Ron* [*Theories of Church Growth*] (Seoul, Korea: Emmaus Publishing House, 1983), p. 261.

[7]David B. Barrett, "The World Religions," in: *Times* 9 (May, 1982), p. 67; Dick Van Halsema, "Korea Impression," in: *Missionary Monthly* 88 (November, 1983), p. 9.

[8]Patrick Johnstone, *Operation World* (Grand Rapids, MI: Zondervan Publishing House, 1993), p. 337.

[9]*A Handbook of Korea,* 1993, p. 132.

[10]*A Handbook of Korea* (Seoul, Korea: Hollym Co., 1993), p. 132; Cf. Seong-tae Kim, *Hankuk Kitokkyo-eui Yeksa-jek Bansung* [*Historical Reflection of Korean Christianity*] (Seoul, Korea: Dasan Publishing Co., 1994), p. 284; Don Richardson, *Eternity in Their Hearts* (Ventura, CA: Regal Books, 1987), p. 21; Johnstone, *op.cit.,* p. 337.

[11]Ro and Nelson, *Korean Church Growth Explosion,* rev., 1995. Pp. 16-17.

[12]Donald McGavarn, *Understanding Church Growth* (Grand Rapids, MI: Eerdmans Publishing Co., 1970), p. 337.

[13]Roy E. Shearer, *Wildfire: Church Growth in Korea,* pp.143-151, Robert Recker, "What are People Movements?," in: Harvie M. Conn, ed., *Theological Perspectives on Church Growth* (Nutley, New Jersey: The Presbyterian Publishing Company, 1976), pp. 76-77.

[14]Alfred W. Wasson, *Church Growth in Korea* (Concord, NH: Rumford

Press, 1934), pp. 153-157; Shearer, *op.cit.*, p. 140; Tae-whan Kim, *An Empirical Study of the Factors Contributing to Rapid Church Growth in Korea* (Philadelphia, PA: Dissertation, Eastern Baptist Theological Seminary, 1984), p. 95-96.

[15]Marlin L. Nelson, "A Foreigner's View of the Korean Church," in: Bong-rin Ro and Marlin L. Nelson, eds. *Korean Church Growth Explosion* (Seoul, Korea: Word of Life Press, 1983), pp. 182-196.

[16]C. Peter Wagner, ed., *Understanding Church Growth* (Grand Rapids, MI: Eerdmans Publishing Co, Third edition, 1990), p. 4.

[17]*Ibid*, pp. 136-137.

[18]Shearer, *op.cit*, p. 64; Wagner, ed., *Understanding Church Growth*, p. 184.

[19]Charles Van Engen, *God's Missionary People* (Grand Rapids, MI: Baker Book House, 1991), p. 160; John N. Vaughan, *The Large Church* (Grand Rapids, MI: Baker, 1985), pp. 61, 105-106.

[20]John Wimber, "Signs and Wonders in the Growth of the Church," in: C. Peter Wagner, ed., *Church Growth: State of the Art* (Wheaton, IL: Tyndale House Publishers, 1986), p. 216; Wagner, *How to Have a Healing in Any Church* (Ventura, CA: Regal Books, 1988), p. 70-72; Holistic evangelism: Harvie M. Conn, *Evangelism : Doing Justice and Preaching Grace* (Grand Rapids, MI: Zondervan Publishing House, 1982), pp. 104-105.

[21]James H. Grayson, "Elements of Protestant Accommodation of Korean Religious Culture: A Personal Ethnographic Perspective," in Darrell L. White, ed., *Missiology*, Vol. XXIII, 1 (Jan, 1995) (Scottdale, PA: American Society of Missiology, 1995), p. 44.

[22]Samuel I. Kim, "Area Reports : Korea," in: David J. Cho, ed., *New Forces in Missions*: *The Official Report of the Asia Missions Association* (Seoul, Korea: East-West Center for Missions Research & Development, 1976), pp. 123; Cf. Spencer J. Palmer, *Korea and Christianity* (Seoul, Korea: Hollym Corporation, 1967), pp. 7-8.

[23]Harold S. Hong, "General Picture of the Korean Church, Yesterday and Today," in: Harold S. Hong, Wong-young Ji, Chung-choon Kim, *Korea Struggles for Christ*: *Memorial Symposium for the Eightieth Anniversary of Protestantism in Korea* (Seoul, Korea: Christian Literature Society of Korea, 1973), p. 13.

[24]Taikpoo Chun, *Hankuk Kyohoe Baljunsa* [*The History of Church Development in Korea*] (Seoul, Korea: The Christian Literature Society, 1987), p. 14.

[25]Bong-rin Ron, Marlin N. Nelson, eds., *op.cit.*, pp., 163, 167, 174-179; Nak-joon Paik, *Hankuk Kaehsinkyosa* [*History of Protestant Mission in Korea*] (Seoul, Korea: Yunsei University Press, 1973), pp. 442; Kwang-sun Suh, *Hankuk Kitokyo-eui Sae Euishik* [*New Consciousness of Korean Christianity* (Seoul, Korea: The Christian Literature Society, 1985), p. 9-39.

[26]Sung-bum Yun, *Kitokkyo-wa Hankuk Sasang* [*Christianity and Korean Thought*] (Seoul, Korea: The Christian Literature Society, 1964), pp. 248-250.

[27]Wan-sang, Han, *Hankuk Hoyohoe-eui Yangjek Sungjang-kwa Kyoinduel-*

eui Gachikwan [Quantitiative Growth of Korean Church and the Values of Korean Christians] (Seoul, Korea: Sungjon University, 1983), pp. 125,139,

[28]Harold S. Hong, "Social, Political, and Psychological Aspects of Church Growth," in Ro and Nelson, *Korean Church Growth Explosion*, pp. 171-179.

[29]Byong-il Chang, *"Yuheyung-jek-euro Bon Kitokkyo-wa Shamanism"* [A Typological Approach to Christianity and Shamanism], *Kitokkyo Sasang Yungu* [*Studies on Christian Thought*] (Seoul, Korea: Kitokkyo Moonhak, 1971), pp. 174-179.

[30]*Ibid.*, pp. 218-219.

[31]Byung-suh Kim, "The Explosive Growth of the Korean Church Toda: A Sociological Analysis," *International Review of* Mission 64 (293): pp. 61-74.

[32]Shearer, *op.cit.*, pp. 35, 81.

[33]Eugene A. Nida and William A. Smalley, *Introducing Animism* (New York, NY: Friendship Press, 1959), p. 59; *The Christian Hope and the Task of the Church* (New York, NY: Harper and Brothers, Publishers, 1954), p. 11.

[34]Donald A. McGavran, *Church Growth and Christian Mission* (New York, NY: Harper & Row, 1976), p. 48.

[35]*The Growth of the Church*, a statement drawn up by a special consultation convened by the W.C.C. Department of Missionary Studies (Iberville, Quebec: July 31-August 2, 1963); See Ralph D. Winter, "Quality or Quantity," in: ed., Donald McGavran, *Crucial Issues in Missions Tomorrow* (Chicago, IL: Moody Press, 1972), p. 178.

[36]McGavran, *op.cit.*, p. 178; See C. Peter Wagner, *Church Growth and the Whole Gospel* (San Francisco, CA: Harper & Row, Publishing Co. 1981), p. 62-64, 75.

[37]Jong-yoon Lee, Ho-jin Jun, Marlin L. Nelson, *Kyohoe Sungjang-Ron* [*Theories of Church Growth*] (Seoul, Korea: Emmaus Publishing Company, 1983), p. 228.

[38]The Korean Peninsula with associated islands lies latitudinally between 33 degrees 06'N and 43 degrees 36'N and 124 degrees 11'E and 131 degrees 52'E. Korea is approximately 670 miles (1,078 kilometers) long and 320 miles (515 kilometers) wide with a total coastal line of nearly 1,484 miles (2,388 kilometers). More than 3,000 islands lie off the southern and western coasts of the peninsula. The peninsula and the islands cover a total area of 85,049 square miles (220,276 square kilometers). See Korea Overseas Information Service, *A Handbook of Korea* (Seoul, Korea: Hollym International Corp, 1993), pp. 12-23.

[39]S. E. Solberg, *The Land and People of Korea* (Philadelphia, PA, New York, NY: J. B. Lippincott Co., 1966), p. 5; In its mountain area Korea has a good supply of minerals such as coal, iron, tungsten, copper, graphite, magnetite, fluorspar, mica, gold, and silver.

[40]*Paektu San* [the Ever-White-Head Mountain], the so-called 'most holy mountain in Korea,' is a dead volcano with a large crater named *Chonji*, or the heavenly lake, on its top, shrouded with a mystical aura as the site of the first kingdom in Korean history dating back some 5000 years. South Korea's highest mountain, *Halla San,* rises 6,980 feet (1950 meters) on *Cheju* Island, the

largest Korean Island.

[41]Samuel Moffet, *The Christians in Korea* (New York, NY: Friendship Press, 1962), p. 12;

[42]I. B. Bishop, *Korea and Her Neighbors* (New York, NY: Fleming H. Revell Co., 1897), p. 144.

[43]Both of the two longest rivers, the *Amnok* river [*Yalu*, 493 miles; 790 kilometers] and the *Tuman* river [*Tumen*, 325 miles], originate from Mt. *Paektu* and flow to the west and the east, along the peninsula's northern border. The two major rivers, the *Daedong* river which flows through *Pyongyang*, capital of North Korea, and the *Han* river which flows through Seoul, capital of South Korea, have played a significant part in the development of Korea's ancient civilization.

[44]Cf. Si-in Bak, *Altai Moonwhasa Yungu: Hankuk Pyun [A Study of Altaic Civilization; History of Korea]* (Seoul, Korea; Tamgu-Dang Publishing Co., 1973), pp. 25-47.

[45]See Kuk-sung Suh, et.al. *The Identity of the Korean People; A History of Legitimacy on the Korean Peninsula* (Seoul, Korea: National Unification Board, 1983), pp. 11-14.

[46]Altaic language group includes Turkish, Hungarian, Finnish, Mongolian, Tibetan and Japanese. Cornelius Osgood, *The Koreans and Their Culture* (New York, NY: The Ronald Press Co., 1951), p. 326.

[47]H. B. Hulbert, *The Passing of Korea* (New York, NY: Doubleday Page Publishers, 1906), p. 92.

[48]Tai-hyung Min, *Korean Statistical Yearbook 1992* (Seoul, Korea: National Statistical Office of Republic of Korea, 1992), p.139.

[49]Gyu-tae Kim, *Hankuk Sinwhawa Woncho Euisik [Korean Mythology and Consciousness of Origin]* (Seoul, Korea: Ewoo Publishing Co., 1980), pp. 248-254.

[50]See Ki-baik Lee, Hyun-Ku Min, *Saryoro Bon Hankuk Moonwhasa Koryo [Cultural History of Korea]* (Seoul, Korea: Iljisa, 1984), pp. 9-28.

[51]See *Korea: Its People and Culture* (Seoul, Korea: Hakwonsa, LTD. 1970), p. 55. In this period, in 1234, the world's first moveable metal type was invented by Korean artisans, which preceded Gutenberg by two centuries. See Ki-baik Lee, *A New History of Korea*, pp. 170, 196, 238.

[52]George T. Brown, *Mission to Korea* (New York, NY: Board of Missions, Presbyterian Church. U.S.A. 1962), p. 5.

[53]Woo-keun Han, *History of Korea,* trans. Kyung-shik Lee, ed. Grafton K. Mintz, (Seoul, Korea: The Eul-Yoo Publishing Co., 1970), pp. 371-383.

[54]Cf. Ki-baik Lee, *A New History of Korea,* trans. Edward W. Wanger with Edward J. Schultz, (Cambridge, Massachusetts, London, England: Harvard University Press, 1984), pp. 69-73.

[55]Ki-baik Lee, *op.cit.,* p. 380

Chapter Two

SHAMANISTIC FAITH AND RELIGIONS IN KOREA

INTRODUCTION

It has often been said that the Koreans were a people without a religion of their own.[1] Koreans, however, are very religious. In all countries, social patterns and philosophic beliefs are rooted in religious ideas that developed in the early phases of the development of the society. This land of Korea, too, has always had its own religious climate, and the vast majority of Koreans practiced their religious life by way of six traditional expressions, namely, shamanism, *Taechongkyo* [The Great Religion], Confucianism, Buddhism, Taoism, and *Chundokyo* [Heavenly Way Religion]. George Herbert Jones, president of the Biblical Institute of Korea in the early 1900's, described the religious life of Korea as follows:

> The Korean is a religious man. He is no atheist. It might be said of him as Paul said of the Athenians of old, he is very religious, for he finds gods everywhere. All nature is animated with them. He has a dim conception of continued existence after death, as his worship of the dead clearly indicates.[2]

The first and most ancient of these religious expressions was shamanism, or spirit worship, and large numbers of Koreans still practice this form of animism which dates back to the dawn of Korean history. *Taechongkyo* is a belief about 4,000 years old and embodies the concept of a triune god: creator, teacher, and temporal king, whose name is *Hanul*. Confucianism became established in Korea so early that its introduction cannot be even approximately pinpointed. No doubt, Confucian classics entered the peninsula with the earliest specimens of written Chinese material well before the beginning of the Christian era.

Buddhism came by way of China to the Korean peninsula in AD 372.
It is difficult to pinpoint the exact date when Taoism came to influence
Korea, but Korean history states that in 624 AD. *Chundokyo* was a
native and indigenous movement which actually later broke out as the
Eastern Learning in 1864. In this chapter the author discusses the ori-
gin, development and belief of the six traditional religions in Korea.

SHAMANISTIC FAITH IN KOREA

The most typical original Korean religious phenomenon can be called
animistic shamanism, which is the oldest form of religious practice of
all of Korea's faiths.[3] Korean shamanism is essentially animistic. It
involves a strong belief in the influence of departed ancestral spirits as
well as nature spirits who inhabit trees, rocks and other natural phenomena. These in turn must be propitiated or otherwise controlled
either by individuals or by priests [shaman, *Mudang*] to ensure health,
fertility and success in life's ventures. There is a strong emphasis on
exorcism and healing, with extensive use of chanting and drums.
Before Confucianism, Buddhism, and Taoism even entered Korea, this
Korean animistic faith had been founded in every part of the Korean
culture. Korean culture and its folk religious faith are so closely tied
and difficult to separate that Korean culture is often regarded as *musok
munwha,* or shamanistic faith culture. Shamanism is still perhaps the
most fundamental and influential religious faith of the Korean people.[4]
It is impossible to give an official estimated number of shamanistic
believers in Korea. One source, however, revealed that more than
eighty percent of the South Korean population today join in shamanistic practices even though many of them believe in one of the major religions.[5]

    In Korea, however, shamanistic faith is not considered a religion
but a primitive folk practice or belief. The definition of religion
includes only such religious bodies as have been recognized and are
organized as religious organizations for civil purposes. In the authoritative six-volume *Dae Baekwasajun* [Korean Encyclopedia], under the
definition of *Chongkyo* [Religion], the religions of Korea are listed in
order of their size: Buddhism and Christianity, Confucianism,
Chundokyo, Taechongkyo, and Islam with several other small religious
bodies.[6] Any mention of animism or shamanism is missing under this
heading of religion. Animism and shamanism are both listed in the
Korean Dictionary of Philosophy as primitive folk practices or

beliefs.[7] However, Korean shamanism has retained the most powerful religious influence on the population as a whole, even though the major religions have permeated the social and political life of the Korean people.[8] Therefore, Korean shamanism is a kind of animistic folk religion indigenous to Korea.

Origin of Shamanistic Faith in Korea

But in the light of the history of religion, old shamanism is a primitive religious phenomenon universally found among ethnic groups in northern Asia, Indians and Eskimos in the North American continent, and natives of the African continent and Southern Pacific areas. It is generally recognized that old shamanism originated in the Mongolian countries and includes the belief in spirits, common ceremonies and a vision of the world, nature and the inner world. One can observe these beliefs and practices in areas of the northern cultural circle such as Mongolia, China, Manchuria, Siberia, or Japan.[9] It is believed that shamanism originated in and was transmitted from the Paleolithic age, approximately 20,000 years ago, but it is not known exactly when old shamanism was introduced to the Korean and appeared in the Korean peninsula.[10] In Mircea Eliade's study of shamanism, he writes,

> In Korea, where shamanism is documented as early as the *Han* period, male shamans wear women's dress, and are far outnumbered by shamanesses. It is difficult to determine the origin of Korean shamanism; it may include southern elements, but the presence of stag horns on the shaman's headdress of the *Han* period indicates relations with the stag cult characteristic of the ancient Turks...The present predominance of shamanesses in Korea may be the result either of a deterioration in traditional shamanism or of influences from the south.[11]

It is almost impossible to determine the origin of Korean shamanism simply because of its complexity and its diversification of practice according to different provinces. It may be safe to say that long before the ancestors of modern day Koreans migrated to the continent into the peninsula, they must have believed in a magico-religion and practiced animistic shamanism. On shamanistic beliefs of Neolithic man in Korea, Ki-baik Lee writes,

> Neolithic man in Korea held animistic beliefs, being convinced that every object in the natural world was possessed of a soul. Man, too, of course had a soul and it was believed that this soul was immortal...The souls of natural objects such as mountains, rivers, and trees were thought of in the same

way as those of men, and certain of these were accorded status as divinities. Accordingly, it was necessary that there be adepts-in-magic, intermediaries with the ability to drive off evil spirits and invoke the gods so as to bring about a happy outcome. It is supposed that these tribal magicians performed ceremonies designed to foretell calamity by means of chants and dancing...[12]

According to traditional historical literature on Korea, such as the *Samkuk Sagi* [*History of Three Kingdoms*], ancient people used to worship the heavenly spirit and other spirits in the fifth and tenth months of the lunar year, dancing and singing and drinking for many days. These rites of heaven worship were called by different names in different states, such as *Yonggo* [a shamanistic ceremony of invoking a spirit] in *Puyo* and *Tongmaeng* [an ancestor worship ritual] in *Koguryo*, and *Muchon* [a dance performed to worship heaven] in *Tongye.*[13] The masters of ritual were called *Chungun*, meaning Heavenly Prince, and the prayer site was called *Sodo*. It was recorded that a tall wooden pole was erected in the *Sodo* on which were hung bells, a drum and a mirror, and that these were used in religious rituals. *Sodo* is a sacred place dedicated to the Heavenly God. If someone who had committed a crime sought asylum in this place, he could not be arrested and could stay as long as he wished.[14] This immediately calls to mind the staging of a *kut* rituals by modern female shamans who hang their drums, mirrors and bells on poles even today. *kut* is a shamanistic ritual for welfare and blessings of the home and individual. We shall return to this later.

In order to understand the origin and formation of Korean shamanism, it is necessary to go back to the oral traditions. It is believed that the *Tangun* myth had been transmitted by word of mouth for many generations before it was finally written down. It is recorded in *Samguk Yusa* [*Memorabilia of the Three Kingdoms*] authored by Ilyon, who was a renowned Buddhist monk in the *Koryo* Dynasty in the 13th Century A.D. The oral tradition of the *Tangun* mythology might have existed from the ancient past of *Chosen*, the old Korea, probably about the twentieth century B.C. The following is the story written in the *Memorabilia of the Three Kingdoms*:

> In ancient times *Hwan-in* [heavenly King] had a young son whose name was *Hwan-ung*. The boy wished to descend from heaven and live in the human world. His father, after examining three great mountains, chose *Taebaek San* as a suitable place for his heavenly son to bring happiness to his human beings. He gave *Hwan-ung* three heavenly treasures, and commanded him to rule over his people. With three thousand of his loyal sub-

jects *Hwan-ung* descended from heaven and appeared under a sandalwood tree on *Taebaek* Mountain. He named the place *Sinsi* [city of God] and assumed the title of *Hwan-ung Chewang* [another title meaning heavenly king]. He led his ministers of wind, rain and clouds in teaching the people more than 360 useful arts, including agriculture and medicine, inculcated moral principles and imposed a code of law. In those days there lived a she-bear and a tigress in the same cave. They prayed to *Sin Undo* [another name of *Hwan-ung*] to be blessed with incarnation as human beings. The king took pity on them and gave them each a bunch of mugwort[15] and twenty pieces of garlic, saying, "If you eat this holy food and do not see the sunlight for one hundred days, you will become human beings." The she-bear and the tigress took the food and ate it, and retired into the cave. In twenty-one days the bear, who had faithfully observed the king's instructions, become a woman. But the tigress, who had disobeyed, remained in her original form. But the bear-woman could find no husband, so she prayed under the sandalwood tree to be blessed with child. *Hwan-ung* heard her prayers and married her. She conceived and bore a son who was called *Tangun Wanggom*, the King of Sandalwood. In the fiftieth year of the reign of *Tang Kao* [legendary Chinese emperor Yao, traditional date some time before 2000 B.C.] in the year of *Kyong-in Tangun* came to *Pyongyang*, set up his royal residence there and bestowed the name *Chosen* upon his kingdom.[16]

It is believed that Korean shamanism is the structural foundation on which the *Tangun* myth was built. *Tangun* mythology is a theory of the origin of Korea as a nation and of its religion, shamanism.[17] The *Tangun* story is regarded as mythology by many scholars, but it is also regarded as a real and factual history by many Koreans.[18] It is unnecessary to present here endless debates on the verification of the authenticity of *Tangun* story.[19]

However, it is a fact that the *Tangun* myth has been deeply imprinted in the minds of the Korean people since the beginning of their history and has been a part of them. This mythology is perhaps the oldest and common faith of most Korean people. Thus, the Korean people are often called the children of *Tangun* of the race of the sandalwood. In this mythology, Korean people make an attempt to declare the pride and glory of Korea as a unique nation, since its founder was *Tangun*, the son of God. This mythology presents *Tangun* as a direct descendant of the heavenly King. The *Tangun* myth reappeared in *Chewangungi* [Songs of Emperors and Kings] by Sung-hyu Yi(1224-1300), in which the story of the life of *Tangun* is rather succinct. One of the obvious differences in the Songs of Emperors and Kings from the Memorabilia of the Three Kingdoms is the incarnation of *Tangun* through the granddaughter of the Heavenly King rather than through the bear-mother.[20]

In Songs of Emperors and Kings, the story of *Tangun* begins with his relation to Korea and his grandfather: "He who has founded this nation is the grandson of the Heavenly King, who is known by the name of *Tangun*."[21] *Tangun* was not only the founder of the nation but also the religious head of the nation, in which there was no separation of religion and state. Some scholars of interpret the three seals given to the legendary founder of Korea, as a drum, a mirror and a bell. If this interpretation is acceptable, then *Tangun* himself may be considered to be the first shaman. If the shaman is defined as the intermediary of spiritual beings, *Tangun* is the archetype of shamans of Korea, because in this myth *Tangun* was the symbol of an intermediary or mediator between the spiritual world of heaven and the material world of earth.[22]

In *Tangun* both the heavenly spiritual world and earthly material world are brought together, personified in him. It is considered that *Tangun* was the first great shaman to be initiated and capable of worshiping and praying to the Heavenly God on behalf of his people for an intimate relationship between the Heavenly God and earthly life. George Heber Jones, one of the early missionaries, writes that he believed that *Tangun*, the founder of Korea, was simply a great shaman.[23] It is believed that *Tangun* performed shamanistic rituals to the heavenly God on the great altar on *Mani* Mountain on *Kangwha* island, located near modern Seoul, which has become a focus for shamanistic ritual performances in which *Tangun* himself is worshiped today. According to variant tradition, *Tangun* first performed a shamanistic ritual to the Heavenly God on the island of *Kangwha*, located at the mouth of the *Han* river, twenty miles below modern Seoul. Later he erected on *Mani* mountain on this island a large altar of stone and earth, measuring approximately seventeen feet high and more than six feet square at the top.[24] Therefore, in the *Tangun* mythology we find the original pattern and essence of Korean shamanism and the archetypical symbol of shamanistic mediation as well as traditional thought of Koreans concerning their establishment as a nation in 2333 B.C.[25]

However, it is believed that the most important characteristic of the *Tangun* myth is that the relation of *Tangun* with the Heavenly King led to belief in the Heavenly King as the highest God of all other gods. Deuk-hwang Kim writes that faith in the Heavenly God is the most important characteristic of early animistic and shamanistic faith, calling it *Shinkyo* or religion of spirits. Belief in the Heavenly God as the highest God is the characteristic of shamanistic faith which predominates down to this day.[26] Kyung-cho Chung writes that Korean shamanism signifies one God, which embraces the idea of one supreme mind.[27] Thus, Korean shamanism, based on the *Tangun* myth, is more than just traditional animistic faith. This traditional faith in a Heavenly God precedes the influence of major religions from neighboring countries. According to archeological studies made by Nam-sun Choi, there are vestiges of ancient Korean temples that were dedicated to the "God of Heaven" together with other gods. It is believed that these temples were built before the introduction of the imported Eastern religions such as Confucianism and Buddhism.[28] Thus, the native faith or religion of Korean people was certainly animistic shamanism, which emphasized the worship of the God of Heaven. George H. Jones indicates that the ideogrphs for "heaven" or for "God" in Korea are just as old as the ideogrph for "spirit" or "ghost."[29]

Hulbert writes in his book on the history of Korea that *Yekook*, one of the primitive peoples to the east of Seoul, "worshiped the heavens in the tenth month of each year."[30] Griffs writes on the heaven and spirit worship of the early Korean people, "They sacrifice to Heaven, to the spirits of the land, to the morning star and to the celestial and invisible powers."[31] It may be safe to say that the central emphasis of Korean traditional and indigenous faith is its animistic and shamanistic faith, and this Korean shamanism is basically the worship the highest God of all others. The old Korean form of shamanism was soon influenced by Confucianism, Taoism and Buddhism. In contemporary shamanism, it is almost impossible to separate these elements. In other words, traditional shamanism emphasizing the highest God of Heaven seemed to disintegrate radically under the influence of magic and the Chinese popular Taoism, which came to Korea probably in the middle of the seventh century A.D.[32] The religious activity of early shamanism is described as follows:

> The *Han*, or genuine Koreans of the third century after Christ, are described (in Chinese Literature) as worshipping the spirits in the fifth and tenth months when the sowing and reaping of the year were concluded. On such occasions, they sang, danced, and drank wine. Several tens of them took part in the dance, and their hands and feet kept time carefully. One particular person was set apart to sacrifice to the Spirit of Heaven, and He was called the "Heavenly Ruler."[33]

These seasonal and thanksgiving rituals seemed to be primarily performed for the worship of the Heavenly King in traditional shamanistic faith. However, in contemporary shamanism this thanksgiving ritual came to be known as *Chonsin Kut* or *Chaesu Kut,* meaning ritual of welfare and blessings of the home and individual. Through the years shamanism became increasingly more interested in magic and divination rather than worship of the highest Heavenly God in order to meet the immediate desires of people, such as worldly happiness and prosperity of the individual. It is assumed that Korean traditional faith began to deteriorate with the coming of Chinese sorcerers and magicians. Charles A. Clark writes,

> In our discussion of Confucianism, we noticed in the story of *Keuija's* coming to Korea in 1122 B.C., that he "brought sorcery and incantation..." This was probably the first injection of Chinese influence into the aboriginal Shamanism. Down through history, the cult continued to develop under the influence of those two strains. The history states that in 773 B.C., there was one king who forbade sorcery and incantation... Magic and divination of the Koreans is said to have followed the teachings of Wun Chang Kang, an ancient Chinese sorcerer.[34]

Development of Korean Shamanistic Faith

During the period of the Three Kingdoms, this degenerated form of Korean traditional shamanism sustained its tenacity of survival as a cultic worship among common people even though it was rejected by people in the dominant classes on the occasion of the introduction of Buddhism, Confucianism and Taoism. *Samkuk Sagi* carries several records of shamanistic rituals in the Three Kingdoms. For example, there is a story of a *Koguryo* King, who punished by death two of his servants for mutilating a sacrificial pig that escaped before it could be sacrificed. The king punished the servants by burying them alive, but he soon became ill himself. He summoned the shaman, who explained the reason for his illness as being the two souls of the dead servants threatening the King's life. The story goes that the King confessed to these servants' souls and was forgiven.[35]

The Shamanism in *Shilla* Kingdom was so strong that Buddhism received forceful resistance from shamanism at the early stage of its introduction, and as a result the great monk, Lee Cha-don, was martyred. *Wharangdo* [an order of knighthood], which played a major role in the unification of the three kingdoms by *Shilla*, was actually a shamanistic organization. The name *Wharangdo* [*Wharang* means literally flowering youth, and *do* indicates the movement] refers to a spiritual movement as well as to the politico-social stratum and the elite stratum of the society.[36] *Wharangdo* was a movement that resulted from the merging of the indigenous and foreign religions, such as Buddhism and Confucianism. An outgrowth from the native shaman culture, *Wharangdo* was affected by the Buddhist belief in the future and the Confucian ethics, such as loyalty and filial piety. The *Wharang* were selected for their refinement. Their functions were singing and dancing on the one hand and military skills on the other. They wandered among the mountains, spiritually and physically cultivating their minds and bodies. The *Wharang* were instrumental in providing the spiritual and military skills for the unification of the three kingdoms which eventually became the United *Shilla* Kingdom (AD 668).[37] During the period of the *Shilla* Kingdom a ritual, called *Palgwanhoe,* evolved (AD 551), which the *Wharang* are believed to have presided over. It was nominally a Buddhist ritual, but in fact reflected the merging of shamanistic ritual traditions with those of Buddhism. While including various entertaining activities, the ceremony was performed in honor of heavenly, mountain and dragon [water] spirits, and it was also an occasion for lay people to renew the eight precepts of Buddhism. *Shilla* and *Koryo* kingdom observed a variety of state Buddhist festivals. The largest were the *Yondunghoe* on the fifteenth of the first month and the *Palkwanhoe* on the fifteenth of the eleventh month. Both these festivals combined Buddhist rites with indigenous practices, and in celebrating them the king and his subjects entreated the various Buddhas and the spirits of heaven and earth to bring tranquillity to the nation and the royal house by presenting performances of music, dance, and various entertainment.[38]

The *Koryo* Dynasty had Buddhism as its national religion, but its kings had a great zeal for shamanism, and they frequently invited shamans into the palace and made them sing and dance. It is a well-known fact that the founder king *Koryo Wanggon* (877-943) designated *Palgwanhoe* as a national ritual, which was a shamanistic ceremony worshipping the heavenly spirit, mountain spirit, and dragon spirit, along with *Yondunghoe*. *Yundunghoe* was one of the largest state Buddhist festivals in *Shilla* and *Koryo* kingdom.[39] In addition to Buddhist ceremonies, the government of the *Koryo* dynasty sponsored various other religious rituals. According to the chronicle of *Koryo*, many Taoist and Confucian rituals were performed at court. As seen in an appeal by *Chong Tonnjon* (AD 1391), the mixture of various traditions was carried on until the reign of the last king of the *Koryo* dynasty, *Kongyangwang*.

After you assumed the throne, the Taoist temples were built higher than the palace. There were rituals often performed in the Buddhist temple and Taoist rituals were also offered very frequently. Above all, the *Mudang* affairs were chaotic and troublesome.[40]

The religious culture of the *Koryo* court was such a conglomeration of different religious traditions that in some religious doctrines or ritual customs, it was hard to distinguish one from the other. In the *Koryo* Dynasty there are numerous records indicating that from its founder to the last king, they held shamanistic rituals presided over by shamans, particularly at the times of severe drought. The *Koryosa* records two hundred rain praying ceremonies, and the number of shamans who participated in a large performance was as many as three hundred or more.[41] The *Koryo* court sponsored prayer ceremonies for royal prosperity performed four times a year in accordance with the change of the season and, additionally, on special occasions. The shamans were favored by the people of the court. They were often called upon by the queen or queen mother to perform ceremonies for the king or other royalty who were sick. In *Koryo* society shamanistic faith permeated people's everyday life. "According to the old custom of *Koryo*," states the *Koryo Dogyong*[42] by So Kung, "the people did not take medicine when they became sick. Instead, they worshiped spirits. By means of rituals, they appeased the spirits who might be the cause of their sickness."[43] The people of all strata of society, from royalty and court officials to common provincial folk, relied on the shaman to prevent unpleasant events, such as sickness and natural disasters, and also to pursue fortune and happiness.

The *Yi* Dynasty rejected Buddhism and had Confucianism as its national religion. During the *Yi* Dynasty shamans belonged to one of the inferior professions, along with Buddhist monks. Throughout the history of the *Yi* dynasty Confucianism was influential, especially among the ruling and male segments of society. Government officials tried to establish Confucian customs in various court rituals honoring spirits and also tried to establish rites of passage for individuals, including those of initiation, marriage and death. In doing so, they not only criticized the belief system of the shaman and their ritual performances as superstitious, but also severely persecuted their practitioners. The shaman were periodically forced to remain outside the boundaries of the capital city or other districts. In spite of their banishment, however, they were often called upon by the queen and the queen mother to perform rituals at court. There they were confronted with overt antagonism from Confucian scholars and officials, who did not hesitate to use physical action to disrupt the ritual scenes. The governing policies of the ruling class regarding this matter were often contradictory. In spite of their hatred and scorn for shamanistic beliefs, the ruling class seemed to believe in two important concepts: 1) that the spirits caused sickness in and brought disasters to people; and 2) that the shaman could manipulate these spirits. Literature written during the period of the *Yi* Dynasty records many instances of the shamans' work. Not only were there private and family services, but the shaman had important ceremonies in the palace and in the nation. She officiated at national rites and filled the role of prophetess.[44] Particularly in times of drought the shamans were invited by kings to perform shamanistic rituals for rain.

King *Sejong* (1397-1450), inventor of *Hangul* [the Korean alphabet] established what was called *Tongseo Hwalinseo* to let official shamans treat patients. The organization was once closed down, but it continued as a kind of clinic until later.[45] During the reign of King *Sungchong* (1457-1494) and Regent *Yonsangun* (1476-1506), a special organization called *Seongsook Cheong* was established; an official shaman was appointed, and he foretold the kingdom's fortune and misfortune.[46] It was recorded that in the reign of *Sunjo* (1552-1608) of the *Yi*-Dynasty, the total number of registered shamans was approximately 2,600.

According to testimonies from early missionaries and foreign writers in Korea, shamanism with its ritual practices was and continued to be one of the most conspicuous features of Korean society in the early 19th century. They acknowledged it as the most powerful religious force among the Korean people. Karl Gutzlaff, the first Protestant missionary visitor to Korea, described spirit houses of shamanistic practice on his trip to Korea in 1832.[47] In the era of Queen *Min* (1851-1895), world traveler, Mrs. Isabella Bishop wrote that one time the police would raid the shamans and try to subdue them, and in another time the sisterhood of shamans would be flourishing.[48] George Herbert Jones depicted an accurate picture of shamanistic faith in Korea as follows:

Korean belief [shamanism] is that earth, air, and sea are peopled by demons. They haunt every embargoes tree, shady ravine, crystal spring, and mountain crest. On green hill-slopes, in peaceful agricultural valleys, in grassy dells, on wooded uplands, by lake and stream, by road and river, in north, south, east, and west, they abound, making malignant sport out of human destinies. They are on the roof, ceiling, fireplace, *kang* [river], and beam. They filled the chimney, the shed, the living-room, the kitchen, they are on every shelf and jar. .Spirits waylay the traveler as he leaves home, beside him, behind him, dancing in front of him, whirring over his head, crying out upon him from earth and air and water. They are numbered by thousands of billions, and it has been well said that their ubiquity is an unholy travesty of the Divine omnipresence. This belief keeps the Korean in a perpetual state of nervous apprehension, it surrounds him with indefinite terrors, and it may truly be said of him that he passes the time of his sojourning here in fear. Every Korean home is subject to demons, here, there, and everywhere. They touch the Korean at every point in his life, making his well-being depend on a series of acts of propitiation, and they avenge every omission with merciless severity, keeping him under the yoke of bondage from birth to death.[49]

In 1898, Gifford said, "It is estimated that demon worship costs the people of Korea two million five hundred thousand dollars a year"[50] for shamanistic rituals. In 1908 one of the first Protestant missionaries in Korea, Horace G. Underwood, wrote, "It is the strongest power from a religious point of view in Korea today."[51] James Gale wrote, "the whole land is shadowed by these [shamanistic beings] as was Egypt by the swarms of locust which came up to strip her."[52] Later he penned again that Korean people held shamanistic beliefs and that the cause of sickness was popularly thought of as evil spirit possession.[53] W.M. Clark, in 1925, wrote, "Today it may be safely said that this shamanism is the strongest power, from a religious point of view, in Korea."[54] Charles A. Clark writes,

> Similar testimony could be brought from numerous writers who have lived between these dates (1832-1925). Confucianism was their religion of state and, as such, a charge upon the national revenue. Buddhism throughout Korea's history was a state cult or a semi-state cult. Shamanism has been often condemned publicly, as noted above, and has always been despised by the literati, and more or less shamefacedly practiced by everyone, yet it has had more vitality than them all.[55]

It is a widely known fact that Queen *Min*, the wife of the last king of the late *Yi* Dynasty, probably raised shamanism to its glory, for she was a devout believer in shamanism and brought shamans right into the palace itself. She appointed a female shaman named Chi-yong Yi as *Chonyonggun* and even allowed her to participate in the decision-making process of national affairs. In fact, it was Queen *Min* who attempted to organize the cult of the whole nation under a centralized system by elevating Chi-yong Yi to the rank of princess. However, when the Queen was murdered by the Japanese in 1895, all of this came to an end.[56] It is then no wonder that even during the time of the Confucian Dynasty, shamanism had an important place in the kingdom and that shamans performed their rites in the palace to propitiate the spirits on all important feasts. In 1930, the *Chosen* Governor General estimated there were 12,380 shamans, which means an increase of about 10,000 shamans in the span of 100 years.[57]

In 1980 the Fifth Republic began with a new constitution which, among other things, stressed the preservation of ancient cultural traditions without prejudice. Thus, during the term of office of one of the former presidents, Doo-whan Chun, *kuts* were always openly permitted. It has been said that a large ritual was performed in honor of the Mountain Spirit, which included prayers directed towards the peninsula's unification in a democratic manner. A representative of the president was present to receive whatever "message from the gods"[presumably from the Mountain Spirit, who is related to the nation's progenitor, *Tangun*] was received by the *manshin*, Ok-hi Oh, when she went into an ecstatic trance. From the foregoing descriptions, perhaps it is not difficult to conclude that shamanism was found effortlessly and practiced vigorously at all social levels in Korea, from the highest ranking persons to the lowest ones.

Rituals of Korean Shamanistic Faith

There are many types of rituals in which shamanists often participate, for instance, those related to the belief in house gods, fertility gods, village gods and other nature spirits. All of the above belief systems have common bases in animism, fetishism, magic and taboos, and all can be categorized in the folk belief systems of Korea. The *mu*, either male or female, refers to certain types of ritual specialists who are often called "shamans," "an exorcist," "a sorceress," and "a female shaman," in Korea and the Western world. The word is a Sino-Korean term, *mu*, connoting two people who connect heaven and earth by singing and dancing. They are also variously called *manshin,* a female shaman, or *packsoo*, a male shaman, according to geographic or sexual distinctions. The function of shamans are as follows: first, a priestly role intermediating between human beings and divine spirits; second, a prophetic function conveying the will of the divine spirit to the followers; third, a role of relieving the sick from their disease; fourth, entertaining the public with singing and dancing.

The *mudang* perform the major ritual, called *kut*, a performance of a shaman, to bring fortune and expel misfortune through contact with spirits for a family or a village. *Kut* is a collective ritual. It is not simply a symbolic action of the folk belief system, but a complex of cultural expression. It integrates many different elements, both art-shamanistic and otherwise. Singing and dancing are of central importance in the *kut* performance, during which poetry and myth are chanted. Magic acts and exciting feats are interspersed with humorous episodes and dramatic actions. People learn and relearn the stories of god and human life. In the ritual, gods and humans laugh together and share other emotions. People gather to share food with the gods and reaffirm their harmony as a member of a family within the local community.

The integrity of the rituals makes one wonder how long it has taken them to reach their present stage of development, and the great variety suggests that many artistic talents and much imagination have gone into their making. Every idea and art of the Korean people finds expression in *kut* performances. *Mudang* have firm faith that the *kut* is the only means of enabling all sorts of human desires and prayers to achieve accomplishment. Therefore, one may claim that the rites of *mudang* are spell-bound ritual magic; there are a variety of different *kut*s for each separate occasion, such as that at the occasion of giving birth to a baby, dedicated to the three gods [*samsin*]-god of heaven, god of earth, and god of the ancestors; exorcism and *kut* for spelling disease when one gets sick; a rite for a wedding; *charigoging* or *chipkashim* (right before heading to the burial site, the coffin is moved outside of a house, when the whole interior of it is to be cleaned up at the funeral); *tang kuk* or *todang kut* for a rich crop or for the welfare of a village, and so on. Additionally, we may recognize numerous other *kut*, such as *chaesu kut* for good luck, a rite for a good fishing haul, *chino kut* for the sake of the other world to which one is heading soon after his death, and so forth.

One of the most prominent and representative *kut* is the twelve-scene *kut*. This is a rite of exorcism with twelve different scenes or series, among which the most important is the prayer to *Songju*, a spirit who guards the home site. The purpose is to worship him and inform him of a happy event, or a house newly built, or one's intention to worship him for the first time, or after one's absence from the house for a while, or *chonsin kut* as it is called, which is extremely colorful and dramatic. The scenes of *chonsin kut* may be classified into three groups: first, a dancing stage in which the related spirit god is invited, second, an incantation stage during which the spirit's will is relayed, and then, a singing stage when the spirit god is entertained. If asked what is the real motivation of the *kut,* it is to bring one happiness, and the desire to drive out calamity and possibly latent ill-luck. This indicates that we are right in calling shamanism a beneficial religion. The instruments employed in their exorcism rites are called *mugu,* the shamanistic tools. The *mugu* Siberians ordinarily use consists of a drum, bells and a mirror. However, the *mugu* Koreans make use not only of the above three but also of additional ones, such as fans, swords, three-pronged spears, gongs and many others. Each tool has a different purpose—the rite, exorcism, fortune telling or wearing divine clothes—a token of its having been developed in an organized and complicated pattern. These tools in fact have the power of inviting spirit gods or of expelling evil spirits; they give absolute protection to shamanism.

The *kut* is performed at a particular holy place such as a divine hall [*shindang*], a shrine [*sadang*], an altar [*chedang*], or a square for the spirits to fall into, the places where spirit gods reveal themselves. These are the sanctuary, they believe, in which is located the "cosmic axis" that provides a communication passage by shamans in their ecstatic experience so that they may spiritually transact with spirit gods. According to Yim Seok-che the program of a greater *kut* consists of the following:[58]

(1) Report of the name and rank of the supplicant
(2) Narration of the material and spiritual devotion of the supplicant to the performance of the ritual
(3) Narration of the process in which the offerings were made and prayer for the god's acceptance of the feast
(4) Narration of prayer for blessings and elimination of all misfortunes in the forthcoming year
(5) Narration of the mythology of the god being invoked
(6) Narration via *taryung* [ballad], dance, jugglery, talent show designed to please the invoked god
(7) Narration of jubilation for having achieved aspirations by the grace of the invoked god
(8) Narration of offering food for the assorted demons, accompanied by the following in some religions
(9) Opening song for a lesser *kut*
(10) Concluding song for a lesser *kut*
(11) Words of the invoked god to human beings
(12) Narration of the god's will by divination
(13) Narration of sending back the invoked god

Lesser *kut*, in which the name of a god is not invoked, are performed in most cases in a theatrical way as the opening process of a greater *kut*. Such lesser *kut* are designed to purify the hall for the greater *kut*, for relieving people of grievances, for paving the road to the other world, and for helping the dead who have not reached the other world. Every greater *kut*, after sending back the invoked god at the end, is followed by a lesser *kut* designed to placate the assorted gathered demons by inviting them to partake of the offerings. In light of the purpose and the performing scale of a shamanistic ritual, the Korean shamanistic rituals are largely classified into three types, which are the god ritual, the family ritual, and the village ritual. Each of them has its own purpose.[59]

Those who performed the so-called greater *kut* are commonly referred to as shamans, but the specific name by which each is known varies according to the region. In the eastern seaboard region, shamans are simply called *mudang* In the northern part of Korea, most shamans become professional when the spirits appear in them, regardless of sex or age. In most cases, this happens between the ages of ten and thirty. When the spirits dwell, the recipient suffers from an indeterminable ailment, behaves oddly, and divines things at the prompting of the spirits. With the performing of a ceremony, the recipient recovers from the illness. The assistants, or *kidae*, who beat double-headed drums, play accompanying music, and sing in alternation with them, are in most cases female, but occasionally there are males among them. *Kidae* are mostly those in whom the spirits have not appeared.

A recent survey reported that one in every 380 Koreans has had some psychic experience in his or her life. Shamanism is currently undergoing somewhat of a revival due to recent efforts to reconstruct Korea's cultural "roots" before they disappear under the march of industrialization. The fifth Republic government (1980-1987) has been more open to studying and retaining Korea's ancient cultural roots. Thus *kut*s can publicly be mentioned. There have been announcements of shamanist performances listed in the English language newspapers in Seoul. These include *kut*s held at places like Korea House, the Space Theater, and even provincial performances. Some years ago, two deluxe hotels of international reputation held rituals to celebrate some sort of "opening of the building." The Hyatt Regency scheduled a *kosa* to celebrate the opening of two refurnished private dining rooms on its second floor.[60] Modern five-star international luxury hotels now hold *kosa* to initiate construction or mark the completion of renovation.

Kosa is a celebrative shamanistic sacrifice to the spirits for opening of business and initiation or completion of construction For example, a *kosa* ritual was held at the *Chosun* Hotel on September 4th in 1981. Here Bob Chamberlain of the executive staff of the Hotel could be seen bowing before the altar. Even though this hotel is owned by one of the biggest chains in the hotel business, they followed local custom when a *kosa* was deemed appropriate at the end of the 12 million dollar renovation projects.[61]

In 1973 members of an organization comprised of *mudangs* and fortune-tellers, known as the *Kyungshinhoe*, which claims a total membership of 48,980, stated that there are estimated to be a total of 208,424 practitioners (*mudang* and fortune-tellers) around the country. However, a member of the management staff asserts that because 80 percent are uneducated, guidance and organizational structure are difficult to maintain.[62] According to a discovery made by Shu-Keun Chang a *mudang* serves between 100 and 200 households in a large town, but it is difficult to know who the believers are. Nevertheless, the previously quoted total estimates of the 50,000 *mudangs*-fortune-teller membership and the 200,000 around the countryside is a surprising figure.[63] Today Seoul boasts a headquarters building at Mount *Samgak* for an organization that claims 70,000 dues-paying members of a *mudang* Association in Seoul.[64]

Korean shamanism may have adopted ideas from higher religions, such as, 1) from Confucianism, ancestor worship, heaven worship, the rites; 2) from Buddhism the idea of the existence of heaven and hell; 3) from Taoism the pursuit of long life and immortality and the desire to live in harmony with nature. A relationship of the different religious beliefs and the primacy of shamanism has been well stated by H. B. Hulbert:

> As a general thing, we may say that all-round a Korean will be a Confucianist when in society, a Buddhist when he philosophizes and a spirit-worshipper when he is in trouble. Now, if you want to know what a man's religion is, you must watch him when he is in trouble. Then his genuine religion will come out, if he has any. It is for this reason that I conclude that the underlying religion of the Korean, the foundation upon which all else is mere superstructure, is his original spirit worship.[65]

However, it should be remembered that shamanism nowadays is the synthesis of Confucianism, Buddhism, and Taosim. All these imported Eastern religions became so intimately united with Korean shamanism that it is almost impossible to disconnect them. It was right when Jones said, "Shamanism has absorbed from the other cults, Confucianism and Buddhism, nearly every thing of supernatural character which they possessed."[66] Knowing this characteristic of Korean shamanism Hulbert once described it as a religion of the mosaic.[67] A modern Korean scholar puts shamanistic belief in the place of primary importance, although he notes that the four basic elements of the religious beliefs of the majority of the Koreans are shamanism, Confucianism, Buddhism, and Taoism.[68]

As such, shamanism has been dwelling in the hearts of Korean ancestors from the time of preliterate societies. Although it was rejected by people in the dominant classes, occasionally Korean shamanism has imbibed the higher religions and maintained its influence on religious life as a cultic worship among common people. It is believed that all the customs, thought patterns, mentality, and practices of Korea's individual life had their roots in animistic shamanism, which had preceded the major religions, and influenced and remained the underlying religion of all Korean people.[69]

TAECHONGKYO

It is said that Korea's oldest religion is *Taechongkyo*. *Taechongkyo* was called *Koshindo* until the early 20th century. There are very few adherents today of this religion, but it has obviously influenced later religious developments. *Taechongkyo* is a resurgence of ancient Korean shamanism in a more organized, theoretically more systematized form.[70] *Taechong* refers to the great ancient shaman or god-man or triune god, and *kyo* means religion.[71] The great ancient shaman or god-man that the *Taechongkyo* particularly refers to is *Tangun* who, as indicated above, is said to be the founder of the Korean nation in 2333 B.C. *Taechongkyo* claims that *Tangun* is the founder of that religion.

Therefore, *Taechongkyo* is about 4,000 years old and embodies the concept of a triune God: creator, teacher and temporal king, whose name is *Hanul* or Heavenly God. This God took human form in the person of *Tangun*, the father, teacher and king of the Korean people, who descended from heaven onto the highest peak in Korea. *Tangun* became the great teacher and law-giver of the tribes he found living on the Korean peninsula, reigning over them for 93 years until he ascended to heaven. In order to propagate worship of *Hanul*, the Heavenly God, *Tangun* established rituals for offering prayers of praise and propitiation to heaven. *Tangun* respected and worshiped his father

Heavenly God as the ancestor of all humans and the world. *Tangun* erected an altar at Mt. Hanbalg to worship his father *Hanul*, the Heavenly God. The teachings of *Tangun* were to worship the Heavenly God, respect our ancestors and love human beings. It was the chief influence over the Korean people in their customs and way of living for five thousand years.[72] These rituals became strongly established among nobles and commoners alike by the time of the Three Kingdom period, but with the introduction of foreign religions, purity in the practice of *Taechongkyo* gradually declined. By the 15th century, this religion as such had practically disappeared.

However, the beginning of *Taechongkyo* in its modern form goes as follows. In October 1904, a man by the name of Paik Pong proclaimed that he received a direct revelation from *Tangun*, by whose holy guidance he went to Mount *Paektu,* which is located in the northern-most area and is the highest in Korea. There he located a temple in which the principle image of *Tangun* was installed and religious services for *Tangun* were held. In that temple he also found a stone-box in which there were scriptures. These scriptures he gave to his disciples, whose names were Paik-too Ihl and Chun Paik, who, in turn, transmitted them to Chul Rha, or In-young Rha, in December 1908.

On January 15, 1909, in Seoul, Chul Rha became the first man who started to proclaim this religion, organizing and theoretically systematizing it. He called it *Tangungkyo* (*Tangun* Religion) and became the chief-leader. Hence, the date of the fifteenth of January 1909 became "*Choong Kwang,*" the day of Re-creation. Later in September 1910, its name was changed into *Taechongkyo*, because the name *Tangun*, which had been identified with Korean nationality, could not be used after the Japanese government annexed Korea in 1910. From the time of its first proclamation, it enjoyed a wide acceptance from most of the Korean people because Koreans thought that this religion was indigenous and nationalist. In fact, its members actually participated, during the Japanese occupation from 1910 to 1945, in the independence movements, and many of the leaders were put into prison and died there.[73] Some scholars, such as Chong-Ho Pyun, say that *Taechongkyo* is only a Korean nationalist religion without any possibility of becoming a universal religion, because it appeals largely to the narrowly nationalistic consciousness and spirit of the Korean people.[74]

After the liberation from Japanese rule in 1945, many leaders of *Taechongkyo* became leading scholars and politicians. It is, however, noted that *Taechongkyo* absorbed, or syncretized, three religions, namely, Confucianism, Buddhism and Taoism.[75] According to the latest statistics available compiled by the ministry of Education in 1973, the number of *Taechongkyo* followers totaled around 150,000 throughout the southern part of the country.[76] It is said that there were about 1,000,000 *Taechongkyo* believers in southern Manchuria alone when Japan lost the war in 1945.[77]

IMPORTED EASTERN RELIGIONS IN KOREA

Having come from China, these three great religions, Confucianism, Buddhism and Taoism, were introduced to the Korean people as part of the advanced civilization of China. They were first taken over by the ruling elite, and it was some time before they became the faiths of the common people. The three religions were always thought to be mutually complementary, and each was important in different areas of moral life. They formed an integral whole, for when one of the three occupied a dominant position, the other two continued to play important parts in the spiritual life of the people. History records this as early as 372 AD. Buddhism reached the northern kingdom of *Koguryo* that divided the Korean peninsula at the time. As to the other two legs of "the tripod on which the spiritual life of the kingdom may stably rest"— Confucianism and Taoism—history gives us no definite date of official introduction. This is specific reference to a passage under the heading of the second year of King *Bochang* (643.A.D) of the *Koguryo* Kingdom in *Samguk Saki* [History of the Three Kingdoms]; *Samguk Saki* is a 50 volume compilation under the editorship of Kim Bushik. The corpus was completed in 1145 A.D. The analogy of the three religions to a tripod can be found in many writing throughout East Asia. To this end he sought to send an emissary to *Tang* to acquire a better understanding of the religion.

The first specific reference to Taoism in the historical records is found the year 624 A.D. In that year Tang sent a Taoist with icons and literature to *Koguryo*. But the introduction of that religion seems to antedate this event considerably. It seems quite probable that Confucianism and Taoism reached the northern region of the Korean peninsula as early as the first century B.C. when the *Han* Empire colonized that religion. In this chapter the three established religions relatively dominant prior to the coming of Christianity, Confucianism, Buddhism, Taoism, which have always been religions deep-rooted in the Korean thought and behavior, will be introduced in an historical order.

Confucianism in Korea

Confucianism has been most important in terms of its cultural impact upon Korean society throughout history, especially in the area of ethics, politics, literature and arts.[78] Confucianism, as a system of moral teaching and behavior, teaches a series of social relationships and codes of morals consisting of five-fold loyalties: ruler and subject, father and son, husband and wife, elder brother and younger, and friends, a belief formulated to promote the organization of family unity and the reverence of elders. It is not known when Confucianism, which is a system of political and social ethics rather than a religion, first entered Korea. One recorded event is that in the third century B.C. a Chinese man by the name of Wiman occupied territory in Korea and brought Chinese literature with him at that time.[79] The records during the Three Kingdom period indicate that there was an early existence of Confucian influence. On the basis of the dated records, *Koguryo* had the earliest university in 372 A.D. and taught the Confucian scriptures.[80]

Until the *Yi* dynasty, Confucianism was much neglected and limited only to scholars and the people of the government who used Confucian principles to rule the country. Confucianism became the state religion with the birth of the *Yi* dynasty in 1392. During the *Yi* dynasty period, Confucianism in all its glory was brought into power, influencing the thinking and conduct of Korean people. Even in modern Korea, Confucianism penetrates deeply to the roots of Korean society. For the last five hundred years, Confucianism has held unlimited sway over the minds and hearts of the Korean people.

One of the chief religious elements of Confucianism remaining is ancestor worship, which is regarded as the foundation of Confucianism; it is practiced widely in Korea. Korea, having been dominated for five hundred years by the Confucian rule of the *Yi* dynasty, regarded ancestor worship as a most important national ritual. Thus, everyone in those days, regardless of his religious preference, was expected to participate in the practice. The development of the Korean form of ancestor worship occurred through the process of combining the shamanistic forms of worship with the Chinese form of Confucian ancestor worship.

The earlier shamanistic forms of worship that appeared in *Yonggo, Tongmaneng, Muchun* and *Sodo* had continuously influenced the later forms of ritual and worship, including ancestor worship.[81] The ancestor worship ceremony was gradually accompanied with the religious idea of reward and blessing. It was believed that the faithful practice of filial piety and the faithful performance of the ancestor worship ceremony would please Heaven and ensure heavenly blessings. This led to the belief that not Heaven but the deceased souls themselves were able to bless their descendants. Thus, the deceased souls were given a position of deity and became the object of ancestor worship ceremonies.[82] Worshippers understand their rites as ways of dealing with the departed; as L. Shirley Prive writes,

> We look for them, but do not see them; we listen to them but do not hear them; yet they enter into all things, and there is nothing without them. They cause all the people of the empire to fast and purify themselves, and array themselves in their richest robes, in order to attend at their sacrifices.[83]

Because Confucianism is a philosophy of life rather than a religion, there is no strong sense of worship of a divine. However, it is interesting to note that Korean Confucians discovered a personal God and even spoke of the "love of God," and believed in a personal God as a source of life and held the idea of an overruling providence about four centuries ago.[84] However, despite the ethical teachings of Confucianism, George Paik pointed out that this

> ...did not prevent the oppression of the masses, general poverty, the treachery and corruption of officialdom, and the degradation of womanhood which were characteristic of Korea in the last century...it encouraged selfishness, exalted filial piety to the position of the highest virtue and made this hide a multitude of sins; it imbued every follower with a hunger for office which resulted in simony and sinecure.[85]

Yong-choon Kim makes the same point.

> But Korean Confucianism also greatly damaged the health and progress of Korea as a nation through its degeneration into party struggle and by almost absolutizing the feudal system in which the upper ruling class monopolized the wealth and power, suppressing the lower-class peasants for centuries.[86]

Today, not many Koreans would acknowledge their religious affiliation as "Confucianism." Few young Koreans would profess any interest in its doctrines, but Confucianism still remains the moral foundation of the nation. From family life to the standard of morality, the Confucian heritage is still making itself felt in every facet of the nation's life. According to the 1991 census Confucianism numbered 421,000 or 1.8 percent of the religious population whose number was 23,364,000.[87]

Buddhism in Korea

Buddhism is a religion as well as a philosophy. Buddhism immeasurably enriched the Korean culture. It is a part of Korean cultural heritage and left an indelible mark on language, manners and customs, arts, folklore and all branches of scientific learning. The secret of Buddhism's success and its great and important contribution to the Korean people was that it gave Korea a sense of security and a feeling of hope. Buddhism was introduced into the Korean peninsula by way of China in A.D. 372, in the form called "*Mahayana*," or "the Great Vehicle." A Chinese monk named *Soondo* was the first Buddhist missionary sent by Fu-Kien, a king of Chin Dynasty.[88] In relation to the doctrine of Korean Buddhism, one Korean scholar writes,

> The Korean Buddhists believe in individual immortal souls, in a vicarious salvation through Amida Buddha, in reincarnation, in confessional, and in hell and a heaven achieved through faith. They believe that six virtues; charity, morality, patience, energy, contemplation, and wisdom must be attained in order to pass from this world of misery to the shore of holiness of the Buddhist heavens. They believe in a host of gods and Buddhas, represented by idols or images. Many forms of sacrifice or of recognition of these spirits are practiced.[89]

Buddhism spread rapidly through the Three Kingdoms and was transmitted to Japan before the close of the sixth century. Korean Buddhism developed into an indigenous religion during the unified *Shilla* and *Koryo* kingdom period, and Buddhism reached its peak and became the state religion. Clark writes,

> "In 1036 A.D. it was decreed that if a man had four sons, one of these must become priest, and in 1080 it was changed to one son out of three. A decree was passed requiring any family having four sons to dedicate at least one to the priesthood."[90]

When Buddhism was the predominant religion in *Shilla* and *Koryo* kingdom, the most popular rituals, both sacred and secular, were *Palkwanhoe* and *Yondunghoe*. Despite their formal relationship with Buddhism, these rituals reflected the Korean native religiosity and indigenous forms of worship.[91] The focal point in these rituals was the well-being of the community or, sometimes, that of the entire state and nation. These rituals entailed a certain shamanistic belief system that were the means for preventing calamities, involving God's blessings, and for protecting the nation with the help of the departed spirit.[92]

The significant feature of *Koryo* Buddhism was the publication of Buddhist 5,048 books and the printing of the eighty thousand wood blocks tripitaka, which is the oldest existing and the most sizable Buddhist scripture in the world. However, by the end of the *Koryo* kingdom, Buddhism exchanged its religious character for a political one. The priest-ridden government became thoroughly corrupt. When the *Yi* dynasty (1393-1910) came into power in Korea, Buddhism fell into disfavor, a condition from which it has never recovered until the beginning of this century. At the time of the introduction of Christianity into Korea, Buddhist priests were prohibited from even entering the capital city of Seoul. After the liberation from Japan, Buddhism was split into two main sects. One of them, the *Taejong*, was a liberal sect of married monks. The other, original sect, the *Chogyejong*, was conservative and refused matrimony. The *Chogyejong* won government support for its position in 1954, and it is now the most influential sect of Buddhism in Korea. In the post-Korean War years, Buddhism in Korea has been undergoing a considerable revival and is making efforts to adapt to the changes brought about by a modern industrial society. With this revival movement, Buddhism began to divide into numerous sects. Today there are at least 17 different Buddhist groups in Korea.[93]

Chogeyjong:	Buddha's idea of self-consciousness, 372
Taegojong:	Belief in idea of self-consciousness, 372
Chinonjong:	Teachings of the Buddhist Goddess of Mercy, 665
Popsangjong:	Belief in Maitreya's Ten Teachings of Goodness, 766
Yonghwajong:	Worship of Maitreya as its principal image, 777
Pomunjong:	Belief in idea of salvation of the Buddhist, 1115
Llsungkong:	Worship of Buddha as its principal image, 1916
Chonghwajong:	Belief in the Yonhwa Buddhist Scriptures, 1931
Mirukjong:	Belief in harmony among heaven, earth and man, 1942
Chondaejong:	Belief in Buddha's idea of self-consciousness, 1945
Pophwajong:	Belief in the Sutra of the Lotus, 1946
Chingakjong:	Worship of Buddha as its principal image, 1947
Chonhwa:	Worship of the Holy Mother as its founding image, 1951
Chontaekjong:	Worship of Amitabha as its principal image, 1958
Wonhyojong:	Belief in Buddhist scripture and Monk Wonhyo, 1963
Bulipjong:	Belief in the Sutra of the Lotus, 1965
Hwaomjong:	Practice of Buddha's conduct and enlightenment,1966

Buddhism is an integral part of modern Korea. Even today Buddha's birthday draws multitudes to numerous temples throughout the country. It is still the most important religion in Korea, although few Koreans are willing to claim it as the religion they believe in. According to statistics in Korea there were 7,253 Buddhist temples,

20,755 Buddhist clergymen as of 1982.[94] According to 1991 statistics there were 11,962,000 Buddhists or 51.2 percent of the religious population of Korea that numbered 23,363,000.[95]

Taoism in Korea

Taoism as a philosophy occupies an important place in Korean history. Its influence on Korean culture was not as great as Confucianism and Buddhism; however, it continued to permeate all strata of the Korean populace because Taoism's worship of the multiplicity of gods readily fit in with Korea's aboriginal animistic beliefs. According to legend *Lao Tzu,* the founder of Taoism, lived in the sixth century B.C. and was about twenty years older than Confucius. Taoism is a natural philosophy of speculative and metaphysical insights with respect to the nature of Reality, the universe, and man. The name Taoism is derived from *Tao*, the Way. *Tao Te Ching* [The Book of the Way and Its Virtue] or the *Lao Tzu*, which is the Bible of Taoism, was written by Lao Tzu.[96] It is not known exactly when Taoism came into Korea, but according to Korean history in 643 A.D., and again in 649, the king of *Koguryo* sent to China for Taoist books and teachers.[97]

Taoism has never been known in Korea as a separate religion with its own temples, and it failed to be productive as an unrelated system of belief. However, all of the religions of Korea are filled with Taoistic ideas which were originally influenced by early shamanism in Korea. The Taoism that came to Korea borrowed religious ideas, divinities and cults from Buddhism. The popular Taoism had met the need of the shamanistic-animistic Korean people. To the Korean people, Taoism always stood for the technique of acquiring the power of command over the life force of the cosmos. It promised longevity. *Tao*, the way of ultimate reality, appeared to the popular mind as the fountain of life force. By manipulating this cosmic ether, popular Taoism promised health, strength, longevity, and fecundity. It was the ability of Taoism to enjoy hospitality not only at the Confucian ancestor worship rite and at the Buddhist temple, but also at the shamanistic ecstasy that made it an important part of the folk religion of the Korean people.[98] Taoism is mainly a philosophy of nature concerned with the transcendent; it tries to bring people into closer harmony with nature by having them remove themselves from the world of human culture into the mountains where they practice a certain kind of moral training and asceticism, which results in good health and a long life. In this sense, then, Taoism is a religion of governing the body.

Table 2.1: Status of Religions in Korea

	1964	1969	1972	1975	1988
Protestant	812,254	3,192,621	3,463,108	4,019,313	10,337,075
Catholic	754,471	751,219	790,367	1,012,209	2,312,328
Buddhism	962,225	4,943,059	7,985,773	11,972,930	14,813,675
Confucianism	62,821	4,425,000	4,425,000	4,723,493	10,184,976
Chundokyo	623,397	636,067	718,072	815,385	1,079,901
Won Buddhism		619,219	681,783	740,362	1,098,537
Taechongkyo	30,815	113,720	145,002	128,198	507,533
Others		1,023,133	1,496775	1,864,263	3,127,251
Total	3,571,438	15,702,036	19,613,880	25,276,153	43,420,774

(Sources: Yung-Jae Kim, *A History of the Korean Church*, 1992, p. 355)

CHUNDOKYO

Chundokyo, literally "The Religion of the Heavenly Way," is a native and indigenous movement, the only mass religion originating in Korea. There were 600,000 members in the 1960s. Fifteen of the thirty-three signers of the 1919 Korean Declaration of National Independence were *Chundokyo* leaders.[99] It has a strong nationalistic tendency and yet a broad perspective of the universal salvation of mankind.[100] It had its origin in the time when the *Yi* dynasty was in turmoil in terms of both her internal domestic politics and her external foreign relations. Political and social unrest were widespread.[101]

The *Yi* Dynasty, at the time of *Chundokyo*'s formation in the 1860s, followed a disastrous road of decay, treacherous corruption and extreme nepotism. Money politics and power politics went together, influencing the government's personal administration. Against this background, the common people in Korea desperately were in need of some god or some religion or even someone to comfort them, to save them from the totally dehumanizing conditions, and to give them hope and salvation. Here came a man by the name of Che-woo Choi, the founder of *Chundokyo*, who was born in 1824. He felt the hope of the people and proclaimed the new religion, that he called the *"Tonghak,"* Eastern Learning. He lamented that "even the politics of *Yao* and *Shun*[102] could not do anything with this world, and even the ethics of Confucius and Mencius could not improve this world."[103] He also commented on Buddhism, "After the domination of Confucianism and Buddhism for several thousand years, has not their destiny not run its course?"[104]

Che-woo Choi had an initial contact with Roman Catholicism, from which he could not get any satisfaction at all. He called it the Western Learning, criticizing it as being too selfish, having no truth, containing self-contradictory doctrines, and with no genuine service by its egoistic adherents to their god.[105] Finally, on April 5, 1860, after about twenty years of seeking in vain after truth from Confucianism, Buddhism and Roman Catholicism, Che-woo Choi suddenly fell into a strange state of shock with his body shaking with chills. Enlightenment was bestowed upon him, and his awakening to the truth or Way became eventually *Chundokyo*.[106] Tong-shik Ryu says that Che-woo Choi expressed his deeply emotional experience of enlightenment in many ways; the following is typical:

> It was April and my heart was strangely fresh, and my body shaking with chills. Even though I thought it must be a sickness, I could find no symptoms and could not express my state. Just then a Heavenly Being spoke, and when I heard his voice I was greatly amazed. 'Fear not, be not troubled. I am He who is called God by the people of the world. Do you not know me?... Inquiring of him further, he replied,... I humbly send you into the world to teach this Way. Be not doubtful, have no doubt at all. Then, shall I teach the Western Way? Not so. I have a spiritual mark which is called *Son Yak* [miraculous drug], its form is like the *Tae Guk* [the ultimate reality of the universe, the symbol of the universe in Chinese philosophy] and also like the Kung Gung [an ambivalent, curved, bow-like figure], Receive this mark and deliver the people from their diseases. Take my mark and teach men. If you do these things for me you will enjoy long life and your virtue will spread throughout the earth.[107]

The founder of the *Tonghak* movement, Che-Woo Choi, had a vision regarding the realization of *Chundo* [Heavenly Way] in 1860, and developed this syncretistic religion, taking elements from Confucianism, Buddhism, Taoism, spirit worship, and Roman Catholicism.[108] Che-woo Choi had believed that all religions, from primitive animism to Western Christianity, were good and embodied one truth. And he said that each man had to seek truth according to his own way, but for Koreans *Tonghak* [*Chundokyo*] was the best way to

seek truth. He proclaimed this religion to be unheard of and incompa-
rable in the present and even in the past. It is the totally new way and
learning. He began to preach and became the founder of this religion,
which the god *Han Ool Nim* revealed to him.

The propagation of this new way and learning was very successful
among the common people in Korea, who eagerly accepted it. Tong-
shik Ryu points out that "the common people used the ambivalent
superstition of the traditional faith of the people," and "by shouting
that the Eastern learning, which was in conflict with the Western learning, was the Truth of Korea, they were able to stir up the nationalistic
feelings of the people."[109] In other words, *Chundokyo* was thought by
the masses to be indigenous. Ryu identifies the words which Choi Che-
Woo received with the *Logos* from God in the Gospel of John in his
book.[110] According to Sung-bum Yun, *Chundokyo* is Roman
Catholicism indigenized by Choi Che-Woo on the foundation of
Korean shamanism. In 1905, the name *Tonghak* was changed into
Chundokyo, with an eye to the claim that it alone constitutes the only
way to heaven.

Chundokyo is a monotheistic religion emphasizing the unity of man
and the universe. Man and God are one, and there would be perfection
here on earth if this unity were properly realized. *Chundokyo*, as a religion with a political movement, instigated the *Tonghak* rebellion in
1894 and the Independence Movement of 1919, which made the most
significant impacts upon modern Korean society. At one time in the
early 1940s it had more than one million adherents.[111]

CONCLUSION

Several religious systems or ethical systems with a religious base have
helped shape the course of Korea's religious development. The first
was shamanism or spirit worship of a type commonly found in
Northern Siberia. Shamanism has had the role of expelling people's
anxiety, of sublimating the inner conflicts of its followers and making
their naive dreams come true. Shamanism infiltrated into and dominated the thought and everyday life of every class of people, ultimately
exercising decisive influences to form a unique pattern and structure of
consciousness in Korean people. We can see clearly that it exists with
a certain dominant power among the people. Each New Year, the
Tojong Book of Fortune-Telling is shown and consulted in many

Table 2.2: Number of believers in Korea

Year	Confucianism	Buddhism	Catholicism	Protestantism
1962	3,426,120	481,292	559,713	
1969		4,903,110	751,000	3,167,100
1972		11,767,000	1,012,000	3,720,000
1974		11,973,000	1,012,000	4,019,000
1975	4,723,493	12,154,779	1,052,691	4,658,710
1976	4,723,000	12,907,000	1,904,000	5,001,000
1977	4,824,000	13,386,000	1,484,000	5,981,000
1978	4,920,000	13,386,000	1,184,000	5,981,000
1979	5,177,000	12,324,000	1,315,000	7,175,000
1980	5,201,000	11,130,000	1,440,000	7,637,000

Table 2.3: Number of clergy in Korea

Year	Confucianism	Buddhism	Catholicism	Protestantism
1962		5,800	652	4,110
1969		14,300	3,000	12,600
1972		18,629	3,487	17,562
1974		19,783	3,952	18,281
1975		19,982	3,952	19,066
1976	11,944	21,612	3,921	21,948
1979	9,572	23,480	4,339	27,721
1981	11,950	20,755	4,797	33,851
1983				40,717
1988				45,000

(Sources: *Ministry of Culture and Information,* Seoul, Korea, 1986;
Kyomunsa Statistics, 9 Feb, 1991)

places. The villages have their shrines, and fishing boats and ferries set up only after exorcism by a witch. From place to place we can see types of totem poles, and as for a wedding or moving a household, even the intellectuals would like to have an auspicious day selected.

Evidence of the ruling power of shamanism in Korea is seen in the present number of shamans or witches. It also played the role of storehouse, in the course of long history, in which Korean traditional culture has been well-preserved. The record of Korean mythology, singing and dancing in shamanisitic rites, and the folkloristic games have been faithfully handed down within the frame of shamanism. Such has been the functional influence of shamanism.

Therefore, shamanism, infiltrating into every nook and cranny of Korean society, dominates the way of thinking as well as the manner of behavior of the majority. Some Korean scholars such as Tong-shik Ryu and Tai-rim Yun claim that shamanism has determined the mentality and mental structure of the Korean people.[112] Tong-shik Ryu continues to say that in Korea shamanism has formed the religious foundation.[113] S. J. Palmer writes that "the primitive ethos of the Korean people derives from shamanism."[114] The average Korean does not look upon the three ancient religious faiths, Shamanism, Confucianism and Buddhism, as mutually exclusive. One of the very common ways to summarize these four religious thoughts is to say that Confucianism rules the political society of the world, Buddhism the mind, Taoism the body, and the *Chundokyo* man and heaven. Nida calls the religions - such as Confucianism, Buddhism, Taoism, and shamanism, which combine to cover the total area of man's concern for life - multireligion.[115] The Korean will recite the classics of Confucius, pray to the Buddhist deities, offer sacrifices to his ancestors and tremble in dread as he passes the shrines of the mountain demons. These three religions existed side by side, or rather interpenetrated and blended with each other. George H. Jones describes the Korean concept of religion as embracing three main beliefs:

> Anyone acquainted with the Korean people will know that they have a religious sense, though it may be on a low plane of exercise. 1) They possess a sense of dependence on that which is above and superior to themselves. They look out of themselves in time of need. It may be only into the great blue firmament above, but it is a look of expectation and hope. 2) They firmly believe that the human and the divine find a plan of intercommunication and relation. 3) We find everywhere among them an earnest striving of the soul after freedom from annoyance and pain. [116]

Indeed, Korea has been in some sense a melting-pot of faiths and religions for several thousands of years. Historically some foreign religions have been absorbed by Korea's indigenous religions. Religious consciousness of believers of overlapping religions naturally tends to contain elements of both. The three religions, Shamanism, Buddhism and Confucianism, are the relevant ones today. According to a 1991 national census, 54 percent of all Koreans follow specific religions. Of these, Buddhists number 11,962,000 or 51.2 percent; and Confucianists 421,000, or 1.8 percent.[117] And *Chundokyo* now has over 150 places of worship and 3,246 clergy members.[118]

Table 2.4: Number of Temples and Churches in Korea

Year	Confucianism	Buddhism	Catholicism	Protestantism
1962		2,161	710	5,793
1969		2,100	400	12,700
1972		1,912	428	13,417
1974		19,783	3,952,	18,281
1975		5,692	2,319	16,089
1976	232	6,780	2,265	17,846
1977	232	7,412	2,308	19,457
1978	232	7,448	2,339	20,019
1979	232	8,086	2,332	21,243
1980	232	7,244	2,342	21,243
1981	232	7,253	2,353	23,246
1988				30,016

(Sources: *Ministry of Culture and Information,* Seoul, Korea, 1985; Kyomunsa Statistics, 1991)

NOTES

[1]W. E. Griffins, *Corea the Hermit Nation* (Philadelphia, PA: The Presbyterian Board of Publication, 1885), p. 161; Percival Lowell, *Chosen: The Land of the Morning Calm* (Boston, MA: Tichnor and Company, 1886), p, 182; Louse J. Milan, *Quaint Korea* (London, UK: Osgood, McLivaine & Company, 1895), p. 226.

[2]G. Herbert Jones, *Korea: The Land, People, The Custom* (New York, NY: Easton and Mains, 1907), p. 49.

[3]Cf.Deuk-hwang Kim, *Hankuk Chongkyosa* [*A History of Korean Religions*] (Seoul, Korea: Haemunsa, 1963), p. 41-42; Ho-sang, Ahn, *Paedalui Chongkyo-wa Chulhak-kwa Yeuksa* [*Religion, Philosophy, and History of Korea*] (Seoul, Korea: Omungak, 1959), pp. 25ff.

[4]Homer B. Hulbert, *The Passing of Korea* (New York, NY: Doubleday Page Publishers, 1906), p. 126.

[5]Paul U. U. Park, "A Study on the Relation of Shamanism to Other Religions," *Korean Religions*, Vol. II. (Jan, 1970), p. 1, in: Jung-Yong Lee, *Korean Shamanistic Rituals* (The Hague, Paris, New York: Mouton Publishers, 1981), p. vii.

[6]Hyung-suk Kim, "*Chongkyo*" [Religion], *Dae Bekkwa Sajun* [*Korean Encyclopedia*], Vol.5 (Seoul, Korea: Hakwonsa, 1962), p. 569.

[7]*Chulhak Dae Sajun* [*Dictionary of Philosophy*], rev. ed., (Seoul, Korea: Hakwonsa, 1974), p. 57.

[8]I-seop Hong, "General Remarks on Korean Thought," in: *Korea: Its Land, People and Culture of All Ages* (Seoul, Korea: Hakwonsa, Ltd. 1960), pp. 316-322.

[9]Michael Ripinsky-Naxon, *The Nature of Shamanism* (Albany, NY: The State of New York University Press, 1993), pp. 56-59.

[10]Sang-hee Moon, "Shamanism and the Mental Structure of Koreans," in: Cheong-soo Suh, Chun-kun Pak, eds. *Aspects of Korean Culture*, p. 183.

[11]Mircea Eliade, *Shamanism: Archaic Techniques of Ecstasy* (New York, NY: Bollingen Foundation, 1964), pp. 461-462.

[12]Ki-baik Lee, *A New History of Korea*, trans. Edward W. Wagner with Edward J. Schultz (Ilchikak Publishers, Seoul, Korea), pp. 7-8.

[13]See Tong-shik Ryu, *Hankuk Mukyo-eui Yeoksa-wa Gujo* [*History and Structure of Korean Shamanism*] (Seoul, Korea: Yunsei University Press, 1975), pp. 46-48.

[14]Cf. Ki-baik Lee, *A New History of Korea*, p. 33.

[15]An aromatic Eurasian herb having linear to lance-shaped leaves and small, whitish-green flower heads arranged in loose, spreading panicles. It also called "tarragon," "artemisia," "sagebrush."

[16]Ilyon, *Samkuk Yusa* [*The Memorabilia of the Three Kingdoms*], trans.

Tae-hung Ha, Grafton K. Mints (Seoul, Korea: Yunsei University Press, 1972), pp. 32-33.

[17]In-whe Kim, et.al., *Hankuk Musok-eui Chonghap-jok Kochal* [*A Synthetic Study of Korean Shamanism*] (Seoul, Korea: Institute of National Culture of Korea University, 1982), p. 5-7.

[18]U-keun Han, *Kuksa* [*The National History*] (Seoul, Korea: Suhomyongusa, 1955), pp. 4-5.

[19]Sung-bum Yoon, *Sung-eui Sinhak* [*Theology of Sincerity*] (Seoul, Korea: Seoul Moonwhasa, 1976), p. 21-22. 217; Dae Jong Kyo Chong Bonsa, *Sam Ill Chul Hak* [*Three Days Philosophy*] (Seoul, Korea: Daejong Chong Bonsa, 1949), p. 43.

[20]Jae-won Kim, *Tangun Shinhwa eui Shin Yungu* [*Recent Studies in the Myth of Tangun*] (Seoul, Korea: Chungeumsa, 1947), p. 14.

[21]Yoon, *Theology of Fidelity,* p. 13.

[22]Deuk-whang Kim, *Hankuk Chongkyosa* [*History of Korean Religion*], p. 40; C.A. Clark, *Religions of Old Korea*, p. 176.

[23]George H. Jones, *Royal Asiatic Society Record* (Seoul, Korea: Transactions of the Korea Branch, 1900), pp. 35-41.

[24]Tong-shik Ryu, *Hanuk Mukyo-eui Yeoksa-wa kujo* [*History and Structure of Korean Shamanism*], p. 173; See Spencer J. Palmer, *Korea and Christianity* (Seoul, Korea: Hollym Corporation: Publishers, 1967), p. 10; See *Korean Review* III, (June, 1903), p. 258; and *Korea Magazine* (September, 1917), p. 411.

[25]Koreans have fixed the divisions of time in linear chronological sequence starting with the establishment of *Tangun* in 2333 B.C. so that the year 1995 in Korean reckoning would be *Tangi* 4328.

[26]Deuk-hwang Kim, *Hankuk Chongkyosa* [*History of Korean Religions*], pp. 16-17.

[27]Kyung-cho Chung, *Korea Tomorrow: Land of the Morning Calm* (New York, NY: The Macmillan Company, 1961), p. 53.

[28]Deuk-whang, Kim, *History of Korean Religions*, pp. 58ff.

[29]George H. Jones, *Royal Asiatic Society Records*, 1900, p. 41.

[30]Homer Hulbert, *The History of Korea* (Seoul, Korea: Methodist Publishing, 1905),Vol. pp. 21.

[31]William E. Griffs, *Corea the Hermit Nation* (New York, NY: Charles Scribner's Sons, 1882), p. 24.

[32]Kim, *History of Korean Religions*, pp. 58ff.

[33]Clark, *Religions of Old Korea*, pp. 176-177, in: Edkins' article in *Korea Repository*, 1892, p. 200.

[34]Hulbert, *History of Korea*, I. p. 11.

[35]James S. Gale, "A History of the Korean People," in: *Korea Mission Field* (Seoul, Korea: Published serially from July 1923-September 1927), No

pagination. Chapter 8.

[36]Tong-shik Ryu, *Hankuk Chongkyo-wa Kitokkyo* [*The Christian Faith Encounters the Religions of Korea*] (Seoul, Korea: The Christian Literature Society of Korea, 1965), pp. 24-25.

[37]Ryu, *Hankuk Mukyo-eui Yeaksa-wa Kujo* [*A History and Structure of Korean Shamanism*], pp. 86-97.

[38]Cf. Tong-shik Ryu, *Hankuk Mukyo-eui Yeksa-wa Koojo* [*History and Structure of Korean Shamanism*], pp. 73, 88, 116-133, 210, 230, 259.

[39]Byung-do Yi, *Hankuksa Joongsea-pyeun* [*History of Korea: The medieval ages*] (Seoul, Korea: Eulyoo Munwhasa, 1961), pp. 78. 171. 292-294.

[40]Nung-hwa Yi, *Chosen Musokko*, trans. from an article published in 1927 in *Kyemyong* [*The Morning Star*] (Seoul, Korea: Kyemyong Kurakpu), Vol. 19, p. 13.

[41]Ryu, *A History and Structure of Shamanism in Korea*, pp. 126-127.

[42]*Koryo Dogyong* means literally, "The Scripture of the Way or Enlightenment in *Koryo* Dynasty"

[43]Tong-kwon Im, *Hankuk Minsokhak Nongo* [*A Study of Korean Folklore*] (Seoul, Korea: Sorwhadang, 1971), p. 394.

[44]Tong-kwon Im, *"Mudang"* [Shaman], *Dae Baekwa Sajun,* [*Korean Encyclopedia*] Vol. 2. (Seoul, Korea: Dong-A Publishing Co., 1962), p. 921.

[45]*Ibid.*, p. 198.

[46]Ryu, *History and Structure of Korean Shamanism*, pp. 198-199.

[47]Charles Karl Gutzlaff, *Journal of Three Voyages Along the Coast of China* (London, UK: Frederick Wesley and A.H. Davis Second Edition, 1834), p. 280.

[48]Isbella Bird Bishop, *Korea and Her Neighbors* (New York, NY: Fleming H. Revell Co., 1898), p. 402.

[49]Gale, *Korean Sketch* (Edinburgh, Scotland: Olipant Anderson & Ferrior, 1898), pp. 83-84.

[50]D.L. Gifford, *Everyday Life in Korea* (New York, NY: Fleming H. Revell, 1898), p. 107.

[51]Underwood, *The Call of Korea* (New York, NY: Fleming H. Revell, 1908), p. 85.

[52]Gale, *Korean Sketch*, p. 83.

[53]See Gale, *A History of the Korean People* (Seoul, Korea: Christian Literature Society, 1927), Chapter 26.

[54]C. A. Clark, *Religions of Old Korea*, p. 178.

[55]*Ibid.*

[56]Jung-young Lee, *Korean Shamanistic Rituals* (The Hague, NL: The Mouton Publishers, 1981), pp. 1-2; Clark, *Religions of Old Korea*, pp. 177-178.

[57]Cheong-soo Suh and Chun-kun Park, *op.cit.*, p. 186.

[58]Seok-che Yim, *Hankuk Musok Yungu* [*Study of Korean Shamanism*], n.p, in: Halla Pai Hulm, *Kut: Korean Shamanistic Ritual*, p. 14.

[59]Kim, *Study of Korean Shamanism*, pp. 342-347.

[60]*Ibid.*, p. 92.

[61]*Ibid.*, pp. 56-57.

[62] Sue-keun Chang, "*Musok*, The Shaman Culture of Korea," in: Shin-yong Chun, ed. *Folk Culture in Korea*, p. 60.

[63]*Ibid.*

[64]Allen, *Ecstasy: Shamanism in Korea*, pp. 18-19.

[65]Hulbert, *op.cit.*, pp. 403-404.

[66]Clark, *Religions of Old Korea*, p. 178.

[67]See Hulbert, *op.cit.*, Chapter XXX.

[68]Ryu, *The Christian Faith Encounters the Religions of Korea*, p. 188.

[69]Ryu, *Hankuk-eui Musok Jongkyo-wa Moonwha* [*Folk Religions and Culture in Korea*] (Seoul, Korea: Hyundae Sasangsa, 1978), pp. 103-114.

[70]Tae Chong Kyo Chongponsa, *Taechongkyo Choongkwang Yooksinpnunsa* [*Sixty Year History of Re-creation on Taechongkyo*] (Seoul, Korea: Tae Chong Kyo Congponsa, 1971), pp. 29-32, 80; Sung-bum Yun, *Kitokkyo-wa Hankuk Sasang* [*Christianity and Korean Thought*] (Seoul, Korea: The Christian Literature Society of Korea, 1964), p. 170.

[71]Tai Chong Kyo Chongponsa, *Sixty Year of History of Re-creation of Taechongkyo*, p. 157; Noong-hwa Lee, "*Chosun Musokgo*" [A Study of Korean Shamanism] in: *Kemyung* [*The Morning Star*], No. 19 (February 1929), p. 1.

[72]See Ho-sang Ahn, *The Ancient History of the Korea-Dong I Race* (Seoul, Korea: Institute of Korean Culture, 1974), pp. 74-86.

[73]*Ibid.*, pp. 369-380; Ministry of Culture and Information, *Chongmoo Pyunram* [*Handbook of Religion*] (Seoul, Korea: Ministry of Culture and Information, 1969), p. 237.

[74]Chong-ho Pyun, *Chongkyo eui Bikyo Yunku wa Ku Kyullon* [*A Comparative Study of Religions and Its Conclusion*] (Seoul, Korea: Simwoo Won, 1959), p.104.

[75]Tai Chong Kyo Chongponsa, "*Hoi Sam Kyung*" [Scripture of Assembling Three], in: *Samil Chulhak: Yukhe Chongkyung Happyun* [*Philosophy of Three-One: Commentary on the Scripture*] (Seoul, Korea: Taichongkyo Chongponsa, 1949), pp. 110-113.

[76]Chang, "*Musok*: the Shaman Culture of Korea," Chun, ed. *Folk Culture in Korea*, p. 59.

[77]Ahn, *op.cit.*, p. 95.

[78]Cf. Yu-lan Fung, *A History of Chinese Philosophy* (Princeton: Princeton University Press, 1952), Vol.I., pp. 30ff.

[79]Ki-baik Lee, *op.cit.*, pp. 16-19.

[80]See Sang-yun Hyun, *Chosen Yuhaksa* [*History of Confucianism in Korea*] (Seoul, Korea: Minjungseakwan, 1949), pp. 13-30.

[81]Cf. Byung-do Lee, Jae-Won Kim, *Hankuksa* [*History of Korea*] (Seoul, Korea: Eulyoo Moonwhasa, 1959), p. 220.

[82]Bong-bae Park, "Christianity and Ancestor Worship," Harold Hong, et.al. eds. *Church and Mission in Korea* (C.L.S.K., 1963), pp. 201f.

[83]L. Shirley Prive, *Confucius and Christ* (New York, NY: Philosophical Library, 1951), p. 81.

[84]Gale, "A History of Korean People," *The Korean Mission Field*, Vol.22, No.9, (Sept. 1926), p. 191; No.8, (Aug. 1926), p. 163; No. 10 (Oct. 1926), pp. 222-224, in: Paik, *op.cit.*, 25; Many passages occur in Korean literature that seem to be rephrasing of passages from the Christian scriptures.

[85]George L. Paik, *The History of Protestant Missions in Korea 1832-1910* (Seoul, Korea: Yonsei University Press, 1970). p. 23.

[86]Yong-choon Kim, *Oriental Thought* (Totowa, NJ: Littlefield, Adams and Company, 1981), p. 94.

[87]Korea Oversea Information Service, *Facts about Korea* (Seoul, Korea: Korea Oversea Information, 1993), p. 131.

[88]See Deuk-whang Kim, *Hankuk Jongkyosa* [*History of Religions in Korea*] (Seoul, Korea: Haemoonsa, 1963), pp. 97-98.

[89]Kyung-cho Chung, *Korea, Tomorrow, Land of the Morning Calm* (New York, NY: The MacMillan, 1956), p. 54.

[90]Ki-baik Lee, *op.cit*, pp. 130-131; Clark, *Religions of Korea*, pp. 33-34.

[91]Ryu, *Folk Religion and Culture in Korea*, pp. 151-152

[92]*Ibid.*, pp. 155-156

[93]Chang, *op.cit.*, p. 50. *Creeds and Founding Years of Buddhist Sects in Korea.*

[94]Byung-kil Chang, *Religions in Korea* (Seoul, Korea: Korea Overseas Information Service, 1984), p. 51.

[95]Korean Overseas Information Service, *Fact about Korea* (Seoul, Korea: Shamhwa Printing Company, 1993), p. 130.

[96]See Keith Crim, *Abingdon Dictionary of Living Religions* (Nashville, TN: Abingdon Press, 1981), pp.742-45; Yong-Choon Kim, *Oriental Thought* (Totowa, NJ: Littlefield, Adams and Company, 1973), pp. 63-71.

[97]Nung-wha Lee, *Hankuk Dokyosa* [*History of the Taoism in Korea*] (Seoul, Korea: Dongkuk Moonwhasa, 1959), pp. 40-45.

[98]Joo-whan Cha, *Hankuk-eui Dokyo Sasang* [*A Taoistic Thought in Korea*] (Seoul, Korea: Dongwha Publishing Co., 1984), pp. 105-112; Cf. Nung-wha Lee, *Chosen Dokyosa* [*A History of Taoism in Korea*], p. 46.

[99]Clark, *Religions of Old Korea*, p. 144; Yong-choon Kim, *Oriental*

Thought, p. 95; Cf. Deuk-whang Kim, *A History of Religions in Korea*, pp. 452-457.

[100]Tong-shik Ryu, "*Chundokyo*: Korea's Only Indigenous Religion." *Japanese Religions* 5, No. 1 (July 1967), pp. 59; Sung-bum Yun, *Religions Around Us*, p. 101; Yun also says that *Chundokyo* is the only religion that has been founded in Korea by a Korean.

[101]*Chundokyo, Chundokyo Sachun* [*A History of Chundokyo*] (Seoul, Korea: Chundokyo, 1964), pp. 3-4; Hahn, *A Comprehensive History of Korea*, pp. 450-452.

[102]The two most famous legendary kings in ancient China.

[103]Paik, *Tonghak Kyungchun Haeui* [*Commentary on the Scriptures of the Eastern Learning*] (Seoul, Korea: Illshin Publishing Co., 1963), pp. 253-254.

[104]*Chundokyo, Scriptures of Chundokyo*, p. 71.

[105]*Chundokyo, Chundokyo Kyungchun* [*The Scriptures of Chundokyo with Notes*], (Seoul, Korea: Chundokyo Choongang Chongpoo, 1956), p. 38.

[106]Tong-hee Choi, *Hyundeyuk Tonghak Kyungchun* [*Modern Translation of the Scriptures of the Eastern Learning*] (Seoul, Korea: Kowoo Publishing Co., 1961), pp. 16-17, 24-29, 72, 76-78.

[107]Tong-shik Ryu, "*Chundokyo*: Korea's Only Indigenous Religion," *Japanese Religions*, pp. 63-64. (This text of the Scripture of the *Chundokyo* is translated by Tong-shik Ryu.)

[108] Che-woo Choi, *Dongkyung Taejun* [*Great Canon of the East*], trans. Man-sung Nam (Seoul, Korea: Eulyoo Moonwhasa, 1973), pp. 33-41; Deuk-whang Kim, *History of Religions of Korea*, pp. 437-60.

[109]Ryu, "*Chundokyo* : Korea's Only Indigenous Religion," *Japanese Religions*, p. 65.

[110] See *The Christian Encounters the Religions in Korea*, pp. 103-108.

[111]Se-myung Paik, *Tonghak Sasang kwa Chundokyo* [*The Thought of the Eastern Learning and the Heavenly Way Religion*] (Seoul, Korea: Tonghak Co., 1956), pp. 6-7, 11.

[112]Ryu, *Religions of Korea*, pp. 15ff; Cf. Tai-rim Yun, *Mental Structure of Korean People*, p. 31.

[113]*Ibid.* p.15. See also Sung-bum Yoon, *Kitokkyo-wa Hankuk Sasang* [*Christianity and Korean Thought*] (Seoul, Korea: The Christian Literature Society of Korea, 1964), p. 161.

[114]Palmer, *Christianity in Korea*, p. 5.

[115]Nida, *Religion Across Culture*, pp. 14-16.

[116]Jones, "The Spirit Worship of the Korean," *Transactions of the Korean Branch of the Royal Asiatic Society*, Vol.II, part 1 (1901), pp. 38-39.

[117]Korean Overseas Information Service, *Facts About Korea*, 1993, p. 130.

[118]Yunhap News Agency, *Korea Annual 1993* (Seoul, Korea: Yunhap News Agency, 1993), p.133.

Chapter Three

BASIC BELIEF SYSTEM AND THE STRUCTURE OF RELIGIOUS CONSCIOUSNESS IN KOREAN SHAMANISM

INTRODUCTION

Since it lacks an established sociological structure, there is debate over whether shamanism can properly be called a religion. The author refers to shamanism not as a religion but as a religious faith, implying that it has definite religious elements even though it may not always meet sociologists' technical definition of religion. According to Michael Harner shamanism ultimately is only a method, not a religion with a fixed set of dogmas.[1] From the middle of the twenieth century Korean folklore scholars began to study Korean shamanism systematically. They gathered the elements of shamanistic belief from the shaman's songs, dances and rituals, which were the expressions of shamanistic belief. It is believed that in Korean shamanism today there are several basic elements which are common to all forms of shamanism, phenomena such as the shaman's mystic experience, her or his view of God, myths, divine songs and rites. It is commonly believed that the heart of shamanistic belief expressed in rituals comprises the characters and fortune of the spirits, of the universe and of the human being. In other words, it concerns the relationship between three areas: the universe, human beings, and spirits and gods.

Today shamanistic faith is still the most fundamental and influential religious practice have by no means disappeared from Korea; it remains the most of the Korean people.[2] Because shamanism has little external organizational form it is impossible to estimate the exact number of believers in Korean shamanism. Nevertheless, it is supposed that more than 80 percent of the South Korean population in our time adhere to shamanistic practice.[3] It is a fact that shamanistic faith has revived in Korea under the banner of "Resurgence of National and Traditional Culture" supported by the government, along with Buddhism, Taoism and Confucianism. In 1973, *Kyungshinhoe*, an organization of *Mudang* [shamans] and fortune-tellers which claimed a total membership of 48,980, states that there are estimated to be a total of 208,424 practitioners [*Mudang* and fortune tellers] around the country.[4] In this chapter the author discusses the basic belief system and the religious and mental structure of Korean shamanism and its relation with ancestor worship in order later to be able to understand how Christianity in Korea has been influenced by shamanistic belief and practice.

BASIC BELIEF SYSTEM OF KOREAN SHAMANISM

Belief about the Universe

The concept of the universe in Korean shamanism is interesting. The universe consists of three stories: the high world, the middle world, and the underworld. The high world, the world of heaven and light where the highest deity and good spirits reside, is ruled by the sun god, the moon god and the star god, as well as the heavenly god. The middle world is the world of man and animals ruled by the earth god, the mountain god and human gods. The underworld is hell, where the evil spirits reside, ruled by the ten royal gods and their messengers. Korean shamanism believed that one ascends into the high world or descends to the underworld according to one's deeds in the present life.[5] Thus, even in Korean shamanism one may find a primitive and simple concept of ethics and after-life. These primitive ideas were later easily incorporated into Buddhism and Confucianism in Korea.

Belief about Human Beings

Korean Shamanism has a notion that human beings are composed of three elements, namely, life, body, and soul. And when one dies, shamanists believe, their life becomes extinct, their body perishes and the soul departs for another world, reflecting their core belief in the immortality of the soul. They hold a common belief that human death

means one's being summoned to the other world, accompanied by a
death messenger from it, that the dead person is to live life there just as
he or she did in this world, and that the soul in the other world may
sometimes be able to return to this world.[6]

Belief about spirits and gods

Korean Shamanism has a notion that depending upon how he or she
dies, a person may become a good or evil spirit, which is a god or devil.
In Korean shamanism, problems of human death or life or matters of
fate depend upon transactions between gods and devils, and it is
believed that the shamans are those who are able through ecstasy to
communicate with the gods and devils. According to Im Sok-Che, the
pantheon of shaman gods are not good or evil spirits per se, even
though there is a distinction between guardian gods and malignant spirits. This is because any gods that are treated well will return the favor,
and those who are neglected or treated badly will punish the individual
with misfortune.[7]

Korean shamanism is basically animistic. It considers that nature is
full of spirits and worships them. It believes that spirits exercise superhuman powers to bring about either blessings or curses.[8] In this
respect, Korean shamanism may be called a kind of religion of polytheistic and polydemonistic belief. The shamans who worship are commonly called "*manshin*," meaning a shaman who serves ten thousands
spirits. According to a shaman in *Chejudo* named *shinbang* [shaman],
there are 18,000 spirits and gods.[9] According to a survey conducted by
Tae-gon Kim, one of the leading scholars on folklore in Korea,
shamanism in Korea knows as many as 273 different kinds of spirits or
gods. They include 73 kinds of spirits responding to *kut* rituals, 115
kinds of spirits appearing on shamanistic paintings, 138 kinds of spirits worshiped in shrines, and 11 different kinds of spirits that are
guardians of households.[10] He classified these 273 as being composed
of twenty-two types of nature gods, eleven types of human gods, and
an unclear category of miscellaneous spirits.[11] Tae-gon Kim claims,

> There are 22 categories of natural gods, 11 in human gods, and another cat-
> egory - 34 in all. The ratio of composition is 63.6 percent natural gods, 33.3
> percent human gods, and 4.1 percent gods falling under other categories.
> Among natural gods, earth gods occupy 9.8 percent, mountain gods 9.5 per-
> cent, water gods 9.5 percent, warrior gods 9.1 percent, and heavenly gods
> 4.7 percent. In other words, the order in the category of natural gods is the
> earth, water, mountain, and the heaven which are most closely connected

with daily human life. In the category of human gods, the order is the warrior gods, royal gods, Buddhist gods, and shaman ancestral gods.[12]

Gods worshiped in Korean shamanism can be classified broadly into two types: natural gods and human gods. The former have their origin in nature worship, and the latter in ancestor and hero worship. These 273 gods, according to this writer's survey, can be subdivided as follows:

A. Natural gods:
    1) Heavenly gods:
        a. Sky or High god   c. Moon god
        b. Sun god   d. Star god
    2) Earth gods
    3) Mountain gods
    4) Road gods
    5) Water gods:
        a. Water gods
        b. Dragon gods
    6) Fire gods
    7) Wind gods
    8) Tree gods
    9) Stone gods
   10) Direction gods
   11) Gate gods
   12) Warrior gods
   13) Demons
   14) Hades gods
   15) Disease gods
   16) Animal gods
   17) Agricultural gods
   18) Birth gods

B. Human gods:
    1) Royal gods:
        a. King god
        b. Queen goddess
        c. Princess goddess
    2) Commander gods:
        a. General god
        b. General's wife goddess
        c. Other goddesses
    3) Lord gods
    4) Madam goddess, bride goddess
    5) Shaman ancestor gods
    6) Buddhistic gods
    7) Taoistic gods
    8) Miscellaneous gods
    9) Other

It is interesting to note that most shamanistic spirits or deities are males; some spirits are acknowledged as females, these generally being classified as "grandmother spirits." Perhaps this may help to explain why the small group of male shamans in Korea today is almost always transvestite, performing in women's costume. These men are not homosexuals, but simply take on feminine attributes in their dance and costume in order to please the male deities, whom they must invite to possess them. However, according to Un-bong Lee, Korean shamanism has two kinds of goddesses: Mother-Earth and Dragon. He writes that Mother-earth and Dragon take dominant parts in Korean faith, more than the heavenly Father God. They usually get married to the Heavenly God and beget a son, who becomes a sacred ruler or a founder of an earth kingdom.[13]

Tae-sok So also believes that the characters of shamanistic gods are vague, and all gods have a common function to bestow longevity and happiness.[14] The gods of Korean shamanism love cleanliness. Koreans take particular care to sanctify the ritual ground before performing a ritual. They avoid unclean people, such as a woman in pregnancy or menstruation, a person who has experienced the recent death of an immediate family member, a murderer and so on. Since the gods of shamanistic faith avoids brightness, Koreans usually perform shamanistic rites after sunset and continue through the night. The gods of shamanism are more properly called spirits, and the old primitive shamanism has names of spirits that have been worshiped, including such names which derive from animism and fetishism. These multitudinous spirits cannot be listed here, we will refer to only a few of them.

The *Obang Changgun*, the general gods, or Five-point Generals, who are the spirits of the heavens, are the green, red, white, black, and yellow generals of the Eastern, Southern, Western, Northern, and Zenith heavens. These spirits are said to be rulers of the five great wards of the heavens, each of whom in his own ward is supreme and each controls a mighty spirit host which does his bidding.[15] These are considered to be very powerful gods.[16] The *Chinchang* are officers under the great *Obang Changgun*, whose numbers are eighty thousand or more, and each of whom has under his direction great numbers of inferior spirits.[17]

The *Sansin*, or mountain gods, are fertility gods and are worshiped particularly just after the harvest. A Korean proverb runs, "Cross over a mountain and you will find another mountain." The Korean people are surrounded by mountains. In no place on the peninsula can the horizon be viewed unobstructed by mountains. Further, the mountains produce the fuel to cook the rice and heat the home. They yield occasional game such as deer, wild pig and pheasant, and also produce that mysterious elixir root shaped like a man: ginseng. Wild animals, including the fierce tiger, roam the mountains. Because of the proximity of the mountains to the people, because of the mystery, and the economic effect the mountains have on the lives of the Koreans, it seems natural that they would believe in the gods of the mountain or *Sansin*. A missionary reports that one will find on the mountainside shrines containing a picture of the god and possibly of a tiger, located where people going to the mountains to hunt, to search for wild ginseng, or to gather fuel will make their offering.[18] It is said that "more people believe in the gods of the mountain than in Buddhism."[19]

The *Sungwhangdang*, referring to mountain pass gods, is the name of the altar where local deities reside and where they are worshiped.[20] *Sungwhang* are spirits to whom passersby over a mountain pass offer the collars off of their coarse clothes. People also offer the clothing of sick children, or the clothing of brides, bits of silk, or cotton, or salt of merchants. These things, and many other objects, are offered to secure the spirits' protection against any harm that might threaten the passersby. At the top of a pass or a critical point on a journey, travellers stopped to make offerings of worn-out sandals and add a stone to an existing stone pile. In Korea this *Sungwhangdang* is the place where both a professional shaman and lay persons make their sacrifices and petitions to the spirits regarding a multitude of desires. According to Jones, a custom of expectorating on the altar may have arisen as a means to divert the attention of the snake spirit which is thought to be evil.[21] An informant told a Korean scholar from *Taegu* that the throwing of a stone on the altar was to keep from getting a sore foot on a journey, and the spitting on the altar was to keep from getting an evil spirit.[22] The *Chunsin* are the gods who are "the tutelary divinities presiding over villages located in a plain." Each is the spirit of the village or a group of hamlets in a valley and is actually a community's god. Their function is almost the same as that of the *Sansin*, but they are perhaps more closely connected with agriculture.

Togebi, ghosts, may have either purely spiritual origins or may be the soul of a departed person. Hurbert divides the spirit world of Korea into two separate orders: that of *Kwisin*, which are of extra-human origin, and the *Togebi*, which represent the souls of the deceased.[23] At any rate, the *Togebi* are usually malevolent, more powerful, and more numerous than the *Kwisin*. *Togebi* will be prevalent at execution grounds, battle-fields and scenes of murder or fatal disaster and resemble the Western idea of a ghost.[24] *Sakwi*, Unclean or Tramp Spirits, are the wanderers and the outcasts of the spirit world of Korea who give a person indigestion and when they have an opportunity, come into a person and cause all sorts of afflictions. The early Bible translators used the term *Sakwi* for unclean spirit, but the present edition of the Korean Bible uses the term, *Kwisin*, to translate unclean spirit, rather than the *Sakwi*, which is of Chinese origin.[25]

Yong, a well-known Chinese dragon god, who lives in and is the lord of all oceans, rivers, lakes, and wells, is also feared by many Korean people.[26] Large number of Koreans believe that the dragon actually exists, and there are many stories about him. Jones states that he generally appears as the herald of the birth of some marvelous child. Also, in times of severe drought, a *mudang* will be called upon to have a dragon *kut* to open the sky which the dragon is supposed to have shut up. Falling under the jurisdiction of *Yong*, it is said, are many water spirits that function as guardian spirits of boats and caretakers of the spirits of drowned people.

Household gods. There are a multitude of household gods surrounding every part of the house and every activity of the family. These gods usually reside in some type of fetish and are often indistinguishable from the fetish itself. A house thus becomes a small peaceful pantheon in itself. Viewed as a pantheon, an ordinary house may be divided into the following six domains, each of which is a sacred spot for contact with its divine occupant: a) the main hall; b) the living room; c) the kitchen; d) the inner court; e) the main entrance; and f) the lavatory. The main hall is the site for the god who protects the master of the house, known as *Sungchosin*. *Sungchosin* is enshrined in a container, usually an earthenware jar, or an envelope placed on the ridge pole or in a corner, and is worshiped as the main patron god of the house, governing the peace and prosperity of the family.[27] In the living room are found three gods of children, *Chosangsin*, *Chesokbulsa*, and *Samsin*. *Chosangsin* are unique figures in that, unlike other house gods, they are souls of ancestors transformed into gods, rejoining their descendants. They are worshiped for bringing prosperity to the family. *Chesokbulsa* is borrowed from the Buddhistic world to ensure the longevity and welfare of the children of the house.

Samsin is the god of fertility, whose origin is unknown. This god is in charge of the fertility of women in the house as well as the welfare of children until they grow to be adults. Although the forms of these three gods of children vary widely, the representative form may be identified as an earthenware jar containing grains, mainly rice, which symbolize fertility and reproduction. The kitchen is ruled by *Chowangsin*, regarded as the god of housewives.[28] The role of *Chowangsin* is rather broadly conceived as rendering divine protection to the housewife for her activities. The kitchen god is not as widely worshiped as the others. *Chowangsin* is typically enshrined in or near the jar filled with water.

There is also the god of the house site, called *Tochu*. *Tochu* governs the material welfare or money matters of the family. His abode is again a jar, usually larger than the ones dedicated to the other gods, placed in the back yard and covered with a bundle of rice straw. The jar is filled with grain or small pieces of clothes, and is not to be accessible to outsiders or expected to be seen by them. The *Tochu* jar is almost always accompanied by another, very much like it, made for *Up*, the god of luck.[29] *Up* is ordinarily represented by a snake or weasel found in the house. If snakes or weasels should come and live near the jar, it is believed that they bring luck to the house. It should be noted that this is not a form of animal worship, but a belief in the spirits of certain animals that can bring luck by moving into the house. Not surprisingly, there is a taboo against killing either of these animals in or near the house. Should they leave the site, the fortune of the house is supposed to wane. Lastly, *Moonsin*, the endurance god, guards the house from the invasion of evil spirits, thereby protecting the family from accidents or other forms of misfortune. No particular abode is designated for this god. Although it is widely recognized, *Moonsin* does not receive sacrifices and prayers from the housewife.[30]

Similarly, *Chiksin*, is supposed to reside in the lavatory, which in the rural areas is built outside the living quarters.[31] This god is referred to as a lavatory maid, and is feared for her vicious, temperamental character. In rural areas, one can still observe people coughing before opening a lavatory door as a way of recognizing her divine existence. The usual interpretation of this practice of coughing is that one avoids accidents at the lavatory by paying respect to *Chiksin*. However, *Chiksin* has never been an object of ritual worship.

Beneath the spirits discussed above come a host of spirits, ghosts, imps and such, which constitute the lowest level of the Korean spiritual realm. There is a class of malevolent spirits full of vengeance towards humanity. These spirits are often souls of those who have died before fulfilling themselves, such as drowned persons, young boys and unmarried girls. All of these spirits have to be appeased to ensure harmony in the home.

Belief about a Supreme God

Generally speaking, shamanism in Korea is polytheistic, polydemonistic, and yet it also contains some elements of monotheism. Even
Korean Confucians and Buddhists recognize this being and its hierarchical supremacy.[32] In Korea, there is hardly a unified conception of
God, due to the fact that Korea has a varied cultural, historical, and linguistic background. But in Korean shamanism we find an idea that
there is to be, in a hierarchy of the gods, one supreme God that reigns
over all other gods. *Hananim* is the word for this supreme God used by
Korean shamanists. The most striking importance of *Hananim* is that
here is the conception of one supreme God. According to Nam-Sun
Choi the shamanist believes in the supreme God, living in heaven, who
is the creator and ruler of the whole universe, giving rain and grain to
harvest. Koreans worshiped *Hananim* who was the object of sacrificial
rites for the blessings of rain and harvest which were most important
for the agriculturally-oriented people in traditional Korea. This
supreme deity created human beings and is the loving and good god,
and is the ruler of the world.[33]

The ancient Koreans, therefore, had a primitive type of vague
monotheism or polytheistic monotheism. Not only did ancient Koreans
regard *Hananim* as the highest deity, but also Confucians and
Buddhists in Korea regarded him as such, and Christians in Korea
adopted the same word to designate their God.[34] After a study of books
on Chinese and early Korean religions, Underwood found that in the
time of *Koguryo* [probably *Koguryo* 37 B.C.- 668 A.D.] *Hananim* was
worshiped as one God. Then it was a descriptive term signifying "the
only one." Some missionaries claimed that *Hananim* was the chief of
all spirits.[35] This concept of *Hananim* probably was not acceptable to
a pre-Christian era Korea. There is no evidence to show that the
Korean people, in pre-Christian days, associated the God of the sky or
Hananim with the spirits they dealt with daily. Korean shamanists
believe that this supreme God, the creator of the universe, is too great
to be concerned with the personal affairs of the people, so it lets its
lower spirits or gods control these lesser things. It has been said that
Hananim was called on to bring rain.[36] The god worshiped to bring
rain is of Chinese origin and "can be said to have only such connection
with the Korean *Hananim* as grows out of a common but independent
concept of Divinity in the two countries."[37] That is why a Korean
shamanist performs to *Hananim* only a service of prayers for rain, but
they offer their prayers and rites for common daily personal affairs to

all sorts of gods and spirits that are under the control of *Hananim*.[38] In Korean shamanism, *Hananim* is remote from the world and does not interfere with every detail of the daily life of man. Thus, the ancient Koreans worshiped other deities, who were regarded as the controllers of many things.

THE STRUCTURE OF RELIGIOUS CONSCIOUSNESS IN KOREAN SHAMANISM

Faith in Fatalism and Divine Determinism

One of the main characteristics of Korean Shamanism is dependence on others or other forces for calling for blessings and fortunes. Making no decisions by himself, a person just lets the *mudang* or witch take charge of eliminating calamities.[39] In spite of the fact that it is his own life and destiny, he does not take responsibility himself for it, but he depends on others such as gods or witches. This means a complete loss of subjectivity and ethics by letting himself be governed by mere fatalism. Accordingly, here follows the conservatism or stagnancy.[40] The reason why shamanism cannot be productive nor can prompt cultural development is sometimes seen to be its conservative and stagnant nature.[41] The fatalistic concept of shamanism breeds relinquishment and sluggishness in the minds of those who follow it. In reality, they would take everything that occurs around them as fate and complain about it as such; they are losing their sense of initiative. Such a mental climate rooted in the belief in fatalism sometimes puts them at variance with reality, not allowing them to renovate their mentality or develop their minds.

Another characteristic of Korean shamanism is earthly pleasure, amusement.[42] The shallow realism and fatalism bring in the long run a present pleasure and amusement as their purpose. They are just interested in enjoying every present moment of their lives by having fun and eating, etc. Korean shamanism has been particularly associated with this amusement and has promoted this Korean characteristic. It is a truth that shamanism encourages people to sit around waiting for a stroke of good luck.

Faith in Magic and Divination

Korean Shamanism is a pragmatic belief system, primarily concerned with the seeking of fortune and the avoiding of misfortune with the aid of superhuman power. Korean Shamanism is closer to incantatory religious phenomenon than to established religions. It was already discussed earlier that the shaman's *kut* consisted of magic ritual. Those who have belief in magic tend to totally rely upon it in order to be relieved from whatever frustration or conflicts they may have around them.[43] Magic, as it were, is a sort of projective system of the mind for those who are directly or indirectly related to it. It is apparent that the magic gives some slight consolation; however, it obviously stands in the way of rationalization of thought and formation of a scientific mind. Shamanism and faith in magic and divination are so intimately related that it is not possible to separate one from the other. Thus Eliade says, "divination and clairvoyance are part of shaman's mystical technique."[44] Without divination shamans cannot exercise their authority to command the obedience of their people. It is mainly divination which becomes an effective instrument of their power.

Therefore, divination is an intrinsic part of shamanistic practices. Divination is a technique of realizing spirits of our unknown world. Perhaps one of the basic characteristics of divination in Korean Shamanism is the use of various objects which are common to daily life. It is also important to observe that the *I-chin,* or *Book of Change,* has been the primary source of most divination processes in Korean shamanism. Shamanistic faith in magic and divination not only encourages the fatalistic attitude of the believers in their future but also serves as a therapeutic instrument to relieve the emotional burden of decision-making and to give immediate satisfaction in the concrete expression of divine will. Divination has been an important means by which Korean people in a crisis try to gain guidance and consolation.

Lack of Ethics and Historical Sense

There is a sense of reproving vice and rewarding virtue in Korean shamanism; however, it is rather vague. This actually means that shamanism itself does not have a code of morality in a strict sense. Shamanists believe in good gods who bring happiness and evil spirits who bring calamity. The good or evil with which shamanists are concerned is not related to any ethical norm whatsoever, only to the norm of economic or material gain. As to ideas of sin and questions of morality, Shamanism does not seem to be very much concerned. They have no doctrine of a judgment day or anything resembling it. It is outside their line of vision. As a result shamanistic believers make no effort to admit their problems as being their responsibility or that they could solve them by themselves. Rather they chronically shift the responsibility of whatever troubles they may come across to the shoulders of gods or their ancestors. There can never be a healthy formation of personality where no fragment of consciousness of responsibility exists. Even the spirit gods of shamanism lack a definite frame of personality. Pyong-choon Hahm writes,

> Just as the shamanistic man lacks any ideal of permanence, he lacks also any ideals which can be described as 'absolute convictions.' Since he lacks an absolute god to define ethical standards, the shamanistic man has no simple black-and-white dualism against which to judge the goodness, justice, or righteousness of his actions.[45]

Shamanism is also lacking in historical sense, without the slightest consciousness as to the direction, goal, or meaning of history; what exists is of a cyclic nature, harping always on the same string. There actually exists not a linear "historical history," but a "non-historical history" ever repeating itself, a nature that is cyclic forever and ever. All the interests and desires of shamanism are concentrated on the present.[46] Their great interest is focused on how to get away from disasters and how to lead a peaceful and enjoyable life. Therefore, such people can not have any fundamental reconstruction or reformation. It is not for the future but for the present that they go to the fortune-tellers. Shamanism does not have any interest in the profound root of human existence nor does it plan for the future. It is a sort of short-term realism.

Personal Well-being

Personal well-being has an age-long history in the devotional life of shamanistic faith in Korea. The happiness the shamanistic faith seeks is this earthly present life, and the content of happiness is to live long, to have many children, to get wealthy, and to maintain health, etc. Happiness is usually regarded as a token of God's blessing for one's religion and good faith. In shamanistic faith, suffering is regarded usually as a spirit's retribution against one's displeasing gods. In such a way faith is regarded as the sole means of getting one's happiness, and as the sole ground of one's self-satisfaction or self-reliance.

ANCESTOR WORSHIP AND KOREAN SHAMANISM

Ancestor worship was one of the integral parts of shamanistic faith and practice in Korea. Ancestor worship was not only a part of the religious practice of Confucianism, but was a component of the shamanistic faith that held a stronger place in the totality than all the other religious tenets. In Korea, while there are syncretistic practices in all the religions represented, shamanism and ancestor worship remain quite connected throughout the religious history. However, the shaman was not recorded as having participated in the actual rituals of ancestor worship. Rather, ancestor worship has always been centered in the family without any professional participation of a shaman. The practice of ancestor worship is known to have existed in pre-Confucian China. Confucianism formalized the rituals of ancestor worship in China and presented the rationale of filial piety for the practice of ancestor worship. While there are some minor differences in practice, the meaning and the essentials of ancestor worship in Korea are the same as in China.

During the *Yi* dynasty Korean culture was saturated in Confucianism, which centered on the life principles of patriotic loyalty and filial piety. Filial piety was regarded as the basic ethical principle of Confucianism, and filiality was necessary in following the mandate of Heaven, which resulted in union of Heaven and man. For example, Confucius taught that "you should serve your parents as you serve heaven, and serve heaven as you serve your parents." In Confucianism teachings, one's civility tends to be extended to the civility of the ancestors who are already dead.[47]

It was also intended to bring unity and harmony to the large family system and to the sociopolitical structure of a nation. Filial piety was practiced through propriety and rites for the living and the deceased ancestors. Even though Confucius did not teach immortality of the soul or life after death, the Confucian tradition taught that when a man dies his soul goes up to Heaven and his body goes down to earth. The two are united at the ancestor worship ceremony.[48] Yul-gok Yi, a saintly Confucian scholar (1536-1583), once stressed the necessity of ancestor worship on the basis of such a religious belief.

> When a man dies, his soul might be said [to be] either existing or non-existing. It is because a soul exists with sincere devotion and a soul dissolves with devotion... When a man's soul is separate after death and has not yet dissolved, it could be moved and elevated and united through my sincere devotion... Even after a man' soul has dissolved, his reason does not dissolve, and his reason could be removed and elevated... This is why descendants remember their ancestors and perform ceremonies in an utmost devoted manner.[49]

The ancestor worship ceremony was gradually accompanied with the shamanistic religious idea of reward and blessing. It was believed that the faithful practice of filial piety and the faithful performance of the ancestor worship ceremony would please Heaven and ensure Heavenly blessings. This led to the belief that not Heaven but the deceased souls themselves were able to bless their descendants. Thus, the deceased souls were given a position of deity and became the object of worship.[50]

The actual practice of ancestor worship varied slightly from place to place, as can be seen by the different description of the worship given by several literary and living sources. Sometimes ancestral tablets were used, but sometimes now only a curtain is hung in a room of the house of the deceased. The offering before this soul of the departed person is food. Placed in front of the tablets was rice, bread, beef, greens, dates, chestnuts, walnuts, persimmons, honey cakes, oil candy, and other articles of food. The ceremony of ancestor worship seems to be providing food for the honored ancestor while greeting the honored personage with a low bow. This is simply an extension of the way a revered living grandfather is treated in a traditional Korean home. The best food of the house is always given to the grandfather, who is greeted with a ceremonial bow. After this simple ceremony has been completed, it will be repeated at the graveside. The food that has been ceremonially offered to the ancestors at the grave mounds finally will be eaten by the family with great gusto. The spirit portion or aroma of the food is considered by some to be eaten by the spirit of the ancestors.

The occasions for observing this ancestor worship are not rigidly fixed, but almost everyone who worships his ancestor will have a service on the lunar New Year and on the first three anniversaries of the death of the person. There may be ceremonies on the birthday of the deceased, and there may be simple, abbreviated daily ceremonies such as bowing to the tablets and offering a bit of food from the eldest son's rice bowl. Ancestor worship for the previous three generations seems to be common. At times the previous ten generations all received sacrifices. Obeisance with the accompanying food and drink is carried out before the graves or the shrines at the birthplaces of famous men. Such a shrine is found in *Kangnung* to the philosopher-moralist, Yul-gok Yi, whose mother dreamed of the dragon when he was born. Men from all over Korea come to pay obeisance to this man. Also, services are conducted at the places of origin of the clan name. There are about 1100 clans in Korea.[51] It is reported that all of these clans originated in South Korea. Taxes were collected each year for ceremonial worship before the shrines of the clans.

CONCLUSION

Korean shamanism considers basically the relationship among three areas: the three stories of the universe, the three elements of human beings, and the spirits and gods. The belief system is a primitive and simple concept of ethics and after-life. It is animistic faith which views the universe as full of spirits and gods and worships them. It is believed that spirits and gods exercise supernatural powers to administer either blessings or curses upon human life. Although Korean shamanism is polytheistic and polydemonic, there is an idea of one supreme god, *Hananim*, that reigns over all other gods. Korean shamanists believe that *Hananim* is remote and too great to interfere with the personal affairs of the daily life of man.

The main characteristics of Korean shamanism are fatalistic belief in divine determinism, and earthly pleasure and amusement. Korean shamanists believes in magic and divination as a means to achieve fortune and avoid misfortune. Shamanists are not concerned with any ethical norm, but with the norm of economic or material gain. Korean shamanism is also lacking in a sense of the direction and meaning of history. Personal well-being and happiness in this earthly life are considered as God's blessing in shamanistic faith. Ancestor worship is an elemental part of the shamanistic faith and the religious practice of Confucianism. Ancestor worship and shamanism in Korea remain connected and are practiced together as a form of religious syncretism. The practice of ancestor worship is always centered in the family without any professional participation of a shaman. It is believed that shamanistic faith and practice was accompanied with formalized rituals of ancestor worship originating in Confucianism. The ancestor worship ceremony was expanded to include the shamanistic religious idea of heavenly blessings.

The core of folk religion in Korea is in fact shamanism, underlying the fundamental stratum of Korean culture. Shamanistic faith is sometimes said to be a kind of indigenous religion of incantatory reference, passed on in such lower classes as illiterates or farmers, who form the base of Korean society. However, in a stricter sense, it is not a phenomenon exclusively limited to any particular class. One may easily come across it even among intellectuals or middle class people. Thus shamanism has infiltrated into every nook and corner of Korean society, dominating the way of thinking as well as the manner of behavior of the majority of Korean people. Even some of the newly created religions in this country are nothing else, in a precise sense, than modernized forms of conventional shamanism. Korean shamanism is still viable as a religious faith. If shamanism was mankind's earliest religion, it has largely disappeared in most areas when they become industrialized. Korea is perhaps an exception. Shamanism still flourishes as a religious faith of south Korea, even influencing - as we will see - Christianity.

NOTES

[1]See "The Ancient Wisdom in Shamanic Culture," S. Nicholson ed., *Shamanism* (Wheaton, IL: Quest, 1987).

[2]Chong-ho Pyun, *Chongkyo-eui Bikyo Yunku-wa Keu Kyulon [A Comparative Study of Religions and Its Conclusion]* (Seoul, Korea. Simwoo Won, 1959), p. 69.

[3]Park, Paul U. U. "A Study on the Relation of Shamanism to Other Religions," *Korean Religions*, Vol. II. Jan 1. 1970.

[4]Chun Shin-Yong, ed. *Folk Culture in Korea* (Seoul, Korea: International Cultural Foundation, 1974), p. 60.

[5]Tong-shik, Ryu, *Hankuk Mukyo-eui Yeksa-wa Kujo [History and Structure of Korean Shamanism]* (Seoul, Korea: Yunsei University Press, 1975), pp. 306.

[6]Tae-gon Kim, "Components of Korean Shamanism," The Korean National Commission for UNESCO, *Korean Folklore*, p. 15.

[7]Sok-che Im, "*Hankuk Musok Yunku Seoseol*," [Introduction of Korean Shamanism], *Asea Yeoseong Yunku [A Study of Women in Asia]* (Seoul, Korea: Sungmyung Yoja Taehakko, 1971), Vol. 9, p. 167-168.

[8]Deuk-hwang Kim, *Hankuk Sasangsa [A History of Korean Thought]* (Seoul, Korea: Baekamsa, 1958), pp. 26-30.

[9]Yong-un Hyon, *Chejudo Musok Charyo Sajon [Chejudo Folklore Dictionary]* (Seoul, Korea: Singu Munwhasa, 1980), p. 868; Sang-hee Moon, "Shamanism in Korea," *Hankuk Sasang [Korean Thoughts]* (Seoul, Korea: International Cultural Foundation, 1979), p. 27.

[10]Hyon, *Chejudo Folklore Dictionary*, p. 868.

[11]Tae-gon Kim, *Hankuk Musok Yunku [A Study of Korean Folklore]* (Seoul, Korea: Chimmundang,1981), 280ff. See also his book, "Components of Korean Shamanism," Korean National Commission of UNESCO, *Korean Folklore* (Seoul, Korea: The Sisayongosa Publishers, Inc., 1983), pp. 12-14.

[12]Tae-gon Kim, *Hankuk Musok Yunku [A Study of Korean Folklore]* (Seoul, Korea: Chimmundang,1981), p. 14.

[13]Un-bong Lee, *Hankuk Kodae Chongkyo Sasang [A Study of the Korean Ancient Religion]* (Seoul, Korea: Chimmundang, 1974), pp. 210-211.

[14]Tae-sok So, *Hankuk Muga-eui Yunku [A Study of Songs of Korean Shamans]* (Seoul, Korea: Munhak Sasangsa Chulpanpu, 1980), pp. 1-10.

[15]*Ibid.*, pp. 197-198.

[16]George Herber Jones, "The Spirit Worship in Korea," *Royal Asiatic Society*, Vol.II. (Seoul, Korea. 1901), pp. 42-43.

[17]*Ibid.*, pp. 198-99.

[18]Jones, "The Spirit Worship in Korea," pp. 43-44.

[19]John Ross, *Corea: Its History, Customs and Manners*, p. 356.

[20]Clark, *Religions of Old Korea*, p. 200.

[21]Jones, "The Spirit Worship in Korea," pp. 45-48.

[22]Chin-tae Son, *Chosen Minjok Munwha Yungu* [*A Study of Korean People's Culture*] (Eulyou Munwhasa, 1948, Seoul, Korea), p. 164.

[23]Hulbert, *The Passing of Korea*, p. 405.

[24]Yun-shik Chang, "Shamanism as Folk Existentialism," Earl H. Phillips, Eui-young Yu, eds., *Religions in Korea : Beliefs and Cultural Values* (Los Angeles, CA: California State University, 1982), pp. 27-29.

[25]Jones, "The Spirit Worship in Korea," pp. 51-52.

[26]James Huntley Grayson, Korea: *A Religious History* (Oxford, England, UK: Clarendon Press, 1989), p. 264.

[27]Chu-kun Chang, "Introduction to Korean Shamanism," Richard W.I. Guisso, Chai-shin Yu, *Shamanism: The Spirit World of Korea* (Berkeley, CA: Asian Humanities Press, 1988), p. 35.

[28]Chang, *op.cit.*, p. 35.

[29]*Ibid.*, p. 36.

[30]Yun-shik Chang, "Shamanism as Folk Existentialism," Chang, et.al, eds. *Religions in Korea: Beliefs and Cultural Values*, p. 31.

[31]*Ibid.*, p. 32.

[32]Horace G. Underwood, *The Religions of Eastern Asia* (New York, NY: The Macmillan Co., 1910), p. 110.

[33]Duk-whang Kim, *Hankuk Chongkyosa* [*A Shaman History of Religions in Korea*] pp. 42-53.

[34]Hulbert, *op.cit.*, p. 405.

[35]Moose, *op.cit.*, p. 191.

[36]Robert J. Moose, *Village Life in Korea* (Nashville, TN: Publishing House of the Methodist Episcopal Church South, Smith and Lamar, Agents, 1911), p. 191; However, Palmer points out that this is in error. Cf. Palmer, *Christianity in Korea*, p. 7.

[37] Hulbert, *The Passing of Korea*, p. 405.

[38]Ryu, *Hankuk Chongkyo-wa Kitokkyo* [*The Christian Faith Encounters the Religions of Korea*], pp. 196-197.

[39]Choon-bang Lee, *Shamanism-kwa Hankuk-In-eui Shimsung* [*Shamanism and Korean Mentality*] (Seoul, Korea: Kunkuk University Press, 1978), pp. 34, 61.

[40]Ryu, *The Christian Faith Encounters the Religions of Korea*, p. 34.

[41]Tai-rim Yoon, *Hankuk-In* [*Korean People*] (Seoul, Korea: Hyunamsa, 1979), p. 24.

[42]Ryu, *Hankuk Mukyo-eui Yeksa-wa Kujo* [*History and Structure of Korean Shamanism*] (Seoul, Korea: Yunsei University Press, 1975), pp. 345-346.

[43]Kwang-il Kim, "Kut and the Treatment of Mental Disorder," Richard Guisso, Chai-shin Yu. eds., *Shamanism: The Spirit World of Korea*, pp. 132-133.

84 *Protestant Church Growth in Korea*

[44]M. Eliade, *Shamanism: Archaic Techniques of Ecstasy*, p. 184.

[45]Pyong-choon Hahm, "Shamanism: Foundation of the Korean World-View," Hong-goo Lee, Seung-Doo Yang, Byongie-Jon Hahm, eds. *Korean Jurisprudence, Politics and Culture* (Seoul, Korea: Yonsei University Press, 1986), p. 333.

[46]Ryu, *The Christian Faith Encounters the Religions of Korea*, p. 35.

[47]Sung-bum Yun, "Korean Christianity and Ancestor Worship," *Korea Journal* 13 (2), 1973, pp; 17-21.

[48]Ki-bock Choi, *Yukyo-eui Sangrye-ae Kwan-han Yungu* [*A Study of the Confucian Ceremony of Mourning*] (Seoul, Korea:Sungkyunkwan University Press, 1979), pp. 128ff.

[49]*Ibid,* pp. 129ff.

[50]Bong-bae Park, "*Kitokkyo-wa Josang Sungbae*," [Christianity and Ancestor Worship], Harold Hong, et. al. eds. *Hankuk-eui Kyohoe-wa Sunkyo* [*Church and Mission in Korea*] (Seoul, Korea: The Christian Literature Society, 1963), pp. 20ff.

[51]C. Osgood, *The Koreans and Their Culture* (New York, NY: The Ronald Press, 1951), p. 37.

Chapter Four

HISTORY OF PROTESTANT MISSION AND SOCIOPOLITICAL CONTEXT FOR CHURCH GROWTH IN KOREA

INTRODUCTION

Korea was called the "Hermit Kingdom" because of her persistent resistance to making any contact with a Western country until the commencement of Western missionary work in the nineteenth century. Prior to the Roman Catholic missions in the eighteenth century, Christianity made several contacts with Korea. There is a suggestion that Nestorianism was the first form of Christianity to come into contact first with Koreans and that it had been introduced into Korea by the end of the seventh century.[1] The Nestorian sect, *Kyungkyo*,[2] persecuted in the West, fled to Persia. From there it sent twenty-one missionaries led by Alopen to China in 635 A.D., which was then in close relationship with the *Shilla* Dynasty. The rumored entrance of the Christian faith into Korea during the *Shilla* dynasty has some support.[3] In recent years, it has been insisted that Nestorianism was transmitted to *Shilla* because some Nestorian stone crosses were excavated in *Pulkook* temple yard, which was built in the tenth year (751 A.D.) of King *Kyugduk* of *Shilla*. The Christian gospel was brought to Korea by Nestorianism.

In 1628 a Dutch sailor, Jan Jansen Weltevree, was shipwrecked on Korean shores and took the Korean name Park Yon and lived out his life in Korea. He is assumed to be the first European Protestant Christian who landed and lived in Korea. He, as the first Westerner naturalized in Korea, rendered distinguished service in a battle against China. He, highly respected as a religious man, married a Korean woman and had one son and one daughter.[4] In 1653 Weltevree was followed by Hendrick Hamel and his company of Dutch sailors, who were cast ashore on *Cheju* Island. They were captured and held in Korea for fourteen years until Hamel and seven others made good their escape to Nagasaki and returned to the Netherlands in 1668. Hamel published the book called *Narrative of an Unlucky Voyage and Shipwreck on the Coast of Korea* from his experience in Korea. Hamel was believed to be the first Protestant from Europe to introduce direct knowledge of Korea and its people to Western European countries.[5] Hamel writes at the end of his an account:

> On the 20th of July 1668. We arrived at Amsterdam, where gave thanks for having delivered us after a captivity of fourteen years and twenty-eight days, and we besought him to have compassion on our poor comrades who were left behind.[6]

Since that time the Protestant mission and its Korean church fruit have many times been noted for their remarkable growth. In this chapter the author will discuss the contacts of Christian missions with Korea and developments culminating in the dispatch of Protestant missionaries to the Korean people. The author also wants to analyze in particular the sociopolitical factors and to what extent they contributed to the growth of the church in Korea.

ROMAN CATHOLIC MISSION AND CHURCH GROWTH

In the thirteenth century a Franciscan father named William de Rubruck was sent to Mongolia by the king of France to convert the officials of the royal court.[7] Father Rubruck happened to visit the border of Korea, in the vicinity of the *Yalu* River, anticipating the days of missions to this land of Morning Calm. In his letter to the Pope the name of Korea was first mentioned in Europe. Father Rubruck writes in his record of travel: "Master William told me that he had seen envoys of people called *Caule* [Korea] and *Manse* who inhabit islands in the sea around which the water freezes, so the Tartars can cross to them."[8]

In the year 1592, Japan invaded Korea. One of the two commanders of the force was General Konishi Yukinaga, a converted Roman Catholic. It is said that there were eighteen thousand Christian soldiers in Konishi's division. It has been suggested that the reason for this historic invasion was Toyotomi's wish to crush the majority of the Christian soldiers in the army. In order to minister to these Christians,

General Konishi asked for a priest. Father Gregorio de Cespedes, a Jesuit missionary from Spain, reached Korea in the winter of 1594 and spent about half a year ministering to the Japanese Christian soldiers.[9] The Edinburgh Review of 1872 says that of the Christian soldiers who crossed the strait in 1592, few returned to their native land when Korea was finally abandoned seven years later.[10] His stay was brief, and his ministry was limited to the Japanese soldiers. There were no intentions of ministering to Korean people. He was the first to set foot in Korea as a Western missionary,[11] but this contact did not accomplish any mission work in Korea.[12]

The next contact with the Roman Catholic faith was made in 1631 when Du-won Jung, a member of the annual tributary mission to Peking, carried back with him copies of Catholic missionary Matteo Ricci's works in Chinese, including the *Chonju Silru*, or *The True Doctrine of the Lord of Heaven*. The True Doctrine of the Lord of Heaven by Matteo Ricci. In the two volumes of the *Chonju Siru* [*The True Doctrine of the Lord of Heaven*] which he wrote, he discusses how God created the Heavens and the earth and how he governs them in peace and how the immortality of the soul of man makes him different from the birds and beasts. He also reasons that man's nature is innately good; therefore, he must respect and serve God.[13] But for almost a century and a half, Roman Catholic books brought into the country were ignored by Korean people. In 1777, however, a group of Western Learning Korean scholars rediscovered the books. During the 18th century they studied them and even began to practice the teachings of the books and launched a religious movement for the spread of Catholicism.[14] However, the official date given for the beginning of the Roman Catholic missions to Korea is 1784. That year Sung-hun Yi, one of the Western Learning participants, went to Peking as a member of a diplomatic mission and returned from Peking, baptized with the name Peter and bringing along a large number of books, crucifixes, and other religious objects. Sung-Hun Yi, Peter Yi, became the cornerstone of the Catholic church in Korea.[15]

The next hundred years, from 1785-1884, have been called "the century of Roman Catholic Mission" by Korean Catholic Christians. It was a century of persecutions and martyrdoms. Christians were initially persecuted in Korea on the ground that Christianity was opposed to Confucianism, especially to ancestor worship, a key part of Korean Confucian practices. In 1785, just one year after the Catholic church had been introduced, we find the first martyr for the faith, Pum-wu

Kim, baptized "Thomas."[16] To the memory of Pum-wu Kim, the first martyr, the first Catholic church, *Myungdong* Cathedral in Seoul, was built on its present position, which is the site of the home of Kim Pum-Wu. In 1794, ten years after the baptism of Sung-hun Yi, there were four thousand Christians in Korea in spite of severe persecution and lack of spiritual shepherds.[17] The first large-scale persecution of Catholics occurred in 1801 when more than 300 Catholic believers, including some female members of the royal family and church leaders, were executed. This is known as the Catholic Persecution, and during its course such prominent Korean Catholics as Sung-hun Yi, Ka-hwan Yi, and Yak-chong Chong, as well as the Chinese priest Chou Wen-mo who was sent by Pope Pius VI in 1794, were put to death.[18] The 1801 persecution was the occasion when Sa-young Hwang, a devout Catholic who worked with Father Chou Wen-mo, a Chinese priest sent from Peking in 1795, wrote a secret letter of 13,000 Chinese characters on a silk sheet of 63cm x 38cm to the bishop of Peking asking to send a military force of sixty thousand men and fifty battle ships to conquer Korea and Christianize the whole country, but Hwang was found out and was executed at the age of twenty seven.[19]

However, at the persistent request to the Bishop of the Peking Diocese and upon direct appeals to the Pope by native believers, in September, 1831, Pope Gregory XVI decreed that a Korean bishopric was to be founded independent of the Peking diocese, under the responsibility of the French Society of Foreign Mission. Assignment to Korea of French priests, training of Korean priests, and other related programs soon followed. This action was taken to be significant by Christians in Korea, for it recognized the independence of Korea from China, even if only in ecclesiastical affairs.[20] The church, which had numbered 3,000 in 1836, had grown by 1838 to 9,000 members. With a vision to the future, three young Koreans had been sent to study theology in Macao, of whom two became priests.[21]

The second great persecution broke out in 1839. At that time three French priests were executed, along with 113 Korean converts.[22] In 1846, Tae-gon Kim, the first Korean priest educated at the Portuguese Seminary in Macao, was killed along with eighteen adherents.[23] One result of this widespread persecution was that Catholicism became known to every corner of the land of Korea. By 1850 the number of known Catholics reached 11,000, and fifteen years later that number had more than doubled. In 1855, the report to the Vatican showed 13,638 Christians, 15,206 in 1857, 16,700 in 1860, 18,000 in 1863, 23,000 in 1865.[24]

In 1866, the last full-scale persecution broke upon the church. It lasted three years. Before it was over, nine French missionaries had been executed, and about eight thousand Korean Catholic Christians were beheaded.[25] This massacre was carried out due to the violation of the royal decrees on religions. The Korean Roman Catholic Church has gone through severe persecutions. Stephen Neill remarked that the suffering and humiliation of Korean Christians in the 18th and 19th centuries was just incredible.[26] C. H. Robinson has this to say: "It is doubtful whether the Roman Christians in the early Roman Empire suffered more than the Christians of Korea in the 18th and 19th centuries."[27]

However, upon the affirmation of a friendship treaty with the United States in 1882, the Korean government finally gave implicit sanction for the Catholic Church movement. The era of persecution was over. From that time on the Catholic Church came increasingly to public attention. By the beginning of the twentieth century, the Roman Catholic Church had fifty-two priests, including twelve Koreans, forty-two thousand believers and forty-one churches. By 1910 there were seventy-one priests, including fifteen Korean clergy, fifty-nine Korean sisters, forty-one seminarians, over seventy-three thousand believers, and sixty churches. The church had entered on a period of unprecedented growth.[28] By 1932, the Catholic Church had over 127,643 believers, 312 church buildings and 183 priests, 85 of whom were Koreans. During this decade, the Vatican recognized the suffering of the Church during its first century with the beatification of seventy-nine Korean martyrs.[29] In 1944 the Catholic Church in Korea possessed seven bishops, 234 priests, of whom 132 were Koreans, and a body of believers numbering 186,666.[30]

On the eve of the Korean War, Catholics numbered only 157,000. The war decimated the ranks of Korean priests, making the church once again dependent on foreign clergy for an additional period. Through the 1950s the leadership had a strong foreign component: the missionary orders carried the interest of the worldwide church to Korea and made critical contributions to the postwar relief effort and the reconstruction of church institutions. In the decade commencing with the end of the Korean war in 1953, the Korean Roman Catholic Church experienced great growth. Through the determined efforts of this combined Korean and foreign force, church membership grew from 160,000 in 1953 to 530,000 in just nine years. In the next ten year period the Church experienced a rapid increase in her size to one million twelve thousand Catholics with fourteen Episcopal jurisdictions organized. In 1953, there were six dioceses in South Korea, but by 1963, this had increased to ten. The 166,000 Catholics in 1953 had by the end of the ten year period become 575,000.

From 1963 to 1974, the Vatican continued to give recognition to the rapid increase in the size of the Korean Catholic Church. In 1968 Archbishop Kim Sun-Whan was made a cardinal by Pope Paul VI. In 1984 the Catholic community in South Korea was estimated at over 1.6 million members in 633 parishes. There were 11 dioceses, the archdioceses of Seoul, Tague, and Kwangju, and 21 male and 42 female religious communities. In 1985 the Roman Catholic Church in Korea celebrated its bicentennial with a visit to Korea by Pope John Paul II and the canonization of 93 Korean and 10 French missionary martyrs of the persution in 1784.[31] Though the Catholic Church is growing at a rate that matches many a Protestant denomination's statistics in Korea, its growth has not been as great as that of Protestant Christianity as a whole.

There are several reasons for this. Catholic converts were not taught the Scripture. From the foundation of the church by Sung-hun Yi in 1784 to 1866, no attempt had been made to translate a single Gospel or any portion of the Bible.[32] Another important factor was the Catholic emphasis on hierarchical organization rather than growth in the Christian life of individual believers. One might also cite the direct Roman Catholic involvement in political activities. In the case of Alexander Hwang, as mentioned earlier, Roman Catholics actually invited an armed intervention. It was natural for Korean officials to view the Roman Catholic church as an agent of aggression and imperialism. According to a 1991 national census, there are 2,477,000 Catholic Christians in Korea, which represents 10.6% of the total population.[33]

HISTORY OF PROTESTANT MISSION AND SOCIOPOLITICAL CONTEXT FOR CHURCH GROWTH

Prior to the official arrival of American missionaries in the nineteenth century, there had been slight contacts with European Protestant Christians in Korea. To bring about understanding of the factors contributing to Korean church growth in the next chapter, the present section on the history of Protestant church growth will be divided into five different periods according to the significant periods of Korean church history: early contacts and beginning of the Protestant mission (1832-

1885), Protestant mission and the attraction of modernization (1885-1890), the period of the formation of the early church (1890-1910), church growth and search for national independence (1910-1953), church growth and anti-Communism (1953-1970), and church growth and economic boom in South Korea.

Early Contacts and Beginning of the Protestant Mission (1832-1885)

The first Protestant missionary who is known to have made efforts to begin the work of evangelism in Korea was Carl Friedrich Augustus Gutzlaff. For Korean documentation on Gutzlaff's visit, see the entry on the seventh Month of the 32nd year of the reign of King *Sunjo* in the Annals of King *Sunjo*. Carl Gutzlaff was a native of Pomerania and a graduate of the theological school at Halle and served with the Netherlands Missionary Society until 1828. And he moved from Batavia to Macao, where he became an intimate friend of Robert Morrision, the first Protestant missionary to China.[34]

Gutzlaff, unlike the Roman Catholic missionaries, gave himself to Bible distribution. In 1832, he sailed with the British ship *Lord Amherst*, which had been sent to open trade relations with Korea and did visit two points on the west coast of Korea.[35] He tried to witness to the Koreans he met and distributed Chinese Bibles and religious tracts for more than forty days.[36] He even succeeded in sending two copies of the Chinese Bible to the king.[37] It has been said that Gutzlaff's visit to Korea was so brief that no recognizable result was produced. However, this first Protestant missionary on the peninsula wrote about his visit with faith in the work of the Lord, saying,

> At all events it is the work of God, which I frequently commanded in my prayers to His gracious care. Can the divine truth, disseminated in Korea, be lost? This I believe not: there will be some fruits in the appointed time of the Lord. In the great plan of the eternal God, there will be a time of merciful visitation of them. While we look for this we ought to be anxious to hasten its approach by diffusing the glorious doctrines of the cross by all means and power... The Scripture teaches us to believe that God can bless even these feeble beginnings. Let us hope that better days will soon dawn for Korea.[38]

No Protestant missionary was to visit Korea for the next thirty-three years after Carl Gutzlaff said his missionary prayer for that country. In 1865 the Rev. Robert J. Thomas, a missionary from the London

Missionary Society to China, spent two and one-half months in Korea's west coast area, studying and distributing Chinese Bibles as Gutzlaff had done before. Robert J. Thomas was graduated from New College, University of London, and ordained and appointed to labor for China under London Missionary Society.[39] The following year he returned to Korea on the American trading ship *General Sherman*. When the ship ran aground on a sandbar in the *Daidong* river on the way to *Pyongyang*, it was set afire by fear-stricken Koreans, and the escaping sailors were massacred. Thomas was killed as he distributed his copies of the Bible to those around him, even the last moment of his life to the man who beheaded him.[40] According to an eyewitness, Thomas made his way to shore with his arms full of Gospels and thrust the Scriptures into the hands of the very men who killed him. Robert J. Thomas became the first Protestant missionary to shed martyr's blood in Korea. Samuel A. Moffett, who was a pioneer missionary in *Pyongyang,* found in 1893 "a man who had received a Chinese New Testament from the unfortunate missionary."

> Later, some representatives of the Government went down the *Daidong* River and collected and destroyed all the Gospels they could find; but they could not erase from men's minds the eager face of God's messenger, neither could they find and destroy all the books. Some were hidden and read and became good seed in fertile ground.[41]

In spite of the devotion and zeal of both Gutzlaff and Thomas, neither of them lived to see the fruit of their labor. Alexander Williamson, an agent of the National Bible Society of Scotland, made a tour through Manchuria and got as far as the customs barrier between China and Korea in 1867. He came into contact with some Koreans and was able to sell them copies of the Bible. In 1873, John Ross and John McIntyre, who have been called the "Wycliffes of Korea," missionaries from the United Presbyterian Church of Scotland, worked among Koreans in Manchuria. In 1876 they began to translate the Gospel of Luke from Chinese characters into Korean script with a man named Sang-Yoon Suh, who was one of the first four Korean Protestant converts in Manchuria.[42] The other three initial believers were Jin-gee Kim, Ung-chan Lee and Hong-joon Paik. Ross' missionary method was "Pauline," as he termed it. Feeling that native evangelists were far more effective than western missionaries could be, he laid great emphasis on colporteur work.

In the spring of 1883, Sang-yoon Suh, one of the colporteurs, left Manchuria with a load of Scriptures, with instructions to reach Seoul with them if possible. In 1884, Hong-jon Paik and Sung-ha Lee made another attempt to bring the Scripture into Korea. But the border was so carefully guarded that this was very difficult. So Sung-ha Lee left quantities of Scriptures in an inn on the Manchurian side. When the inn-keeper found the forbidden Scripture, he threw some into the river and some into the fire. When Ross heard of it, he said, "The water of life" to Koreans, and "the ashes will be fertilizers to bring about a great growth in the Korean church." Sure enough, this region later became a strong Christian community and many church leaders came from this area.[43]

After varied experiences, he was successful in reaching the capital with only a few copies in his hand. After making other attempts to bring the Scriptures into Korea, he returned to his native village of *Sorai* on the west coast of Korea, and there he preached and established the first worshipping Korean Protestant congregation. Within six months, about twenty people gathered together every Sunday to read the translated Scripture and worship.[44]

> Suh Sang-Yoon brought us word of the good work in the village of *Sorai*, where he lived, and where he said there was a small company of Christians, and earnestly entreated us to visit his home and oversee the work. This we were unable to do at that time. In the following spring, a delegation of the Christians in this village waited upon us, seeking baptism. They were examined before the whole mission, and finding they had been believers for some years, and were able to state intelligently the ground of their faith.[45]

In November of 1884, hearing a report that there were believers who asked for baptism in the Korean valleys of Northern Manchuria, where many copies of the gospels had been sold by colporteurs, Ross and his colleague J. Webster decided to visit these areas. They baptized 75 people in four villages there and placed many others on the waiting list for further instruction. This group of baptized people, who were all farmers and heads of families,[46] became the first Christian Korean community in Manchuria.[47] When Ross returned from his first visit among the Koreans in their villages in 1884, he reported to the society:

> Besides those already baptized there are 600 men applicants for baptism in the *Corean* Valley." Reporting on Colporteur Suh's work in Korea, the Bible translator said: "As the result of his two years' labor there, he has now over 70 men applicants for baptism...He has opened what he calls a 'Preaching Hall' in a city to the west of the capital, where he has 18 believers, and another convert in a city to the south of the capital has 'over twenty' who are applying for baptism.[48]

It was reported that by the end of 1884 there were already more than 100 baptized believers, and about 600 men requesting baptism. There were also thousands of families that had been reading the Scriptures in their family devotions,[49] and the congregation built the first Korean church building with their own financial support in 1885.[50]

It is interesting to note that before the Protestant missionaries arrived in Korea, the Ross version of the New Testament was already circulating throughout the country, and little bands of believers had begun to form as churches were waiting only to be baptized by missionaries.[51] From all these preliminary activities and efforts by Gutzlaff, Thomas, Williamson, Ross, and others we find that from the beginning Protestant Missions in Korea emphasized the importance of spreading the Bible as the main missionary method. They made efforts to translate Biblical passages and the Lord's prayer into the vernacular Korean language, cooperating closely with Koreans, teaching them and learning from them as well. As observed earlier, Korean Protestant Christians have always been one step ahead of the Western missionaries in propagation and establishment of the church. Koreans in Manchuria and Korea had already been converted to Protestant Christianity by the efforts of their native Christians. The church was already established before the first official Protestant missionary ever set foot in Korea in 1884.

In 1884, two years after the signing of the treaty between the United States and Korea, the American Presbyterian Church sent the first Protestant missionary to Korea, Horace Newton Allen. Allen, physician, missionary and diplomat, was graduated from Ohio Wesleyan University in 1881 and from Miami Medical College, Oxford, Ohio in 1883. And he was appointed by the Presbyterian Board of the Foreign Missions to China as a medical missionary and reached Shanghai in October, 1883. Allen was a medical doctor who had already seen service in China. Upon his arrival he was able to save the life of the queen's nephew by the providence of God. By saving the life of a wounded prince, Min Young-ik, at the point of death, he won the favor of the court and was made the court physician. In April 1885, the first government hospital using Western medicine was opened and bore the name *"Kwanghyewon"* or "Widespread Relief House" under the charge of Dr. Allen. Thus was laid the foundation of resident missionary work in Korea.[52]

Six months after Horace Allen's arrival, on Easter Sunday, 1885, two American missionaries arrived in Korea via Japan. They were

Horace G. Underwood, sent by the Northern Presbyterian Board of Missions, and Henry Appenzeller, sent by the Foreign Missionary Society of the Northern Methodist Episcopal Church. Upon arrival on the shore of *Chemulpo*, Appenzeller offered this prayer: "We came here on Easter. May He who on that day burst the bars of death, break the bonds that bind the people, and bring them to the light and liberty of God's children."[53]

The Rev. Horace Grant Underwood was born in London, England, July 19, 1859. At thirteen years of age he came to the United States with his father. He graduated from the Theological Seminary of the Dutch Reformed Church in America, located at New Brunswick, New Jersey. He was appointed the first clerical missionary of the Presbyterian Mission Board on July 28, 1884. He was missionary, author, Bible translator, editor, educator and preacher. He died on October 12, 1916, at Atlantic City, New Jersey. Dr. Arthur J. Brown paid a fitting tribute, when he said, "He will live in the history of Christianity as one of the founders and builders of the church in Korea."[54]

The Rev. Henry Gerhart Appenzeller was born on February 6, 1858, in Sonderton, PA. In 1882, being a member of the German Reformed Church, he studied at German Reformed Franklin and Marshall College in America. After an experience of personal conversion, he changed to the Methodist Episcopal Church. While he was on his honeymoon during Christmas week, 1884, he received his appointment for mission work in Korea from the Foreign Missionary Society of the Methodist Church. On June 11, 1902, while he was on his way from Seoul to the meeting of the Union Board of Bible Translators at *Mokpo*, he drowned when the steamship he was traveling in was sunk in a collision. William E. Griffs, his biographer, pays him the following tribute: "Appenzeller of Korea built himself as a living stone into Christian *Chosen*...As traveler, explorer, teacher, organizer, evangelist, and Bible translator, his labors were manifold, while his temper was ever sweet. His seventeen years of service were crowned with success."[55]

Protestant Mission and the Attraction of Modernization (1885-1890)

Protestant Christianity came to Korea at a critical and providential time in the nation's social and political life. The five-hundred-year *Yi* dynasty was about to fall, and Korea had been forced to open to the outside world and was slowly losing its independence to the rising empire of Japan. Christianity came as something new to the people in times of insecurity and was therefore easily accepted. The sociopolitical situation was very unstable. After Japan defeated Russia in the Sino-Japanese War, China lost her influence over Korea. Japan's victory over Russia made many people think that modern civilization was superior to traditional Chinese culture. Japan won the war after she began modernization. "Missionaries said that had the Chinese won, mission work in Korea might have been stopped."[56]

Also Christianity came from the West, and it brought modernity with the same colonial hang-up as elsewhere. Since there was no feature of modernization immediately at hand to attract the people, they turned to Christianity, and Christianity had the advantage of entering the ancient kingdom before other forms of modern civilization had taken possession of the people.[57] According to the Rev. C. E. Sharp in his writing in 1906, the primary motives were dissatisfaction due to political oppression and poverty, and the quest for western learning.[58] The missionaries brought this western civilization and, therefore, appealed to the young and active reformers who were impatient for the modernization of Korea. Therefore many Koreans saw Christianity as a powerful force to serve national interests. Western powers of the United States and other European colonial powers also put pressure on Korea for diplomatic treaties. In addition to external pressure from neighboring invaders and internal political disintegration through factionalism, Korea had no strong philosophical rationale that provided a basis for any political or intellectual ideologies. The country was in deep trouble in every way. Won-Sul Lee succinctly describes the condition of Korea at the end of the 19th century:

> Politically inept, economically stagnant, socially disequilibrated, and morally corrupt, the old system could not cope with the tidal challenge of the West, and people were in the state of total despair.[59]

The Christian church played the key role in the modernization of Korean society. The term "modernization" here is broadly defined as the process of social and cultural changes of the traditional ways. It may include the economic changes of industrialization, value change from traditionalism toward modernism or rationalism. Some say when Korea was still in the traditional state, Christianity opened a door to other nations for what might have been one of the initiating forces of Korean modernization. Christianity was identified with modernity and attracted young people. The common people were attracted by the pioneer missionaries. They were attracted because of the possibility of social advancement. Therefore, the sociological condition and modernization of the nation caused the growth of the church in this early stage of the Korean Church.

When the first two American Protestant missionaries arrived in Korea, they began direct evangelism work very cautiously. Allen Clark has explained the reasons for this cautious beginning as follows,

> First, the new missionaries did not know the language well enough to be able to do much preaching in Korean. They had no grammars or language textbooks. Second, the government's attitude was not favorable to Christianity... Further, it must be remembered that the treaties included no provision to allow for missionary work. It was well to move slowly, lest the future of the work be hindered by rushing too fast.[60]

At that time the political situation was very unstable because of the unsuccessful coup d'etat of December, 1884. The law which had forbidden the acceptance of Christianity on penalty of death was not yet repealed. Therefore, the people were afraid to make contact with these missionaries. However, the Presbyterian mission emphasis was on direct evangelistic work along with church planting, while the Methodist mission stressed educational and medical work. Presbyterian missionary Underwood tells us about his early direct evangelistic work by way of street discussion:

> As soon as we had secured a little knowledge of the language, we regularly went out in the lands and by ways, sitting down under some tree near a frequented road, or beside some medicinal spring to which the people were in the habit of flocking. We would take out a book and start reading and when several gathered around us to ask questions, we would attempt to explain to them the book, its truth, and what it meant.[61]

Later these street evangelistic efforts developed into opening a street chapel in Seoul. The first fruit of this street discussion evangelism was the conversion of To-sha No, Allen's interpreter, who was baptized on July, 1886. This first baptism was only the beginning. After him, many other Koreans would follow. Underwood writes in 1887,

> We are to have several baptisms on next Sunday and the men who have applied seem to be thoroughly in earnest. They are some of the offshoots, as it were, from some of Ross' work in the North.[62]

In fact, the early Presbyterian missionaries reaped the harvest of converts of John Ross from Manchuria. Underwood explains the growth of the church in Korea in 1888 in the following words,

> Throughout the whole of the northern province it seemed evident that the wide seed-sowing that had been carried on from China, and the books that had been circulated, had their effect, and opportunities for effective work seemed more numerous in that direction than elsewhere. While, therefore, natives were employed to distribute and sell books in other parts of the land, the efforts of the missionaries were merely directed thither, and their trips were almost entirely toward the north. A most promising work was opening up at *Euiju*, and at one time there were gathered at this city from the surrounding villages and counties men to the number of over a hundred who asked to be received into full membership.[63]

In September 1887 the Presbyterian mission organized the first Protestant churches of Seoul and *Sorai* on Korean soil. The first church of Seoul was organized with a roll of fourteen members, of whom thirteen were converted by a man trained by Mr. Ross in Manchuria.[64] In the village of *Sorai* on the west coast of Korea Underwood found a company of seven ready for baptism. The church of *Sorai*, the second Protestant church in Korea, called "the cradle of Protestant Christianity in Korea," claimed the adults of fifty out of fifty-eight homes in the village and produced leadership for the Presbyterian Church and showed the pattern of "self-support." The missionaries went to the villages not to convert the people but to baptize and instruct those who were already won by their countrymen. Underwood writes again, "Wherever the seed is sown it seems to take root, and bear fruit...There are today two organized churches in this land, with a total membership of over a hundred."[65]

In this period of establishment, there was moderate growth in the Methodist Church compared with that in the Presbyterian Church. From the beginning, the methods and practices of Methodist missionaries in Korea were much different from those of the Presbyterians. Early Methodist missionaries who arrived in Korea did not begin determined evangelistic work as early as the Presbyterian missionaries such as Underwood did. The Presbyterian missionaries made long trips because of the demands from all quarters for instruction and baptism. Some of them traveled one thousand miles on foot during a year.[66] Stokes gives two reasons for this: first, there was the difficult language barrier; and second, Methodists were most sensitive to the governmental opposition to Christian evangelism. "The memory of the earlier Roman Catholic persecutions hovered over them like a shadow."[67] However, it is a fact that the Protestant missionary movement never received any official opposition from the Korean government in this period. The Rev. Samuel Moffet writes,

> There are at present no signs of opposition to our work, but our position here is not assured and the present king is not secure on his throne. A revolution might bring to power the man who twenty years ago had 20,000 Christians put to death.[68]

However, in the field of education the Methodist Mission was far in advance of the Presbyterian Mission. The Presbyterian Mission put its emphasis on evangelistic efforts, using education for the training of Christians, while the Methodist Mission laid strong stress on education in general for both Christians and non-Christians as an evangelistic instrument. Just four months after Appenzeller's arrival in Korea, he opened a boys' school with two students, which made such progress as to have eighty-two students enrolled in 1889. At about the same time that the boys' school was founded, Mrs. Mary F. Scranton founded a school for girls with one student. By 1888, there were eighteen students enrolled.[69] Both schools were given royal approval, and the king and queen gave them the names of the schools: *Baejae Hakdang* [Hall for Rearing Useful Men] for boys and *Ewha Hakdang* [Hall for pear blossoms] for girls.

In June 1887, Appenzeller baptized the first Korean Methodist convert, one of his students in the school. And in September Appenzeller bought a small house in Seoul for Sunday worship and called it "Bethel" chapel, in which a public service for Koreans was held. The first Korean Methodist Church was organized on October 9, 1887.[70] The total adherents in Seoul reported in 1890 were one hundred and sixty-five.[71] As Methodist converts grew in numbers, they began to lead their own people to Christ. One of the missionaries, W. B. Scranton, writes, "The seekers come seeking us out and asking for instruction...We do not need to hunt them, but they come to us openly."[72] In fact, the early trips of missionaries had been in response to new Korean-Manchurian converts who sought instruction and baptism. In 1894, in *Inchon* city (twenty miles west of Seoul on the coast), twenty-two out of the mission's total of seventy communicants were recorded. There, in 1894, *Inchon* Methodist Christians constructed the first Methodist chapel, which was called the banner of the Korean Methodist Mission.[73] Along with the church, a boys' school was opened there as an evangelistic agency with the intention of reaching not only the students themselves but their parents also.[74]

There were a number of other mission societies founded during this establishing period. First, the Korean Religious Tract Society was organized in 1889. As observed earlier, the circulation of Christian books and pamphlets had been one of the most effective missionary methods. Ross' work among the Koreans in the Manchurian valley and the seed-sowing in Korea during the beginning days of the mission were all done through Christian literature circulation. In order to publish and circulate Christian tracts and periodicals throughout the Kingdom of Korea, in 1889 the Korean Religious Tract Society was organized with financial aid from the Toronto Tract Society, the American Tract Society and the Religious Tract Society of London.[75] The Tri-lingual Press of the Methodist Mission was begun in order to give employment for self-support and to print Christian literature.[76] The most important task undertaken in this period was the translation of the Bible into Korean. Although there were both the Ross and Su-Jung Yi versions of the New Testament, a meeting of all the missionaries in Seoul was held to improve these translations in 1887. By 1890, the Gospels of Mark, Luke and John had been published. Su-jung Yi was converted by Japanese Christians in Japan in 1883, the first translator of the four Gospels into Korean. Later on he taught Korean to H. G. Underwood and Henry Appenzeller. In March of 1884, he sent out a special plea to the American churches to send missionaries to evangelize his homeland. Upon returning to Korea, he was murdered in May of 1886 by members of a faction at court.[77]

The year 1890 was a very significant one in Korean history. In response to the invitation of missionaries to Korea who were impressed with the plan presented in his series of articles,[78] John L. Nevius visited Korea in 1890. Nevius was born in Ovid, New York, March 4th, 1829. He was graduated from Union College and from Princeton Seminary. He went to *Shantung*, China, as the first missionary of the Northen Presbyterian Church in 1880. Although he worked there for more than ten years, he was never able to practice his method of operation in China, because it depended upon the unified support of a whole mission working in a given area, and from the beginning his plan was not too well received by his China colleagues. In fact Calvin Mater, one of his colleagues, actually published a small book in which he tried to refute Nevius' ideas and to prove that they had not and would not work in *Shantung*, China.

His two-week visit with seven young Presbyterian missionaries had its immediate and profound effect on mission policies. Underwood writes,

In the spring of 1890, Dr. and Mrs. Nevius, of *Cheefoo*, China, visited

Seoul, and in several conferences, laid before the missionaries there the methods of mission work commonly known as the Nevius method. After careful and prayerful consideration, we were led, in the main, to adopt this, and it has been the policy of the mission first,...[79]

Nevius was well known throughout the entire missionary world for the advocacy of his three-self-movement, namely, Self-Propagation, Self-Government, Self-Support, for planting and developing of younger churches. It is very interesting to note that Nevius never published a book containing one comprehensive and systematic mission methodology. Rather he published his various ideas in several articles which were later collected in the booklet *Methods of Mission Work*. Nevius' publications are as follows: *China and the Chinese*; *Demon Possession and Allied Themes*; *Methods of Mission Works; Planting and Development of Missionary Churches*; and books and pamphlets in Chinese. In 1928, Charles Allen Clark made an attempt to present Nevius' principles in a systematic way through the publication of a book entitled *The Korean Church and the Nevius Methods*. In this book he traced the application of these principles to the Korean situation through the mission history of Korea until 1928. He reported that whereas in 1898 there were fewer than 10,000 Christians, in 1928 there were over 160,000 Presbyterians alone.[80]

Formation of the Early Protestant Church (1890-1910)

It was a period of social and political unrest when Christianity was brought into Korean society. Society was under intense pressure both from within and without. Threats of the disruption of the traditional social structure were all around. Search for new ideas and new social-cultural goals was prevalent among many of the lesser elite and even among some of the simple folk. Under these circumstances, Christianity with her new value system could be accepted in society and could spread all over the country in spite of strict control and severe persecution by the government. The pioneer missionaries revolutionized the feudalistic and aristocratic society by their message. Such pioneer missionaries as Underwood and Appenzeller successfully made contacts with the common people. This meant that they attacked the *Yangban* class.

The Korean society was divided into several classes in the late 1890s and early 1900s. The main classes were the *Yangban* class (the class of nobility), the *Sangmin* class (the class of commoners as the farmers and merchants) and the *Chunmin* class (the class of humble people as the slaves and Buddhist priests and shamans).[81] Christianity appealed to the people who had no power in the society. People who had never enjoyed a social status were welcomed by the church. The missionaries preached that before God every person is equal.[82]

In this period the result of implementing the Nevius Method was great success and brought about tremendous growth of the church, and it took place mostly through self-propagation. The propagation of the gospel was done not only by the native evangelists in the church, but also by new converts who became witnesses to their own people. In the 1890s, the missions and the missionary work which had been undertaken by the Northern Presbyterian and the Northern Methodists from the U.S.A. was augmented by the arrival of missionaries from other churches and mission bodies.

> 1889: The Presbyterian Church of Victoria, Australia, Y.M.C.A. Mission;
> 1890: The Church of England;
> 1892: The Presbyterian Church in the United States;
> 1895: The Ella Thing Memorial Baptist Mission;
> 1896: The Methodist Episcopal Church, South;
> 1898: Canadian Presbyterian Church.[83]

In 1890 three baptized communicants were recorded in *Pyongyang* city. By 1893 a church had been organized, and in 1894 fifty-two communicants were recorded in the two *Pyongan* Provinces. In 1890 an average Sunday attendance in the *Pyongyang* city church was about five hundred people. Every Sunday new people were welcomed by this church.[84]

In 1893 different foreign missionary organizations came to an agreement as to how to divide the Korean mission field. The first Presbyterian committee on comity was appointed in January, 1892 at the annual meeting of the mission. Its purpose was to confer with the representatives of the Methodist Mission regarding the matter of comity agreement. Again on January 23, 1893, the Presbyterian Mission appointed a committee on comity consisting of three members, D. L. Gifford, W. L. Swallen, and S. F. Moore to confer with the Methodist representatives regarding the rules of comity. On October 24, 1893 the report of the committee on comity was adopted and the committee discharged.[85] In that year a Comity Agreement between the Northern Presbyterian Mission and the Methodist Episcopal Mission was created. Comity Agreement was a territorial mission agreement of the Presbyterian USA Mission, the Canadian Presbyterian Mission and the

Australian and Methodist missions for their settlement of the territorial divisions in Korea.

> First, Resolved that we advise that as a general rule the common occupation of smaller cities and the districts around them is not the most profitable way of utilizing our forces, but that open ports and towns having a population of over 5000 should be open for common occupation, and especially so when they are needful bases for the occupation.[86]

The increasing number of missionaries and mission societies necessitated such an agreement. This Comity Agreement favored the emphasis on the growth of the churches in Korea. A set of Rules for Comity were adopted on the field for the Methodists and Presbyterians. The Presbyterian U.S.A. Mission had a chain of mission stations from the north-west to south-east corner; the Presbyterian U.S. Mission had the south-west corner; the Canadian Presbyterian Mission had the southeast; the two Methodist Missions had strong missions in the peninsular. This agreement had been kept in effect until the missions withdrew in 1941, the advent of World War II.[87] The rules adopted are as follows:

I.   Resolved that, as a general rule, the common occupation of small cities and the districts around them is not the most profitable way of utilizing our forces; but that open ports and towns with a population of over 5,000 should be open for common occupation and especially so when they are useful and needful bases for the occupation of the regions beyond.

II.   When a town of less than 5,000 has been established as a sub-station by a missionary in charge of the district (a "sub-station" being understood to be a place where inquirers or Christians regularly assemble for worship on the Lord's day, or a place visited not less than four times a year, two visits at least to be made by the missionary in person), it should be considered as occupied, and we deem it inadvisable for another Mission to begin work there; but the discontinuance of work for six months shall leave an open field.

III.   Societies wishing to begin work or to extend it, are strongly recommended to take into consideration unoccupied territory so as speedily to cover the whole field.

IV.   We recognize the inherent right of every church member to change his membership to another denomination; but persons whose names are on the records of a church as members or candidates shall not be received by another church without a letter of recommendation from those in charge of that church.

V.   Resolved that we mutually respect the acts of discipline of the various churches.

VI.   Students, teachers and assistants in any department of the work shall not be received in any capacity whatever by another Mission without the written permission of the person to whom he is responsible.

VII. As a general rule, books should be sold and not given away, and there should be uniformity in prices.[88]

Once mission stations had been established almost everywhere in Korea, the growth of the Korean Protestant church began. Beginning in 1895 and continuing for about fifteen years, until 1910, there was a dramatic explosion of church growth in Korea. Roy Shearer writes,

> ...the communicant membership of the Church began to grow in 1895, and it did not slow down until 1914. At the turn of the century the Church showed better than a thirty percent increase in communicant membership for the year 1900 alone. People were flocking to the Church in tremendous numbers and the annual report of the mission board asked, 'Are not these people going too fast?'[89]

In 1897, the Northern Presbyterians opened a mission in the city of *Taegue* in the southwest. In *Taegue* in 1899, there was one church with twenty-five adherents. In *Kyunggi* Province the Presbyterian Church grew from one hundred to fourteen hundred members between 1890 and 1900. By 1905, there were forty-two churches with nearly two thousands adherents.[90] The Northern Presbyterian Mission in the northwest reported three thousand members by 1902, and in central Korea, registered over four thousand six hundred adherents by 1906. Elsewhere, this pattern of steady increase can be shown to be the norm. And by 1905 there was a firm agreement between the Northern Methodist and Presbyterian Missions and by 1907 with the Southern Methodist Mission. In 1909 two thousand Presbyterian adherents of *Whanghai* Province, including four hundred and sixty baptized members from 49 churches, were transferred to the Methodist Church, while two hundred adherents were received by the Presbyterians from the Methodists in the same province. When Southern Methodist missionaries arrived in Korea they began immediately with evangelistic work in Seoul. Within ten years they had firmly established the Methodist-Episcopal Church in the cities of Seoul, *Songdo*, and *Wonsan*, the territories to which they were assigned in the Comity Agreement.[91]

As mentioned earlier, a large part of the success of this evangelistic work was caused by an emphasis on self-support and self-propagation. Characteristic of the church and mission during this time were the evangelistic activities, the movement toward the formal establishment of the organizational church, and the evangelistic movement which grew out of the 1907 Revival.[92] The origin of the Great Revival may be traced to a meeting in 1903 when Hardie expressed his thoughts in a prayer and Bible study meeting of some Methodist missionaries. Mrs. Underwood, the wife of Horace G. Underwood, one of the pioneers in Korea missions, writes,

> He was asked to prepare to lead the missionaries in some weeks of Bible study, but, as he tried to make ready, he himself was convicted with deep and overwhelming grief and repentance for coldness and shortcomings. He openly confessed before both the Korean church and the missionaries and begged for their prayers. Others were overcome with like conviction and repentance until all the missionaries and the native Christians had received a baptism as of fire.[93]

In 1904, the Bible conference at *Wonsan* was repeated, with a similar experience. In August 1906, the missionaries from *Pyongyang* invited Hardie to lead them during a Bible conference. The Rev. H. A. John of New York, who visited Korea in September, told them about the great revivals in India and Wales. All the Christians who heard this story were eager for a similar experience. Graham Lee says, "His telling of it gave some of the people a great desire to have the same blessing."[94] The evenings preceding the Bible conference, which started on the 6th of January, 1907, were entirely devoted to prayers and special evangelistic preaching. At one of these evening sessions, the outbreak of the revival took place. William N. Blair of the Northern Presbyterian Mission, who had worked for four years in the area north of *Pyongyang*, gives the following account presented at an annual Bible conference in January of 1907,

> The evening meeting connected with the Bible conference began January 6, in the Central Church in *Pyongyang,* with more than 1,500 men present. Women were excluded for lack of room. Different missionaries and Korean leaders had charge of the evening meetings, all seeking to show the need of the Spirit's control in their lives and the necessity for love and righteousness.[95]

In his book, *Gold in Korea*, Blair describes the events that took place that evening:

> After a short sermon Mr. Graham Lee took charge of the meeting and called for prayer. So many began praying that Mr. Lee said, "If you want to pray like that, all pray." And the whole audience began to pray out loud all together. The effect was indescribable. Not confusion, but a vast harmony of souls and Spirit, a mingling together of souls moved by an irresistible impulse of prayer. The prayer sounded to me like the fall of many waters, as an ocean of prayer beating against God's throne.[96]

Graham Lee says of that particular meeting,

> As the prayer continued, a Spirit of heaviness and sorrow came down upon the audience. Over on one side some began to weep, and in moments the whole congregation was weeping. Man after man would arise, confess his sin, break down and weep, and then throw himself to the floor, beat with his fists in perfect agony of conviction...[97]

This public confession of sin was a unique experience in Korea because it never happened again and never before on this large scale. Blair and Hunt write, "The whole church was washed and made clean and sweet and new."[98] After the meeting, the Pentecostal fire flamed forth and spread continually everywhere the story was told throughout the peninsula. The important outcome of this great religious awakening to Korean Christians was that this revival showed that Christianity met the needs of the people and promoted the establishment of religious habits in the Korean Christian community.

At the beginning of this revival movement, daybreak prayer meetings that often began at 4:30 each morning became a way of life for the Korean Church. Still another effect of the great revival of 1907 was widespread church evangelism in cooperation with different denominations. Denominational barriers were broken down and Christians were minded to join together in witness. One Korean leader said to the missionaries, "Some of you go back to John Calvin, and some to John Wesley, but we can go back no further than 1907, when we first really knew the Lord Jesus Christ."[99] The great revival movement in 1907 gave to the Korean church a more zealous and passionate driving power of winning new converts. In 1904 there were reportedly 2,773 adult baptized communicants, and 23,700 adherents in the Methodist and Presbyterian churches in Korea. Six years later in 1910, there were 13,939 adult baptized communicants, and 107,717 adherents.[100] During this period the church nearly doubled its membership every twelve months.

The dramatic explosion of Protestant church growth in Korea between 1895 and 1910 startled the Christian world. In those crucial fifteen years, the Protestant church grew from only 802 to an astonishing 167,352.[101] Comparative Roman Catholic figures for the whole period are unavailable, but from 1900 to 1910, while the Protestants reported a phenomenal 900 percent increase in adherents, the number of Catholics rose only 25 percent, from 60,000 to 75,000.[102]

A new vision of a nationwide evangelistic campaign began to grip the hearts of the Korean Christians. A daring step toward the realization of the vision was launched under the name of "Million Movement" in 1909 and 1910.[103] In fact, in 1909, three missionaries of the Southern Episcopal Mission felt that the spirit of the 1907 revival was waning. They influenced the adoption of the bold watchword "Two hundred thousand souls for Christ" at the Annual Meeting of the Mission. The three missionaries of the Southern Episcopal Mission who authored the bold watchword were M. B. Stokes, F. K. Gamble, and a woman missionary, W. T. Reid.[104] The General Council of Evangelical Missions changed and adopted the slogan "A Million Souls for Christ" for the Evangelization of all Korea.[105] When this slogan was adopted there were only 8,000 church members enrolled in all the Protestant churches, including catechumens. But it was estimated by the foreign missionaries that there were about 200,000 believers connected with the Christian church. At that time the missionary force numbered about 200 members in Korea.[106] The movement began with tremendous enthusiasm and evangelical fervor. G. T. Brown described three of the methods in the plan for evangelistic advance.

> First, there would be mass evangelistic rallies in the various centers. The second, a novel idea with a distinctive Korean flavor, was called the "collection of days." At a mass meeting, the Christians would be asked to donate a number of days of full-time preaching or personal evangelistic work. Third, a major effort would be made in the distribution of gospels and tracts.[107]

Many millions of religious tracts and 700,000 Gospels of Mark were purchased by Korean Christians and distributed to unbelievers among them. All the Christians spent a part of their time doing home-visitation. Nearly every home in Korea had been visited and daily prayer had been offered by these thousands of Korean Christians for realization of the watchword.[108] However, the results of this effort were discouraging. In 1910, 2,010 were received into the church by baptism in the area worked by the Southern Presbyterians,[109]and 2,022 members and probationers for the Southern Methodists, and 15,805 for all the churches in the General Council.[110] These numbers look discouragingly small by the side of the hoped-for 200,000 and 1,000,000. However, the missionaries were not discouraged. Baird said:

> The whole church entered into the campaign with faith and unparalleled enthusiasm. The gospel was preached as never before all over Korea. We do not know how many were saved, but we do know that a great multitude have been persuaded to enter the churches and express a desire to believe. Personally, I believe that when all is known, more than a million souls will be found to date their interest in the kingdom from this Million Year.[111]

Most of the workers probably accepted the watchword not as a definite numerical goal but as a slogan. Many, however, accepted it as a definite goal. Some have criticized the way in which the movement was carried on, calling it a "worked-up Campaign with too little antecedent preparation."[112] However, it goes without saying that the Million Movement was tremendously beneficial. No doubt the church was strengthened by the active members having the experience of witnessing, and the movement did serve to stir up the nationwide Christian community to evangelism, to produce a feeling of national solidarity, and to prepare the church for the lean years which were to come. In 1910 the "Commission for Carrying the Gospel to All the Non-Christian World" reported to the World Missionary Conference at Edinburgh the following facts with regard to the missionary situation in Korea:

> The missions in Korea maintain 307 missionaries including wives, who occupy twenty-three mission stations...and through the work of Korean evangelists, Christianity has secured a foothold in greater or lesser degree in nearly every one of the 330 counties which constitute these provinces. The work done at some of the stations has been remarkable both for its rapidity and its permanence. One of the *Pyongyang* churches, in the course of a history covering only sixteen years, has become five churches and still the congregation of the parent church numbering 2,500 is so large that men and women have to meet separately.[113]

Search for National Independence and Church Growth (1910-1953)

Considering the explanations given for church growth, it can be seen that rather quite a few Korean scholars assume that the nationalism of the Koreans contributed to church growth.[114] These scholars want to show that the Koreans' nationalism played an important part in the widespread Korean acceptance of Christianity. According to them the Korean Christians identified with the Korean nation and the people and thus roused the national pride, especially in the time of the Japanese occupation. In contrast to other areas, the Christian mission in Korea has not been identified with Western colonialism. Kane, in his book about Western colonialism, *A Global View of Christian Missions*, has said the following.

> In Africa and Asia the Christian mission has been identified with colonialism. In India it was British colonialism. In the East Indies it was Dutch

colonialism. In Indo-China it was French colonialism. In the Philippines it was American colonialism... Elsewhere Christianity suffered from an unholy alliance between the gospel and the gunboat.[115]

However, Korea is a different story. Korea was colonized by the neighboring Asian power, Japan. The year 1910 marks a distinct turning point in the fortunes of the Christian church in Korea. In that year Korea lost her independence with the treaty of annexation by Japan, which was signed on August 22 and promulgated on August 29. The Japanese occupation brought many hindrances to the activities of Christian movements in Korea. In 1911, one hundred forty-nine Koreans were arrested; among them there were 98 Christians. The charge was that they had conspired to kill the Japanese governor-general Terauchi as he passed through *Pyongyang*. After severe torture and some years of imprisonment, some of these people were released in 1915. However, during this period the communicant membership figures for the Presbyterian church record a good growth.[116]

During the time of national crisis (1910-1945) in Korea, Christianity played a very significant role. Belief in Christianity gave a sense of patriotic national identity as an alternative force to Japanese colonial assimilation. Korea welcomed Western powers which were "Christian" as a means to restore political independence and to introduce political democracy. Christianity introduced the new concept of modern education and injected a new Christian ethical standard. Unlike China, where the colonial powers were Western nations, Korea faced colonialism from Japan. Therefore, the Korean people welcomed Western influence including Christianity in order to liberate themselves from the hands of the Japanese. While the gentry class in China rejected Christianity, many Korean intellectuals eagerly grasped Christianity. For example, the Korean Independence Association at the beginning of this century had several key leaders.

Christianity played a vital role in Korean nationalism. Korean nationalism awoke when the people felt oppressed by Japanese imperialism. When the Korean Christians from over-seas who studied in the West came back to Korea during this period, they identified with the nation and the people. This gave new hope to many Koreans.[117] A number of them saw Christianity as a powerful force to serve national interests. Sun-Ae Chu writes,

> The awakening to a new civilization was understood as a movement to save our nation and its people. This awakening was encouraged by the spirit of patriotism in the Christian faith. Churches initiated and promoted this

awakening to Western civilization and the Christian spirit fostered the idea of political independence and patriotism.[118]

The March First Movement of 1919 gave a positive image of Christianity to the people, because Christians played a leading role in this Independence Movement. The Inspiration for the March First Independence Movement came from American President Woodrow Wilson's "Fourteen Points" which included in Point Five the right of small nations to self-determination as an integral part of the post-World War I peace settlement. On March 1st, 1919, in Seoul, the Korean Declaration of Independence was publicly read from the pavilion in *Pagoda* Park, but simultaneous meetings also occurred all over the country. The opening lines of the declaration read as follows, in a translation made shortly after the event.

> We herewith proclaim the independence of Korea and the liberty of the Korean people. We tell it to the world in witness of the equality of all nations and we pass it on to our posterity as their inherent right. We make this proclamation, having back of us five thousand years of history and twenty millions of a united loyal people. We take this step to insure to our children for all time to come, personal liberty in accord with the awakening consciousness of this new era. This is the clear leading of God, the moving principle of the present age, the whole human race's just claim. It is something that cannot be stamped out, or stifled, or gagged, or suppressed by any means. [119]

A Declaration of Independence was prepared and signed by a group of thirty-three outstanding religious leaders who chose martyrdom for the freedom of the country. Two were Buddhist, fifteen were *Chundokyo* believers, and sixteen were Christians, twelve of whom were prominent Protestant ministers.[120] Stephen Neill writes,

> In some countries the Christian, because of his association with the West, was suspect and in danger of being regarded as a second-class citizen. In Korea exactly the opposite was the case; to be a Christian was to be a patriot; the churches were widely identified with the Korean national causes.[121]

Many intellectuals accepted Christianity not only for spiritual reasons but also because of its political persuasion. The first president of Korea, Syngman Rhee, was a Christian.[122] Syngman Rhee had been involved in the independence movement. For many years he lived in the United States. The fact that he was a Christian contributed to the further spread of the Christian faith and attracted many Koreans to join the church.

Rhee exemplified the new power elite: Christian with an American education or people who had learned English at Missionary schools and thus developed access to the United States military government which administered the South until 1948. Christians represented a new modernizing force.[123]

However, some of the foreign missionaries who worked in Korea during the Japanese annexation never subordinated Christianity to nationalism. Their idea was more or less: When you are Christian, you should also be a patriot and love your country. Indeed, many Korean Christians were real patriots. Some of these missionaries, however, did not stimulate the nationalistic sentiments, because they thought that every person should "be subject to the governing authorities"(Rom. 13:1), in this case the Japanese. Some American missionaries from a conservative and fundamentalist background advocated that the church distance itself from political issues. For example, A. J. Brown argued, regarding the Korean church's involvement in the independence movement, that

> It is not right for Jesus' disciples to be against the government, but they should simply obey it, ...It is not wise for the young church to join the anti-Japanese movement, ...We are concerned about religious salvation of individuals rather than about social justice. The latter is to be achieved only through the former. The church should be right away from any political movement.[124]

Most of the missionaries tried to be neutral, although most supported the Korean people in cases of real oppression. In the case of the March First Independence Movement, Martha Huntley, who had worked as a missionary's wife in Korea since 1905, clearly described the attitudes of the missionaries.

> This incident [The March First Independence Movement] vividly points up the position of the Protestant missionaries, who had no leadership roles in the movement. Instead, they were literally caught in the middle; their sympathies were with the Koreans, but they were not and did not want to be involved in a crusade for independence. They were, both by mission policy and their personal inclination, basically apolitical. They were committed to the Biblical injunction to obey government authority, to be subject to the powers that be. [125]

At this time in Korea four percent of the population was Christian.[126] Indeed, the historical event of March First of 1919 gave a positive image of Christianity.[127] The credibility of Christianity increased because of the promotion of patriotism by Christians. The suffering and punishment by the Japanese after the failure of the movement increased the credibility even more. As far as the Christian church was concerned, Allen D. Clark notes three important results from this Independence Movement: a man could be a Christian and still be an ardent patriot; Christians were as willing to suffer for their country as anyone else; and the imprisoned Christians, when released, testified to the great spiritual blessings they had received in prison.[128] Most of the church pastors were jailed and not a few churches were burned, and some villages were burned to the ground. The tragic *Jaeam*[129] incident was one of the worst cases in point, where the church was set afire while the Christians were in it, and all the people were killed as they tried to escape.[130]

Table 4.1: School Enrollment in Korea by Nationality in 1925

School Level	Nationality	Enrollments	Pop. (per 10,000)	Ratio
Elementary	Koreans	386,256	208.2	1:6
	Japanese	54,042	1,272.35	
Boys Higher Schools	Korean	9,292	5.01	1:21
	Japanese	532	106.70	
Girls Higher Schools	Korean	2,208	1.19	1:108
	Japanese	5,458	128.50	
Vocational Schools	Koreans	5,491	2.96	1:21
	Japanese	2,663	62.70	
Normal Schools	Korean	1,703	0.92	1:16
	Japanese	611	14.39	
Colleges	Koreans	1,020	0.55	1:26
	Japanese	605	14.24	
University	Koreans	89	0.05	1:109
	Japanese	232	5.46	

(Sources: Ki-baik Lee, *A New History of Korea*, 1984 , p. 367)

Meanwhile, in order to cooperate in evangelistic work "The Federation Council of Churches and Missions" was organized in 1919, whose members were the delegates of the Korean Methodist church, the Presbyterian church and foreign missionaries. In 1924 the name was revised to "The National Christian Council". The purpose of the National Christian Council was to unite the Christian bodies in Korea to cooperate (1) preaching the Gospel, (2) in promoting the public morals, and (3) in spreading the Christian cultures.[131] The most important function of the Council was the joint work among Koreans in Japan. By 1930 there were almost a half million Koreans scattered from *Kogoshima* to *Sapporo* with Christian churches established in nearly 40 places.

However, when in 1930 the Japanese began forcing Korean Christians to participate in *Shinto* worship, the gap between liberal and conservative theologians grew; internal disagreement about *Shinto* worship made the National Christian Council more difficult. The imperial government of Japan in Korea pressed *Shinto* worship upon the Korean churches and Christian schools. Kun-sam Lee writes,

> The emperor was considered to be a god, and the spirits of departed emperors and of their Sun-goddess ancestries were worshiped in the great national shrine in Tokyo and other places. Prayers of adoration and thanksgiving were offered at these shrines and petitions were offered to the gods of Japan.[132]

To encourage the students and teachers to do Shinto worship, the Japanese government insisted that this was not so much a religious act as an act of patriotism. The ruler declared that bowing to the state shrine was not a religious act: "A Japanese out of duty as a citizen must honor the ancestors of the emperor. This cannot be regarded as a religion. It is a ritual. It is the ceremony of gratitude to ancestors."[133] The Presbyterian Mission decided to close their schools rather than compromise with the Japanese religion. The Japanese authorities worked methodically to break down the whole church. They began with individual Christians, then addressed the presbyteries, and finally they put pressure on the General Assembly.

In 1938 the Presbyterian General Assembly convened at the West Gate Church in *Pyongyang*. Before the assembly four hundred delegates were called to the police station and ordered to approve a motion relative to the approval of a *Shinto* shrine. It was passed. This action gave the police a powerful weapon with which to destroy all resistance within the church. However, Korean Christians stood against the

Japanese authorities, suffering torture, imprisonment and even martyr-dom. According to Clark, the number of Christians who suffered imprisonment for their faith is estimated to have been about 3,000, of whom some 50 paid the price of martyrdom.[134]

Despite this suffering and persecution, the Korean church grew under the Japanese rule. Finally the Korean church enjoyed a period of popularity, and many unbelievers came into the church. A mission station reports for 1920 read, "perhaps the work of no year ever began under such adverse circumstances or closed with such bright prospects as the year 1919-1920."[135] Thus, the church grew as a result of that historical event under the Japanese oppression. According to Roy Shearer, in 1911 the number of communicants of the Presbyterian Church was 46,934. This number had grown to 69,047 in 1919, 72,138 in 1920, and 89,000 in 1925. By 1936 the total number of believers amounted to 341,700.[136] In 1939 the communicant membership was 134,000.[137] The outbreak of World War II in 1941 brought even more severe oppression to the churches. Many more church leaders were imprisoned. The Presbyterian Board of Foreign Missions reported that at that time 1,200 out of 5,000 Protestant churches closed.[138] All the foreign missionaries were forced to leave the country. However, the Japanese failed to destroy the Christian Church in Korea.

CHURCH GROWTH AFTER KOREAN WAR

Anti-Communism and Church Growth in South Korea (1953-1970)

In order to understand the characteristics of the Korean church, one has to remember how she suffered for many decades from external invasions and internal revolutions. In 1950, Korea once again became a victim of a larger power. The ideological struggles between Communists and the free people mushroomed and ultimately divided the country. By the thousands, Koreans under the Communists in the North began to escape to find freedom in South Korea. The tragic Korean War impoverished the people and brought added sufferings to the nation. North Korea, where the Northern Presbyterian Mission was particularly successful, had the largest Christian population in the nation. A Korean Christian historian has said that in 1945 in North Korea, approximately 18 percent of the population was Christian, and that in South Korea only 3 percent claimed to be Christians.[139] In fact, three-fourths of all the members of the Korean Presbyterian church were in North Korea. Before 1945, approximately ten percent of *Pyongyang*, the capital of North Korea, claimed to be Christians, and more than fifty percent of *Sunchun* city was Christian.

Table 4.2: Foreign Mission Societies in Korea before 1945

	Mission Societies	Missionaries	Rate
1	Northern Presbyterian U.S. Mission	339	22.1%
2	Northern Methodist U.S. Mission	241	15.7%
3	Southern Presbyterian U.S. Mission	191	12.5%
4	Southern Methodist U.S. Mission	162	10.6%
5	Salvation Army Mission	125	8.2%
6	Australia Presbyterian Mission	84	5.5%
7	England Episcopal Mission	77	5.0%
8	Canada Presbyterian Mission	65	4.2%
9	Seventh Adventist Mission	28	1.8%
10	Oriental Mission Mission	26	1.7%
	The others	192	12.5%
	Total	1530	100%

(Source: Seung-tae Kim, Hae-Jin Park, *Review of Missionaries in Korea: 1884-1984*, 1993)

In the five year period 1945-1950, before the invasion, some five million people evacuated from the north and crossed the 38th parallel to get away from communism with all its supposed economic benefits, but with its denial of freedom. When the United Nations forces arrived, more than 100,000 Northern Christians, many of them pastors and church workers, fled south. The result was a great impetus to the Christian movement in the south.[140] Great new churches were established and many new converts were made among the people. For example, Kyung-chik Han, well-known pastor of *Youngnak* Presbyterian Church in Seoul, began a prayer meeting which by 1946 had developed into a congregation of some 500 members. By the summer of the following year membership had risen to 2,000 and by 1948 to a membership of over 3,000. In the late seventies the membership was 50,000.[141]

On June 25, 1950, the Korean War broke out. During the war the Christians were beaten and scattered. It is believed that one-third of all church buildings were damaged or destroyed throughout the whole country.[142] More than four hundred Christian pastors were killed by the communists because of their faith, and Roman Catholic sources give the names of over a hundred martyred priests in the whole of Korea.[143] The Korean War (1950-1953) also produced many Christian martyrs in South Korea. At the end of 1950 some 500 Christian leaders in Seoul alone were either killed or kidnapped by the Communists. A Korean church historian writes that about 400 pastors of all denominations were lost.[144] During the war, 727 pastors and evangelists were arrested, 360 captured, and in Seoul 39 prominent Christian pastors were martyred.[145]

During the Korean War, the Korean churches received enormous amounts of assistance from the West and played a major role in distributing food and clothes to the hungry and destitue. Of these the many war widows with their children were the most needy. Members of the missions established homes for them, and most women were provided with some form of employment. Much help was also given to amputees, lepers, blind and deaf, tuberculosis patients and crippled children.[146] All these good works created a positive image of Christianity among the Koreans. The help of the Korean Christians during and after the Korea War, the contribution of the Korean War to church growth, can be characterized in two ways. First, the Korean War brought not only an invasion of North Korean Communists but also an invasion of North Korean Christian refugees to the south. Before the war majority of Christians had always lived in the north. Once these refugees had settled down, they established churches in the cities and rural areas. The theological knowledge and the evangelistic zeal of these North Korean Christians enriched the undeveloped South. Secondly, according to Andrew Choi, a Roman Catholic priest, "the Korean War left a permanent scar on the psyche of most South Koreans."[147] As so many times after terrible wars, "a huge vacuum appeared,"[148] in addition to the tremendous suffering in non-spiritual matters. Christians both tried to fill that spiritual vacuum and to relieve the non-spiritual suffering. Thus, "The Korean War and its miserable aftermath offered another boost to Christianity in South Korea."[149]

Roy Shearer, an American missionary, once made a close observation to find the reason for the remarkable growth in the years immediately following the end of the Korean War. He pointed to three reasons. First, the relief work of American churches provided a favorable atmosphere for people to respond to the Gospel. Secondly, military help from the United States during the Korean War intensified a pro-American attitude among the people and, to many of them, America was regarded as a Christian nation. American aid after the Korean War is seen as an example of love. Contact with Westerners has always given hope to any group of Koreans who struggled for a better society. The relationship with the Christian nation, America, since the late 19th century was particularly precious to many Koreans. The American aid which came after the Korean War in order to re-establish the damaged country was very welcome. Many Koreans regarded this material help as "an example of Christ's love, and many recipients of this aid responded to that love and became Christians."[150] At the time of the growth of the Korean church there was an element of opportunism, as food and other material relief many times have been easier to obtain if one expressed the right Christian sentiment. Thirdly, the painful experiences of war smashed some of the old traditions and meaning of life and caused the people to be receptive to something new.[151]

In the midst of intense suffering and toil, the Korean churches in the South were able to give hope to the hopeless, food to the hungry, and shelter to the homeless. Christians looked forward to their heavenly home as a relief from the painful earthly conditions that surrounded them. Yang-sun Kim, the late Korean church historian, said in 1955 that the Korean church, long known for its emphasis on evangelism, sought for spiritual revival after living through the communist invasion. He says, "the spiritually revived Korean church today has twice as many churches and members as before June 25th, 1950."[152] A missionary, who experienced the growth in southwest Korea during the post-war period, said that in 1954 church members and officers called on the members of their villages. These church leaders brought their relatives, friends, and fellow clansmen into their congregations.[153] Once again Korean Christians led their own people to Christ, and missionaries were kept busy doing the best they could to help build a strong church. But this time, there was existent a strong body of experienced pastors and seminary graduates who trained the young church which was growing by a people-movement. People Movement is a process of the joint decision of a number of individuals all from the same people group that enables them to become Christians without social dislocation, while remaining in full contact with their non-Christian relatives, thus enabling other segments of that people group, across the years, to come to similar decisions and form Christian churches made up primarily of members of that people group. McGavran said, "People like to become Christian without crossing racial, linguistic, or class barriers."[154]

As an indication of the amazing open door for the gospel in the post-war period, it is interesting to note how many new church buildings were erected. In 1955, the Presbyterians reported 1,200 new churches built; the Methodists, 500; and Holiness Church, 250. New denominations coming into the country built hundreds more. In all, a total of over 2,000 new church buildings were constructed by 1955.[155] In the 1950s many new Christian organizations and missions began to work in Korea. Many Koreans responded to the gospel. Bruce Hunt, a missionary of the Orthodox Presbyterian Church in America, wrote in 1958: "There were only 100 communicants at the time the principles were adopted, but today there is a full grown, self-propagating, self-supporting and self-governing church of 800,000 members."[156]

Another reason for huge growth during this time may be that several incidents after the Korean War indicated that there was a constant threat of Communist attack from the North. These incidents, together with the presence of the De-Militarized Zone, still provide "a very important motivating factor to many Christians to renew their faith. People look for spiritual security rather than earthly uncertainties."[157] The uncertain situation in the country made many non-Christian Koreans look for security in the churches. Many churches preached anti-Communism messages, which probably attracted the frightened Koreans. In many churches they found a faithful ally against communism. Tae-whan Kim writes,

> many people have attended church for their security and peace of mind... the teaching of anti-communism by the church compelled the Korean people to trust God because the future of the country depended on God for his deliverance from communist oppression.[158]

Ever since the war in 1950, the Korean Protestant Church has been struck with a plague of virulent schisms. Presbyterians have split into four rival factions. In May 1951 the Presbyterian General Assembly took the decision not to recognize *Koryo* Theological Seminary in *Pusan*, which had been founded in 1946 by a group of church leaders who had opposed firmly the participation of the Korean churches in the *Shinto* Shrine Worship. In 1952, the second split took place. A Presbyterian group had its own Theological Seminary in which "liberal theology" was taught since 1939. In 1954 this group founded a new church with the name: Christ Presbyterian Church in Korea or Presbyterian Church in the Republic of Korea. And the third split in the Presbyterian Church took place in 1959. They accounted for 66 percent of the 5,281 churches.

The Presbyterian Church in Korea at its 44th General Assembly in September 1959 was rent asunder when the anti-ecumenical minority broke away over the issue of membership in the World Council of Churches. The schism was healed five months later when a Special Assembly decided in the interest of local unity to withdraw from the WCC.[159] However, a group of Christians within the General Assembly did not agree with the theology of the WCC. In 1960 the anti-WCC conservative group organized the Presbyterian Church *"Haptong*; the pro-W.C.C. ecumenical group remained under the name Presbyterian Church *"Tonghap."*[160]

The Methodists divided twice, but are successfully reunited again. Both the Baptist and Holiness Church were pulled apart by fractional disputes.[161] But even in the midst of divisions the churches continued to grow.[162] After the Korean war there was rapid development and urbanization in Korea and there was a growing emphasis on urban evangelism which changed the mission policy of the churches. However, in 1960, about 80 percent of the population lived in the rural areas. The churches, therefore, decided to emphasize rural evangelism. It was reported that the receptivity ratio of response to the Christian message in the rural areas had greatly increased. According to Korean Campus Crusade for Christ, 80 percent of the farmers who heard the gospel in the summer of 1978 responded positively as against 40 percent in 1976.[163] From the 1970s the growth became explosive in Korea. In 1970 there were about 3,235,000 Protestants in Korea, 4,868,000 in 1979, and 7,181,000 in 1982.[164]

Economic Boom and Church Growth in South Korea after 1970

The Korean church grew with the economic growth and development and the industrialization and urbanization during this period. The economic growth of Korea has been one of the fastest among the developing countries in the Third World during this period. The growth of economy between 1953-1970 has been shown to be at the rate of 8.0 -15.0%.[165] In fact, after the Korean War, the industrialization of Korea has been intensively stressed by the government and the people. As the industrial facilities and factories were sprouting near the cities and towns, the rural population started to move into the urban areas. Before 1960, the migration of the agricultural population was only 14.7 percent. During 1962-1967, the rate of urbanization had increased 22.8 percent. Marked progress has been achieved in various aspects of the Korean economy since the end of the Korea War (1953).

Table 4.3: Statistics of Protestant Churches in Korea (1970-1979)

Year	Denominations	Churches	Ministers	Members
1970	59	13,007	15,708	3,235,475
1975	50	12,979	22,483	3,154,738
1979	64	17,793	24,035	4,867,657

(Source: *Ministry of Culture & Information,* 1979)

South Korea's significant economic improvement came only after 1972. The achievement of self-sufficiency in rice supply by 1987 was one of the most significant aspects of economic development. Another significant aspect of the economic change of South Korea was the strong development of industry from the early 1980s onward.[166] For instance, the Korean per capita GNP was $846 in 1977 compared to $195 in 1969, and reached $1,735 in 1980 (Report of Korean economic planning board). By 1975, South Korea's GNP grew to $18.8 billion from $2.3 billion in 1962, with the average annual GNP growth rate of 10% between 1962 and 1975, despite the oil shock of 1973.[167] Economic growth continued after 1980 and by 1986 the GNP grew to $95.1 billion with per capita GNP of $2,296. The GNP growth rate of 1986-88 was 12.6%, bringing the GNP up to $150 billion and per capita income of $4,738 in 1988.

South Korea's economy continued to grow with an annual GNP of 6.6% in 1989 and 8.4% in 1991, bringing the GNP to $295 billion and per capita income to $6,749 in 1992.[168] However, the economic development caused social unrest because the growth was not balanced and was developed by the politically privileged classes, and because the market was subject to sharp fluctuations. B. S. Kim, a Korean socialist, says that the relationship of economic development and church growth is as follows:

1) While the rapid economic development made the living circumstances more convenient than the past, the distance between the rich and the poor is greater.

2) The progress of economic development is a serious fluctuation.

3) The freedom and equality of the people were distributed by the development of political initiative.

4) The industrialization and centralization of the city made the poor farmer come to the cities. Because the people have the confusion, unrest, and stress by such modernization, they have to go to the church to get the rest and peace.[169]

Table 4.4: Statistics of Denominations in Korea (1979)

	Denominations	Churches	Ministers	Members	Rate
1	Presbyterian	9,923	13,691	2,798,191	57.5%
2	Methodist	2,384	3,116	721,167	14.9%
3	Holiness	1,216	1,483	416,158	8.6%
4	Pentecostal	1,008	1,312	368,947	7.6%
5	Baptist	913	1,041	227,540	4.7%
6	Salvation Army	166	375	86,429	1.8%
7	Seventh Adventist	664	297	50,796	1.0%
8	Nazarene	140	153	40,282	0.8%
9	Christian	360	520	40,179	0.8%
10	Episcopal	71	58	15,031	0.3%
11	Gospel	19	28	4,712	0.1%
12	Lutheran	10	12	2,456	0.1%
	The Others	894	1,949	95,679	2.0%
Total					100%

(Source: *Institute of Korean Church & Society Study*, *Compressive Study of Korean Church for 100 years*, 1982, p. 163)

The growth of industrial facilities in and around large cities brought about rapid urbanization, attracting an increasing number of people away from rural areas. The urban population grew at an annual average rate of 5%, increasing the percentage of urban population from 28 in 1960 to 74.4 in 1990.[170] It is interesting to note that recently the greatest growth in Protestant adherence took place precisely during the period of greatest urban industrial development, when large numbers of people moved from the country to the city, and when with rapid industrialization there was an accompanying rapid change in social values and social dislocation. These conditions permitted an already strong Protestantism to enlarge its adherents because it could offer meaning for life amidst social change, and through the church community it could offer a replacement for the face-to-face village community which had been lost when people moved to the anonymous cities.[171] The church growth of Seoul is based on the increase of its population. The population of Seoul increased from 777,000 in 1940 to 2,445,000 in 1960 and to 8,367,000 in 1980, and the population today is over ten million. In 1990, about 25% of the nation's population lived in the metropolitan area of Seoul while 48% were in the six largest cities.

The radical industrialization and urbanization, which began in the 1960s and became explosive in the 1970s and 1980s, destroyed the ancient securities, led to new challenges, and caused many problems. Kil-myong Noh, a professor of Korea University in Seoul, "attributes the popularity of Christianity in South Korea to the consequences of radical industrialization."[172] These consequences were mainly bad for the many farmers who migrated to the large cities where they met indifference and depersonalizing living conditions.

> They have nowhere to turn to but the church. Brutalized urban slum-dwellers respond much more enthusiastically to messages of immediate salvation and success than to traditional virtues of hard work, dedication and honesty.[173]

This conspicuous process made many scholars think that there is an interrelationship between the two developments. Kim Byung-suh states that there is an interrelation.

> The development motif which has been encouraged by the military government has greatly influenced the Korean church. The development motif has a philosophy of material success at any cost. A sense of fierce competition often makes individuals extremely self-centered, egoistic and selfish; thus a dog-eat-dog competition, particularly over land and space in the extremely congested cities, may be observed. The development psycholo-

gy, along with industrialization, brought about the "Bigness syndrome." The size of an institution is understood as a measure of success. The Korean churches also experience the same bigness syndrome and many churches concentrate on the expansion of the congregation, the budget and the church building by means of highly technological systems.[174]

In any case, the tremendous growth of the Korean churches since the 1970s occurred simultaneously with the enormous economic growth and radical industrialization. In this period, the message of immediate material success based on Possibility Thinking Theology was introduced by Norman Vincent Peal and Robert Schuller in many Korean Churches. According to them, God performs miracles in the people who, unafraid of failure and public embarrassment, move boldly and bravely forward attempting big things for God and expecting great things from God. The principles of possibility thinking are these: 1) Possibility thinking assumes that there must be a way to achieve desired objectives. 2) Possibility thinking makes great pronouncements. 3) Possibility thinking results in brainstorming. 4) Possibility thinking brings in support from unexpected sources. 5) Possibility thinking is simply opening your mind for God to unfold the ways in which His will can be accomplished. Schuller writes,

> The greatest power in the world is the power of possibility thinking. If your dream has come from God then you need only to exercise this miracle-working power, and you can reach the seemingly unattainable goal!... So what then is possibility thinking? Possibility thinking is the maximum utilization of the God-given powers of imagination exercised in dreaming up possible ways by which a desired objective can be attained.[175]

Explosive church growth from 1970-1990 has resulted in the development of some of the largest churches in the world: the *Yoido* Full Gospel Church (706,000 members), Yongnak Presbyterian Church (60,000 members), and Kwanglim Methodist Church (73,000 members). In the capital city of Seoul alone with eleven million people there are more than 6,533 churches. According to the 1993 Christian Almanac, there were over 12.6 million Protestant Christians, 36,832 churches, and 67,008 pastors and evangelist in South Korea. In the nation-wide election of the National Assembly in April 1992, 90 Protestant Christians out of 299 seats were elected.[176]

The early Protestant missionaries emphasized evangelistic work in North Korea because there was a greater response there than in the South. Since its seizure of power in North Korea in 1945, the North

Church Growth in North Korea after 1953

Table 4.5: Statistics of Denominations in Korea (1980)

	Denominations	Churches	Ministers	Members	Rate
1	Presbyterian (29)	12,270	17,613	3,999,137	55.7%
2	Methodist (4)	2,793	3,461	819,725	11.4%
3	Holiness (3)	1,303	1,713	452,618	6.3%
4	Pentecostal (7)	961	1,585	440,557	6.1%
5	Baptist (4)	965	1,189	306,984	4.3%
6	Salvation (1)	173	393	88,222	1.2%
7	Adventist (2)	654	255	68,222	1.0%
8	Nazarene (1)	148	156	75,191	1.0%
9	Christian(2)	209	269	37,388	0.5%
10	Episcopal (1)	66	81	45,284	0.6%
	The Others (12)	1,701	5,025	847,319	11.8%
	Total (67)	21,243	31,740	7,180,627	100%

(Source: *Ministry of Culture & Information.* The Present State of Religious Organization in Korea, 1980; *The Christian Academy*, The Phenomenon and Structure of Holy Spirit Movement in Korea, 1982, p. 229)

Table 4.6: Statistics of Protestant Churches in Korea (1980-1991)

Year	Denominations	Churches	Ministers	Members
1980	67	21,243	31,740	7,180,627
1983	69	26,044	40,717	5,337,308
1984	-	22,871	36,351	8,460,135
1985	-	-	-	6,489,282
1987	74	30,321	48,334	10,337,075
1989	87	29,820	55,989	10,312,813
1990	112	34,407	58,288	11,888,374
1991	-	37,190	67,398	12,571,062

(Source: Seung-tae Kim, *Historical Reflection of Korean Christianity,* 1994, p.284)

Korean Workers Communist Party began thoroughly suppressing all religions for ideological and political reasons. Some 2,000 churches were destroyed one by one, leaving 50,000 Catholics and 300,000 Protestants with no place to hold religious gatherings. Since the Korean war, a policy of severely punishing religious leaders has been added to the full-scale religious suppression which began as the North Korean regime became stabilized. North Korean religious followers welcomed the South Korean troops and the United Nations forces who advanced into North Korea during the Korean War and voiced their opposition to North Korean Communist regime. This has, undoubtedly, contributed to the North Korean regime's decision to persecute religious believers. And so North Korea arrested and executed clergy, accusing them of "being bribed by U.S. imperialists." The practice of murdering "vicious, reactionary" religious followers was practiced before, during and after the Korean War.

It was after the Korean War that the crosses and statues of St. Mary in Christian churches and Buddhist images in Buddhist temples were all removed, and church and temple interiors were renovated to remove the religious atmosphere. Before the war, Communists had used Christian churches as kindergartens, nurseries or class-rooms without removing the crosses or other religious symbols. The execution of clergy was reduced from 1958 on. More than 150 clerics including 52 Koreans, 4 Americans, 15 Frenchmen, 66 Germans, 1 Austrian, 5 Belgians, 6 Dutchmen and 1 Australian were imprisoned for an extended period of time; they were executed, or they died in prison.[177] After 1958, these executions were curtailed. However. the churches north of the 38th parallel were almost completely wiped out by the Communist regime during the Korean War. Many of the five million refugees who fled south from North Korea were Christians. Some denominations lost half their membership when the country was divided. From 1950 to 1955, the religious policy of North Korea changed to persecution of Christians. From 1955 to the present time, the destruction of religions has been the policy of the government. Since then many religions simply went underground. In 1959 the Labor Party declared its opposition to religion as an enemy of science and development, supposedly hindering the conscious struggle for self-understanding. Religion, as the root of this non-scientific and superstitious thought, must be eliminated.

By the early 1960s, religious activities virtually disappeared in North Korea, though the North Korean Constitution of 1947 still guaranteed the freedom of religion. *Pyongyang* anti-religious stance is partly attributable to the view on religion maintained by the late President Kim Il-sung, who wrote:

> Religion is a superstition. All the religions, be they Christianity or Buddhism, belong in essence to the superstition. Historically, religion has always been the tool of the ruling class who want to deceive, suppress and exploit the working class for the benefit of their interests. In the modern age, the imperialists have been using religion as an ideological tool to invade the underdeveloped countries.[178]

Until 1972, freedom of religion in North Korea had been guaranteed based on Article 14 of the constitution that read: "All the people shall enjoy the freedom of religion and religious activities." But in December 1972 North Korea adopted a new constitution and inserted a peculiar phrase in Article 54: "Citizens have freedom of religious belief and the freedom of anti-religious propaganda." This gives people freedom for faith and freedom for anti-religion.

On July 4th 1972, the North-South Joint Communiqué started dialogue between North and South Korea and the ideological walls began to be shattered through the efforts of the World Council of Churches (WCC) and other organizations. After working out measures to prevent the ideological sway of the populace, North Korea re-activated "religious organizations." Activities of "religious organizations" included propaganda-agitation against South Korea attempts at the infiltration of international religious organizations and the approaching of overseas Koreans who were sympathetic in an attempt to win them over to North Korea. In August 1974, Pastor Koh Ki-Joon in North Korea attempted to gain membership in the World Council of Churches but failed in the bid because he could not present appropriate data concerning the status of Christian circles in North Korea, such as the number of churches, congregations, ministers, etc. In 1975 the Communist party, in an attempt to enhance diplomatic relations with other countries, formed a pro-government Christian religious group as a tool that was also used to discover members of the underground church. In January 1975 the North Korea Communist Party sent three representatives from the *Chosen* Christian Corporation to attend the Asian Christian Peace Conference in India.

In 1981, November 3-6, there was a conference held on North Korea in Vienna, Austria. The meeting brought 15 Korean delegates from northern Europe and North Korea. In the 40 years since Korea was divided, this was the first meeting in which Christian delegates from North Korea met with South Korean Christians living abroad. Pastor Koh Ki-Joon from the North reported that there were about 5,000 practicing Christians, and about 500 house churches worshipping regularly throughout the country in 1980.[179] However, only after 1984 did the North Korean government allow people to hold religious meetings, but no proselytizing was permitted. In 1986 a Japanese reporter wrote an article on the situation in which he described a house-church: There was no organ, no electronic organ, and no piano. Even the cross was not in the 33 meter square *ondol* room.[180] A Kim, Il-sung portrait was on the wall, and the eight members, including a missionary, had Il-sung Kim badges on. Also, Han-chul Yu, a missionary of the Propaganda Department of the North Korean Christian Federation, told the reporter that there were about 40 house-churches in *Pyongyang* and each had about 10 members. Throughout North Korea there were over 500 places of worship, 30 ministers and about 10,000 followers; 15 students were attending the three year theological school opened in the office of North Korea Christian Federation.[181] In June 1988, one more organization, the "Association of Catholics," was established in North Korea.

Today North Korea claims that it has some 10,000 Protestant Christians and 15,000 Catholics. Recently North Korea built a Protestant church and a Catholic church in *Pyongyang*, naming them *Bongsu* Church and the *Changchung* Church, respectively. On April 29-May 4, 1991, South Korean lawmakers visited *Pyongyang* to attend an International meeting. During their stay there, Choong-soo Park, Won-ki Kim and Se-hyong Cho were able to attend a Sunday service at the *Bongsu* Protestant Church. They found only about 150 elderly persons, and they noticed that Rev. Li Sung-bong in his sermon neither quoted from the Scripture nor touched on any religious subjects; instead he concentrated on anti-South Korean propaganda. Hyon-wook Kim and Kwan-yon Park attended a Sunday mass at the *Changchung* Catholic Church, but they only saw a government-appointed vice chairman of the church, Sung-kun Cha, say mass. They were told by a North Korean guide that "there are no Catholic priests in North Korea."[182] A peculiar phenomenon in North Korea is that church-goers are not allowed to take Bibles out of the churches. This means that the Christian life is still forbidden in homes in North Korea.

CONCLUSION

Protestant Christianity came to Korea at a time of total breakdown in the nation's social, political and religious life, when the nation had been rudely opened to the outside world. The five-hundred-year-old *Yi* dynasty was tottering, and Korea was slowly, but inexorably, losing its independence to the rising empire of Japan. In the process, Confucianism, the official faith of the doomed dynasty, was becoming thoroughly discredited. Buddhism had been in decline even longer. It had lost its hold on the nation in the fall of an earlier Buddhist dynasty. The traditions of centuries were failing. Into this vacuum of faith and meaning, with its loss of national pride, came the gospel. Protestant Christianity offered a new hope for the future during periods of social and political turmoil. While the objective of the Christian mission was strictly religious, people in Korea responded to the message with a social and political hope for liberation. Koreans took the Christian message politically and nationalistically, as well as religiously. As indicated, beginning in 1907, Korean churches became crowded, and membership increased. Churches became centers for the nationalist movement and the salvation of the nation. During the time of Civil War and Reconstruction, Korean Christians tried not only to fill the spiritual vacuum but also to relieve material and physical suffering. The strong apocalyptic hope of Korean Christians and the relief work of Western churches provided the atmosphere for Koreans to respond to the gospel positively. After 1970, the enormous economic growth and radical industrialization of Korea contributed to church growth because of migration of many farmers to the larger cities. In the time of economic growth whereby many are moving to the city, it turned out that the Christian church has been able to cater to the needs and demands of the new society. Another factor for recent church growth was the messages of immediate material success in the churches. Unfortunately growth during this period had been obscured by serious divisions of the Presbyterian Church. However, during the last two decades the Korean church has experienced remarkable growth by new evangelical fervor demonstrated in great crusade meetings. The purpose of what follows now is to study in full the reasons for church growth and the different factors contributing to it.

Table 4.7: Korean Protestant Church in 1994

Denominations	Churches	Members
Presbyterian: 61 denominations	25,331	7,771,665
6 of the large Presbyterian denominations		
Haptong	5,447	2,158,000
Tonghap	5,330	2,101,000
Reformed	2,000	650,000
Conservative	1,454	562,000
Republic of Korea (ROK)	1,379	345,000
Koryo	1,319	372,000
Methodists: 4 denominations	4,564	1,369,092
Largest Methodist denomination:		
Korean Methodist Christian Church	4,361	1,240,000
Penetecostal: 8 denominations	1,429	1,252,535
Yoido Full Gospel Church	10 Satellite churches	70,6000
Evangelistic Holiness Church:		
2 denominations	2,542	1,067,534
Baptist: 5 denominations	1,910	850,384
Totals	35,776	12,311,210

(Source: 1994 Statistics from the *Christian Newspaper,* 1995; Young-je Han, ed., *1993 Christian Almanac*, Christian Literature Press)

NOTES

[1]Cf. Phillip Schaff, *History of the Christian Church* III (Grand Rapids, MI: William Eerdmans Publishing Co., 1953), p. 731; Yun-tae Oh, *Hankuk Kitokyosa Hankuk Kyungkyosa Pyun [History of Korean Christianity: Nestorianism]*, (Seoul, Korea: Haesun Moonwhasa, 1973), Chapter III; Deukwhang Kim, *Hankuk Jongkyosa [A History of Religions of Korea]*, p. 302-03; Yang-sun Kim, *Hankuk Kitokkyosa Yungu [History of the Korean Church]* (Seoul, Korea: Christian Literature Company, 1971), pp. 27-29.

[2]*Kyungkyo* in Chinese literally means "Religion of light."

[3]Duk-whang Kim, *A History of Religions in Korea,*(Seoul, Korea: Daeji Moonhwa, 1988), pp. 271-272.

[4]Gari Ledyard, *The Dutch Come to Korea* (Seoul, Korea: Royal Asiatic Society, Korea Branch, 1971), pp. 25-37; Roger S. Greenway, ed. *Lengthened Cords* (Grand Rapids, MI: The Christian Reformed Board of Foreign Missions, 1975), p. 161; Cf.Yang-Sun Kim, *Hankuk Kitokyosa Yungu [History of the Korean Church]*, pp. 37-38.

[5]Ledyard, op.cit., pp. 121-134. Hendrick Hamel, *Narrative of an Unlucky Voyage and Imprisonment in Korea 1653-1677*, English Version, (Seoul, Korea: Reprinted by Korea Branch, Royal Asiatic Society, 1918); Pyong-do Yi, trans. *Hamel Pyoryuki [Narrative of an Unlucky Voyage and Shipwrecked on the Coast of Korea]* (Seoul, Korea: Iljokak, 1954).

[6] Hendrik Hamel, *Journal of the Unfortunate Voyage of the Yacht Sparrow* (Seoul, Korea: Iljokak, 1954), pp. 218-219.

[7]Kyung-bae Min, *Hankuk kitokyoheasa [History of Christianity in Korea]* (Daehan Kitokyo chulpnssa, 1982), pp. 36-38.

[8]William de Rubruck, *The Journey of William Rubruck to the Eastern Parts of the World*, 1253-1255. trans. W.W. Rockhill (London, UK: The Hakluyt Society, 1900), pp. 200-201, in: Kwang-soo Kim, *Hankuk Kitokyo Junraesa [A History of the Introduction of Christianity in Korea]*, p. 38.

[9]Ralp M. Cory, "Some Notes on Father Gregorio de Cespedes, Korea's First European Visitors." *Transactions of the Korea Branch of the Royal Asiatic Society*, Vol. 27, 1937, pp. 9-10.

[10]Otis Cary, *A History of Christianity in Japan* (New York, NY: Fleming H. Revell, 1909), p. 115; *The Edinburgh Review*, Vol.136, 1872, p. 303. in: Kyung-bae Min, *Hankuk Kitokkyoheosa [A History of Christianity in Korea]*, p. 43.

[11]Cory, "Some Notes on Father Gregorio Cespedes, Korea's First European Visitor," *Transactions of the Korean Branch of the Royal Asiatic Society*, Vol.XXVII for 1937, pp. 1-55.

[12]C.C. Dallet, *Historie de l'Eglise de Coree*, Paris, 1874, I. pp. 3-4, in: Min, *op.cit.*, p. 46.

[13]Yi Su-kwang (1563-1628), in his *Chibong Yusol [Collected Essays of Chibong]*, writes about the *T'ien-chu Shihi [Chonju Sirui]* in Korean. See Su-

kwang Yi, *Chinbong Yusol* [*Collected Essays of Chibong*] (Seoul, Korea: Kyungin Moonwhasa, 1970), p. 36; Cf. Joe, *Traditional Korea A Cultural History*, pp. 410-411.

[14]Kenneth Scott Latourette, *A History of the Expansion of Christianity*,Vol.VI, (New York, NY: Harper & Row, 1944), p. 414.

[15]Hong-yeul Yoo, *Hankuk Chuju Kyohoesa* [*History of Catholic Church in Korea*] (Seoul, Korea: Catholic Publishing House,1962), pp. 82-87; H. G. Underwood, *The Call of Korea* (New York, NY: Fleming H. Revell Company, 1908), p. 127.

[16]Kwang-soo Kim, *Hankuk Kitokyo Junraesa* [*A History of Introduction of Christianity in Korea*], pp. 90-91.

[17]Charles A. Clark, *Religions of Old Korea*, p. 234.

[18]Joe, *Traditional Korea A Cultural History*, p. 414; Jerome Breunig, Cf. S J., *Have You Had Your Rice Today* (Chicago, IL: Loyola University Press, 1964), p. 27; Ki-baik Lee, *A New History of Korea*, p. 240.

[19]Hong-yeul Yoo, *Hankuk Chunju Kyohoesa* [*History of Catholic Church in Korea*], p. 167; Kwang-soo Kim, *Hankuk Kitokkyo Junaresa* [*A History of the Introduction of Christianity in Korea*], pp. 99-102.

[20]Min, *op.cit.*, pp. 78-82.

[21]Grayson, *op.cit.*, p. 78.

[22]Taikpoo Chun, *Hankuk Kyohoe Baljunsa* [*The History of Church Development in Korea*] (Seoul, Korea: The Christian Literature Society, 1987), p. 47.

[23]Won-sun Lee, Huh In, *Kim Tae-gon-ui Pyongyang* [*Letters of the Priest Kim Tae-gon*] (Seoul, Korea: Jungmunsa, 1975), pp. 29-36.

[24]Cf. Won-Soon Lee, *Hankuk Chunju Kyohoesa* [*History of Catholic Church in Korea*] (Seoul, Korea: Tamgoodang, 1980), p. 213.

[25]Jindanhakhoe Pyun, *Hankuksa* [*History of Korea*] *Hyundai Pyun* (Seoul, Korea: The Eluoo Moonwhasa, 1964), p. 274; Yoo, *Hankuk Chunju Kyohoesa* [*History of Catholic Church in Korea*] p.624; About Catholic persecution under the Regent, Taiwonkun, 1866-1871, Cf. Yoo, *Studies on Catholic Persecutions During King Kojong's Reign (1863-1907)* Part I.

[26]Stephen Neill, *A History of Christian Mission* (New York, NY: Penguin Books, 1964), p. 415.

[27]C.H. Robinson, *History of Christian Missions* (Edinburgh, UK: T.&.T. Clark, 1915), p. 249.

[28]Chun, *HankukKyohoe Baljunsa* [*History of Church in Korea*], p. 181.

[29]Yoo, *Hankuk Chunjoo Kyohoesa* [*History of Catholic Church in Korea*], pp. 1000-1001.

[30]Chun, *Hankuk Kyohoe Baljunsa* [*History of Church in Korea*], p. 183.

[31]Korean Overseas Information Service, *A Friend from Far* (Seoul, Korea: Samwha Printing Company, 1984), p. 5.

[32]For the list of Catholic publication in Korean, See C. Dallet, *op.cit.,* p. 504.

[33]Korean Overseas Information, *A Handbook of Korea* (Seoul, Korea: Hollym Corporation, 1993), p. 132.

[34]Cf. Byung-gil Lee, *Joongkuk Sunkyo-eui Yeaje-wa Oneul* [*Yesterday and Today of Mission in China*] (Seoul, Korea: Gaehyukjueui Shinhang Heybhoe Press, 1987), p. 35; *Hankuk Kitokysa Yungoohoe, Hankuk Kitokkyo-eui Yeksa* [*A History of the Korean Church*] Vol. (Seoul, Korea: The Christian Literature Press, 1989), p. 129.

[35]Jin-ho Lee, *Dongyang-eul Sumgin Gutzlaff* [*Gutzlaff who Ministered to the Orient*] (Seoul, Korea: Department of Methodist Church in Korea, 1988), p. 39; Cf. *Journal of Three Voyages along the Coast of China in 1831,1832 & 1833, with Notices of Siam, Corea, and the Loo-Choo Islands* (London, UK: Frederick Westley & A. H. Danis, 1834).

[36]Kwang S. Kim, *Hankuk Kitokyo Junraesa* [*A History of the Introduction of Christianity in Korea*], pp. 233-239.

[37]Yang S. Kim, *Hankuk Kitokyosa Yungu* [*History of the Korean Church*] (Seoul, Korea: Christian Literature Company, 1971), p. 42.

[38]Gutzlaff, *Journal of Three Voyages along the Coast of China*, p. 355.

[39]Cf. Sir John Edward Lloyd & R. J. Jenkins, eds. *The Dictionary of Welsh Biography, down to 1940* (Oxford, UK: B.H., Blackwell, 1959), *Congregational Year Book*, 1940, p. 225.

[40]M.W. Oh, "Two Visits of the Rev. R. J. Thomas to Korea," *A Transaction of the Royal Asiatic Society*, Korean Branch,Vol.XXI. (Seoul, Korea: The Royal Asiatic Society, 1933), p. 104; Paik, *History of the Protestant Missions in Korea: 1932-1910*, pp. 50-51.

[41]T. Stanley Soltau, *Korea: The Hermit Nation and Its Response to Christianity*, p. 86.

[42]William E. Griffis, *Henry G. Appenzeller: A Modern Pioneer in Korea* (New York, Chicago, Toronto, London and Edinburgh: Fleming H. Revell Co., 1912), pp.45-46.

[43]Harry A. Rhodes, *History of the Korea Mission*, p. 74.

[44]J. Ross, "The Christian Dawn in Korea." p. 247. in: *The Institute of Korean Church History Studies, Hankuk Kitokkyo-eui Yeuksa* [*A History of Korean Church*], Vol. I., (Seoul, Korea: The Christian Literature Press), p. 155.

[45]Horace Underwood, *The Call of Korea*, pp. 136-137.

[46]G.T. Brown, *Mission to Korea* (New York, NY: Board of World Mission, Presbyterian Church, U.S.A., 1962), p.10.

[47]J. Webster, "Journey to the Corean Valleys," *The United Presbyterian Mission Record* (Oct. 1885), pp. 321-326; J. Ross, "Corean Converts," *The Missionary Review*, (May, 1885), pp. 207-209, in: *The Institute of Korean Church History Studies, A History of Korean Church*, Vol.I (Seoul, Korea: The Christian Literature Press, 1989), p. 153.

[48] *British and Foreign Bible Society Annual Report for 1885*, pp. 215, 216, 361.

[49]J. Orr, "The Gospel in Corea," *The United Presbyterian Missionary Record* (June, 2, 1890), p. 188.

[50]*British and Foreign Bible Society Annual Report for 1887*, pp. 271-272. and *H.G. Underwood's Letter to Dr. Ellinwood*, 1887, January 22.

[51]Regarding the Mission Methods of John Ross, See John Ross, *Mission Methods in Manchuria* (New York, NY: Fleming H. Revell Co., 1903).

[52]Allen D. Clark, *History of the Korean Church* (Seoul, Korea: The Christian Literature Society, 1916), p. 61; Sun-keun Lee, *Hankuksa; Choikeunsesa* [*History of Korea: Modern History*] (Seoul, Korea: Jindan Hakhoe, 1951), p. 950.

[53]R. S. Maclay, "Commencement of the Korea Methodist Episcopal Mission," *The Gospel in All Lands* (August 1885). p. 328.

[54]A. J. Brown, "The Rev. Horace Grant Underwood, D.D., LL. D.," *The Korean Mission Field*, Vol. 13, No.2 (February, 1917), p. 24.

[55]W. E. Griffis, *A Modern Pioneer in Korea, the Life Study of Henry G. Appenzeller* (New York, NY: Fleming H. Revell Co., 1912), p. 7.

[56]Shearer, *op.cit.*, p. 49.

[57]Rak-joon Paik, *Hankuk Gaeshin Kyohoesa* [*History of Protestant Church in Korea*] (Seoul, Korea: Yunsei University Press, 1973), pp. 440-441.

[58]*Far Eastern Economic Review,* April, 19, 1984, p. 55.

[59]Won-sul Lee, *Gospel Light*, February-March 1983, p. 9.

[60]Allen D. Clark, *History of the Korean Church*, p. 70.

[61]Underwood, *The Call of Korea*, pp. 106-107.

[62]Underwood, *Letter to the Board of Foreign Missions of the Presbyterian Church U.S.A.*, (Seoul, Korea: January 22, 1887).

[63]Underwood, *op.cit.,* pp. 137-138.

[64]*Annual Report of the Board of Foreign Missions of the Presbyterian Church U.S.A* (New York: 1890), p. 134.

[65]Mr.Underwood's letter from Seoul, Dec. 23, 1888. *The Missionary Review of the World, North Presbyterian Church*, Vol.2, No.4 (April, 1889), pp. 288-289.

[66]Cf. Shearer, *Wildfire: Church Growth in Korea*, pp. 45-46.

[67]Charles Davis Stokes, *History of Methodist Missions in Korea: 1885-1930* (New Haven, CN: Yale University Doctoral Thesis, 1947), p. 81.

[68]Samuel A. Moffet, *Letter to the Board of Foreign Missions of the Presbyterian Church U.S.A.* (Seoul, Korea: March 18, 1890).

[69]Paik, *Hankuk Gaeshinkyosa* [*History of the Protestant Church in Korea*], pp. 126-129.

[70]C.A. Sauer, *Within the Gale*, p. 10.

[71]Gil-sub Song, *Jundog Jeil Kyohoe Gushib Yensa* [*The Ninety Year History of Jundong First Methodist Church*] (Seoul, Korea: Jungdo Jeil Kyohoesa Pyuchan Wewonhoe, n.d.), p. 58.

[72]*Methodist Episcopal Church North Report for 1890*, pp. 272-273.

[73]Charles D. Stokes, *History of Methodist Missions in Korea*, p. 112.

[74]George H. Jones, "Mission Work on the *Chempulpo* District" in: *Gospel in All Lands* (September, 1984), p. 415.

[75]George Bonwick, "The Birth of the Korean Religious Tract Society," *The Korean Mission Field*, Vol. 10, No.1 (January,1914), p.12; "The Korean Religious Tract Society," *The Korean Repository*, Vol.3 (October, 1896), pp. 413-414.

[76]*Methodist Episcopal North Report for 1888*, p. 339.

[77]Cf. Duk-ju Yi, "A Study on Translation of the Korean Bible," Man-yeul Yi, and others, *Hankuk Kitokkyo-wa Minjok Wundong* [*Christianity and National Movement in Korea*] (Seoul, Korea: Bosung, 1986), pp. 107-127.

[78]*Planting and Development of Missionary Churches, Methods of Mission Work, The Korean Church and the Nevius Methods*.

[79]Underwood, *The Call of Korea*, p. 109.

[80]C. A. Clark, *The Korean Church and the Nevius Methods*, p. 5.

[81]For further information about the different classes in the Korean feudal society, Cf. Hugh H.W. Kang, ed., *The Traditional Culture and Society of Korea: Thought and Institutions* (Honolulu, HI: Center for Korean Studies, University of Hawaii, 1975).

[82]Harold S. Hong, "Social, Political and Psychological Aspects of Church Growth," Ro and Nelson, eds. *op.cit.,* pp. 174-175.

[83]Paik, *History of the Korean Church in Korea: 1832-1910*, pp. 184-198.

[84]Shearer, *op.cit.*, pp. 81-82.

[85]Cf. *The Presbyterian U.S.A. Korea Mission*, Report on Comity by C.C. Vinton, Chairman; January 23, 1893.; *The Presbyterian U.S.A. Korea Mission, Minutes* (1885-1899), p. 149, 186.

[86]C. A. Clark, *The Korean Church and the Nevius Methods*, p. 90; The Presbyterian U.S.A. Board, Report C. C. Vinton, in: C. Chun Sung, *Schism and Unity in the Protestant Churches of Korea* (Seoul, Korea: Christian Literature Society, 1979), pp. 115-116.

[87]Cf. Horace G. Underwood, "Division of the Field," *The Korea Mission Field*, Vol.5, No.12, Dec.1909, p.211. Charles A. Clark, *The Korean Church and the Nevius Methods*, pp. 118-119. C.D. Morris, "Division of the Territory between the Presbyterian and Methodist Missions," *The Korea Mission Field*, Vol. 10, No.1, Jan., 1914, p. 18-19. "Agreement on Division of Territory," *Annual Meetings of the General Council of Protestant Evangelical Missions in Korea*, Oct.,1909, pp.32-34; F.E.C. Williams & G. Bonwick ed., *The Korea Missions Year Book* (Seoul, Korea: The Christian Literature Society of Korea, 1928).

[88]R.E. Speer, *Report of a Visit to Korea, 1897*, p. 41. in: C. Clark, *The Korean Churches and the Nevius Methods*, pp. 118-119.

[89]The first converts were baptized in 1886; by 1894 the number had grown to 236. By 1910 there were nearly 30,000 communicants of the Presbyterian and Methodist Churches. Cf. Stephen Neill, *A History of Christian Missions* (New York, NY: Penguin Books, 1964), pp. 343-344.

[90]Paik, *Hankuk Gaeshinkyosa* [*History of the Korean Church in Korea*], p. 286.

[91]Shearer, *op.cit.*, p. 172.

[92]In 1907 two great events of Korean church history had been marked. The first was the Great Revival and the second was that the seven Korean graduates of the Union Presbyterian Theological Seminary, which was organized in 1901, in Pyongyang were ordained as ministers in order to serve the Korean Church, which became independent in the same service. Cf. Taikpoo Chun, *Hankuk Kyohoe Baljunsa* [*The Development of Church in Korea*], p. 159.

[93]Lillian H. Underwood, *op.cit.*, p. 224.

[94]Lee Graham, "How the Spirit Came to *Pyongyang*," *The Korean Mission Field,* 3 (March 1907), pp. 33-37.

[95]William N. Blair and Bruce F. Hunt, *Korea Pentecost: The Suffering Which Followed,* (Edinburgh, UK: Banner of Truth Trust, 1977), p. 26.

[96]William N. Blair, *Gold in Korea* (New York, NY: The Presbyterian Church in the U.S.A., 1957), p. 62.

[97]*Ibid.,* p. 63.

[98]Blair and Hunt, *op.cit.*, p. 78.

[99]G. H. Jones and J. Fowler-Wiling, *The Lure of Korea*, p. 21, in: Hoke, Donald E., ed. *The Church in Korea* (Chicago, IL: The Moody Press, 1975), p. 378.

[100]A.W. Wasson, *Church Growth in Korea* (New York, NY: International Missionary Council, 1934), p.66; C.A. Clark writes: "Between 1897 and 1909 the total of Protestant communicants sprang from 530 to 26,057," in: C. A. Clark, *Korean Church and the Nevius Method*, p.151; The Seoul Conference reported that the number of the baptized Christians in Korean churches increased from 14,000 in 1902 to 68,000 in 1912. *The Continuation Committee Conferences in Asia 1912-1913* (New York, NY: The Chairman of the Continuation Committee, 1913), p. 390.

[101]The first converts were baptized in 1886; by 1894 the number had grown to 236. By 1910 there were nearly 30,000 communicants of the Presbyterian and Methodist Churches. Cf. Stephen Neill, *A History of Christian Missions* (New York, NY: Penguin Books, 1964), pp. 343-344.

[102]Charles D. Stokes, *History of Methodist Missions in Korea, 1885-1930* (Ph.D. dissertation, Yale University, 1947), pp. 10-15.

[103]George T. B. Davis, *Korea For Christ* (London: Christian Worker Depot, 1910), p. 67.

[104]Cf. G.T.B. Davis, *Korea for Christ: The Story of the Great Crusade to Win One Million Souls from Heathenism to Christianity* (London, UK: Christian Workers Depot, 1910), p. 6-7.

[105]The General Council of Evangelical Missions was constituted on September 15, 1905. The purpose of this council was to cooperate in Christian work and eventually to organize one Evangelical Church in Korea. "A Bold Watchword for Korea," *The Missionary Review of the World*, Vol. 33, No. 4 (April, 1910), p. 242.

[106]A person who promises to lead a Christian life, regularly attending worship services and studying prescribed Biblical material in order to be examined for church membership six months after being admitted to the catechumenate.

[107]Brown, *op.cit.*, p. 79.

[108]Yang-sun Kim, *op.cit.*, pp. 90-91; "The Million Movement and Its Results," *Korean Mission Field*, Vol. 7, No.1 (January, 1911), p. 5.

[109]Brown, *op.cit.*, p. 79.

[110]Wasson, *op.cit.*, p. 61.

[111]W. M. Baird, "An Address to the Presbyterian Mission on the Million Movement," *Korean Mission Field* 7 (November 1911), p. 210.

[112]C. A. Clark, *Korean Church and the Nevius Method*, p. 155.

[113]Report of Commission I, "Carrying the Gospel to All the Non-Christian World," *World Missionary Conference* (1910), pp. 74-75.

[114]Kyung-bae Min, *Hankuk Kitokkyohoesa* [*History of Christianity in Korea*]_(Seoul, Korea: The Christian Literature Society, 1982), pp. 193; Taikpoo Chun, *Hankuk Kyohoe Baljunsa* [*The History of Development in Korea*] (Seoul, Korea: The Christian Literature Society, 1987), pp.200-205; Tong-shik Ryu, *Hankuk Jongkyo-wa Kitokkyo* [*The Christian Faith Encounters the Religions of Korea*] (Seoul, Korea: The Christian Literature Society, 1965), pp. 136-139.

[115]J. Herbert Kane, *A Global View of Christian Missions* (Grand Rapids, MI: Baker Book House, 1971), p. 267.

[116]See Yang S. Kim, *Hankuk Kitokyohoesa Yungu* [*A Study of Christianity in Korea*] Seoul, Korea: The Christian Literature Society, 1971), p. 115

[117]Kyung-ro Yun, "*Shinminhoe-eui Changrim Kyungwe-wa Yibhoe Julcha*," [The Foundation and the Process of Association of New Nation], *Kristokyowa Gyerea Munwha* [*Christianity and National Culture*] (Seoul, Korea: Kotokyomunsa, 1987), pp. 233-234.

[118]Sun-ae Chu, "Korean Church Growth and Christian Education," Ro and Nelson, *op.cit.*, p. 311.

[119]Cf. Ki-baik Lee, *New History of Korea* , pp. 338-342.

[120]Ji-ho Cho, *Hankuk Toknip Undongsa* [*The History of Korean National Movement*] (Seoul, Korea: National History Completion Society, 1964), pp. 647-649.

[121]Stephen Neill, *Colonialism and Christian Missions* (New York, NY:

McGraw-Hill, 1966), p. 219.

[122]In June 1953 Syngman Rhee (1875-1965) released about 27,000 anti-Community prisoners of war from the North Korean Army. Although this action of Rhee was not so much approved in international politics, it gave many Koreans the conviction that Christians were fighting for a good cause, namely liberating the North Korean brothers from the Communist oppression.

"Phenomenon of the Cross: Confucianist South Korea Rapidly to Christianity," *Far Eastern Economic Review*, April, 19, 1984, p. 44.

[123]Yohan Chom *"Hankuk Kitokyo-eui Konan* [The Struggles of the Korean Christianity], Seoul, Korea: Sungjon University, 1984, pp. 53,54.

[124]Martha Huntley, *To Start a Work: The Foundation of Protestant Mission in Korea* (1884-1919) (Seoul, Korea: Mokyangsa, 1987), p. 540.

[125]Kane, *Global View of Christian Missions*, p. 268.

[126]Kim Yong-bock, *Minjung* theologian, evaluates this Independent Movement from the perspective of the *Minjung*. The Messianic traditions of Buddhism, the *Tonghak* religion and Christianity united into a messianic religious foundation of the *Minjung*, which became the backbone and the dynamic power of the March First Movement. This movement marks the turning-point in Korean history, it became the pragmatic, the basic experience of the Korean people. From this experience the *Minjung* derives its motive, horizon and goals for the creation of its own, new future. See Young-bock Kim, *Minjung-Theolgie des Volkes Gottes ni Sudkorea* (Neukirchen-Vlyun, 1984), p. 224.

[127]Clark, *History of the Korean Church*, p. 173.

[128]*Jaeam* is a small town in *Kyunggi* province near Seoul.

[129]Choon B. Kim, *Hankuk Kitokkyo Sunan Sahwa* [*Historical Story of Persecution in Korean Church*] (Seoul, Korea: Sung Moon Haksa, 1969), pp. 53-57.

[130]Korean National Christian Council, Minutes, 1928, p. 6; Cf. Chun, *The History of Church Development in Korea*, pp. 219-210.

[131]Kun-Sam Lee, *The Christian Confrontation with Shinto Nationalism* (Philadelphia, PA: The Presbyterian and Reformed Press, 1966), p. 4-5.

[132]D. C. Holton, *The National Faith of Japan; A Study in Modern Shinto* (New York, NY: E. P. Dutton, 1938), p. 69.

[133]See Allen D. Clark, *History of the Korean Church*, p. 202.

[134]*Annual Report of the Board* (New York, NY: 1922), p. 146.

[135]C. A. Clark, *Nevius Plan and Missions Work*, p. 320.

[136]Shearer, *op.cit.*, pp. 59-79; Another report reveals that in 1938 about 80 percent of the churches and Christians lived in the territory of the Northern Presbyterians, which is now in North Korea. At that time there lived about 600,000 Protestant Christians in that area. Cf. Rhodes and Campell, *A History of the Korean Presbyterian Church in the U.S.A.1884-1934* (Seoul, Chosen Mission Presbyterian Church, 1934), pp. 209-210.

[137]Shearer, *op.cit.*, p. 207.

[138]J. D. Douglas, *Let the Earth Hear His Voice* (Minneapolis, MN: World Wide Publication, 1975), p. 58.

[139]Yang-sun Kim, *Hankuk Kitokkyosa Yungu [A Study of the History of Christian Church in Korea]* (Seoul, Korea: The Christian Literature Society, rev. 1980), pp. 79-81.

[140]Larry Ward, "Dr. Han Kyungchik, Korea's Quiet Dynamo," *World Vision*, 12 (March 1968), pp. 16-19; Bong-rin Ro, "Do Theological Schools Help Local Churches?" *Asia Theological News* (January-March, 1982), p. 4.

[141]Robert H. Glover, *The Progress of Worldwide Missions* (New York, NY: Harper and Row Publishers, 1960), p. 201.

[142]Jang-moon Kim, *Catholic Korea, Yesterday and Today* (Seoul, Korea: Catholic Korean Press, 1964), pp. 341-384.

[143]Chun, *op.cit*, pp. 307-313.

[144]Kim, *Catholic Korea, Yesterday and Today*, pp. 341-384; Kim, *History of the Christian Church for Ten Years after Liberation:1945-1955*, p. 78.

[145]Rhodes and Campell, *op.cit.*, pp. 320-344.

[146]*Far East Economic Review*, April, 1984, p. 44.

[147]*Ibid.*, p. 44.

[148]*Ibid.*, p. 55.

[149]Shearer, *op.cit.*, p. 211.

[150]*Ibid.*, pp. 210-212.

[151]Yang-sun Kim, *History of the Korean Church in the Ten Years since Liberation,* p. 20.

[152]Shearer, *op.cit.*, p. 210.

[153]D. A. McGavran, *The Bridges of God: A Study in the Strategy of Mission* (New York, NY: Friendship Press, 1955), p. 71.; See also, Harvie M. Conn, ed., *Theological Perspective on Church Growth* (Nutley, NJ: Presbyterian Reformed Publishing Co., 1976), pp. 76-77.

[154]Allen D. Clark, *History of the Korean Church*, p. 251.

[155]Nevius, *Planting and Development of Missionary Churches*, Preface to the fourth Edition by Bruce F. Hunt.

[156]Ro and Nelson, *op.cit.*, pp. 163-164.

[157]Tae-whan Kim, *An Empirical Study of the Factors Contributing to Rapid Church Growth in Korea* (Philadelphia, PA: Dissertation from Eastern Baptist Theological Seminary, 1984), p. 95-96.

[158]John C. Smith, "Policy Lessons from Korea," in: *The International Review of Missions 50* (July 1961), pp.320-324.

[159] Cf. Yung-hun Lee, *Hankuk Kyohowsa [The History of Korean Church]* (Seoul, Korea: Concordia Press, 1978), p. 348; See Glover, *op.cit.*, pp. 201-202.

[160]Moffett, *The Christians of Korea*, p. 27.

[161]Samuel H. Moffett, *The Christians of Korea* (New York, NY: Friendship Press, 1962), p. 119.

[162]Joon Gon Kim, "Six New Churches Every Day: Korean Church Growth," *Asian Perspective* 17 (n.d.), p. 1-2.

[163]Cf. Ministry of Culture and Information, *Hankuk Jongkyo Pyunlam 1979* [*Annual Report of Religions in Korea 1979*]

[164]David J. Cho, ed. *New Forces in Missions: The Official Report of the All - Asia Mission Consultation.* Seoul '73 and the Inaugural Convention of the Asia Missions Association, 1975 (East-West Center Missions Research & Development, Seoul, Korea, 1975), pp. 127-128.

[165]Cf. Korean Overseas Information Services, *A Handbook of Korea*, 1994, pp. 382-390.

[166]Andrew H. Nahm, *Introduction to Korean History and Culture* (Seoul, Korea: Hollym Corporation, 1993), pp. 322-323.

[167]*Ibid,* pp. 323-324.

[168]Byung-suh, Kim, *A History of the Growth of Christianity in Korea* (Seoul, Korea: Christian Literature Society, 1971), p. 703.

[169]See Nahm, *Introduction to Korean History and Culture*, p. 332.

[170]Grayson, *Early Buddhism and Christianity in Korea: A Study in the Emplantation of Religion*, pp. 127-128.

[171]*Far East Economic Review* (April, 1984), p. 55.

[172]*Ibid.,* p. 45.

[173]*Ibid.*, p. 71.

[174]Cf. Robert H. Schuller, *Your Church Has Real Possibilities* (Ventura, CA: Regal Books, 1975). pp. 85-87.

[175]Ro and Nelson, *Korean Church Growth Explosion*, rev, 1995, pp. 15-16.

[176]Tae-Woo Ko, *Religions in Korea* (Seoul, Korea: Institute of Korean Religion, 1988), p. 58.

[177]*Kim Ilsung Sunjib* [*A Selection of Kim Il-sung's Work*], Vol.1 (Pyongyang, North Korea: Korean Workers' Party Printing House, 1967), p. 173.

[178]Wi-Jo Kang, "Conference on North Korea," *Missiology: An International Review* 10 (October 1982), pp. 487-488.

[179]A hot-floored room.

[180]Ko, *Ibid.* p. 75.

[181]The Institute for South-North Korean Studies, *The Human Rights Situation in North Korea* (Seoul, Korea: The Korean Herald Inc., 1992), pp. 70-71.

Chapter Five

FOREIGN MISSIONARY POLICIES AND METHODS AND NATIVE KOREAN EVANGELISTIC WORK FOR CHURCH GROWTH IN KOREA

INTRODUCTION

The present numerical growth of Korean Protestant churches is itself showing evidence of influence of the foreign missionary method and policies. In order to understand church growth in Korea, in this chapter the author first deals with how the missionary methods and policies of the foreign missionaries was employed in their work and contributed to church growth through their methods, such as Nevius, their Bible translation, literature work, education and humanitarian work. In the past, when reasons were sought for the tremendous, fast growth of the Korean church, the writers often implied that missionaries and their methods were the primary causes of this miracle of church growth in Korea. The foreign missionary does not rank, however, first in his influence on the growth of the church in Korea.

Korean church history indicates that the Korean church was started by the Korean people and stood foremost among all modern mission fields for the rapidity with which its converts have been won and a strong church established. A. J. Brown, former Far East Secretary of the Presbyterian Board of Foreign Missions, and C. Darby Fulton, Southern Presbyterian Board of Foreign Mission Executives, were forced to conclude that the constant stream of new believers was due to the work of native Christians rather than to the foreigners in charge.[1] Darby Fulton saw a striking difference between the missionary work of Korea and that of other Far Eastern fields. He said,

> In China and Japan the evangelist...uses street preaching and such pioneer work, seeking to awaken a spiritual response to find an entrance for the Gospel. In Korea, on the other hand, the spread of the gospel has usually outrun the missionary. Groups of believers have come together in distant villages and are sending delegations to the mission stations, pleading for spiritual oversight and leadership.[2]

Therefore, in the later part of this chapter the author also will trace and analyze how the gospel penetrated swiftly in Korea and will consider certain evangelistic models and methods and practices used by native Korean Christians, such as personal evangelism, Bible study groups, family evangelism, mass revival meetings and the army Christianization movement, and their influence on Korean church growth and revival.

FOREIGN MISSIONARY POLICIES AND METHODS FOR CHURCH GROWTH IN KOREA

Nevius Methods and Policies of Mission Work

In fact, the consideration of the policies and methods of early missionary work is not undertaken merely out of general interest. On this point, Horace G. Underwood, one of the earliest pioneer missionary leaders in Korea for many years, writes,

> Very early in the history of the work, almost at its beginning, God in his providence led us to adopt methods that have been said by some to have been unique, but in reality are simply those that have been adopted by numbers of missionaries in different parts of the world. The only unique feature has been the almost unanimity with which these have been followed by the whole missionary body in this land.[3]

The Nevius method has been regarded as one of the main reasons for the success of the mission in Korea by the mission scholars.[4] Charles A. Clark writes, "Come and see for yourselves what great things the Lord is doing here!"[5] Kenneth S. Latourette has stated, "Distinctive of Protestantism in Korea was the active part of the Korean Christians in the spread of the faith. One reason for this was a policy adopted early at the suggestion of John L. Nevius, a Presbyterian missionary in China during a visit in Seoul."[6] Bishop S. Neill commented in his book, "The fruits of the Nevius method were clearly to be seen in the character of the church...The Korean Christians have shown of independence which would not lie down under any kind of missionary domination."[7] Sherwood Eddy writes,

Christianity in Korea has been characterized by its rapid growth and its apostolic zeal. In self-support, self-expansion, and self-government, it has furnished in many respects a model for all mission fields. The church in Korea has been a witnessing church, a praying church, a Bible-studying church, and a giving church...[8]

It is the Nevius method which most of the eminent scholars recognize as one of the chief factors in her rapid and faithful growth in the early years. David Cho writes, "There seems to be a consensus among people that the phenomenal growth of the Korean church is a result of the adaptation of the so-called Nevius method by the early missionaries."[9] Nevius writes,

> Some have felt that we are warranted, in the first presentation of Christianity, in withholding those doctrines which antagonize Chinese system and are apt to excite prejudice and opposition, presenting only those features which are conciliatory and attractive, thus drawing the people to us and gaining an influence over them, and afterwards giving them instruction in the complete system of Christian truth, as they are also able to bear it. I doubt whether such a course is justified by the teachings of Christ and the Apostles. God may and does, in His mercy and grace, make use of our incomplete presentation of His truth, and an imperfect apprehension of it in the conversion and salvation of men, but have we still not greater reason for expecting His blessing in connection with His truth given in its completeness?[10]

A framework of the Nevius methods in his book is as follows:[11]

1. **How to begin a mission work.**
   Missionaries should be able people, educated and thoroughly prepared for their work. Each missionary should associate himself with, as a personal helper, some native Christian who will always be with him and help interpret him to the people and the people to him. Missionaries starting on a new field should itinerant widely as suggested by the great commission. During the itineration the missionary should seek and contact curious crowds. He should not concentrate on a specific class, but seek all social classes impartially, not neglecting the officials, literati or women. Many churches have been started first by women, who have maintained great influence, even after men have come forth as the nominal leaders. Private conversation is more successful than public preaching.

2. **How to deal with new converts.**
   Self-propagation. Each individual Christian should be led to work for his neighbors and friends, without pay, remaining in the vocation in which he was called. The testimony of such a man has an effect upon his neighbors and friends which simply cannot be measured. Make the people see that Christianity does not necessitate their retiring from and renouncing the world in religious devotion, as their old religions taught

them, but that the best Christian is one who practices the doctrine while living an ordinary, normal life. Utilize and capitalize the new enthusiasm of the young Christians to the limit. Every man, woman and child in the congregation should be at the same time a learner from someone better informed, and a teacher of anyone less informed. The laymen shall select their own leaders. Mostly this will be a process of natural selection; charismatic leaders will emerge automatically. The church shall extend itself through this layering method.

3. **How to deal with financial responsibility.**
Self-support. Christians should provide their own chapels according to their needs and financial possibilities. These should be built in indigenous style in order not to cause village hostility. Only a few leaders shall be full-time employed and paid. They shall be paid for their work by the churches which they supervise. We, Christians, should care for the poor of the Church particularly. There should be pressure to increase gifts. Eventually the Christians should finance their own home and foreign mission work. Schools and Christian institutions should receive only partial subsidy, and that only when being founded.

4. **Instruction of inquirers and Church members.**
Basic instruction should be given by local lay-leaders. Emphasize teaching, more than preaching of the Gospel, since the oriental peoples are less accustomed to our western methods of long rhetorical addresses. Manuals of instruction should be provided. In all teaching, lay heavy stress upon the Scripture text itself. Bible classes should be established. The Bible is the basis of all the work, and the aim is to fill the minds of the people with it so that it will control conduct. The Bible is the only authoritative guide to answer questions. Depend in all teaching upon the guidance of the Holy Spirit.

5. **Discipline.**
There should be strict discipline according to Biblical guidelines. Further, discipline should be such as public opinion will approve.

6. **Church organization and ecumenism.**
Do not pay too much time and attention to the enforcing of a highly sophisticated church system in an early stage of work. Make the basic of the church the voluntary activities of the ordinary Christian. Once again, have no professional pastors of local churches before the people feel the need for them and are willing to pay for them. There should be no waste of energy in competition with other denominations on the mission field. At least territorial division should be secured.

7. **Educational and medical work.**
The great mission of the Christian Church is not to teach mechanics and civil engineering or foreign languages or science, nor to Christianize heathen nations by civilizing them, but to Christianize them and then leave them to develop their own civilization. No feature of the labors of the first propagators of Christianity was more prominent than this, that

the Gospel was proclaimed in connection with acts of kindness and humanity, healing the sick, raising the dead, comforting the distressed. This great principle and rule of action, illustrated in the life of Christ and the apostles, is as important and applicable as ever. The cooperation of foreign Christian physicians in the work is of the greatest importance.

8. **The foreign missionary.**
   The missionary should remember that it is not his appropriate work to assume the personal care of a single native church longer than such a course is absolutely necessary, and that by doing so, he may inflict a positive injury upon it. His business is to plant independent, self-supporting, Christian institutions and to raise up native ministry. The missionaries are temporary messengers sent into an alien population to do a certain task. When it is accomplished, they must withdraw.

9. **Test of the Mission field.**
   The first test of any mission method could be its adaptability to the end in view, and the second its Scriptural authority. A final test of any method is whether it works or not. Any method applied without trust in God is doomed to failure.

10. **Attitude towards non-Christian faiths.**
    Christian doctrine should be presented in its fullness, without - temporarily - withholding doctrines that might be offensive to the beliefs of the people on the mission field. Missionaries should make our teaching as full and clear as possible.

In 1891, just a year after Nevius' visit, at its first Annual Meeting, the Korea Mission had adopted and codified these principles into strict rules and By-Laws.[12] Although the Korea mission codified Nevius' principles, the rules have been changed according to the changed conditions. For instance, in his book *The Nevius Plan for Mission Work in Korea*, Charles A. Clark indicated several changes in regard to the mission school policy, to the Winter Bible classes for leaders, and to lay leaders in the churches.[13]

It is well known fact that the strong emphasis laid on financial self-support of the Korean congregations has been the most prominent feature of the application of the Nevius methods to Korea. As early as 1902, we find *Methods of Mission Work* by Nevius in the list of books which first year missionaries were required to read. As a general rule, no financial assistance was given by the mission in building country churches. All other local expenses also were borne by the Koreans themselves.[14] In fact, one of the main reasons that the Nevius methods had been so attractive to the missionaries to Korea was the lack of sufficient funds and personnel.

In 1888 the Presbyterian missionaries felt keenly the limitations of personnel and finances from the board. In the same year in which the Methodists received more than $28,000, the Presbyterians received only $14,000.[15] For months Allen, Underwood, and Heron pressed the need for more personnel. Lamenting the board's lack of response, Underwood wrote in despair, "I have given up hope, I have written letter after letter. They seem almost to have forgotten they have a mission out here at all."[16] During this time of stress due to a lack of adequate funds and personnel, Underwood became aware of the method of missionary activity being suggested by Nevius. The principle of self-support put an obligation on every believer to contribute financially to the local congregation, which meant that the survival of the local church was dependent on the motivation of the Christians and their financial resources.

The underlying thought of many missionaries who implemented this principle of self-support was that western funds would spoil the Korean Christians. Besides, these funds would give the image that a missionary is a money handling business man rather than a preaching missionary. Roy E. Shearer writes regarding the cause and effect relationship between self-support and rapid growth in comparing Korean Methodist and Presbyterian Churches.

> We must here examine more closely the policy of self-support the Presbyterian missionaries adopted as a result of hearing the experiences of Nevius. Presbyterian William B. Hunt, who worked beside Methodists in *Whanghai* Province, writes that, while the Methodist Church in *Pyongyang* and *Whanghai* Provinces made early gains by building churches and paying helpers with American funds, that same Methodist Church was considerably weaker in 1909. In the *Pyongyang* "western district," Presbyterians had ten times the Christian strength as Methodists had in 1909. Hunt says that Western funds used for paying Methodist helpers attract a type of helper who is adroit in using the missionary's name in civil court cases and who is really a business man first and a preacher second.[17]

However, it should be remembered that the principle of self-support had not always been the best mission policy for immediate church growth in some parts of the nation, especially in the poor farming area of the south. According to Sung C. Chun, the principle of self-support did not cause church growth, but in fact hindered it, because the principle of self-support was strictly enforced throughout all of Korea.[18] Sung C. Chun is very critical of the argument that the church grew because of the adoption of the Nevius methods. For the following reasons, the Nevius Plan was not the main cause of the Korean Church growth in the south of Korea, but rather hindered its development.

First, without specific helps toward self-support, the Nevius Plan assumed that the churches in Korea would naturally become self-supporting. However, particularly in South Korea, the poor tenants had little opportunity to develop the prerequisite self-support. This meant that the program of the missionary effort was hampered by the Nevius Plan. The majority of the population in Korea is composed of poor farmers who desperately needed guidance prior to attaining any degree of self-support.

Second, the advocates of the Nevius Plan failed to recognize the value of the culture maintained by the *Yangban* class.[19] By ignoring this cultural stratum, the planners brought upon themselves hostility from the *Yangban* class concerning Christianity. Individual dignity tended to be overlooked in the plan. In addition, hostility was generated among missionaries toward the *Yangban* class because of their misunderstanding of the cultural heritage of the class.

Third, the Nevius Plan resulted in an imbalance of the Christian population. One small area, the Northwest, obtained two-thirds of the total Protestant church constituency. The exclusive concentration in this one area of the country accentuated the spirit of conflict between the Protestants in the Northwest and those in the rest of the land.

Fourth, the Nevius Plan favored isolationism. Information concerning social and theological developments from abroad was curtailed because few students were sent overseas for further education.[20]

However, the policy of self-support was made a basic principle for the operation of churches and in education. Most congregations were self-supporting. According to the Nevius method, if a congregation was not ready to pay the full salary of a pastor, it had to use a volunteer minister and become a surcharge of a larger congregation. For instance, the Presbyterian Church in Korea grew to 350 congregations in 1900, and of those, 270 were self-supporting churches. And according to the report on elementary education of the Northern Presbyterian Church, in 1907, 334 out of 337 schools were entirely self-supporting,[21] and in 1923, 386 out of 400 schools (96.5%).[22] In all, the Korean government paid about 75 percent of the costs of elementary schooling and around 25 percent of higher education in 1923.[23]

Along with self-support, there was the principle of self-government in Korean churches. As for self-government, temporary officers would be appointed by the missionary for each congregation, but as soon as possible the church would choose its own deacons and elders. It was felt best not to superimpose upon an infant church a highly complex system of church government, but to encourage church machinery to develop only as far as the church was able to manage to support. On September 17, 1907, the principle of self-government became official when the National Presbyterian Korean Church was organized as a presbytery and assumed independent jurisdiction over its own affairs. In the first meeting of this presbytery there were present thirty-eight missionary pastors and elders and forty Korean elders. From its first session there has been a majority of Korean delegates in the highest court, and that majority has always been well over two thirds.[24] In September, 1912, the Korean church became fully organized as a national church, and a complete constitution, written by the Korean church staff, was adopted for self-government in 1922. It was evident that the Koreans were much involved in the government of the church from the beginning. This created a strong church government which affected the church growth.

However, the real core of the Nevius methods was originally not its financial strategy or church government or self-propagation, but its emphasis on the Bible study system as the basis of all mission work, which encouraged every Christian to study the Bible and to be able to pass on to others what he found there. An impressive system of Bible classes was established. When the first class was held in Korea in 1890, there were seven men studying, which was exactly in accordance with Nevius' plan. William B. Hunt, one of the strongest of all the supporters of the Nevius principles on the field, wrote of the classes in 1909:

> The education of the whole church, all of its membership, young and old, literate and illiterate, is being undertaken systematically and largely by Training Classes in which the textbook is the Bible... Bible study is the object of the class, but prayer, conference and practical evangelistic effort are prominent parts of the work.[25]

Samuel A. Moffett says that it was in these classes that Korean Christian workers were first trained and developed, and here that colporteurs, evangelists, helpers and Bible women were discovered and appointed to the work.[26] In fact, from the very beginning of mission work the authoritative and supernatural character of the Bible as the Word of God has been taken for granted, and it has been assumed also that if its teaching enters into the heart of a man it will manifest itself in the transformation of his life and practice. After 25 years of mission to Korea, Samuel A. Moffett made comment as follows:

> The Bible itself has been, of course, pre-eminently the greatest factor in the evangelization, as in all other countries, but it has certainly occupied a rather unique position in the work of Korea, and the Korean church derives its power, its spirituality, its great faith in prayer, and its liberality from the fact that the whole church has been, as it were, saturated with the knowledge of the Bible.[27]

Korean Bible women, evangelists and colporteurs traveled throughout the country, and all were witnesses to the fact that the primary mission method was the spreading of the "inspired Word of God, given of God to reveal His holy will as to men's earthly lives and as to their eternal salvation."[28] The phenomenal growth of the Korean Protestant church, within half a century of its founding, having a constituency of over 265,000, naturally raises the question in the minds of all those interested in Christian missions as to what has been the cause or causes of this growth.[29] One has undoubtedly been the point of view which from the beginning governed the methods of the work and its development. Needless to say, much of the credit for the rapid growth of mission work in Korea was attributed to the Nevius method. Writing in 1919, Charles A. Clark says of the Presbyterian Church in Korea:

> ...somehow or other we find in that little country of Korea, today, apparently one of the most remarkable churches on any mission field in the world - an independent, national church of 161,000 believers, fully self-governing in every sense of the word, preeminently self-propagating, and almost self-supporting: a church which seems to have solved most of the problems of comity or organic union with its neighbor churches and to have attained a large measure of control over the former mission institutions, yet with the most cordial relations continuing between itself and the missionaries and the boards that helped to found it fully without sacrificing its own autonomy.[30]

W. D. Reynolds of the Southern Presbyterian Mission who held an important position in the Presbyterian Theological Seminary for many years wrote about certain principles for training the Three-Self ministry. Reynolds outlined three negative and four positive principles which had been based on the Nevius Methods: [31]

Negative;
1) Don't let him know for a long time that you have any idea of training him for the ministry.
2) Don't employ him as a preacher or evangelist on foreign pay, if you can help it.
3) Don't send him to America to be educated, at any early stages of Mission Work.

Positive;
1) Seek to lift to a high plane of spiritual experience.
2) Ground him thoroughly in the Word and in the cardinal facts and truths of Christianity.
3) Train the young pastor-to-be to endure hardness as a good soldier of Jesus Christ.
4) As Korean Christians advance in culture and modern civilization, raise the standard of education of the native ministry.

Within the lifetime of the pioneer Protestant missionaries, a self-governing and largely self-supporting church with a vigorous native leadership had grown up. Although the Nevius methods had been despised as a main hindrance to a balanced development of Korean Christianity,[32] it is an undeniable truth that the application to Korea of a mission policy based on the Nevius methods, summarized as self-support, self-propagation and self-government, has been decisive in the history of the church growth in the north of Korea from the beginning, later in the south of Korea, and for the history of the Korean Christian as a whole.

What made the Nevius method so attractive to the missionaries in Korea? There were several reasons. Perhaps one of the main reasons was the fragile political condition in Korea. If the church in Korea was to survive without the protection of America or other Western countries, the Nevius method of self-support, self-propagation and self-government had to be stressed. The missionaries were very much aware of the "hands-off" policy of the American government and the eventual annexation of Korea by Japan.[33] Arthur Brown said in 1912,

> We saw long ago that the independence of Korea was impossible and that the only practical question was whether Russia or Japan would rule the country. America generally believed that it would be better for both Korea and the world that Japan should dominate.[34]

Through the Nevius method, the Korean church learned self-confidence and gained a new sense of self-respect and independence of spirit which was so vital to their survival under the humiliation of foreign domination.[35] Stephen Neill writes,

> The fruit of the Nevius method was clearly to be seen in the character of the church; there have been periods of tension between missionaries and Korean Christian leaders, but on the whole relationships based on mutual respect have been good; the Korean Christians have shown a spirit of independence which would not lie down under any kind of missionary domination, and they were thereby prepared to hold on in faith in the periods of trouble which were to come on this sorely tried church.[36]

It must also be noted that this rapid growth of the church in Korea is to be attributed in part to the policy and methods of early missionary work. This emphasis on self-support and self-propagation and self-government made the Korean church grow and mature even during the Japanese occupation and the period of the communist war. The convergence of the mission policy with the Korean socio-culture and personality of the people made Christianity in general easily acceptable for many Korean people. As a result of the success of the application of the mission policy in the past, many Korean Christians continue to regard this mission policy as a key to success. The Nevius method of church extension or church planting is also responsible for church growth today. However, in addition to the the good points about the mission policy as a factor in church growth, many negative points are also raised. Roy Shearer says, in relation to the Nevius methods, that these could not answer the question why the church was growing so rapidly.

> I am not convinced that the traditional Presbyterian answer for growth in Korea ("we used the Nevius Method") was correct. As I study the Methodist Mission, which did not conscientiously follow the Nevius methods, it is increasingly clear that any single answer is dangerously inaccurate. The reasons for growth in the Korean church are complex. Some areas where Methodists and Presbyterians worked side by side, each using slightly different methods, achieved the same amount of church growth.[37]

However, following Nevius' indigenous principles of mission methodology, the Korean church has practiced and taught tithing to its members for the support of the church. For example, Kim Ik-du was a very well-known Korean evangelist:

> When he preached in an evangelistic campaign, the people were so moved and blessed by the Holy Spirit that they gave just what they had. At one time when the offering was collected he was surprised to find many personal items in the offering boxes. There were 200 finger rings, 22 silver and gold watches, 200 silver ladies hairpins, $17,000 in cash.[38]

Other Christians did not have much to give, so they brought their grain and clothes to the church to support the work of Christ. With the offerings four Christian evangelists were supported for one year. Many years ago Jones reported:

> Korean men have been known to mortgage their houses that mortgages might be removed from the houses of God; to sell their crops of good rice intended for family consumption, purchasing inferior millet to live upon through the winter, and giving the difference in cost for support of the workers to preach among their own countrymen. Korean women have given their wedding rings, and even cut off their hair that it might be sold and the amount devoted to the spread of the gospel.[39]

This kind of emphasis is found in the Korean church today. When they plan to build the church, many Korean Christians sell their houses, land and sometimes their blood (for hospital use), and they make these sacrifices enthusiastically. Moffett writes that stewardship has become an integral part of their Christian faith.

A story is told of a family of refugees making their painful way back to their home village after the communist invasions. The home was gone; the church destroyed. But five bags of rice were still left under the courtyard where the family had buried them before fleeing south. It was all they had left, but the little Methodist family carefully set aside three of the precious bags of rice as a thank offering for their deliverance, giving them for the rebuilding of the church.[40]

The Korean church history indicates that the Korean church stood foremost among all modern mission fields for the rapidity of growth and a strong church established through implementation of Nevius methods. Therefore, the missionary methods such as the Nevius method laid the foundation for a church which has become famous for its rapid church growth in the modern history of missions.

Bible Translation and Literature Work

From the commencement of Protestant mission work in Korea, the Bible translation and gospel literature work have occupied a peculiarly prominent place and have influenced significantly the progress of missionary work in Korea. It has been said that one of the predominant means of early missionary work for the growth of the Korean church was literature.[41] The real beginning of mission work in Korea was made by foreign missionaries in neighboring countries by way of the Bible translation and literature work for Korean people. The first translation of the Gospel portions into Korean were made in Manchuria and in Japan. The literature prepared in Manchuria had been secretly brought into Korea even before any missionary had placed his feet on Korean soil.[42]

The Gospel portion that was printed in Japan was brought into Korea by the very first missionaries who made a stopover in Japan. This means the literature ministry in Korea had an advantageous beginning. When the first missionaries came to Korea, they laid strong emphasis on the importance of literature and many got involved in this work. During the first eight years of the Presbyterian Mission in Korea, thirty missionaries came to the Korean field. Among those, ten of them, who were gifted with literary and linguistic abilities, produced a great deal of literature. This laid a firm foundation for the literature ministries of the Korean church.[43] In 1876, the first converts, who had been contacted and baptized by Ross and McIntyre working among Koreans in

Manchuria, were engaged to make a translation of the Gospels from the Chinese into the *Hangul,*the vernacular language of Korea.

Korean, as a unique language, has been used in the Korean peninsular over the centuries, and is now spoken by nearly sixty million people including 3,000,000 Korean settlers in Manchuria, about 600,000 in Japan, and some 600,000 in North America. As for the script, Korean can be written in two ways. One is in Chinese characters and the other is in the Korean alphabet, which is called *Hangul*. *Hangul* is regarded as one of the most ingenious and perfect phonetic scripts in the world. Concerning the superiority of this alphabet and the unfortunate attitudes toward it. Hary A. Rodes writes, "This was a great blessing to the missionaries also as they could learn the '*Unmun*' [*Hangul*] in a few days and be reading the Korean Bible and studying the Korean language both written and oral."[44] If it were not for this simple script, the modern educational development of the nation would not have been possible.

In 1882, the Gospel of Luke was published, a total of 3,000 copies, and in 1883, 3,000 copies of the Gospel of John were printed, and these two Gospels were published by the British and Foreign Bible Society.

> In preparing a translation of the N.T. he was assisted by his colleague John MacIntyre of *Newchang*, and a Korean named Suh Sang-yun. The first draft was made from the Chinese delegates' version by the Korean assistant, who used the dialect of North-Western Korea, and it was then corrected by the two missionaries. In 1879 the N.B.S.S., undertook to provide type for a tentative edition S. Luke and John's Gospels and in 1882 an edition [3,000 copies] of each was printed at *Mukden*, with type obtained from Japan.[45]

The rest of the New Testament was similarly prepared, and, after editions of the Gospel of Matthew and Mark were issued in 1884, and the Gospel of John and Ephesians in 1885, the complete New Testament appeared in 1887, published by the British and Foreign Bible Society with the consent of the National Bible Society of Scotland. Meanwhile, the newly printed gospels were sold among the Koreans in the eastern Manchurian villages.

However, books of a foreign source were not allowed to come into the Hermit Kingdom, and now that the edition of the Gospels was printed the problem was how to get them into the country and circulate them. Korean merchants went to Manchuria periodically to buy the old official papers which were offered for sale and brought into Korea on the backs of coolies. The suggestion came to John Ross and John McIntyre that if the Scriptures were made up into bundles, unbound, they might be carried into the country without detection. It was in this manner that the Scripture in Korean was first introduced into the country. In a short time there was a small company of believers among the merchants on the Korean valleys on the northern border of the country. Three of these men were employed as colporteurs, to sell Scriptures and to preach to their fellow-countrymen.

Between 1883 and 1886, no less than 15,690 copies of this translation were circulated in Korea through the colporteurs.[46] From the beginning, the work of Suh, the colporteur, was very successful. Ross writes that the first congregation of Korean converts was almost entirely those who had been led by Suh.[47] It was thus the circulation of Scriptures which introduced Christianity to the Hermit Kingdom, and it is recognized that the wonderful progress of mission work in northern Korea is due in no small measure to the seed-sowing of those early days. It is worthy of notice that in *Euiju* there was a strong church of 1500 believers with no missionary resident in the city.[48] It was the Ross translation which laid the foundation for the Protestant mission work in Korea.

Meanwhile, a Korean student named Lee Soo-Jung, studying in Japan, had been contacted by some Japanese pastors, and in April 1883 he was baptized[49] as the first Korean Protestant Christian in Japan.[50] In 1885, he was asked to translate the Gospel of Mark into Korean by Henry Loomis, agent of the American Bible Society in Yokohama. He used the Chinese Bible and the Japanese Bible as texts and translated a portion of the Scriptures into Korean. In 1885, the Gospel of Mark was published in Japan. When the first missionaries, Horace Underwood and Henry Appenzeller, came to Korea, they first stopped in Japan and brought Lee Soo-jung's translation of Mark with them to Korea. This was one of the few cases in the history of missions where the missionaries reached the country in which they were to labor carrying with them the Scriptures in the language of the people.[51] Horace G. Underwood, one of the first missionaries, writes,

> Before our arrival, not a little introductory work had been accomplished through the labors of Messrs. Ross and McIntyre, in China, who, being on the main road between Peking and Seoul, had seized the opportunity presented by the passing of Koreans, to learn the language, preach the Gospel, and prepare tracts and portions of the Bible. Several of their converts had returned to Korea and, as colporteurs of the British and Foreign Bible Society, had been engaged in a widespread seed-sowing, that did much to prepare the way.[52]

However, as soon as the American missionaries in Seoul had acquired a knowledge of the language, they began to direct their attention to

Bible translation work. Even though the Ross translation of the entire New Testament was available, it could not be accepted as the standard Bible because of its strong northern dialect and poor rendering. In 1887, the need for a better translation was so urgent that "Committee for Translating the Bible into the Korean Language" was formed. The purposes of organization were stated to be "translation, revision, publication, and conservation of the text of the Holy Scriptures in the Korean tongue." Underwood and Gale of the Presbyterian U.S.A. Mission, Appenzeller and Scranton of the Methodist Episcopal Mission, and Reynolds of the Southern Presbyterians served on the Board of Translators.[53]

It is said that some members of the committee met over 500 times to complete the translation. With their efforts and sound cooperation, the New Testament translation was accomplished by 1900 and the entire Bible by 1910.[54] Thus, in 1900, a tentative version of the New Testament was published, and 98,498 copies of the New Testament had been sold by 1905.[55] Between 1899 and 1909 the circulation of the Scriptures in Korea went forward with unparalleled progress. The total number of portions and Testaments issued in 1900 amounted to 44,000 copies; in 1909 the circulation was about 400,000.[56] Finally, it was only during the year 1910 that the translation of all the books of the Old Testament into the Korean language was completed, and within a year 8,000 copies of the entire Bible were sold.[57] Now with the whole Bible available, the church laid great emphasis on the importance of each believer owning a personal copy and reading it. This had a tremendous impact on Bible distribution, and 2,379,751 copies of the Scriptures were sold by 1918.

The work of the Korean Religious Literature Society was of the utmost importance in the growth of the Church in Korea. The annual reports of the Bible Committee of Korea are filled with stirring incidents of the influence of distribution of the Scripture and Gospel literature in transforming the lives of the Koreans.[58] In October 1889, plans were made to form a society for publishing Christian literature at the suggestion of Horace Underwood.[59] The following year, the Korea Religious Tract Society was established in order to provide suitable literature for Christian propaganda and has since then carried on a work which has had an amazing growth and has been of invaluable assistance to the whole cause of Christianity throughout the country.[60]

The Korea Religious Tract Society was supported by the six missions of the Federal Council and received generous assistance from societies in England and the U.S.A. The first publications were a booklet called *The Salient Doctrine of Christianity* and ten different Gospel tracts. The Gospel tracts published in the early years: *The Pilgrim's Progress. The True Plan of Salvation. True Savior, Leading the Family in the Right Way. Story of the Gospel, Jesus our Pattern. Introduction to Christianity. How to Escape Calamity. The Story of Old Chang. Introduction to the Bible.*[61]

In 1919, the Society's name was changed to The Christian Literature Society of Korea (CLS). In order to produce better literature, a new editorial committee was formed. The committee was engaged in the translation and publication of helpful books ranging from tracts, children's literature and Sunday School lessons to dictionaries and a series of important Bible commentaries for pastors and theological students.[62] The chief publications of the Society were the *Bible Magazine, The Sunday School Magazine* used by all the Korean churches, *The Presbyterian Theological Review, The Korean Bookman, The Children's Magazine, The Union Hymnal* and *The Christian Messenger.* The annual report for 1931 said that "Over thirty editions of the *Chansonga* [Union Hymnal] have been sold in the last 20 years."[63] *The Korea Mission Field* (1905-1941), the official magazine of the General or Federal Council of the Protestant Mission in Korea, was the most successful publication of the Society. The Society was the only union publishing institution in Korea, and it had support of and fulfilled the needs of practically all the Protestant missions working in Korea.[64]

It has been said that the Korean people on the whole were not naturally great readers, and the task of distribution of the literature was not an easy one. Thus, various methods were employed in connection with book rooms and colporteurs to increase the sales and to develop an intelligent reading Christian constituency. However, Korean people became good readers through literacy education training. C. C. Vinton, custodian of the Society, reported in 1905,

> Perhaps there is nowhere in the world a population so imbued with reading and studying habits as that of Korea. We doubt if in any other country in the semi-civilized world, books are so eagerly sought and read of a quality and cost apparently out of proportion to the purchaser.[65]

It must be said that the Bible translation and literature work of the Protestant missions have been excellent tools to evangelize Korea and yielded outstanding results in the early years of the Protestant missions. Literature work found very fertile soil in Korea with its closely knit, basically animistic society which had one standard language that was easy to learn to read. Furthermore, the dedicated and skilled missionaries had translated the Scriptures very early, and they widely distributed them as well as preached the gospel and led Bible studies. All of this, in turn, brought thousands to Christ and helped build them in faith; the Bible translation and literature work contributed to early church growth in Korea.

Missionary Modern Educational Work

In the beginning of the Protestant mission in Korea, direct preaching to the common people was not allowed when the pioneer missionaries arrived in Korea. The missionaries adopted the policy of non-aggressive evangelistic activity of modern Western Christian education through schools founded by Protestant missionaries in the 1880s.

> When the early missionaries reached Korea, the old anti-foreign laws were still in force. The only religious liberty that these foreign missionaries possessed was the right granted by treaty to hold their own religious services, and to erect chapels... The government's reaction toward the foreigners was unfavorable. The missionaries consequently adopted the policy of non-aggressive evangelism...Evangelistic activities were, however, quietly carried on through hospital, schools, and private conversations... The patient work of the missionaries was not without fruit.[66]

The openness of part of the Korean population to accept modern education made it also easier for them to welcome the Gospel. Only the elite minority had educational opportunities to learn from the Chinese classics, and the majority of Korean people were illiterate in the 19th centuries.[67] Pioneer missionaries translated the Scriptures into the Korean language and taught Koreans, through Sunday schools, vacation Bible schools, and Bible institutes, how to read the easy Korean phonetic script rather than the difficult Chinese characters. Chinese education was a privilege for the high class people. The western missionaries taught not only Christian doctrine, but also secular knowledge. They introduced modern education, its form as well as its content.

To all intents and purposes, the first modern school was established by an American missionary. It was *Ewha* Girl's School founded by Mrs. Mary F. Scranton, who came to Korea in June 1885 with her only son, William B. Scranton, but who acted independently to open a girls' school.[68] The Rev. Henry G. Appenzeller founded the school for boys,

Baejae Hakdang, in 1885. Severance Medical School was opened in 1886, and *Soongshil* Christian school was founded in 1897. In addition, institutions of higher education were started by Protestant missionaries. The aim of these schools was to enlighten the unlearned masses.[69] These modern educational institutions offered new courses in mathematics, geography, history and natural history as well as English, Chinese classics and Bible.[70] These institutions were at first the target of aversion on the part of the traditional gentry class so that the first students consisted mainly of orphans or lower class converts. But later they attracted the attention of elite classes and produced many leading figures not only in the Christian movement but also in the social and political movement, especially that of independence.

The growth of Korean Christian schools contributed to Korean church growth. According to the statistics of each denomination in 1909, Presbyterian schools numbered 605, with 14,708 students, Methodist schools numbered 200, with 6,423 students, and other denomination schools numbered about 150.[71] Several Christian colleges were opened at the beginning of the 20th century: *Soongshil* College in 1906, *Ehwa* College in 1910, and *Yunhee* College in 1915.[72] And *Yonsei* University in Seoul developed from *Yunhee* College with 17,947 students, and *Ehwa* College grew to be one of the largest Christian women's universities in Korea with 15,340 students. When the Japanese annexed Korea in 1910, there were 2,250 private schools in Korea, among which 1,402 were Chinese character learning institutes, 25 were secular modern schools, and 823 were Christian schools. The missionaries emphasized female education through Christian schools, in contrast to Confucians' lack of respect under Confucianism. Korean Christianity gave women freedom. The education of women and girls affected Korean church growth in the evangelism of women.[73] The second statement of the Mission Council wrote about the education of women as follows: The conversion of women and training of Christian girls should be a special aim, since mothers exercise so important an influence over future generations.[74]

According to Yun-ok Lee, who was actively involved in the National Organization of Presbyterian Women, "Korean women have contributed much to the growth of the Korean church during the 100 year history of Protestantism in Korea."[75] An essay in the *Chosun Christian Bulletin* on December 29, 1898, said, "Education of housewives is such an urgent task. The thriving of the household, revival of the nation and power of people depend upon the education of Korean

Table 5.1: Private Schools of the late *Yi* Period

Founded	Name of School	Founder	Location
1883	Wonson Academy	Chong, Hyun-sok	Wonsan, Hamkyung
1886	Baejae Academy	US Methodist (North)	Seoul
	Ewha Girls School	US Methodist (North)	Seoul
	Kyonsin School	US Presbyterian (North)	Seoul
1890	Chongshin Girl School	US Presbyterian (North)	Seoul
1897	Sungsil School	US Presbyterian (North)	Pyongyang
1898	Baehwa Girls School	US Methodist (South)	Seoul
1903	Sungeui Girls School	US Presbyterian (North)	Pyongyang
1904	Hosudon Girls School	US Methodist (South)	Kaesong
	Young Men's Academy	Chon, Tok-ki	Kyunggi, Seoul
1905	Posong School	Yi, Yong-ik	Seoul
	Yangjong School	Um, Chu-ik	Seoul
	Hwimun School	Min, Yong-hwi	Seoul
1906	Sinsong School	US Presbyterian (North)	Sonchon
	Posong Girls School	US Presbyterian (North)	Pyongyang
	Chinmyung Girls School	Lay Um	Seoul
	Poin School	Poin School Association	Seoul
	Yanggyu Girls School	Chin, Hak-sin	Seoul
	Sojon Lyceum	Yi, Sang-sol	Kando, Manchuria
1907	Shinhung School	US Presbyterian (South)	Chonju, Cholla
	Kijon Girls School	US Presbyterian (South)	Chonju, Cholla
	Taesong School	Ahn, Chang-ho	Pyongyang
	Osan School	Yi, Sang-hun	Pyongyang
	Osong School	North & West Assoc.	Chongju
	Pongmyung School	Yi, Pong-nae	Pyongyang, Seoul
1908	Kiho School	Kiho Educational	Seoul
	Tongdok Girls	Yi, Chae-guk	Seoul
	Taedong Technical	Taedong School	Seoul
1909	Soui School	Chang, Chi-yong	Seoul

(Sources: Ki-baik Lee, *A New History of Korea*, 1984 , p. 333-334)

women." Truly, the missionaries' founding of women's schools based on the spirit of equality of the sexes was the first torchlight for liberating Korean women and opened the way for Korean women's education. The purpose of this education was to equip church women to awaken fellow Koreans from the deep sleep of social and political ignorance.[76] Speer at one time said,

> The Korean woman is somewhat like the Moslem woman in her home life. The women's quarters are separate and she must not be too much seen if at all, by any man outside her immediate family. The Gospel meant liberty and love for her.[77]

This is quite true. The gospel has been a large factor liberating women in Korea and giving them almost complete freedom. Outside of surrender of her old religion, the Korean woman had everything to gain and nothing to lose by becoming a Christian. Her circle of social contacts was immediately widened and enriched. During the long rule of Confucianism, Korean women suffered most. They always had to obey the Confucian law, which set them in very low position. A. J. Brown wrote of the Korean women:

> Women, in old *Chosen*, had a low place. Her function was merely to drudge at home and to bear him converted sons. Respectable women of social standing were expected to seclude themselves in a separate part of the house.[78]

When these uneducated women started reading the Bible with the help of the missionaries' wives, they realized that they should have equal rights with men. The church women began to mobilize themselves. From the beginning, church women, believing they were doing God's will, took the initiative in seeking social justice and in recovering women's rights. Certainly women play an important role in democratizing their homes and society. They initiated strong protest against the evil social system, which allowed powerful and rich men to have concubines, and they became leaders in the education of girls. Many Christian women participated in the Independence Movement of 1919. The Presbyterian Assembly of October 1919 reported that 531 women from Presbyterian churches had been imprisoned because of their participation in the Independence Movement.[79] Thus the Christian schools were the most influential modern education institutions in Korea at the turn of the century. Man-kyu Lee pointed out the contributions of Christian schools in his book *The History of Korean Education* as follows: [80]

1. Reconstruction of life based on the Christian faith
   a. Prohibition of drinking and gambling
   b. Wiping out of superstitions

2. Improvement of the way of thinking
   a. Correction of stubborn Confucian ideas
   b. Break-down of class-consciousness
   c. Equality of man and woman
   d. Establishment of the monogamic pattern
   e. Freedom of women from man's domination in the family
   f. Promotion of women's education

3. Improvement of the way of life
   a. Emancipation from the rigid Confucian tradition and simple reverent ceremonies of weddings and funerals
   b. Free and natural human relations and recreation

4. Promotion of intellectual knowledge
   a. Self awareness for the need of intellectual growth
   b. Need of education of children by the parents
   c. Familiarization of attending the meetings for speech and discussion
   d. Expansion of knowledge about clothes, foods and gardening
   e. Promotion of modern music
   f. Introduction of modern medicine
   g. Expansion of the ideas of modern education

5. Promotion of national consciousness
   a. Use of the Korean language and its promotion
   b. Access of over-seas information and contacts
   c. Propagation of the Korean Independence Movement over-seas through the missionaries.

The western missionaries opened the doors of their schools to everyone, the rich and the poor, the powerful and the powerless, in a society where education was limited to the privileged. Christian education was open to the oppressed and the deprived, and it was the nurturing ground of Protestant church growth. Indeed, many Koreans came to know about the Christian faith through these Christian schools. The objects of educational work of the Protestant missionaries were primarily to gain access to non-Christians to lead them to Christ, and to train up children from Christian homes and especially to prepare them for positions of leadership within the church. Therefore, though modern education and the establishment of Christian schools for men and women to reach out to non-Christians, missionaries contributed to early church growth in Korea.

Table 5.2: Foreign Missionaries in Korea before 1945

	Nationality	Missionaries	Rate	Remarks
1	USA	1,009	65.9%	
2	UK	199	13.0%	
3	Canada	97	6.3%	UK Mission Society
4	Australia	85	5.6%	UK Mission Society
	The others	140	9.2%	
Total		1,530	100%	

(Source: Seung-tae Kim, Hae-jin Park, *Review of Foreign Missionaries in Korea: 1884-1984,* 1993)

Humanitarian Social and Welfare Service

Throughout the history of foreign missions, social services and medical work have proven a great factor in breaking down barriers of unfriendliness and suspicion and in preparing the way for the reception of the Gospel.[81] In Korea, where perhaps fewer of these barriers exist than elsewhere, and where the people have shown greater readiness to receive the Gospel than in many mission fields, the beneficent work carried on by Christian doctors and in mission hospitals has exercised a tremendous influence in the lives of countless individuals and in the growth and development of the early Korean church. Korea was first opened to Protestant missions through the medical skill of Dr. Horace Allen. The medical work was begun by Dr. Horace N. Allen, an American who came on September 20, 1884, served as physician to the United States Legation while being under appointment by the Board of Foreign Missions of the Presbyterian Church in the U.S.A. However, because of government restrictions, Dr. Allen's work was limited to the American Embassy until, on December 4, 1884, there came about an event that prepared the way for open missionary work.[82] The Royal Hospital called *"Kwanghyewon"* [Widespread Relief House] was opened in the capital city of Seoul on April 10, 1885, just five days after the arrival in Korea of the young Horace G. Underwood, who, although he was a minister, had studied medicine for a year and so was immediately able to help Dr. Allen in the hospital.

When medical doctor Scranton, a Methodist, arrived, he began to assist the former in his work in the Royal Hospital with medical doctor Allen. However, with the subsequent arrival of medical doctor John Heron, another Presbyterian, Dr. Scranton left the Royal Hospital dispensary. By September of 1885, he had established a dispensary of his own, which became the basis of the hospital of the Methodist Episcopal Mission.[83] However, his patients were not the people of the court, but the poorest and the neediest. Dr. Scranton was particularly concerned with people suffering from contagious diseases who had been driven from their homes and left to become helpless beggars on the streets. Dr. Scranton's mission hospital later evolved into a hospital exclusively for the treatment of women and children. The Methodists emphasized medical care for the poorest strata of the society, while the Presbyterians concentrated on the development of hospital work and the training up of a native medical profession. Methodist medical work was augmented in October of 1887 with the arrival of a woman doctor and the establishment of a women's dispensary.[84] In the 1890s, 18 large hospitals were opened throughout the country.[85]

The first medical missionaries were interested in using their medical training for the evangelistic advance of the church.[86] The pioneer missionaries introduced western medicine to Korea. Western medicine proved to be effective in healing sick people. Therefore a positive attitude towards the missionaries meant that the influence of the Gospel, which the missionaries brought, grew. As the people began to realize the ineffectiveness of the Korean doctors' concoctions and magical practices as compared with Western medicine, they turned to foreign doctors. Thus, these physicians opened the way for the preachers, broke down prejudices and suspicion, and won the confidence of the people.[87] Quite early, when it became apparent that hostility was being replaced by cordial acceptance, the Northern Presbyterian Mission wanted to give up medical work in large hospitals. As early as 1891, Dr. Gifford says,

> The day for preliminary work so ably conducted by Dr. Allen and Dr. Heron is now past and a foothold in the land is secured. The Koreans know we are here for evangelizing and consent to this.[88]

The medical missionaries traveled with their fellow American preachers and their main purpose was to win a welcome for the Christian enterprise. As they treated their Korean patients, they hoped to win them to Christ. In fact, quite early the mission saw medicine not so much as a Christian service of love, but as a way of gaining a foothold in this land where churches could be produced.[89] Soon they no longer saw the necessity of using medicine as a means for evangelism. In 1897, medical work in the northwest of Korea was also affected by the

Table 5.3: Foreign Denominations in Korea before 1945

	Denomination	Missionaries	Rate
1	Presbyterian	679	44.4%
2	Methodist	403	26.3%
3	Salvation Army	125	8.1%
4	Episcopal	77	5.0%
5	Seventh Adventist	28	1.8%
6	Oriental Mission	26	1.7%
	The others	192	12.5%
Total		1,530	100%

(Source: Seung-tae Kim, Hae-jin Park, *Review of Foreign Missionaries in Korea: 1884-1984,* 1993)

amazing church growth. By 1902, it had become the practice of all missionary agencies in Korea that no station should be opened in the interior without a doctor on its staff.

The tradition of medical service has been a well-known characteristic of the Protestant missionaries for the beginning of their activities. It was not limited to believers; it was open to everyone. Again and again, patients who have been restored to health have, at the same time, been led to Christ. They have returned to their distant villages and, through their personal testimony, have there formed little groups in their homes which have later developed into flourishing little churches. In 1926, J. M. Rogers of *Soonchun* described his hospital's emphasis on holistic healing.

> This is a mission hospital; therefore, our main object is to preach by word and deed the gospel of our Lord and Savior Jesus Christ. We believe that the Great Commission includes healing as well as teaching and preaching, and that Christ healed many who never believed in him as personal Savior... So we feel it is his will for us to take healing to all whom we may, and to do this we want to give the best service we can enabled by all that modern scientific medicine has to offer...We also hope and believe that by our service we help to turn many to a saving knowledge of Christ... In short, this a fertile field for the gospel message.[90]

In the 1950s after the Korean War, medical work aided the advance of the church. Many men and women have been converted to Christianity through treatment received in hospitals connected with the Korean church. The large mission hospital at *Daegu* has been instrumental in planting over one hundred churches during its history of continued evangelistic effort.[91] The superintendent, Dr. Howard Moffett, describes the evangelistic work of that hospital:

> At the center of all our hospital work and program... is our evangelistic effort. The staff is voluntarily organized into a "preaching society," in which all participate. A typical medical-evangelistic mobile clinic trip included four doctors, two nurses, one pharmacist, one hospital chaplain and a driver-mechanic. The group took a week's exhausting trek through three provinces, treating patients in the villages, holding roadside demonstrations on health problems, giving medical lectures, making health surveys, and holding evangelistic services every night. They worked from daybreak prayer meeting time until midnight. More than 1,200 patients were given free treatments, and hundreds asked to know more about the Lord Jesus Christ of whom the doctors and nurses spoke so freely.[92]

The Christian social service in the Protestant mission contributed to early church growth. In fact, the first social service work of foreign missions in Korea was begun by the Catholic church in 1880 by the establishment of an orphanage in Seoul.[93] The first Protestant missionaries immediately saw the needy, the poor people, the widows, and orphans etc. In 1892, Horace G. Underwood started orphanage work in Seoul.[94] In 1894, R.S. Hall, a Methodist missionary opened a school for blind girls in *Pyongyang*. This kind of Christian social service continued through Korean church history. Asylums for orphanages and the aged and school for deaf-dumb are as follows: [95]

1890, R. Hall, Methodist Mission, *Pyongyang*

1892, E. B. Landis, *Inchon.*

1903, Methodist Mission, *Pyongyang*

1904, Mrs. Moffet, *Pyongyang*

1916, Salvation Army Mission, Seoul.

1921, Park Kyung-suk, *Pyongyang*

1924, Baby Life Saving Station by Methodist Mission, *Kongju, Choognam*

1925, Lee Byung-joon, *Sunchun*

1934, Kim Jin-kuk, *Wonsan*

1935, Presbytery of *Pyongyang*

1936, Lee Yong-dam, *Hoeryung*

1936, Jung Ji-kang, *Pyongyang*

During the Korean War (1950-1953), the churches received enormous amounts of assistance from the West and played the major role of distributing food and clothes to hungry people. Among the needy people, the many war widows with their children were the most needy. Members of the missions established homes for them, and most women were provided with some form of employment. Much help was also given to amputees, lepers, the blind and deaf, tuberculosis patients and crippled children. Welfare for children organization during and after the war are as follows: [96]

    1951,   Christian Children Welfare Center, V.J. Mill
    1952,   Compassion, Swanson Evangelistic Mission
    1953,   World Vision
    1955,   Holt Children Welfare Mission

Church growth was accompanied by a great extension of compassionate social services through which 560 orphanages, 49 widow's homes, and 25 rehabilitation centers were established.[97] As an indication of the amazing open door for the gospel during this period, it is interesting to note how many new church buildings were erected. In 1955, the Presbyterians reported 1,200 new churches built; the Methodists, 500; and Holiness (sponsored by the Oriental Missionary Society), 250. New denominations coming into the country built hundreds more. In all, a total of over 2,000 new church buildings were constructed by 1955.[98] Following the Korean War American churches sent massive relief supplies to war-stricken South Korea, and many persons joined the church in thankfulness for this material help. The material help America gave to the people in their time of need did serve as an example of Christ's love, and many recipients of this aid responded to the love and became Christians. In the history of the Protestant missions, several missions and Christian organizations were responsible for the care of the needy people such as orphans, disabled people and poor people. All these good works of the Western missionaries paved the way for Protestant evangelization and created a positive image of Christianity among the Koreans and contributed to church growth.

NATIONAL EVANGELISTIC WORK AND FOREIGN MISSION WORK FOR CHURCH GROWTH

National Evangelistic Work

In relation to church growth in Korea, Samuel Moffet suggested evangelistic zeal, fervency in prayer and devotion to the Word of God as an explanation for the church growth in Korea.[99] It should be remembered that the early Korean Christians learned the zeal and the method of personal evangelism from the missionaries. As discussed in an earlier chapter, from the early days it had been the policy of the missionaries to travel over large areas of the country visiting the numerous market towns and villages to preach the gospel to as many as possible. From the beginning, the church grew because of the witnessing activity of Korean Christians implementing the efforts and zeal of evangelistic work learned from missionaries. When on a visit to Korea at the beginning of this century, A. J. Brown, former Far East Secretary of the Presbyterian Board of Foreign Missions, saw that distances prevented frequent missionary visits to each new place of preaching. Blair wrote of his experience of preaching the gospel in the mountainous countryside in the following words:

> As soon as I could speak enough Korean to begin, I had leisure to preach to the people as I walked the roads... most Koreans walk. I am even planning to take out a motorcycle to Korea to use on long journeys. Nevertheless, I mean to walk as much as possible because it is the best way to preach the gospel... There is a system of market in Korea, five towns in a circle. The market town may not have more than twenty houses; but every fifth day it blossoms into a full-grown city, a great beehive of peddlers with their wares spread out on mats along the road, and farmers from miles in every direction. A market is a fine place to meet men and an excellent spot in which to preach the gospel.[100]

After the message has been welcomed in the most unexpected places, groups of believers have come into existence. After following the evangelistic method of early missionaries, the development of the church in Korea from the beginning depended upon the efforts of the personal witness of Koreans themselves.[101] This was underlined by Malcom C. Fenwick, an independent missionary to Korea. "The gospel can best be taught to foreign people by picked native converts."[102] He made this statement after he confessed that he himself failed as a missionary. The thought that it was the Koreans themselves who brought the Gospel to the Korean people has the underlying assumption that this was an advantage for the spread of Christianity.

From the beginning the Korean Christian has been to an unusual degree a witnessing Christian, and the Korean church became a church of personal evangelistic workers. It has been continually emphasized that unless personal faith is awake to the necessity of personal testimony, both in speech and in conduct, it is neither a healthy nor a normal faith.[103] In 1909 James Gale wrote,

> From the early days of the mission there has prevailed among the Korean con-

verts a very high conception of the privileges and responsibilities of church membership; he is a worker giving his service freely and gladly to extend the knowledge of Christ among his neighbors. It has not been an unusual thing for a pastor of a local church to have not less than one-third of the entire membership of his church on the street on a Sunday afternoon engaged in house to house visitation and personal work among their unconverted neighbors.[104]

Whenever Korean Christians have an audience they have been willing to tell "the Good News" to others. James Gale wrote:

Many years of testing by the question, "Where did you first hear the gospel? at church? on the street? at a prayer meeting? by reading the Bible?" bring the characteristic responses "No, I heard it first from brother Kim, or brother Paik, or brother Choi; he came to my house and we read together." From lip to lip and heart to heart it has gone to the distant valleys,...from east to west, all over the land. God will bless Korea, for if ever a land exemplified the Christian principle of passing it on, it is this same country.[105]

Undoubtedly the great majority of Christians in the early Korean Church were the direct result of the personal evangelism of believers. However, it is to be noted that Korean evangelists supported by their churches have also played a major role in personal evangelism. Korean Christians are famed for the zeal with which they have supported and extended the church. Their zeal was fed by their own vivid religious experience, by the teaching and example of the missionaries, and by the fact that from the beginning, responsibility for supporting the local church and for administration taken by the Korean Christians in the enterprise was due in some measure to the deliberate policy adopted by the missionaries, and in some measure to the rapid rise of the church, which made it impractical for the mission to carry the whole administrative and financial load. Sharrocks reported in 1906:

Last year in our station of *Syenchun* we had 6,507 adherents; this year there are 11,943. From whence the 5,436 conversions during the twelve months? — an average of 453 per month. Could it be from the $72.00 spent on local evangelists giving their whole time to the work and receiving their support from the native church... The 5,436 converts of this year will be up for examination and baptism next year. In the face of these facts I think we can call the Korean church self-propagating.[106]

As stated earlier, one of the remarkable methods of evangelistic work in the early church was the implementation of the colportage system. A large use was made of Korean colporteurs. These Christian men were employed by the missionaries to travel about the country and sell scripture portions and tracts. Funds were provided by the Bible societies. The colporteurs worked under the direction of the missionaries and made regular reports to them. These colporteurs were the advance guard of the Christian movement, and in many cases the first believers in a village were due to their efforts. In 1928, 177 colporteurs sold Gospels and Bibles. They also witnessed as they went from place to place, and as a result, they started many churches. It was reported that by 1936, 18,079,466 copies of the Scripture had been sold.[107]

The Korean women were very active in direct evangelism. The evangelistic task of the church women's witnessing Committee was organized at *Nuldahri* Church in *Pyongyang* in 1898. Lee Shin-Haeing was the first president of the committee. She dispatched evangelists to the places where no churches existed and founded many churches.

> Korean women played a remarkable role in establishing new churches. In 1899, about forty house wives gathered and organized a witnessing committee in *Changyun, Kyungsang Namdo*. They opened the map of the five neighboring subcounties and marked where the gospel of Christ should be spread. They visited each place, witnessing for Jesus and established churches. They not only made efforts in establishing churches in our country, but also in evangelizing the whole world. The national Women's Evangelistic Association sent Mr. Kim Soon-Ho to *Sang Dong* city in China along with five women missionaries in 1931.[108]

The outreach was multiplied by the personal evangelism of Korean Christian women, known as Bible women. They visited from house to house, told gospel stories, and sold gospels, and likewise distributed tracts.[109] The personal evangelism of the Bible women was very influential. According to the Presbyterian Rules and By-Laws of 1896, the Bible Woman, *Chundo Puin*,[110] was "a Christian woman employed in the distribution of Christian literature, and in Biblical instruction."[111] Her work was, however, more comprehensive than this definition suggests. The Bible woman was primarily employed to reach the Korean women with the Gospel. It was hard for male evangelists, native or foreign, to reach these women, because of the rigid separation of the sexes in traditional Korean culture. The Bible women made long journeys, selling Bibles, preaching and evangelizing. They led services for women, taught them how to read, and instructed them on various issues, such as the Bible, conduct in the Church, control and care of the family, and health and hygiene.[112] In 1901 Mrs. Campell reported that about 2,632 women had listened to the gospel from the Bible women in Seoul during the year.[113] In 1904 Mrs. Moose said of her Bible woman, Mrs. Kim:

She is very enthusiastic over the work in the vicinity of our new chapel and has recently brought in a number of articles which have been used in the worship of evil spirits, the owners of said articles renouncing their former faith and becoming candidates for membership in our church. From September 1903 to September 1904 Mrs. Kim reports having talked to 6,912 women on the subject of personal evangelism.[114]

Early Korean Christians pledged themselves to spend a certain number of days in personal evangelism and tract distribution. Paik and Clark wrote about two conspicuous methods adopted by the Korean Christians: "the custom of contributing days for evangelistic work and the distribution of Christian literature, especially portions of the gospels." The following is a summary of the extent of these two methods in 1909:

Poor and hard-working Koreans were inspired to give at least 100,000 days of work in all, for 76,000 days of earnest personal work were done last winter, and this fall several hundreds of native workers gave a whole month to special service, going from house to house as well as dealing with men personally in great meetings. Many millions of tracts and 700,000 gospels of Mark were purchased by native Christians and given to unbelievers with prayers and earnest persuasion; nearly every home in Korea has visited and daily prayer has been offered for this by thousands of Koreans.[115]

The missionaries and the Korean pastors regularly gave opportunities to every church member to make such pledges. Even when examing a candidate for baptism it was the common custom to inquire whether or not he personally testified to his new-found faith. One of the usual questions in examining candidates for baptism was, "Have you since you became a Christian led anyone else to the Savior?" In his story of the great crusade to win one million souls from heathenism to Christianity, George T. Davis writes:

Persistent personal effort day after day for the salvation of the lost is the third great method (the first is prayer, the second, the word of God) for the realization of the object in view. The Korean Christian possesses a passion for soul-winning not found in Western lands. It is a kind of unwritten rule in many Korean churches not to admit a believer into full membership until he has led at least one soul to Christ. The most striking method of personal work in Korea is the custom of setting apart whole days and weeks of time to be devoted exclusively to personal dealing with the unsaved.[116]

In the large gathering for Bible study, and in the Bible Institute also, systematic instruction in personal evangelism was often given, and some portion of the afternoon was spent by all who attended putting into practice the principles taught.[117] As one Korean has said:

When a man passes through transforming religious and moral experiences, he naturally desires to share them with others. This spirit is especially characteristic of Christianity, not only because of its claim to universality but because of its ideal of love that urges people to reach others, especially those who are not so fortunate.[118]

The zeal of personal evangelism and gospel tract distribution has been a continuous characteristic and church growth factor of the Protestant church in Korea until today. Today the evangelistic zeal shows itself in the home visitations and other church activities. Home visitation evangelism is to visit non-Christian houses to preach the gospel and to talk to the family or an individual. Today twice a year big home-visitations are done by Christians. Every home is visited and a short service is held. Every Christian gives time for this evangelistic work. When a new church starts in Korea, the pastor and the evangelist or leaders of the church visit house to house, talking with the family, and preach the gospel. In the area of many apartments and the areas where the houses stand close together, many church pastors use this evangelistic method effectively. The para-church organizations for evangelism have sprung up in the Christian community in the closing years of the 1980s.

Table 5.4: The Church Growth Rate of Main Denominations in Korea

Year	Presby *(Hapdong)*	Holiness	Presby *(Tonghap)*	Methodist	Presby *(Kijang)*
1964	1,496	507	2,130	1,200	679
1975	2,484	761	2,685	1,538	738
Ratio	66.8%	50.0%	26.0%	29.0%	8.6%

(Source: Jung-Keun Lee, *Theological Thought,* 1977, p. 363)

Evangelism by private conversion was one of the methdos Jesus used.[119] He spoke to crowds, but a significant part of the gospel records conversations Jesus had in private, such as with Nicodemus, the woman of Samaria and Zacchaeus. Not only did Jesus use this method, but he trained his disciples to use it. Like his disciples toady they were amazed and full of joy at their success (Luke 10:1-20). There was nothing at the time which resembled a professional ministry. The leaders of the churches were diverse in age, social class, sex, education, religious and cultural backgrounds, and race. There was no one group which more than any other had the responsibility for spreading the gospel.

They were all enthusiasts who shared their new found faith with conviction and believed the Bible's commandments to evangelize applied to all believers. Lay evangelism is a biblical norm that is buried under centuries of clerical, ecclesiastical tradition. Lay evangelism is one of the secrets behind the steady and rapid growth of the Korean churches. Lay evangelism training is one of the major factors responsible for the Korean church's spiritual readiness and openness.

Foreign Mission Work by Korean Christians

The missionary minded Korean Christians organized their own foreign Mission Work. As early as 1897, the women organized a missionary society and sent an evangelist to the *Soonan* district.[120] In 1901 the Korean church started sending missionaries to Manchuria. These activities took place long before the constitution of the independent Presbyterian Church in Korea was adopted in 1907. A Foreign Mission Board decided to send Lee Ki-Pung, the first foreign missionary, to *Cheju* Island.[121] Moffett said, "sixteen years ago, he (Lee Ki-Pung) stoned me on the streets of *Pyongyang*, and now he goes as the first missionary of the Presbyterian church in Korea."[122] He was one of the seven pastors ordained in Korea and even though Korea needed many pastors for the national churches, they wanted to share the gospel with the people on this island with its different culture and language. This took place just 23 years after the first Presbyterian missionary, the American Horace N. Allen, arrived in Korea. Underwood wrote that "here was the native church of Korea with only seven ordained native ministers, and yet at its first meeting, setting aside one of its number to go as a missionary to far distant Quelport."[123] Thus, the Korean Presbyterian Church became a missionary church from the very day of its foundation. Allen D. Clark wrote:

> The important thing... was that the Korean Church felt such a deep debt of gratitude to Christ for blessings received that, with only seven precious ministers, newly ordained, they dedicated one of these men to the work of carrying the Gospel to those who did not know the truth of salvation, and so made their thank-offering to the Lord.[124]

In 1909 Chai Kwan-hul was sent by the Presbyterian churches to the eastern part of Russia, and Han Suk-jin was sent to Tokyo, Japan.[125] There were also approximately ten Korean pastors serving in

Manchuria. When the Korean Presbyterian Church's General Assembly was organized in 1912, they voted to send three missionaries to China. The next year they sent pastors Park Tae-ro, Sa Bung-sun, and Kim Yong-hung to *Sandongsung*, China. They were the first missionaries to fellow Koreans living in China.[126] The Korean Presbyterian Church continued to send missionaries to China, including evangelists and medical missionaries, until the end of the Second World War. By the end of the Second World War there were approximately 100 Korean missionaries serving in northeast Asian mission fields.[127] The northern Methodists founded their Home Missionary Society in 1907. In 1910 this became the Foreign and Home Missionary Society of the Methodist Episcopal Church in Korea, sending missionaries to China and Manchura. In 1955, even before restoration from the Korean War poverty, churches sent many missionaries to Taiwan, Thailand, Japan, Hong Kong, Indonesia, Nepal, Pakistan, Ethiopia, Brazil, Mexico, Argentina, Brunei, America and South Vietnam.

The 1970s was the great decade for the Korean church. Korea's young people have been displaying a growing mission concern. According to the Korean Statistical Yearbook of 1978, almost 70 percent of the population in Korea was under 30.[128] In 1978 the *Youngnak* Presbyterian Church held a four-day World Mission Rally. On the last night about 6,000 to 7,000 young people stood up, committing themselves to support, pray for or become missionaries overseas.[129] The church's growth was unprecedented and the awakening to mission was phenomenal. The growth rate continued to accelerate in the 1980s, and the mission awakening continues to deepen. More new societies have organized and more new missionaries have been sent out during this past decade.

During the '80s, in crusades organized by the Korean Church Evangelistic Association about 100,000 Koreans pledged at least one year of overseas service. Doctors, teachers, pastors, etc. went overseas as self-supporting missionaries, as Christian Service Corps workers.[130] According to a survey of Korean missionaries done by Marlin Nelson in May 1982, there were 47 mission organizations sending 323 missionaries to 37 different countries, and 180 Diaspora missionaries and 143 cross-cultural missionaries. The majority of these 249 missionaries were sent by 8 mission societies, and 31 mission societies were supporting and promoting activities in various ways but were not sending out missionaries This total does not include the University Bible Fellowship staff of 101 Korean and national workers serving the Fellowship with self-supporting lay-missionaries in eleven countries excluding the U.S.A. and Canada. In 1983 the total number of Korean Protestant lay missionaries overseas was estimated as over 1,000.[131] In 1984 32,000 Christians registered to go overseas as vocational missionaries. In 1988 there were 530 missionaries, and in 1990, 687 missionaries was sent to different countries in Asia, Europe, North America, Africa, the Middle East, Australia.[132] According to David Lee, director of the Global Missionary Training Institute in Seoul, there has been an increasing members of Korean missionaries. In 1992, 2,576 missionaries in 105 countries, and in June 1994, 3,272 missionaries in 119 countries.[133]

With the birth of nondenominational faith missions, a new wave of awakening arose so that each church began its own program and new movements came into being. The main Korean Missionary Sending Supporting Agencies are as follows:

Korean Presbyterian Church Mission (*Haptong*); Korean Presbyterian Church Mission (*Tonghap*); Korean Presbyterian Church Mission (*Koryo*); Presbyterian Church Mission; Korean Methodist Mission; Korean Evangelical Mission; Korean Salvation Army Mission; Korea International Mission, Korea Translation Mission; Korea International Mission for Christ; Mission to North Korea; World Omega's Revival Mission Society; Asia Evangelical Mission; Asian Gospel Mission; Agape Mission; Evangelization of North Korea; Presbyterian Inter-Mission Committee; Korean Christian Medical Mission; Korean Christian Entertainer Mission; World Progress Mission; Korean Christian Mission Center; Korean Indonesian Mission Fellowship; Korea Mass-Media Christian Mission; The Christian Service; Council for Mission in North-East Asian Churches; Korea Mission to Bangladesh; Gospel for Asia Foundation; Asian Evangelical Mission; Hankuk International Evangelistic Mission; Korean Christian Mission Society; Korea Gospel Mission; Korea Harbor Mission; Christian Reach out to the World; Korea Inter-Varsity Mission; University Bible Fellowship Mission; Student Fellowship of World Mission; Ewha Women's University Students Mission; Korean Presbyterian Women's Mission (*Haptong*); Korean Presbyterian Women's Mission (*Tonghap*); Women Mission of Presbyterian; Korean Methodist Women's Mission; Korean Women's Evangelical Service; The Wheat Seed Women's Mission; The Signal Fire Women's Mission; The Prayer Partnership Women's Mission. [134]

Today there are 4,321 Korean missionaries in 122 different countries.[135] The Korean church has been extremely conscious of her mission responsibilities from the beginning. A number of churches have sent or plan to send their own missionaries.

Emphasis on Bible Study and Prayer Life

From the beginning the missionaries emphasized and taught the Korean Christians how to study the Bible as the Word of God, taking the position of strong conservative theology. A. J. Brown, who was general secretary of the Board of Foreign Mission of the Presbyterian Church U.S.A., commented on the theological opinion of foreign missionaries in Korea before 1911 as follows:

> The typical missionary of the first quarter century after the opening of the country was a man of the Presbyterian type. He kept the Sabbath as our New England forefathers did a century ago. He looked upon dancing, smoking, and card-playing as sins in which no true follower of Christ should indulge. In theology and biblical criticism he was strongly conservative, and he held as a vital truth the premillenial view of the second coming of Christ. The higher criticism and liberal theology were deemed dangerous heresies.[136]

Samuel Moffet, the founding president of the Presbyterian Seminary in *Pyongyang* did not write many books, but his influence was great and his theology was conservative and Calvinistic. Recalling the first time he came to Korea, he said, "I have done what I prayed and decided before God when I first came to Korea. That is, I decided not to preach anything except the cross of Christ. If I preach any other gospel, I should be cursed."[137] We can see his theological thought in this saying. Kim Chai-Choon writes,

> Since the nation had hopelessly failed to maintain political independence, the people's minds naturally became inclined toward the spiritual, otherworldly realm of religion, and found the answer to their search in Christianity.[138]

Therefore, conservative Bible study made an important contribution to church growth in Korea. Bible Study played an essential role in the early Korean church and has become a main course in the church's growth. Many reports and statements indicate that the early Korean church enthusiastically studied the Bible. Those who gathered for Bible study shared lodging and board together and enjoyed the Bible's teachings in a festive spirit. Korean missionaries at first emphasized Bible study for new Christians to grow well and to be trained as the leaders of the church.

One important reason why the Korean church could overcome the serious historical situation during the Japanese occupation and Korean War, and why the church could grow continually, was its diligent study of the Bible. Shearer described the Bible study as the following.

The use of the Bible study as the basis of training new Christians and intensive Bible teaching are included in Nevius' plan. The Bible training classes also were set up early in mission history. These classes also, especially in the northwest, were a powerful force in producing a strong church.[139]

In the early Korean church, the purpose of Bible study was to strengthen the faith of each Christian and to find and train promising laymen to be pastors. These studies took three different forms. First, one single church or a few neighboring churches held Bible study for the local people individually or as a whole. Once or twice a year local congregations sponsored *Sakyenghoe* (literally, Search the Scripture Conference) lasting five to seven days. During this conference laymen and lay women would stream in from neighboring areas to study the Word of God systematically. Second, Bible study for the church staff was held for two or three weeks in the summer. Third, stemming from those forms, theological education was provided for the pastors.

According to a recent empirical study of Korean church growth and faith, the favorite program of Korean Christians is Bible study; regular Bible study is 50.1 percent, early morning prayer meeting is 24.7 percent and lectures on the Christian life are 14.0 percent.[140] In Korea nowadays, every segment of society is being penetrated through a small group Bible Study movement. Billy Graham said at the climax of his 1973 Crusade in Korea: "I urge church and theological leaders... to come and study the Korean church. I believe the secret of the power and strength of the Korean church is that they believe and proclaim the Bible."[141] William J. Danker comments in his book, *Two Worlds or None*:

Church has been strong in Bible study... the dawn prayer meetings at each local church have been a daily source of spiritual strength. The church has been strong in evangelism. Through the years people would each pledge so many days of evangelistic preaching.[142]

In Korea one of the most active evangelistic movements is campus Bible study and evangelism. Local churches concentrate on evangelizing students and reaching university students through Sunday School, youth ministries, and para-church organizations. Between 1950 and 1980, new kinds of para-church organization began their ministries in Korea. This type of Bible study came into being not through the church but through several student mission groups such as Campus Crusade for Christ (CCC), Navigators, University Bible Fellowship (UBF), Korean Inter-Varsity Christian Fellowship (IVCF), JOY Mission, Youth for Christ (YFC), and Student Bible Fellowship (SBF).

Campus Crusade for Christ was introduced to Korea in 1958. Since that time it has grown rapidly in number and influence and has become the largest Christian student movement in Korea. CCC has contributed much to the Korean churches but most particularly in the matter of training reproductive laymen. In 1984 CCC had about 130 full-time staff members, more than 10,000 college students, and about 180,000 college graduates. The Navigators began its Korean ministry in 1966 as an international and interdenominational Christian mission. The aim of the Navigators is to make disciples all around the world, thus helping to fulfill the Great Commission in Matthew 28:19-20. Disciple making is central to its ministry, based on the multiplicative process shown in 2 Timothy 2:2. University Bible Fellowship began activities in Korea in 1961 and became a nationwide organization by 1968. By 1974 the organization had expanded worldwide with branches in the U.S.A., Germany, Bangladesh, Switzerland, France, Spain, Italy, Japan, Canada, Guatemala, Brazil, Chile, Libya and others. UBF's rigorous and enthusiastic Bible study approach challenges the Korean churches. Inter-Varsity Christian Fellowship, introduced in 1959, has student evangelism as its objective. Participation in church training programs, ministry in local churches by the staff workers and publication and distribution of Christian literature are some of the contributions IVCF has made to the local churches in Korea. JOY Youth Club was formed in 1958 by those who felt the need of evangelism among high school students. In 1966 the name was changed to JOY Club to include all age groups. In 1976 the name was changed again to JOY Mission with the hope of fulfilling Christ's Great Commission. The fundamental purpose of this student group is to train and adequately equip persons on the campuses and also in business offices for world mission. Youth for Christ, which was introduced in 1961, focuses on leading teenagers to Christ. The objective of this group is evangelization on the campuses through Christian fellowships. By 1984 the group had 3,200 members, and more than 21,000 high school student members had graduated. Student Bible Fellowship separated from the UBF in 1976 because of different viewpoints concerning local churches. The SBF desired to have a good relationship with local churches while the UBF wanted to continue as an interdenominational mission group.

We can classify the student mission organization into two categories according to origin: those formed by Korean Christians, and those introduced from other lands. These groups are student-centered, interdenominational, strongly Bible study oriented and enthusiastically evangelistic, with a keen world vision for non-Christians. Summer evangelistic Bible conferences, which are held by these para-church organizations, usually draw over ten thousand university students.

However, as a result of church-centered outreach, many students after their graduation became involved in church evangelism as well as in campus evangelism. At one time the Korean Campus Crusade for Christ surveyed 12,096 Korean students at 129 universities in 24 cities. The survey findings, released in 1981, reveal that Christianity has become a major influence on Korean students.[143] In 1983, 13,000 students were surveyed on 125 campuses and the results showed that 33 percent claimed to be Christians.[144] In 1986, a great evangelistic thrust in primary schools, high schools and universities occurred. Twenty-five percent of all professors claimed to be Christians. Thirty percent of the primary and high school teachers said that they were Christians. Thirty-three percent of all college students responded that they were Christians.[145] Bill Bright, founder of Campus Crusade for Christ International, once said, "Students represent the major source of man power to help change the course of history. They need to be reached for Christ."[146]

It has been said that the Methodist missionaries who came to Korea introduced the Wesley Class Meeting System,[147] which is small group Bible Study and Fellowship, to the Korean churches. This is a so-called cell group movement. In the early churches, it is interesting to note that the apostolic church relied on evangelism in homes with small groups of people. There are repeated references to this. Paul reminded the elders from Ephesus, "I have showed you, and have taught you publicly, and from house to house" (Acts 20:20). Michael Green writes the following concerning the value of small group evangelistic meetings in homes:

> It had positive advantage; the comparatively small numbers involved made real interchange of views and informed discussion among the participants possible... The sheer informality and relaxed atmosphere of the home, not to mention the hospitality which must often have gone with it, all helped to make this form of evangelism particularly successful.[148]

It is assumed that the adoption of this system contributed to the church growth. Marlin L. Nelson writes, "Another major contributor to the growth of the Korean church is the Wesley Class Meeting. This Methodist system is used by nearly every denomination in Korea."[149] In Korea, every church has a small group Bible study and fellowship system which is geographically divided and which meets weekly in the various members' homes according to local districts. One of the main functions of such home cell group meetings is that it is an avenue of outreach to non-Christians. A small number of people meet face to face weekly to study the Bible, pray, exchange experiences, and to be trained for home-visitation. After each meeting, members often go out together to visit non-Christians and to invite them to attend Sunday services and small group Bible study and fellowship.[150]

Small group Bible study and fellowship has resulted in an increase in the numerical growth of the membership of the church. Small group meetings in homes provide an opportunity for the laity to be directly involved in evangelism. Taught the basic Scriptural principles of evangelization, small group members are motivated to search for the receptive. This emphasis on personal evangelism has had effects, such as the development of love and compassion in the hearts of the active small group members, the continual growth of faith, and the continual increase and multiplication of the small groups. This system is particularly fruitful for the big churches. Yonggi Cho, pastor of the Full Gospel Central Church, says that the secret of his successful ministry is the small group Bible study and fellowship. In one article concerning the phenomenal growth at his church, it was written:

> Such growth is all the more remarkable in that 75 percent of it comes from the world, and only about 25 percent from transfer from other congregations or denominations.[151]

Many Korean churches present evidences of numerical church growth by applying and emphasizing the small group Bible study and fellowship system. The Full Gospel Central Church of Seoul, which has more than 706,000 members, with 52,000 small groups, is an excellent example of rapid church growth.[152] This local group has grown from 7,750 members in 1967 to 70,000 in 1978 by practicing this small group Bible study and fellowship system.[153] In 1985, 19,839 small groups composed of no more than fifteen members met usually on Friday evening, in homes, offices and factories across Seoul.[154] This small group Bible study and fellowship system contributed greatly to the growth of the church.

Prayer life is also one of the strengths in the Koran church and has played a vital part in the rise and growth of the church in Korea. Korean church has been known for its emphasis on prayer. Every church schedules a daily early dawn prayer meeting. The origin of this early dawn prayer meeting goes back to 1906 when Pastor Kil Sun-zu started the the pre-dawn prayer meeting at his chruch in Pyonygang, North Korea. This practice dates back to the great Revival of 1907

Table 5.5: Statistics of Protestant Churches in Korea (1960-1969)

Year	Churches	Members
1960	8,005	1,524,258
1965	9,057	2,225,193
1967	9,706	2,899,108
1969	12,987	3,211,614

(Source: *Yearbook of Christianity in Korea,* 1970, pp. 520-521)

which was born out of a five-month period of prayer. In preparation for the "Million Soul Movement" pastor Kil and one of his elders went to church every day at four a.m. for two months. Others heard of it and desired to join them. It was announced that the church bell would ring each morning at four-thirty. One the first morning a large company had arrived by two a.m., and then the bell was rung, five hundred were present. Ever since that time the pre-dawn prayer movement spread to all other churches and has remained a daily part of the church's life.

The most well-known pre-dawn prayer meetings are at the Myungsung Presbyterian Church in Seoul which started with a handful some ten years ago. Today, the church has 30,000 members. The secret of this rapid growth in the ministry of Rev. Kim Sam-hwan, who has faithfully conducted the pre-dawn prayer meetings every morning. The number of Christians who attended the last March 1995 pre-dawn prayer meetings at 4:30, 5:30, 6:30 and 10:00 a.m. reached over 16,000 each morning. Thousands of other Christians who attend pre-dawn prayer meetings in their own church gives similar testimonies; therefore, there is no doubt that God has blessed the Korean church through pre-dawn prayer meetings.[155]

Another aspect of pray emphasis in the Korean church is the all night prayer meeting usually on Friday evening once a week. Christian sing hymns, listen to messages, give testimonies, and pray all night. There also also 521 prayer mountains (*kidowon*) throughout the country, and thousands of Christians go up to prayer mountains for prayer. Besides the church prayer meetings, Joon G. Kim of the Korea Campus Crusade for Christ intruduced the '1.1.1. Prayer Movement' to the Korean Church which encourages Christians to pray "Once a day a 1:00 p.m. for one minute." The emphasis on Bible Study and prayer life have certainly brought about church growth in Korea.

Family Evangelism for Church Growth

In the history of the Korean church, wherever the church grew rapidly, it grew through family evangelism. Even in areas of small growth, because of family solidarity, it is quite probable that believers came to Christ as families rather than as isolated individuals pulled outside their family relationships. Robert Recker remarks in an article entitled, "What Are People Movements?":

> This web is where the most intimate of relationships takes place and provides the natural avenues for the spontaneous witnessing of Christians in their immediate environment, addressed to those who are most vulnerable to that witness, and who are best able to judge the quality of the Christian life of the one who witnesses.[156]

In Korea, people are dealing with a society based on the family, not on the tribe. This family unit is strong and is the basic social unit in the country. The family society refers to the extended family living in one house: grandparents, parents, children, and grandchildren. The society influenced by Confucianism must keep the order of the family. The master of the family is the grandfather; the entire family operates by the grandfather's commandments. If the grandfather decided to believe in Christ, all the family would believe in Christ; if he opposes Christianity, it is hard for one of the family to become a Christian. Paik gives an excellent description of the relationship between family evangelism and church growth:

> A Korean village is generally composed of a number of closely related families. If the father is influential, his conversion might result in the mass conversion of the village... There was a fellowship among converts that was attractive to an outsider. The Christians were sympathetic toward each other and stood together in sorrow and joy. When a man had a friend who was not Christian, he exerted himself to win his friend into the fellowship of the church. Thus self-propagation began within the family circle and with close friends. Not only was the fellowship an attractive feature, but by winning members of his own family and his friends a convert might do away with all possibility of persecution.[157]

As mentioned earlier, Korean Christians engaged in intensive evangelism. In the story of fifty years of the development of the church, Blair concludes that while the Koreans went far with their evangelism, the gospel really followed along family channels. It was in the intimate relationship of the home where firm belief sprang from heart to heart and believers have been harvested. Strong men who became Christians went to their clan villages and convinced their relatives that they, too, should acquire this new life. As an example, Blair tells of a church in the Kyungsang province that was started by Mr. So:

> One day young Mr. So went with a friend across the mountain for a visit to a nearby church; he obtained a Bible and became a believer. His father remained unconverted, but Mr. So soon won his uncles and several cousins, who began meeting in a home on Sundays. The whole village was aroused, discussing the new religion. The community resented the singing of the Christians, but when in early spring Mr. So, the priestly head of the clan, refused to prepare food for ancestral worship at the shrine of their ancestor, the whole clan and community rose in rebellion. The gospel story was spread widely. They studied the Bible, kept the Sabbath, preached, and endured persecution. Finally after much community turmoil, Mr. So turned over the ancestral shrine and its endowed fields to another family. Gradually the followers of Christ increased... The church grew larger and was divided, and a new group sprang up three miles away in a village where other cousins lived.[158]

These were the means by which the Korean church multiplied ahead of the missionaries. Here is one example from among many.

> Away up in the mountains at the head of a little valley we found a whole family, consisting of a man, 74 years of age, his four sons and their wives, and daughters and their husbands who were Christians. No missionary had ever visited them, and a helper but three times. The whole family of 11 persons except one son who was away from home passed a most creditable examination and we rejoiced to receive them as catechumens. The one son-in law had first heard the gospel here in Pyongyang three years ago and was interested enough to buy some Christian books which he took home and which in turn led the whole family into believing.[159]

One missionary, on his first visit to a Korean village, found that all of the village people were Christians and had regular family worship, even though a missionary and that they had never visited them and there was as yet no organized church. Because of the close-knit web of family relationships and the inter-family relationships through the clan, no one wished to make the great step in accepting a new religion which would break down these family ties.[160] A person on hearing of the gospel of Christ, or reading of it from a Bible sold to him, would go back to his own village, talk it over with the members of his family and clan, and if a positive decision were made, the entire group often quite naturally became Christian, still holding fast to its family relationship. If all were not immediately won, each family member in his own time would often become Christian until soon the whole family and sometimes the entire clan turned to Christ.[161] Shearer says the family pattern of the society was as follows:

The family structure has been used by God in Korea to win men and women to Christ. If we are be His servants to assist in further winning, we must study the family structure pattern, and develop a theology congenial to it.[162]

It is interesting to note that a Korean scholar indicates in his Korea research report the percentage of Korean clergy and laymen becoming Christian because of their family. His study indicates that 66.1 percent of the clergy and 47.9 percent of the laymen came to faith this way.[163] This means that family evangelism contributes to church growth in Korea. However, it must be remembered that such family conversions to Christ in Korea were not a mass movement in the sense that mobs of unconverted people were taken into the churches. It was rather a response of faith to the gospel, flowing unimpeded along the web of family relationships. Harry Boer has called attention to the significance of the family unit in the evangelism of the Christian church from its earliest beginning.[164] McGavran has eloquently called us to discern the many "Bridges of God" in the web of relationships provided by the "extended family."[165]

One of the most important methods of spreading the gospel in antiquity was by the use of homes.[166] The apostolic church relied on evangelism in homes. There are repeated referenced to this (Acts 5:42). Paul minded the elders from Ephesus, "I have showed you, and have taught you publicly, and from house to house" (Acts 20:20). In his book, *Evangelism in the Early Church*, Michael Green writes the following concerning the value of family evangelism.

> It had positive advantages; the comparatively small numbers involved made real interchange of views and informed discussion among the participants possible... The sheer informality and relaxed atmosphere of the home, not to mention the hospitality which must often have gone with it, all helped to make this form of evangelism particularly successful.[167]

Nationwide Evangelistic Revival Meetings

The awakening which brought about the revival movement gave to the Korean church a more zealous and passionate driving power for winning new converts. A new vision of a nationwide evangelistic Revival campaign began to grip the hearts of the Korean Christians. As mentioned earlier, missionaries and Korean ministers began holding revival meetings throughout the country in the early 1900s. A daring step toward the realization of the vision was launched under the name of "Million Movement" in 1909 and 1910. This movement began with tremendous enthusiasm and evangelical fervor. G. T. Brown described three of the methods in the plan for evangelistic advance:

> First, there would be mass evangelistic rallies in the various centers. The second, a novel idea with a distinctive Korean flavor, was called the "collection of days.".... Third a major effort would be made in the distribution of gospels and tracts.[168]

The logical outcome of these mass meetings was nationwide revival. One of the effects of the revival was widespread church evangelism in cooperation with different denominations. Denominational barriers were broken down and Christians were minded to join together in witness. This revival movement continued to spread through the whole nation. Two key leaders of the Korean revival movement were Sun-zu Kil (1869-1935) and Ik-du Kim (1874-1950). Sun-zu Kil was renowned as one of the outstanding evangelists in Korea. Sun-zu Kil was born in March 1869 at *Anju*, *Pyongyang* South province, where he spent most of his childhood in studying the ancient Chinese classics but failed in his commercial career. He visited famous temples in his attempts to master the Buddhist Truths, but no longer finding asceticism to his taste, he indulged himself in Taoism without reaching the inner solace he so desperately sought. Kil assumed his career in commerce after mastering the Chinese herb medicine. He was converted to the Christian faith by Jong-sup Kim and discovered that salvation through Christianity satisfied his thirst for faith in religion. He became an outstanding evangelist of the Christian revival movement. He graduated from the Pyongyang Theological Seminary in 1907 and was renowned as one of the seven early Christian ministers; he was assigned to the congregation at *Chandaihyun* church for 15 years, during which time he highlighted the revival movement throughout the country.[169]

The sermons of Sun-zu Kil were not merely authoritative, fluent and graceful in tone but so inspiring that the audience on the floor repented of their sins. He had a miraculous power of alleviating suffering and the spiritual diseases of the congregation. His broad and deep knowledge of the Holy Scriptures and the profound wisdom and biblical research not only elevated him as a scholar of the Bible but also played an essential role in the interpretation of the Book before the foreign missionaries. For ten years after 1924, Kil chiefly engaged in the revival movement throughout the country and preached a number of sermons on more than 20,000 occasions; he converted 70,000, 30,200 of whom were baptized; he established 60 Christian churches.[170] In 1935, he died while leading the morning devotion at *Kochang* church in *Kangsu kun* in Korea. L. S. Kim described the life of the evangelist Sun-zu Kil.

> You are a Korean hero, the Korean church was founded by your faith. The early morning prayer meeting that you started in Korea, became the world prayer meeting. You who were filled with the fire of the Holy Spirit made the Korea revival. More than three thousand people were baptized by you and seventy thousand were converted by just you.[171]

And evangelist Ik-du Kim led many people to be converted through his evangelistic ministry. Ik-du Kim was born in November, 1874, in *Taiwon*, *Hwanghaedo* province. Before his Christian conversion, Kim was a notorious delinquent of the village. He became a reformed Christian in 1900 and was baptized in 1901 in a Presbyterian church, becoming the assisting minister in 1903. Upon his graduation from the Pyongyang Theological Seminary in 1910, he was ordained to ministry at *Shinchon* church in *Hwanghae* province for 20 years and then ministered to the congregation of *Seundong* church in Seoul in 1920.

Although he is less academic, Kim's sermons reached the common strata and his biblical proficiency caught the audience up in an emotional experience. While leading the congregation of *Shinchon* church, Kim continued to motivate the revival movement throughout the country, helping to bring about a remarkable conversion of the people into the Christian churches in Korea. A great number of the multitudes of people in his audiences were both mentally and physically diseased because Kim was widely known to heal and cure. L. S. Kim described his ministry of signs and wonders as follows:

> When he led the revival conference at *Daegu* in April 1920, eight hundred and eight people were converted and one paralytic, Yu-kyuk Chang, was healed. When he prayed laying his hand on a lame man, Du-dyu Kim, in the revival conference, the lame leaped up, stood, and walked in May 1920.[172]

The revivalists led the mass revival meetings throughout the country and brought the great church growth. The mass revival meetings have usually been held for the purpose of evangelizing the whole nation. This kind of revival meeting occurred during the first period of mission until 1910. After the annexation of Korea by Japan, Korean churches decided to evangelize one million. At the time of liberation in 1945 Chi-sun Kim proposed a "Three Million Evangelization Movement" to aspire for national evangelization. At that time, the total Christian community numbered about 400,000.

Table 5.6: Statistics of Denominations in Korea (1980)

	Denominations		Churches	Ministers	Members	Rate
1	Presbyterian	(29)	12,270	17,613	3,999,137	55.7%
2	Methodist	(4)	2,793	3,461	819,725	11.4%
3	Holiness	(3)	1,303	1,713	452,618	6.3%
4	Pentecostal	(7)	961	1,585	440,557	6.1%
5	Baptist	(4)	965	1,189	306,984	4.3%
6	Salvation	(1)	173	393	88,222	1.2%
7	Adventist	(2)	654	255	68,222	1.0%
8	Nazarene	(1)	148	156	75,191	1.0%
9	Christian	(3)	209	269	37,388	0.5%
10	Episcopal	(1)	66	81	45,284	0.6%
	The other	(12)	1,701	5,025	847,319	11.8%
Total		(67)	21,243	31,740	7,180,627	100%

(Sources: Ministry of Culture & Information, *The Present State of Religious Organization in Korea,* 1980; The Christian Academy, *The Phenomenon and Structure of Holy Spirit Movement in Korea*, 1982, p. 229)

In the early 1960's, the General Assembly of the Presbyterian Church made a resolution to plant a new church in every county, the second smallest administrative unit of the government. Through this effort, the Christian people caught a vision for the evangelization of the whole country. It was the first nation-wide undertaking by the Korean church. In 1965 Kyung-chik Han and Helen Kim developed a Korean Evangelization movement with the catch phrase, "Thirty Million to Christ."[173] From the start of that day, the revival meetings spread through out the whole church in Korea. Several nationwide mass evangelistic crusades culminating in the *Yoido* Mass Meetings have helped to boost the evangelistic zeal of Christians and to show the power of the gospel to non-Christians. These crusades seem to be producing unprecedented numbers of converts and a boom in the Christian population. A climatic display of Christian strength in Korea was evidenced in the outpouring of support for the Billy Graham Crusade in the summer of 1973. More than 4.5 million people attended the meetings in six cities, and on the last alone, in Seoul, more than a million Koreans packed the *Yoido* Plaza.[174]

The '80 World Evangelization Crusade was the most recent cooperative mass evangelistic revival meeting. From August 12-15, the '80 World Evangelization Crusade coordinated four days of seminars, rallies, and prayer meetings. For four hours each day, twelve major seminars and fifty area church conferences were held across Seoul. Approximately 60,000 people attended the fifty church conferences. Each evening, over two million people gathered on the *Yoido* plaza for rallies where internationally-known leaders spoke. The goal of two million people attending was reached by assigning one million Christians to bring one million non-Christians. Also, each evening 1,500,000 Christians remained all night on *Yoido* plaza to pray for national reconciliation.[175] The statistics for people participating in '80 WEC - "Here's Life, Korea" were as follows: [176]

Yoido Rally	10,500,000
All Night of Prayer Meeting	5,200,000
Morning Sessions	250,000
50 Church Conference	240,000
12 Major Conference	160,000
Total	**16,350,000**
* Number of Converts	1,000,000
* Missionary Pledge	1,000,000

The results of the Expo '74 and the '80 World Evangelization Crusade have been unprecedented. No one denies the impact of the mass revival meeting; these were having an influence in many areas of society and the church as a whole. The church had grown. The statistics show that mass evangelism has contributed to the increase in church members in Korea. In March 1979, there were 2,050 churches in Seoul. As of August 1981, the Korean Christian Press and government agencies, such as the Ministry of Culture and Information, have published that 4,700 churches in Seoul have been located. This indicates that the number of churches has doubled during these two years.[177] It was reported that one year after "Expo '74," the Mass Evangelistic Meeting held in *Yoido* in July 1975, there was a 33 percent increase in church attendance and a 64 percent increase in church offerings in the various city churches of Korea.[178]

From 1945, World War II, to 1973, the average annual church

growth rate was 6 to 12 percent. But, between 1974 and 1975, there was a 33 percent increase. One year after the '80 World Evangelization Crusade, a similar church growth rate was shown. Many factors contributed to this rapid church growth. However, mass evangelism was clearly one of the keys.[179] For example, when we compare the membership increase of the four major religions for 1977-1981, based on the Ministry of Culture and Information, the peak years of the Evangelization Crusades, we find that the Protestants increased by 19.96 percent, Catholics by 11.06 percent, Confucians by 5.22 percent and Buddhist declined by 7.93 percent.[180] The mass evangelistic revival meeting provided a tremendous spiritual openness across the country. According to the latest statistics, Modern Society Research Institute's report, over 82 percent of Korean Christians have experienced "the baptism of the Holy Spirit."[181] Some leaders of the Korean national mass evangelistic Meetings had developed the criteria characteristic of a mass revival movement as follows:[182]

1. Evangelization. Every Korean must have the opportunity to hear and respond to the message of Christ and the Holy Spirit.

2. Discipleship training. Every Christian must become an effective witness. And in order for him to become an effective oral witness, he must be trained in how to do personal evangelism.

3. Maximize Christian participation and influence. The full participation of educated or uneducated people, rich or poor, workers or farmers, soldiers or students.

4. A combination of evangelism plus national consciousness. A positive form for a spiritual nationalism.

5. A sense of the Kingdom of God. Jesus Christ is Lord of all.

6. Social salvation and reconciliation. Evangelism is the most effective way to bring about social reform because a spiritual group dynamic will change the whole social structure.

7. A sense of eschatological crisis. The hour is urgent; Christ is coming again soon.

8. A unique opportunity and openness. God has uniquely opened our hearts to His message.

9. All Christian resources organized in order to generate energy and power.

Under the above characteristics of the Pentecostal revival movement and spiritual explosion, several strategies have been implemented and major thrusts have occurred in recent years. These all have served as stepping stones to the overall goal of total evangelization of the nation. However, it must be remembered that an individual church revival conference which has been held in spring and autumn, two times a year,

since the Great Revival in 1907 also contributed to the church growth
in Korea. Today the revival conference is usually held for one week in
spring or fall in order to awaken the church's members to do the work
of evangelism. During the conference, church members study the
Bible, pray and have fellowship for their spiritual awakening.

There are biblical and historical precedents for mass evangelism.
Scripture recognized mass evangelism as one of the basic methods for
reaching people with the gospel. Nearly 150 times in the New
Testament we read that the Jesus spoke to "multitude."[183] Jesus often
addressed himself to the city as a whole in his declaration. The apostle
Paul practiced the evangelization of the masses. He usually went after
of all to the marketplace where the masses gathered (Acts 19:28). In
the history of the expansion of Christianity many mass evangelistic
gathering have been held in various countries.

Mass Media Communication

Evangelistic mass communication has played an important role in
presenting the Gospel to the Korean people. It is obvious that mass
communications have contributed to church growth in Korea. [184] Jay-
kwon Kim, president of Word of Life Press in Seoul, illustrates this
efficient use of mass media by the churches and different institutions
and organizations, mentioning the work of Bible Society, the
Christian Broadcasting System, the Far East Broadcasting System
and the Far East Broadcasting Company. Further he mentions the
several Christian newspapers and magazines. From the 1950s, modern mass communications were introduced to Korea, such as radio,
film and television.

> The twentieth century is characterized by rapid communication, mass pro-
> duction, and population explosion. If any business wants to be successful
> in this day and age, it must utilize mass media well. And the same is true
> of successful church growth. For example, the Korean church has utilized
> the mass media efficiently for its growth.[185]

The first Christian programs to be broadcast over government radio
stations were limited to Christian music. After many difficulties the
government granted a permit for a private Christian radio station.
Finally on December 15, 1954, the Christian Broadcasting System
went on the air with 5,000 watts of power and the call letters of
HLKY.[186] The establishment of the Christian Broadcasting Station
(CBS), was very timely and appropriate because it helped meet the

spiritual needs of people who were unmercifully attacked by the Communist invasion. In 1959, four branch stations in *Daegu, Pusan, Kwang-Ju,* and *Iri* were set up so that HLKY reached a potential listening audience of fifteen to twenty million people.[187] A second radio station, the Far East Broadcasting System (FEBS), with the call letters of HLKX[188] and a 50,000 watt transmitter, was established by the Evangelical Alliance Mission. They aired their first message in December 1956. The purpose of this studio is to broadcast the gospel message. Many sermons by local pastors are aired daily to strengthen the believers and to help win new believers. The follow-up department by correspondence and telephone conversations is making every effort to help the new believers grow spiritually. A third radio station, the Far East Broadcasting Company (FEBC) with call letters HLZA[189] and 250,000 watts of power was established in June 1963. Like FEBS, the main purpose of FEBC is to broadcast the gospel in Korea and further into the interior of China and Russia.[190] From 1956, the government television station and two commercial stations had given some free time for Christian programs. During the past 20 years, some hundreds of Christian programs utilizing films, dramas, choirs, puppet stories and panel discussions were broadcasting over these stations to bring about better understanding of Christianity.

In 1983, the *Korea Times* reported the election of Rev. Han Kyungchik as director of the newly organized Korea Video Evangelization Society.[191] The purpose of this society is to do evangelism in hotels, hospitals and military installations by use of video tapes of sermons by noted pastors. Mass media found very fertile soil in Korea with its closely knit, basically animistic society, which had one standard language which was easy to learn to read. Therefore, mass media in a modernizing society is playing the role in making the church and its mission known to people in Korea through channels of television and radio stations.

Army Christianization Movement for Church Growth

One surprising fact in church growth in Korea is the high percentage of Christians in the Armed Forces. The Korean military has chaplain corps organized by the order of the first Christian president, Syngman Rhee, on February 7, 1951.[192] During the Korean War, many chaplains worked among the soldiers in the army of the Republic of Korea. The work among the prisoners of war was very successful. "Some of the statistics given out by Chaplain Voelkel in June 1953, are as follows: Total number of believers, 14,458, baptism, 3,384, catechumens, 4,047."[193] It was reported that 299 chaplains had been serving military mission in 1955.[194] The strong evangelistic movement began to arise in the field after 1970. There is an account as to how this military evangelism first began.

> Some years ago there was a regiment in charge of the Demilitarized Zone area. This regiment, constantly plagued by accidents, was called the "accident regiment." The commander performed all kinds of superstitious religious rites and rituals, offering pigs and oxen to appease the spirits, but things got worse. The commander was replaced but the situation never changed. Finally a Christian colonel was appointed commander. Upon arrival he had all commanding officers under him worship God, pray, and preach and listen to the Word of God. He did likewise for all the soldiers. Then accidents began to decrease and the regiment was renamed the "Joshua Regiment."[195]

Han Sin, the supreme commander, a Buddhist, desperately looked for ideological and spiritual armament as a fighting force against the Communists. He began a campaign called "Religionization Movement of the Korean Army." All soldiers were advised to adopt any one of the these religions: Buddhism, Catholicism or Protestantism. Colonel Junsup Han, chief of the Republic's Chaplaincy corps, spearheaded the Army Christianization Movement in 1969. The chaplains visited every unit of the army, presenting the gospel and evangelizing soldiers.

The movement began to bear fruit from November 1971, and during the next five months to March 1972, 3,965 soldiers were baptized in the several divisions of the Korean Army.[196] On the 25th of April 1972, an epochal baptism occurred on the drill grounds of the Army near the western front lines. Eighty-eight officers and 3,390 soldiers were baptized, a total of 3,478 men. This mammoth baptism was the result of the all Army Christianization Movement.[197] In September and October 1972, a total of 6,700 were baptized in mass baptism ceremonies. Nearly 150,000 soldiers reportedly became Christians during the two years 1972-1973.[198] It was reported that 525 chaplains were in the military mission in 1982[199] and that in early 1983, 60 percent of the commanding officers and soldiers of the Korean Army were Christians.[200] During the 13-year period from 1971 to 1983, 349,041 soldiers and officers became Christians and were baptized.[201] According to Han Kyung-chik, in 1984 forty-five percent of the soldiers were Christian believers. It had been reported that at least 50 percent of the entire army was Christian and 8,460 members in the

Officers Christian Union in the armed forces.[202] Allen D. Clark says of military evangelism:

> This work [military evangelism], if effectively done, could have a tremendous influence on the civilian population as the men went back into civilian life, after their time in the army.[203]

Today about six hundred thousand young men and women in Korea serve in the military. Every year 200,000 young men are discharged form the army. When they return to their homes, 50 percent of them have joined their home churches. Five thousand local church pastors have been commissioned by the Army to preach to the 2,700,000 man Army reserves once a week.[204] Through this All Army Christianization Movement, every soldier is exposed to and urged to hear the gospel at government expenses. According to an official report in 1991, 200,000 young men are drafted and 70 percent of the officers claim to be Christians. There are 50 military chapels and each Saturday between 2,000 and 3,000 soldiers receive baptism.[205]

It is very interesting to note that the first Gentile convert to Christianity was a Roman centurion. Cornelius and his company were won not only by earlier preparatory work through contacts with the faith of Israel through the synagogue but also by the military evangelism done by Peter after the divine visions had been seen. As he and his household and friends listened to Peter's preaching, they believed and received the Holy Spirit, whereupon they were baptized at Peter's command (cf. Acts 10:1-11:18). He seems to have made his house a sort of church, for his relatives and friends were in sympathy with him, and among the soldiers who closely attended him were some devout admission into the Christian church is told in some detail in Acts 10. Nothing further is known of Cornelius, though one tradition asserts that he founded the church in Caesarea, and another legend is that he became the bishop of Samandoros.[206] As in the time of the conversion of Cornelius so too in Korea today there is the encouraging evidence of a spiritual awakening in the military.

CONCLUSION

Protestant missions, with one hundred and ten years of history in Korea, have been most successful in gathering converts into the church and bringing about impressive church growth. Many factors have contributed to the success of the Christian enterprise in Korea. There is no simple answer to the question why the penetration of the gospel was so swift in the Korean church. The first Protestant missionaries began their work as they built modern institutions of education and medical care. Medical work and medical education have been an important tradition of the missionary effort in Korea ever since. The earliest missionary activity was not limited to the care of the sick. They taught not only Christian doctrine, but also knowledge of the world. They translated portions of the Bible, published Christian tracts and taught students the Korean language. The Protestant missionaries respected and used the vulgar script, the language of the common people. They opened the doors of their schools to everyone in a society where education was limited to the privileged. Christian education was open to the oppressed, the deprived, and it was the nurturing ground of nationalism, political resistance, and democracy.

Within twenty years of the arrival of the first resident Protestant missionary, early stirrings of a great revival began to sweep through the staid Presbyterian and Methodist beginnings of missionary effort. From the beginning of the foreign missionary work Nevius methods and policies contributed to the fast growth of Korean churches. These early Nevius missionary methods were evangelical, non-colonial and firmly disciplined. They expected Korean church structures, as they were organized, to be generally self-supporting, and they quickly turned over ecclesiastical authority from the missions to the self-governing national churches. Therefore, it must be noted that this rapid penetration of the gospel in Korea by the early church is to be attributed to the policies and methods of missionary work.

The author has also attempted to show in this chapter that one of the primary human factors influencing church growth was the evangelistic work of native Korean Christians. The credit must be given to the character of Korean Christians, who enthusiastically witnessed to their new faith. The secret of the outflowing vitality and church growth is the personal evangelistic zeal of the Korean Christians. From the beginning of the early church, personal evangelism was not left to professional evangelists and pastors. The urgent speaking of one layman to another struck a responsive note and sparked the turning of great numbers of Korean people to Christ. This word of mouth testimony together with a changed life experience quickly paved the way for the preaching of the foreign missionaries and native evangelists. Even after these first beginnings, the church grew because of the witness activity of Korean Christians. Campbell in *Christ of the Korean Heart* puts it similarly by saying:

> The millions that have come to the Savior and received him into their hearts have not been won by foreign missionaries, only a few of them. Nearly all have heard the good news from the lips of their own countrymen. The story goes from mouth to ear and from heart to heart.[207]

The strength of the Korean church lies in the local church. The local church, under the spiritual leadership of its pastor has organized various activites for its members for worship, fellowship, instruction in the Word, evangelism and missions outreach. The role of a pastor for his congregation is crucial for the growth of the church. In fact, may Christians believe that the most important factor church growht primarily depends on the leadership of its pastor. He trains lay leaders for weekly district Bible study groups and organizes other church activities. Twice a year he organizes a house visitation program to visit the homes of his members and conducts family worship services there.

Church growth was the result not only of organized evangelistic activity of the church and its educational work, but also due to the simple, earnest witness of the Korean Christians as they went about their daily tasks. In the Korean church Christianity was never presented merely as a system of beliefs to be accepted. It was a way of life to be followed. No mere acceptance of a creed or nominal allegiance has ever been sufficient for membership in Korean churches. In the presentation of the gospel of Christ, various ways of communicating the message were carried out by Korean churches according to their social and political situation at a given time. There are probably more models and methods of evangelism contributing to the rise and growth of the Korean church and its strength today than those described in this chapter.

From a different aspect, theological education has also helped the growth of the Korean church. Korea is the country where there is mass production of full time Christian workers. The abundant supply of pastors from theological seminares and fervent dedication of pastors for their congregations have resulted in much fruit. Until 1934 there were only two theological training centers established by Korean Protestants, one Presbyterian and one Methodist.[208] By 1983, however, there were about 80 theological seminaries in Korea. According to *Chosun Ilbo* the number of theological department graduates reached about 10,000 by 1985.[209] Korea has 270 theological colleges and seminares, six of which have more than 1,500 students each. The smallest among the institutions had a minimum of 100 students. The largest boasts a student body of 2,000.[210] David Cho, Executive Secretary of Korea Foreign Missions Association, says in his national report on Korea in 1982, "The Growth of Korean Missions and its Contribution to World Evangelization," as follows:

> In reality the 60,000 or more students in these seminaries are potential fire seeds for the evangelization of Korea. The bulk of 10,000 graduates produced annually from these schools are either planting their new churches or are sent to churches without a leader. Also they have to be sent to the 2,000 new churches being born each year and to the 1,000 or so churches that might see alteration in leadership, not to mention service in the military, in schools, police stations, prison, and in industries.[211]

Pansik Hong, a professor of theology at the Koryo Theological Seminary, asserts that were 6,000 in 1986. Kotokkyo Yunhap Sinmun suggests that there were 15,000 of the by February 1989.[212] The surplus of theological graduates contributed tremendously to the growth of Korean church.

Born in an atmosphere of lay witnessing, national evangelistic work, small group Bible study and fellowship, family evangelism, mass revival meetings, army Christanization, and mass production of full-time Christian workers, the Korean church is thriving and growing remarkably. The Korean Christians are volunteering themselves for evangelistic work and missionary work to extend the Kingdom of God. They believe that God in turn blesses and makes their churches grow. In conclusion, the Spirit of God has used these situational factors combined with the tireless efforts of missionaries and the spiritual fervency of many national Christians. One of the early pioneer missionaries, Underwood, says, "We found that God by his spirit had been at work throughout the length and breadth of this land before we preached here."[213] He was right in this remark. Therefore, working through all human sociopolitical, cultural, and religious factors, the Spirit has brought church growth for His glory.

More than half a century ago Moffett gave an answer upon which few answers have improved. He said, "For years we have simply held before these people the word of God, and the Holy Spirit has done the rest."[214]

NOTES

[1]C. Darby Fulton, *Star in the East* (Richmond, VA: Presbyterian Church Committee of Publication, 1938), p. 174.

[2]*Ibid.*

[3]Horace G. Underwood, *Tragedy and Faith in Korea* (New York, NY: Friendship Press, 1951), p. 23.

[4]Samuel H. Moffett, "Nevius: Starting on the Right Foot," Harold B. Smith and Myung-hyuk Kim, "Will Success Spoil the South Korean Church," *Christianity Today*, Nov. 20, 1987, p. 34; Rak J. Paik, *Hankuk Gaeshinkyosa* [*History of the Protestant Church in Korea*], p. 307.

[5]Charles A. Clark, *The Nevius Plan for Mission Work*, p. 6.

[6]Kenneth S. Latourette, *Christianity in a Revolutionary Age*, Vol. III: *The Nineteenth Century Outside Europe* (New York, NY: Harper and Brothers Publishing Co., 1961), p. 448.

[7]Stephen Neill, *A History of Christian Missions* (Harmondsworth, Middlesex: Penguin Books Ltd., 1964), p. 344.

[8]Sherwood Eddy, *The New Era in Asia* (New York, NY: Missionary Education Movement of the United States and Canada, 1913), p. 69.

[9]David J. Cho, "The Growth of Korean Missions and its Contribution to World Evangelization," Bong-Rin Ro and Marlin L. Nelson, eds., *Korean Church Growth Explosion* (Seoul, Korea: Word of Life Press, 1983), p. 107.

[10]John L. Nevius, *Planting and Development of Missionary Churches* (New York, NY: The Presbyterian and Reformed Publishing Company, 1899). p.88.

[11]*Ibid.*, pp. 16-35.

[12]Clark, *The Korean Church and the Nevius Methods*, pp. 75-82.

[13]Clark, *The Nevius Plan for Mission Work in Korea*, p. 95.

[14]Alfred W. Wasson, *Church Growth in Korea* (New York, NY: International Missionary Council, 1934), p. 29.

[15]Everett N. Hunt, Jr., *Protestant Pioneers in Korea* (Maryknoll, NY: Orbis Books, 1980), p. 77.

[16]Horace G. Underwood, "Korean Missionaries Incoming and Outgoing," *Letters of the Presbyterian Church in the United States of America* (Philadelphia: The Presbyterian Historical Society, 1912 [February 8, 1888]), p. 128.

[17]Shearer, *op.cit.*, p. 185.

[18]Chun, *Schism and Unity in the Protestant Churches of Korea*, p. 71.

[19]*Yangban* was the dominant social class that directed the government, economy and culture of *Yi* dynasty society. *Yangban* married only among themselves and so of course *Yangban* status became hereditary. See Ki-baik Kim, *A New History of Korea*, pp. 172-175.

[20]Chun, *Schism and Unity in the Protestant Churches in Korea*, pp. 95-96.

[21]Underwood, *Call of Korea*, pp. 112-123.

[22]Clark, *Nevius Plan and Mission Work*, p. 171.

[23]Harold S. Hong, Won Y. Ji and Chung C. Kind, eds., *Korea Struggles for Christ* (Seoul, Korea: Christian Literature Society, 1966), p. 78.

[24]Clark, *The Korean Church and the Nevius Methods*, p. 144.

[25]Quarter Centennial Report, *Presbyterian North Mission*, p. 18ff. in: Clark, *The Korean Church and Nevius Methods*, p. 110.

[26]*Ibid.,* p. 20.

[27]Samuel A. Moffett, "Evangelistic Work," in: *Quarto Centennial Papers read before the Korea Mission of the Presbyterian Church in the U.S.A.* at the annual meeting in *Pyongyang,* August 27, 1909, p. 17. in: Clark, *The Korean Church and the Nevius Methods*, p. 107.

[28]Clark, *The Korean Church and the Nevius Methods*, p. 108.

[29]T. Stanley Soltau, *Korea: the Hermit Nation and its Response to Christianity* (New York, NY: World Dominion Press, 1932), p. 24.

[30]Clark, *The Korean Church and the Nevius Methods*, p. 13.

[31]W.D. Reynolds, "The Native Ministry" *The Korean Repository*, Vol.III (May, 1896), pp. 200-201.

[32]See Sung C. Chun, *Schism and Unity in the Protestant Churches of Korea*, pp. 75-96.

[33]Moffett, *Christians of Korea*, p. 62.

[34]*Ibid.*, p. 3.

[35]Paik, *History of Protestant Missions in Korea*, 1832-1910, p. 413.

[36]Neill, *History of Christian Missions*, p. 344.

[37]Shearer, *op.cit.*, pp. 165-166.

[38]Kim, "Six New Churches Everyday," Ro and Nelson, eds., *Korean Church Growth Explosion*, pp. 7-10.

[39]Robert H. Glover, *Progress of Worldwide Missions* (New York, NY: Harper and Row Publication House, 1964), pp. 199-200.

[40]Moffett, *Christians of Korea*, p. 28.

[41]Mahn-yol Yi, *Hankuk Kitokkyo Munwha Undongsa* [*The Cultural History of Christian Movement in Korea* (Seoul, Korea: The Christian Literature Society Press, 1987), p. 23.

[42]Sang-yun Suh and Hong-joon Baik, Eung-chan Yi, translators, were converted by Ross and McIntyre in Manchuria. See J. Ross, "Corean Version of the New Testament: How I Come to Make It." *United Presbyterian Magazine*, May, 1, 1883, pp. 206-208; *Annual Report of the Board of Foreign Mission of the Presbyterian Church U.S.A.* (New York: 1890), p. 134; J. Ross, "Manchuria Mission," *United Presbyterian Missionary Report*, Oct. 1. 1880, pp. 333-334.

[43]See Jay-kwon Kim, "The Impact of Mass Communications," Ro and Nelson, eds., *Korean Church Growth Explosion*, p. 139.

[44]Rodes, *History of the Korean Mission*, p. 90.

[45]Mahn-yol Yi, *Hankuk Kitokkyo Munwha Undongsa* [*The Cultural History of Christian Movement in Korea*], pp. 132-133; *Historical Catalogue of the Printed Editions of the Scriptures in the Library of the British and Foreign Society*, edited by T. H. Darlow and H. F. Houle. P.886, in: Sung C. Chun, *Schism and Unity in the Protestant Churches of Korea*, p. 40.

[46]As of November 30, 1886, the Scriptures distributed were as follows: 1884-7,588, 1885-3,907, 1886-4,197. *Annual Report of the British and Foreign Bible Society for 1887*, p. 272. in: Mahn-Yol Yi, *The Cultural History of Christian Movement in Korea*. p. 136.

[47]Underwood, *The Call of Korea*, p. 131.

[48]Davis, *Korea for Christ*, p. 54.

[49]G. W. Knox, "Affairs in Corea," *The Foreign Missionary* (June, 1883), p. 17.

[50]H. Loomis, "The First Korean Protestant in Japan," *The Korea Mission Field* (July, 1937), pp. 139-141.

[51]Davis, *op.cit.*, p. 54.

[52]Underwood, *The Call of Korea*, p. 107.

[53]W. D. Reynolds, "Fifty Years of Bible Translation and Revision," *The Korea Mission Field*, Vol. 35, No. 6 (Jun., 1936), p. 172; The American Bible Society, *Annual Report*, 1900, p. 142.

[54]W. D. Reynolds, "The Board of Bible Translators," *The Korea Mission Field*, Vol. 2, No. 6 (April., 1906), p. 101.

[55]Mahn-yol Yi, *The Cultural History of the Christian Movement in Korea*, p. 141.

[56]Davis, *op.cit.*, p. 54.

[57]Jay-kwon Kim, "The Impact of Mass Communications," Ro and Nelson, eds. *Korean Church Growth Explosion*, p. 143.

[58]Davis, *op.cit*, p. 55.

[59]L. H. Underwood, *Underwood of Korea* (New York, NY: Fleming H. Revell Co., 1918), p. 46.

[60]Chang-shik Lee, *Taehan Kitokkyo Seahoe Paikyeunsa* [*The Centennial History of the Christian Literature Society of Korea*] (Seoul, Korea: The Christian Literature Society Press, 1984), p. 18; The founding missionaries are Appenzeller, Underwood, Gale, Hulbert, Reynolds, Gifford, Jones, Baird, Moffett, Bunkers, Fenwick, Vinton, Gerald Bonwick, "The Birth of the Korean Religious Tract Society," *The Korea Mission Field*, Vol. 10. No. 1 (Jan. 1914).

[61]*The Korean Repository*. Jan. June. Sept. Dec. 1896; Mar. 1898.

[62]The following figures from the 1930 Report indicate the extent of the

year's work: Copies published-1,392,973;Pages published-33,938,544; Copies distributed-1,532,481; New Titles and Reprints-88. See T. Stanley Soltau, *Korea: The Hermit Nation and Its Response to Christianity*, p. 62.

[63]The Christian Literature Society of Korea, *Annual Report*, 1931, p. 9.

[64]Mahn-yol Yi, *The Cultural History of Christian Movement in Korea*, pp.306-308.

[65]The Christian Literature Society of Korea, *Annual Reports*, 1931. pp. 6-7.

[66]Paik, *The History of the Protestant Church in Korea*, pp. 134-136.

[67]Today there is a high rate of literacy, 92 percent, in Korea.

[68]Cf., Chung Han Chung, *Ewha Palshimyeunsa* [*History of Ewha 80 Years*] (Seoul, Korea: Ewha Women's University Press, 1967).

[69]*The Gospel in All Lands*; 1888, p. 374.

[70]Mahn-yol Yi, *The Christian Cultural Movement in Korea,* pp. 202-204.

[71]Kyung-bae Min, *Hankuk Kitokkyohoesa* [*Korean Christian Church History*], p. 238.

[72]Taikpoo, Chun, *Hankuk Kcyohoe Baljunsa* [*The History of Church Development in Korea*], pp. 190, 259, 283.

[73]Hyo-jae Lee, "*Hankuk Kyohoe Yeasung Baikyeunsa*" [The One Hundred Year History of Christian Women in Korea] *Yeasung Kaelzeiada* [*Women Be Awakened*], (Seoul, Korea: Korean Christian Publishing Co., 1985), pp. 23-26.

[74]Clark, *History of the Korean Church*, p. 112.

[75]Yun-ok Lee, "The Role of Women in Korean Church," Ro and Nelson, eds. *Korean Church Growth Explosion*, p. 231.

[76]Kwang-sun Suh, *Hankuk Kitokkyo-eui Sae Euishik* [*A New Understanding of Christianity in Korea*] (Seoul, Korea: The Christian Literature Society of Korea, 1985), pp. 63-65.

[77]Clark, *The Korean Church and the Nevius Methods*, pp. 284.

[78]A. J. Brown, *Report of a Visitation to the Korean Mission of the Presbyterian Board of Foreign Missions*, p. 393.

[79]*Ibid.,* p. 234.

[80]Man-kyu Lee, *The History of Korean Education*, pp. 22-24.

[81]Cf. J. Verkuyl, *Contemporary Missiology,* trans. & edited by Dale Cooper, (Grand Rapids, MI: 1978), pp. 212-218; Harold R. Cook, *Highlight of Christian Missions* (Chicago, IL: Moody Press, 1967): pp. 71, 145, 199-200, 219.

[82]Cf. H. N. Allen, and J. W. Heron, "First Annual Report of the Korean Government Hospital, Seoul," *Journal of Social Science and Humanities*, December, 42 (Seoul, Korea: The Korean Research Center, 1975), pp. 105-129.

[83]*Annual Report of Missionary Society of the Methodist Episcopal Church,*

1886, p. 268; W.B. Scranton, 'Historical Sketch of Korea Mission of the Methodist Episcopal Church, *The Korean Repository*, July, 1898, p. 258.

[84]*The Annual Report of the Missionary Society of Methodist Episcopal Church,* 1888, pp. 340-341.

[85]Hyu-seung Park, *"Hankuk Kitokkyo Euiryo Eundongsa"* [*History of Christian Medical Work in Korea*], Young-je Han, ed. *Hankuk Kitokkyo Sungjang Baikyeon* [*The Church Growth of One Hundred Year in Korea*] (Seoul, Korea: The Christian Literature Society, 1986), pp. 101-102.

[86]O.R. Avision, Review of Medical Mission Work in Korea, *The Christian Mission Movement in Japan, Korea and Formosa*, 1914, p. 488. Cf. R.F.M.E., 1892, p. 283, 1902, p. 317. See Standing Rules and By-Laws of the Korea Mission of the Presbyterian Church in the U.S.A., Adopted as Working Basis for One Year, October 1st, 1904, *Minutes of Korea Mission*, Presbyterian Church U.S.A., 1904, p. 92.

[87]Paik, *op.cit.*, p. 125.

[88]D. L. Gifford, *Letter to the Board of Foreign Missions of the Presbyterian Church, U.S.A.* Seoul, Korea: June 17, 1891.

[89]Standing Rules and By-Laws of the Korea Mission of the Presbyterian Church in the U.S.A., adopted as Working Basis for One Year, October 1st, 1904. *Minutes of Korea Mission*, Presbyterian Church U.S.A., 1904, p. 92.

[90]R. T. Coit, "What is the Good of a Hospital in Korea?," *Presbyterian Survey* 38 (August 1926), pp. 485-486.

[91]Shearer, *op.cit.,* p. 205.

[92]Moffett, *The Christians of Korea*, pp. 167-168.

[93]Heong-yeul Yoo, *Hankuk Chunju Kyohoesa* II [*History of Catholic Church in Korea*] (Seoul, Korea: Sejong Daewang Kiyeum Sajubhoe, 1976), p. 289.

[94]*The Report of the British and Foreign Bible Society*, 1886, p. 148; 1891, p. 136.

[95]Cf. Mahn-yol Yi, *Hankuk Kitokyo Munwha Undongsa* [*The Cultural History of Christian Movements in Korea*], pp. 278-281.

[96]Rhodes, Harry A. and A. Campell, *History of the Korea Mission Presbyterian Church in the U.S.A. 1935-1959*, Vo.II, pp. 320-344.

[97]Kwang-soo Kim, *Hankuk Kitokkyo Jaekunsa* [*A History of the Reconstruction of Christianity in Korea*] (Seoul, Korea: Hankuk Kyohoesa Yunku, 1981), p. 187.

[98]Clark, *History of the Korean Church*, p. 251.

[99]Cf. Moffett, *The Christian of Korea*, pp. 15-30.

[100]Blair and Hunt, *Korea Pentecost: The Sufferings Which Followed*, pp. 39-41.

[101]T. Stanly Soltau, *Korea The Hermit Nation and Its Response to Christianity* (London, New York, Toronto: World Dominion Press, 1932), pp. 37-38.

[102]Fenwick, *The Church of Christ in Corea,* pp. 191.

[103]Soltau, *op.cit.*, p. 37.

[104]J. S. Gale. *Korea in Transition* (New York, NY: Young People's Mission Movement, 1909), p. 192.

[105]*op.cit.*, p. 191.

[106]*Ibid.,* pp. 195-196.

[107]*Ibid*, p. 144.

[108]Yun-ok Lee, "Presbyterian Women's History," Ro and Nelson, eds., *Korean Church Growth Explosion,* p. 235.

[109]J. Ross, "A Bright Light in Northern Korea," *Foreign Missionary* (Sept. 1886), pp. 151-152.

[110] Literally means, *"chundo"*-evangelism, " *puin"* -married lady."

[111]Marthy Huntley, *To Start a Work. The Foundations of Protestant Mission in Korea (1884-1919)* (Seoul, Korea: 1987), p. 423.

[112] "Native Bible Women," *The Korea Mission*, Vol. VII. No. 5 (June, 1910), p. 119ff.

[113]*Minutes of the Annual Meetings of the Korea Mission of the Methodist Episcopal Church 1901*, p. 21.

[114]*Ibid.,* p. 48.

[115]Anonymous, "The Million Movement and Its Results," *Korea Mission Field* 7 (January 1911), p. 5.

[116]George T. B. Davis, *Korea For Christ* (London, UK: Christian Workers' Depot, 22. Paternoster Row E.C. 1910), p. 10.

[117]Soltau, *op.cit.*, p. 39.

[118]George R. Paik, *The History of Protestant Missions*, p. 286.

[119]Sweazey, *Effective Evangelism*, p. 89.

[120]*Soonan*, a mining town, is located in the Northeast of *Pyungan* province.

[121]A. D. Clark, *Digest of the Presbyterian Church of Korea (Chosen),* pp. 31, 108-109.

[122]Underwood, *Call of Korea*, p. 173.

[123]Quelport is an old name for present *Cheju* island; *Ibid*, pp. 173-174.

[124]A. D. Clark, *A History of the Church in Korea*, p. 174.

[125]Min, *Hankuk Kitokyyohoesa [History of Christian Church in Korea]*, p. 268.

[126]A. D. Clark, *Digest of the Presbyterian Church of Korea (Chosen)*, pp. 109-113.

[127]Won Y. Koh, "The Missionary Vision of the Korean Church," *Church Growth Bulletin* 8 (March, 1972).

[128]Tai-hyung Min, *Korean Statistical Yearbook 1978* (Seoul, Korea: National Statistical Office of Republic of Korea, 1978), p. 39.

[129]Joon G. Kim, "Six New Churches Every Day," Ro and Nelson, eds., *Korean Church Growth Explosion*, p. 10.

[130]Lawrence E. Keyes, *The Last Age of Mission* (Pasadena, CA: William Carey Library, 1983), p. 105.

[131]G. Sweeting, "Land of the Morning Calm," *Moody Monthly*, 84 (September, 1983), p. 91.

[132]Sung-whan Kim, "*Hankuk Kyohoe-eui Sunkyo Hyunhwang-kwa keu Daechak*" [A Survey of Missionary Work in Korean Church and Recommendation], *Chong Shin Daewonbo* [*General Assembly Theological College Newpaper*], September 25, 1990.

[133]Ron and Nelson, eds., *Korean Church Growth Explosion*, rev, 1995, p. 33.

[134]Cf. Cho, ed. "Growth of Korean Missions and Its Contribution to World Evangelization," *The Third Force* (Seoul, Korea: East-West Center for Missions Research & Development, 1986), pp. 120-122.

[135]*The Christian Journal* Vol. No.17. May 8. 1994; Jong-koo Park, *Segui Sunkyo, Ke Dojun kwa Gal Deung* [*An Analytical Study of Contemporary Movement of the World Mission of the Korean Church and a Projection to AD 2000*](Seoul, Korea: Shin-Mang-Ai Press, 1994), p. 19.

[136]A. J. Brown, *The Mastery of the Far East*, (New York, NY: Scribners, 1919), p. 540, in: Harvie M. Conn, "Studies in the Theology of the Korean Presbyterian Church (Part I)" *The Westminster Theological Journal*, Vol. XXIX, No.1 (Nov. 1966), p. 26.

[137]Yang-Sun Kim, *The Ten Year History of the Korean Church After Liberation* (Seoul, Korea: Korean Presbyterian General Assembly Educational Department, 1956), p. 173.; Gal. 1:9.

[138]Chai-choon Kim, "The Present Situation and Future Prospect of the Korean Church" Harold S. Hong, Won-yong Ji, and Chung-choon Kim, eds. *Korea Struggles_for Christ* (Seoul, Korea: Christian Literature Society of Korea, 1966), pp. 27-28.

[139]Shearer, *op.cit,* pp. 196-197.

[140]Byung-suh Kim, ed. *An Empirical Study of Korean Church Growth and Faith* (Seoul, Korea: Institute of Modern Society, 1982), p. 90.

[141]Harvie M. Conn, "The Exploding Korean Church," *Moody Monthly* 74 (June, 1974), p. 24.

[142]William J. Danker, *The Worlds Or None* (St. Louis, MO: Concordia Publishing House, 1964), p. 264.

[143]"Local Churches Win University Students," *Asian Theological News* 8 (Jan-March 1982), p. 16.

[144]J. G. Kim, "How to Spark a Spiritual Explosion," *Asian Theological News* 9 (April-June, 1983); p. 17.

[145]David Cho, ed., *The Third Force*, p. 167.

[146]George E. Sweazey, "Evangelization Among Secondary School Students," J.D. Douglas, ed., *Let the Earth Hear His Voice* (Minneapolis, MN: Worldwide Publication, 1975), p. 759.

[147]Wesleyan Class Meeting is originated from the Wesleyan Revival Movement in 18th century in England by a group of four students meeting together at Oxford University.

[148]Michael Green, *Evangelism in the Early Church* (Grand Rapids, MI: William B. Eerdmans Publishing Co., 1970), pp. 107-108.

[149]Nelson, "Foreigner's View of the Korean Church," Ro and Nelson, eds. *op.cit.*, p. 192.

[150]Cho and Hurston, "Ministry through Home Cell Unit," Ro and Nelson, *op.cit.,* p. 282.

[151]Elmer Town, "The Biggest Little Church in the World," *Church Growth Bulletin,* Vol. XIII, No.1, 1976, p. 83.

[152]Bong-rin Ro, "The Korean Church: God's Chosen People for Evangelism," Ro and Nelson, eds., *Korean Church Growth Explosion*, rev, 1995, p. 32.

[153]J. G. Kim, *Asian Perspective* 17 (n.d.), p. 3.

[154]John N. Vaughan, *The Large Church* (Grand Rapids, MI: Baker Book House, 1985), pp. 105-106.

[155]Sam-hwan Kim and Yoon-su Kim, "Church Growth Through Early Dawn Prayer Meetings," Ro and Nelson, eds. *Korean Church Growth Explosion*, rev, 1995, pp. 96-110.

[156]R. Recker, "What Are People Movements?," Harvie M. Conn, ed., *Theological Perspective on Church Growth* (Nutley, NJ: Presbyterian and Reformed Publishing Co., 1976), pp. 76-77.

[157]George R. Paik, *History of Protestant Missions in Korea*, p. 284.

[158]H. E. Blair, "Fifty Years of Development of the Korean Church," *Jubilee Paper* 16. 1934, p. 84.

[159]C. F. Bernheisel, *Letter to the Christian Endeavors of Chicago Presbytery* December 19, 1901.

[160]Jonathan Goforth, *When the Spirit's Fire Swept Korea* (Grand Rapids, MI: Zondervan Publishing House, 1942), p. 30.

[161]Shearer, *op.cit.*, pp. 147-149.

[162] *Ibid.*, p. 219.

[163]K. Syuk Kim, *Korean Research Report of Korean Mission One Hundred Years* (Seoul, Korea: Christian Institute for the Study of Justice and Development, 1982), p. 40.

[164]Harry Boer, *Pentecost and Mission* (Grand Rapids, MI: William B. Eerdman Publishing Co., 1961), pp. 165-185.

[165]D. A. McGavran, *The Bridge of God: A Study in the Strategy of Mission* (New York, NY: Friendship Press, 1955), p. 71.

[166]George E. Sweazey, *Effective Evangelism* (New York: Harper and Row Publishers, 1953), p. 89.

[167]Michael Green, *Evangelism in the Early Church* (Grand Rapids, William B. Eerdmans Publishing Co., 1970), pp, 107-108.

[168]Brown, *Mission to Korea*, p. 79.

[169]Cf. Min, *Hankuk Kitokyohoesa* [*History of Christian Church in Korea*] , pp. 350-356.

[170]Jin-kyung, Kil, *Yunge, Kil Sun-zu* [*Spiritual Valley, Kil Sun-zu*] (Seoul, Korea: Jong-ro Seajek, 1980), p. 326.

[171]L. S. Kim, *Korean Church Martyrs and Their Sermons* (Seoul, Korea: Kimunsa, 1968), p. 213.

[172]Yung-hun, Lee, *Hankuk Kitokkyosa* [*The History of the Korean Church*] (Seoul, Korea: Concordia Press, 1978), p. 122.

[173]Whal-Ran Kim, "*Junkuk Bokeumwha Undong-eui Meridol-eul Noeumyu,*" [Putting a Corner Stone of National Evangelization Movement], *Junkuk Bokeumwha Undong Bogosea* [*Report of National Evangelization Movement*] (Seoul, Korea: National Evangelization Movement Central Committee, 1965), p. 3-5.

[174]Kane, *Concise History of the Christian World Mission*, p. 135.

[175]Yung-jae Kim, *Hankuk Kyohoesa* [*A History of the Korean Church*] (Seoul, Korea: The Korea Society for Reformed Faith and Action, 1992), p. 326.

[176]Edythe Draper, ed. *The Almanac of the Christian World* (Wheaton, IL: Tyndale House Publishers, 1992), p. 367.

[177]Cf. *Munwha Gongbopu, Hankuk Jongkyo Pyunlam* [*A Handbook of Religions in Korea*] (Seoul, Korea: Munwhoa Gongbobu Press, 1982).

[178]Joon G. Kim, "Six New Churches Everyday: Korean Church Growth," *Asian Perspective* 19 (n.d.), p. 5.

[179]David Cho, ed. *The Third Force*, pp. 168-169.; Joon G. Kim, "How to Spark a Spiritual Explosion," *Asian Theological News*, 7 (April-June, 1983): p. 17.

[180]Cf. *Dong-A Nyungam* [*The Almanac of the Year*] (Seoul, Korea: Tong-A Publishing Co., 1983), p. 638.

[181]Joong-ki Kim, Chin-hong Chung, Hak-sup Chung, eds. *Hankuk Kyohoe Sungjang-kwa Teuksung-ei kwanhan Yunku* [*A Study on the Korean Church Growth and Its Characteristics*] (Seoul, Korea: Hyundae Sawhee Yunguso, 1982), pp. 77-86.

[182]Ro and Nelson, *op.cit.,* pp. 22-23.

[183]Matt. 9:35-38; Luke 4:14-22; Matt. 5:1.

[184]Jay-kwon Kim, "The Impact of Mass Communications," Ro and Nelson, eds. *op.cit.,* p. 136.

[185]*Ibid.*

[186]HLKY is the international radio call letters for the Christian Broadcasting Station, Seoul in Korea.

[187]An-jun Kwak, *Hankuk Kyohoesa* [*History of Korean Church*] (Seoul, Korea: The Christian Literature Society, 1973), pp. 334-337.

[188]HLKX is the international radio call letters for the Far East Broadcasting System, Seoul in Korea.

[189]HLZA is the international radio call letters for the Far East Broadcasting Company, Seoul in Korea.

[190]Taikpoo Chun, *Hankuk Kyohoe Baljunsa* [*The History of Church Development in Korea*], p. 319.

[191]*Hankuk Ilbo* [*Korean Daily News*], November 10, 1983.

[192]Chun, *Hankuk Kyohoe Baljunsa* [*The History of Church Development in Korea*], p. 318.

[193]Rodes and Campell, *op.cit.*, p. 199.

[194]Yang-sun Kim, *Hankuk Kitokkyo Haebag Shimyeunsa* [*History of Ten Years of Korean Church after Liberation*] (Seoul, Korea: Presbyterian Educational Department, 1956), p. 109.

[195]Joon G. Kim, "Six New Churches Everyday," Ro and Nelson, *op.cit.*, p. 4.

[196]Mass Baptismal Ceremony, *Hankuk Ilbo* [*Korea Daily News*], April 26, 1972.

[197]"Revival in Indochina: Action in the Far East," *Christianity Today* 16 (May, 1972), pp. 32-33.

[198]"Korea: GI and Jesus," *Christianity Today* 18 (November 9, 1973): p. 60.

[199]Kie-tae Kim, *Gun Sunkyo-eui Eron-kwa Siljae* [*The Theory and Practice of Amy Mission*] (Seoul, Korea: Voice Publishing Co., 1985), p. 289.

[200]Joon G. Kim, "How to Spark a Spiritual Explosion," *Asian Theological News* 9 (April-June, 1983), p. 17.

[201]Ki-tae Kim, *op.cit.*, p. 295.

[202]J. G. Kim, "The Impact of Evangelization on Korean Society," David Cho, ed. *The Third Force*, p. 168.

[203]Allen D. Clark, *History of the Korean Church*, p. 255.

[204]J. G. Kim, "The Impact of Evangelization on Korean Society," David Cho, ed. *The Third Force*, p. 168.

[205]*The Christian Times*, Feb. 1, 1992.

[206]Geoffrey W. Bromiley, *The International Standard Bible Encyclopedia*, Vol 1 (Grand Rapids: Williams B. Eerdmans Publishing Co., 1979), p. 783.

[207]Campbell, *Christ of the Korean Heart*, p. 12.

[208]Taekpoo Chun, *op.cit*, p. 238.

[209]Feb. 26, 1986.

[210]Cho,"The Growth of Korean Missions and Contribution to World Evangelization," Ro and Nelson, eds. *Korean Church Growth Explosion*, p. 115.

[211]David Cho, ed. *The Third Force: The Official Report of the Third Triennial Convention, Seoul, '82 of the Asia Missions Association* (East-West Center for Missions Research & Development, Seoul, Korea: 1986), p. 68.

[212]Feb. 26, 1991.

[213]Underwood, *Call of Korea*, p. 91.

[214]Samuel H. Moffett, "What Makes the Korean Church Grow?" *Christianity Today* 18 (November 23, 1973), p. 11.

Chapter Six

SHAMANISTIC-SYNCRETISTIC CHRISTIANITY AND CHURCH GROWTH IN KOREA

INTRODUCTION

Korean Christianity has followed a process of growth through coalescence of shamanistic faith and worship and through accretions of religious tenets and rites from primitive indigenous religions. Syncretistic tendencies between Christian belief and traditional shamanism were unavoidable. As mentioned in an earlier chapter, in shamanistic practice the role of shamans is prominent, for they tried to make the gods, demons and ancestral spirits responsive to the people's wishes. Shamanistic Christianity in Korea represents a type of syncretism of the idea of nature worship and Christian teachings. Most of the new Christian shamanistic movements are oriental mystic shamanistic religions because of the syncretistic nature of doctrine, which is a mixture of the *yin-yang* oriental world view and oriental shamanistic mysticism and the peculiar interpretation of the Scripture. In Korean philosophy, the metaphysical ultimate is the *Tao* [in Korean, *Do*]. When regarded as the source of the universe, it is called the Great Ultimate and moves from rest to activity and back to rest. Within the monistic framework of *Tao*, One Totality, there is a division of two opposite elements or principles, namely *Yin* and *Yang*, which may be translated as feminine and masculine, darkness and light, negative and positive, or passive and active principles. Even being and non-being, high and low may fit into this category of *yin-yang*.[1]

In this chapter, the author will discuss how Korean Christians are influenced by several elements of shamanistic faith and how these elements contribute to the numerical church growth. The author, thus, seeks explanations for the remarkable church growth in the specific shamanistic background of the Korean people and their society. Several major shamanistic Christian religious movements which evolved and influenced the Korean church in this century will be introduced historically for a better understanding of the background of Korean church growth. The development of a Christian shamanistic movement is the result of the mixture of Christianity and shamanism in Korea. Most of the new religions in Korea are influenced by shamanistic faith.[2]

SHAMANISTIC GOD AND *HANANIM* IN THE KOREAN CHURCH

The shamanistic Christian faith started right from the beginning with the coming of the gospel as brought by the Nestorians. Nestorian Christianity rendered a great modification to the Korean shamanistic conception of Heavenly God.[3] At the time Nestorianism was introduced to Korea there was a substantial exchange of culture and religion between the Chinese *Tang* dynasty and the Korean *Shilla* dynasty, and the *Shilla* dynasty enriched her civilization by importing and acculturating and later assimilating *Tang*'s culture and religions.[4] While in the process of this assimilation of *Tang*'s civilization into *Shilla*'s traditional cultural forms, there also began an effort in which the Nestorian conception of God became indigenized into the Korean traditional conception of *tengri* which means "heaven." Nam-sun Choi holds that the traditional Korean thought of God originated from "*tengri*," which is a Mongolian word meaning heaven. However, the problem is that when this Mongolian word was mixed and later syncretized with Chinese letters which would express the traditional thought of God in Korea, that mixture and syncretism gave rise to various conceptions of God in Korea. For that reason, *Tien* (heaven), and the Korean thought, *Park* (bright light), are very important factors in formulating the Korean concept of God.[5]

It is interesting to note that the *Tangun* Myth that is claimed to be an indigenized form of the Nestorian concept of God has a concept which is Trinitarian.

> It is further interesting to note that when missionaries translated the Christian scriptures into Korean, they chose the term *Hananim* to stand for God. The name *Hananim* is distinctive and very widely used. In a crucial decision this term was retained by the Protestants in Korea as the one best

suited to be the Christian word for God. As early as 1890 one Protestant pioneer wrote, "The name *Hananim* is so distinctive and so universally used that there will be no fear in the future translations and preachings."[6] From this point, Koreans were prepared to understand God in Christianity. Palmer writes, "They found that their inner thoughts were recorded in the Scriptures; their superstitions were like those in the days of Israel's decline; and their conclusions concerning life and the spiritual world were what the Bible concluded life to be."[7]

Hananim is the shamanist Heavenly Spirit. Jones, a pioneer missionary in Korea, in his study of the spirits, correctly does not deal with the concept of a high God, *Hananim*, the word for God now used by Christians. Jones does not make a mistake of some writers who were prone to read into Korean thought Christian views of God, such as "God is a Spirit," which were not present in pre-Christian Korean concepts of *Hananim*. The belief in *Hananim* was,

> ...far removed from crude nature-worship... The Koreans all consider this being to be the Supreme Ruler of the universe. He is entirely separated from and outside the circle of various spirits and demons that manifest all nature...The Koreans have never attempted to make any physical representation of *Hananim*. He has never been worshiped by the use of any idolatrous rites... As a rule the people do not worship *Hananim*. He is appealed to by the Emperor only...[8]

However, missionaries also confused worship by the Emperor at the Temple of Heaven in times of famine, drought, or other great calamity with the worship of *Hananim*. Hulbert says that because of this belief in *Hananim*,

> The Koreans are strictly monotheists, and the attributes and powers ascribed to this being are in such consonance with those of Jehovah that the foreign missionaries (Protestant) have almost universally accepted the term for use in teaching Christianity.[9]

However, for centuries Korea had been plowed by shamanistic efforts to communicate with higher beings, and when the seeds of Christianity were placed in this rich, plowed soil, they flourished and produced the fruit of Christian disciples. Populations where shamanistic faith flourished were prepared to believe in a higher being.[10] The value of using the term *Hananim* in the Christian church in Korea was greatly enhanced by the fact that this belief, while it was a belief in one god, was a belief in nothing else. Korean shamanistic faith gave the people an awareness of a higher being.[11] They were glad to find a high God of love to replace the gods of fear they had known.

SHAMANISTIC ANCESTOR WORSHIP IN THE KOREAN CHURCH

Since the early days of the Christian missions in Korea, ancestor worship has been the focus of many controversies. The Roman Catholic and Protestant Christians in Korea experienced persecution and martyrdom at the end of the 18th century and in the 19th century because of their opposition to ancestor worship.[12] The Roman Catholic Christianity in Korea met the first persecution at the hands of government because Yun Chi-Choong, a man of the noble class, refused to make ancestral tablets or to offer sacrifices to his ancestors when his mother died in the summer of 1791. He was charged with religious heresy, denying filial piety and abolishing sacrifices to ancestors and was beheaded with his nephew Kwon Sang Yun in December of 1791. It was reported that Yun Chi-choong said as follows:

> Since I accepted the Heavenly Lord to be my great parent, it would not be right and honoring not to follow the order of the Heavenly Lord. Since the religion of the Heavenly Lord prohibits making a wooden tablet, I buried it under the ground. I would rather do wrong to my deceased mother than to the Heavenly Lord.

The question of whether ancestor worship is purely a religious practice or simply a practice of honoring the ancestors as an extension of the filial piety expressed during life is a question that has bothered Christian missions for two centuries. To put it as a question: is ancestor worship conducted out of fear that the soul of the departed will work harm on the people if the worship is not conducted? And similarly: is this a worship of the soul of the departed in order to receive a blessing, or, on the other side, is this a simple ceremony of remembrance to the departed ancestor without any thought of the spirit of the departed person? Blair said that ancestor worship was the great cross of the Korean Church. He writes,

> Almost before they knew it there was a church in *Pyongyang*, a company of men and women professing the name of Jesus and assembling for worship on the Lord's Day. The magistrate heard of it. "Ah," he said, "You can't do that here. If you worship according to the foreigners' religion, how are you going to worship the spirits of your ancestors at New Year's time?" This is the great cross of the Korean church. Each New Year every son of Korea must bow before the tablets that represent to him the spirits of the dead ancestors. Not to bow down, not to offer the yearly sacrifice, is to be guilty.[13]

Westerners in Korea felt strongly that ancestor worship was a religious ceremony, that is, worship of the spirits. Clark concludes that "if it were not real worship, I doubt if it would have had the vitality that it has had as a religion."[14] Korean sources, on the other hand, do not ascribe ancestor worship as motivated by fear or as desire for blessing from the spirit of the departed alone. One informant stated that it is not commonly thought that there is any supernatural penalty connected with non-worship of ancestors. The demand for worship of ancestors seems to come from a social pressure regarding the respect one pays his parents. Because of the high virtue placed upon one honoring his father, a person not participating in this ancestor worship would be said to not know his parent, which in Korean society would be a grave insult if it were true.

A Korean scholar says that while there may be some fear for what the spirit will do if not worshiped properly, the main thrust of ancestor worship is love for the departed and the desire of the living to feel good about the departed person.[15] A missionary says that while some Koreans believe that the fate of the dead depends on the faithful ancestor worship,

> Some believe that the condition of the dead is permanently fixed by the sentence of the ten judges upon their arrival in the other world. Such would hold that whether a man worships his father or not, does not affect the happiness of either the father or the son. But it does affect the reputation and social standing of the son among his acquaintances, as being a man who shows respect or disrespect to the spirit of his father living in the ancestral tablet in his house.[16]

If we cannot eliminate entirely the possibility that there is fear or a religious motive involved in worship of the ancestor, at least we can say there is no formalized system of curses that will come upon a person if he does not worship his ancestors, or blessing that a person may acquire if he does participate in this worship. It is believed by both Christian and non-Christian that the present-day attitude toward ancestor worship is an extension of filial piety alone and the participants, for the most part, deny it is spirit worship. Gifford, quoted above, would support this view in nineteenth century Korea, showing the lack of spiritual meaning in ancestor worship in an early development. Moffet, a long time Presbyterian missionary to Korea, noted that some churches are trying to produce a form of memorial for the dead that would not be considered unorthodox.[17] The Korean Church in general went through much suffering, facing many forms of persecution, because of her strong opposition to Confucian ancestor worship, considering this practice as idol worship. The Korean church has had to show that men can honor parents without idolatry. Jones says,

> Some of the Christians under the propaganda of the Roman Catholic
> Church were executed for this offense, and the opening year of the nine-
> teenth century is marked by the promulgation of a law proclaiming death
> against all Christians because of their sacrilegious immorality in forsaking
> the worship of the dead.[18]

It is reported that the veneration-of-the-dead issue cannot be forever
swept under the rug. Ancestor worship has dominated all the cultural
influences which have been at work throughout the country of Korea.
It is by no means dead. A glance at the statistics on the family system
tells us that the number of those who keep their book of lineage are
63.9 percent of those surveyed. Those who insist on keeping the ancestor worship are 72.2 percent. 75 percent of these people are college
graduates or above.[19] One observer estimated that 80 percent of
Korea's Christian minority do conduct services for the dead covertly,
but that it is simply passed over in the churches. Even today some new
converts face the persistent problem of ancestor worship, for the
Confucian tradition dies hard even in a modernized age. Local pastors
often counsel new converts on the persistent problem of ancestor worship. In the Korean Protestant Churches, *Chudo Yebae*, a formal
memorial service for the deceased parents or other relatives, is usually
held in the home of the person requesting the service and is conducted
by the minister of the church. *Chudo Yebae*, a memorial service, is recognized by the major denominations in Korea and is included in their
authorized books of services. *Chudo Yebae* is offered on behalf of
deceased parents or other near relatives normally up to two or three
ascending generations.

All Protestant denominations now include in their books of service a formal order of the memorial service for the deceased parents.
The service is normally held in memory of a relative in the first two
generations above the person who made the request. In a room a low
table is laid out with various festive foods, fruits, biscuits and meats.
The family gathers around this table with the minister in the center
and the chief mourner opposite. A service of thanksgiving for the life
of the deceased is offered consisting of hymns, reading from
Scripture and a short sermon or talk by the minister. Afterward, the
family and minister eat a communal meal together. There was big
trouble at the largest church in Korea regarding this issue in 1982.
The pastor of this church, Rev. Cho Yonggi, preached on ancestor
worship, saying in his sermon, "honor thy father and thy mother." He

asserted that the command applied whether they are living or dead.[20] Cho further amplified his position by providing an illustration from the counsel he had given to a new convert. Cho preached the following words:

> Ancestor worship is nothing but honoring one's parents. I do not understand why people say it is an idol worship... Parents are parents whether they are alive or dead. Isn't it our custom to visit our living parents and prepare food for them?... It is quite natural that we think of our deceased parents on such days as their birth or death. It is quite all right to prepare food, think of our deceased parents as if they were present, erect a cross instead of ancestral tablet, and bow down... We honor our parents with bowing down. It is not a sin to bow down to deceased parents. It is not an idol... Our deceased parents have gone either to heaven or hell. Even though they have gone to hell, they are our parents. Having an affectionate remembrance of them is keeping God's commandment... Apostle Paul was a great man. To the Jews he became like a Jew to win Jews, to those under the law. To those outside the law he became as one outside the law that he might win those outside law... To perform an ancestral worship is really a good thing. In the past we performed sacrificial rites to God.[21]

This sermon gave rise to a heated discussion and met with nationwide criticism. A whole range of leading Korean pastors, including representatives of the historic Presbyterian and Methodist denominations, attacked this pastor's preaching as falling short of traditional orthodox Christian teaching in Korea. The *Christian Weekly Press*, Nov. 7, 1981, printed critical remarks from ten Christian leaders:

> What Christianity makes important is person. We believe in God as a person. Deceased parents are not persons...Bowing to impersonal beings is nonsense [Chin-kyung Chung]. Sacrificial rules are prescribed in the Scriptures. Ancestor worship is idol worship [Jong-yun Lee]. There have been two kinds of mission policy in Asia, accommodation and transformation. Whereas ancestor worship was tolerated in such countries as India, China and Japan, it was intolerable in Korea. The first mission policy in Korea was transforming old customs. It rejected wine, tobacco, opium, divination, and ancestor worship. Though ancestor worship is a traditional cultural rite, it includes idolatrous elements and cannot be tolerated [Myung-hyuk Kim]. Since the deceased ancestors cannot be the object of worship and since we are not allowed to idolize them, it is not right to bow down to the deceased ancestors [Kim Jong-dae]. Preparing food and bowing to the deceased parents even without making ancestral tablets is obviously idolatry. Jesus himself abolished the Jewish sacrificial system and instituted worship with prayers... Numerous men of faith have suffered because of this problem of ancestor worship. I would be a disgrace to them if we say that bowing without a tablet is not idolatry [Kyung -young Chun].[22]

Sun-whan Pyun, a Korean liberal theologian who is noted as a champion for his willingness to dialogue with other religions, expressed his affirmative view about ancestor worship in the *Dong-A Ilbo,* December 24, 1983, a widely circulated daily news. He said the following:

> Ancestor worship is a social product of a large family system. To express filial piety and perform sacrifices is following the heaven designated ethics. Ancestor worship is an expression of filial affection, not an idolatry.[23]

The Korean Roman Catholic Church takes a rather tolerant attitude toward traditional ancestral worship by allowing the following behavior: bowing before a corpse, a tomb or a picture of the deceased; burning incense in front of a corpse or during an ancestral worship ceremony; and preparing food offerings in memory of the deceased.[24] In a way, the traditional Roman Catholic teaching on purgatory justified Confucian ancestral worship since the Roman Catholic Church had taught its adherents to pray for the dead. The notion of purgatory and the notion of prayer for the dead go hand in hand; the "communion saints" unites the living with the dead in prayer.[25] Today the Roman Catholic Church allows that prayers may be offered for the dead during a funeral service as well as on the third, seventh and thirtieth days following death. The Roman Catholic Church established the date the All Souls Day, November 2, as a day of memorial to encourage Roman Catholics to visit ancestral graves.[26] Jin Hee Lee, Minister of Cultural Affairs and Information and spokesman for the Korean government, has also exhorted Christian leaders to take an affirmative attitude toward Korean culture. He proposed a "Koreanization of Christianity" in a public speech to a gathering of Christian leaders on December 16, 1983.

INFLUENCE OF SHAMANISTIC FAITH UPON KOREAN CHURCH

Shamanistic Faith in Material Blessings

In Korea when a family of the shamanistic faith opens a new business, the *Mudang* is invited for the rituals of material blessings because the ritual of blessing has the power for transforming evil fortunes into prosperity. The rituals are to be performed by the shaman annually at the beginning of the year for a flourishing business.[27] In the countryside, the shaman makes a visitation to each family in her territory at the beginning of the year and after the harvest to pray for the material blessing and peaceful life of the family. The believers, as a response, pay the shaman with money or grain.[28] Material blessing is one of the main goals of the shamanistic rituals. Both the Christians and the church in Korea adopted many elements from the shamanistic rituals, and those elements contributed to numerical church growth in Korea. It is not clear which rituals are meant here. Do you mean Christian rituals or do you mean shamanistic rituals. From the context, it could be eitherThe ceremonial services and special prayers for material blessings are believed to have influenced the idea of blessings among the Christians.[29] For instance, in the Korean church, there is an annual visitation program, which is called *dae shimbang*.[30] The pastors and elders of the churches make a visit to each of their parishioners to bring a blessing for the peaceful life and abundant life of the church members. It is also popular in the Christian Church of Korea for church members to invite their pastor to perform a special ceremonial service of blessing at the birth of children, on the birthdays of the adult members, on the day of opening business.

The former moderator of the General Assembly of the Presbyterian Church of Korea, Tack-jin Im, said, "The reason for the enormous church growth is social anxiety. The people want blessings; blessings are a part of the church, although they are not the only part."[31] From the sociological perspective Byung-suh Kim, a professor of sociology at *Ehwa* Women's University in Seoul, mentions the following influence of shamanism on numerical church growth in early 1980s.

> In the industrialized process encouraged by the New Village movement of the government, the Korean masses wanted to achieve a better life through whatever means was available to them: thus they came to the church as some clergymen stressed, and even promised, a better life here and now. This appeals strongly not only to the poor but also to the middle class who have strong sense of relative deprivation.[32]

In the time of rapid social change, the Korean people lost their basic securities in life, which made them long for other securities. According to some scholars, the Korean churches successfully took action in this situation of insecurity.

> It assumed that one of the main factors for church growth is the extreme anxiety created by rapid social change and the resultant instability. Those who come to the church to escape the worldly vortex of troubles and anxiety are often greeted by the refined drama of religious exorcism and soothing message that caresses the wounded and injured psyche. The masterful performance of "shamanistic" rituals for material growth [appears] in some of the abnormally-expanded mammoth churches in Korea.[33]

The desire for earthly blessings draws many people to churches where the sermon of material blessing is emphasized in preaching. For instance, Pastor Yonggi Cho of the Central Full Gospel Church on *Yoido* Island, stresses God's material blessings in the present life and brings about explosive church growth. The church slogan is from the second verse of the third epistle of John: "Beloved, I pray that in all respects you may prosper and be in good health, just as your soul prospers." That leads to the church's "triple-meter faith" in riches of the Spirit, of the body, and in possessions. Much of the praying focuses on daily problems, and daily problems invariably involve money.

The Central Full Gospel Church claims to be the largest congregation in the world. Its founder, Paul Younggi Cho, became a Christian in 1956 when, he says, he was healed of terminal tuberculosis through the visits and prayers of an itinerant Bible woman. After a period in the Assemblies of God Bible Institute in Seoul, he started leading open-air meetings and doing faith healing on his own. By 1961 he had a proper church building, and by 1968 the church had a congregation of five thousand. Growth has been exponential ever since, and when Korean Christians use the word "explosion" to describe their movement, it is Paul Cho's church that first comes to mind. [34]

Attendance at church and fervent prayer are believed to create a condition in which the person will be blessed. The desire for this state is a clear reflection of the shamanistic tradition of Korea. Somehow this preaching of prosperity fulfills the desire of the people in Korea and brings about numerical church growth.[35] The theology of blessings or the doctrine of prosperity[36] successfully attracts the blessings-oriented Korean people. This theology teaches that if the believer just prays incessantly and gives tithes faithfully and spends all his spare time in church, he can expect from God abundant material blessings as well as success in school or business. Most apparent is the excessive emphasis in sermons on the believers' earthly blessings.[37] This theology of blessing teaches that every believer can receive these material blessings as a reward of faith, prayer and sacrifices in the forms of offerings and services to the church. For the poor people, of course, this theology is very attractive. The middle class people, too, see in this theology a means to improve their wealth and status. Even the rich people are blessing-minded, for they see their wealth simply as a blessing from God. As an evangelistic policy, many pastors promise wealth, health, power and honor in their sermons in order to attract the shamanistically attuned Korean populace. According to many Korean theologians, the need of worldly blessings here-and-now or material blessings is cited more often than any other need. Jin-hong Jung, professor of religion at Seoul National University, describes a motion picture that was shown as a model of prayer in the chapel and related it to the issue of worldly personal blessings.

> It was true that they were praying according to their individual needs and thus, there was not collective prayer with the same subject of prayer. They gathered just within one place and at the same time.[38]

Still, shamanistic faith praying for earthly blessings and happiness is predominant among Christians in Korea. The prayer of shamanistic Christians is primarily a petition for worldly blessings, happiness, health, material success and a higher social status. Having faith in Yahweh God is interpreted not differently from believing in the traditional spirit-gods who bless the followers with material wealth and longevity. The issue of material blessings has become a great concern to Korean Christians who speak of *kibok sinang* (belief in prayers for blessings) as being the principle spiritual problem facing their church.

Shamanistic Faith Healing and Exorcism

In the shamanism of Korea, diseases are believed to be caused by evil spirits.[39] Bu-yong Lee also sees the greed of *wonkwi*, the evil spirits, as the cause of diseases in the shamanistic tradition.[40] He writes, "Korean Shamanistic faith, especially in healing of the body, is flowering under the banner of Christianity."[41] The therapeutic emphasis of the rituals in the Korean church is deeply related to the traditional concept of diseases in Korean shamanism. The general concept of diseases as understood among Korean Christians is not so different from this traditional concept. According to Kwang-Iel Kim's field research, most of the charismatic leaders of the Korean church assert that diseases are caused by evil spirits.[42]

According to a survey published in the *Hankuk Daily Newspaper* on March 10, 1983, a majority of Korea's Protestant pastors still follow a shamanistic attitude towards mental illness. A paper presented by two Seoul National University medical college professors, Sohn Chin-uk and Lee Bu-Yong, of its Medical College, emphasizes that Protestant ministers in Korea believe that mental illness is "the work of devils" (80.6 percent), whereas Korea's Catholic priests recommend a psychiatrist or doctor. Mental illness within one's own family was to be treated by "faith healing" among 65 percent of the Protestant pastors. As for those who become mentally disturbed after a revival meeting or prayer session on a mountain top, 84.6 percent of the Protestants regarded those people as "possessed by the devil."

Thus the shamanistic attitude that the mentally ill are possessed by evil spirits seems to have passed over into Korea's Protestant Christian movement. Presently only a third of the Protestant pastors support psychotherapy or medical therapy for mental illness, but two-thirds of the Catholic priests endorse this more modern method.[43] The Protestants explain that faith healing is more effective than other means; perhaps this reflects both the congregation's and the pastor's belief. It would seem that the Seoul National University's Medical College professors are trying to point out how pervasive is the influence of shamanism in medicine, even today.[44] Jin-hong Chung also reports that about thirty percent of those who attend the Sunday worship service held in *Yoido* Full Gospel Church are people who want to be cured of their illnesses by having the evil spirits that possess them driven out.[45]

In fact, Korean Christians call diseases *byungma*, the demon of illness. Sickness is viewed as a state of possession by the evil spirits. Therefore, illness is identified with a demon or evil spirits. Because of this, they ask God to defeat the power of the demon of illness at the worship service.[46] The rituals of exorcism are performed as an important part of the Sunday service in many charismatic churches. Special occasions, such as revival meetings and house visits by such people as the *yojundosa*, the Bible woman, or *unsaja*, the specially gifted person of spiritual power, are used for exorcism.[47] It is interesting to note that early Korean church history tells us that the Bible women had been playing a role in healing and exorcism. A Korean missionary, Scranton, writes about the ministry of a Bible woman:

> These women are highly respected and are believed to have the ability to offer up prevailing prayer. If anyone is in trouble of any sort, in mind, body, or estate, the Bible woman is sent for to pray and sing Psalms. When anyone gets tired of trying to propitiate the evil spirit, it is the Bible women who must come and take down the fetishes and burn them. They are called upon to cast out devils, as well as to offer the fervent effectual prayer for the healing of the sick. Their faith is often greater than that of their teachers, and the all-loving and compassionate Father rewards them accordingly.[48]

This description of the ministry of a Bible woman shows remarkable similarities with that of a Korean shamanist sorceress, i.e. a Korean shaman. Another article in the Korean Mission Field explicitly points at the Bible woman's ministry as a substitute for the shaman's practice:

A large number of women have been persuaded by Sarah (a Bible woman) to destroy the various things in their house connected with devil worship, and it is now an established custom to send for the Bible woman to pray with and for them when they are sick instead of sending for the *Mudang*.[49]

It is obvious that the missionary ministry of the Bible women went beyond efforts toward conversion and personal salvation, or the establishing of churches, although these notions were certainly indispensable for their missionary consciousness. The inclusion of teaching, healing, and prevailing intercessory prayer in their ministry pointed toward a holistic concept of salvation. This holistic mission approach absorbed and provided a substitute for the function of the *mudang*, who was the central cultic official in the shamanist tradition. The ministry of faith healing and exorcism has been very effective in bringing about the numerical church growth in many charismatic churches in Korea.

Shamanistic Ecstasy and Mystical Experience

In the Korean Christian Church the experience of ecstasy and becoming one with God stands out as the characteristic feature of charismatic movements. At the revival meetings the charismatic leaders emphasize their subjective mystic experiences as the means of control and authority over the believers. The believers also seek spiritual experiences, such as visions, psychic observation, trance, etc.[50] As was found in the shaman tradition, many charismatic Christians consider this ecstatic experience that they seek a mysterious "union with God."[51] In the testimonies of Christians' experience with the Holy Spirit, not a few similar examples are found in shamanistic experience; so that it is reported that it is impossible to differentiate between them.[52]

As a recent phenomenon, mystical experience became a characteristic of the Christian life in the Korean Church. Priests of Korean shamanism get excited by the mystical power of spirits in the midst of their cults, and they show a supernatural ecstasy. It is not different in the charismatic revival meetings in the Korean Church. Songs of fast tempo are popular, particularly with hand clapping, and traditional drums and gongs are used by the leaders to intensify the spiritual experience of participants.

It is popular now in many denominational churches of Korea to employ similar techniques of traditional rituals as a result of the synthesis of the two faiths. In the charismatic Church, prayer with fasting, speaking in tongues, and visible signs of the second birth are excessively stressed. As a result, many Christians who do not have the gift of tongues or an ecstatic experience of the second birth fall into doubt and end up in mental clinics. The majority of the Korean churches, mostly Presbyterian, Methodist, Korean Evangelical, and Roman Catholic, remain rather sound, but very few remain totally unaffected by this shamanistic mysticism. In recent years, it was reported that thirty-two out of sixty Methodist pastors had chosen the ministry as their profession on the basis of their "charismatic experiences in which they heard the call from the Lord."[53] This accounts for 53.3 percent, which is a very high rate compared to other variables, such as "family influence" (18.3%), "advice by relatives" (10.0%), and "advice by pastors" (5.0%).[54] Most revivalists of the Korean church today claim their mysterious experiences and the accompanying spiritual power as the basis of their charismatic leadership. The believers accept their claim and leadership positively with the same mind-set.[55]

Shamanistic Initiation Illness and Spiritual Power

As discussed earlier, the experience of illness is an indispensable condition in the *Mudang*'s initiation. Tae-gon Kim pointed out that a future shaman undergoes a "terrible mental and physical illness with great pain"[56] until this person accepts the will of the possessing spirit and becomes a shaman. The experiences of the initiation illness turn out to be the motif of the ecstasy and source of the spiritual power. Mircea Eliade also pointed out the same phenomenon of initiation illness in Siberian shamanism. He said that the shaman acquires the "technique of ecstasy"[57] through the experience of initiation illness. The problem of the initiation illness seems to be parallel with the experience of the incurable diseases many of the Christian pastors of the Korean church confess to have had. It is considered a necessary condition to have this experience of disease to become a spiritually powerful leader. On the grounds of their experiences of recovery, they become famous healers in the Korean church.

From the early period of the Christian mission, many of the church leaders claimed charismatic leadership on the grounds of divine revelations they insisted they had received during their prayers in the mountains. Pastor Sun-ju Kil, who was the center figure of the early revival meetings, heard the "heavenly voice calling him on the third night of his prayer"[58] before he became the major leader of the early charismatic revival meetings. Even before he was converted into the

Christian faith, this ecstatic experience was not unfamiliar to him. It was reported that Kil had experienced "spirit possession in *Daesung* Mountain while he was chanting a spell."[59] Pastor Ik-du Kim, who led the first revival movement of the Korean church in 1907, had an experience of repentance in a mountain near his house.[60] It was not much different with Pastor Yong-do Lee, another great charismatic leader in 1930s. From the age of thirteen, he dedicated himself to "overnight prayer" and made it a lasting habit. While he was praying and fasting, it was reported, he saw "mysterious visions" through which he convinced himself that it was the call of the Lord. This became the motif of his charismatic leadership in the revival meetings.[61]

Most recently this phenomenon of illness and the commitment to the ministry of healing is commonly found among several pastors of huge congregations. Pastor Yonggi Cho of the *Yoido* Full Gospel Church wrote about his experience of the "incurable state of tuberculosis"[62] before he was converted to the Christian faith. By accepting Christ as the Lord, he was able to recover from the disease, and eventually his ministry was recognized by believers as the "powerful healing of diseases" and the intercession for "material blessing in this world."[63] Pastor Chang-in Kim of *Choonghyun* Presbyterian Church, and pastor Kyung-chik Han of the *Youngnak* Presbyterian Church, and many other pastors of large congregations are well known for their struggles with serious diseases before they came to the peak of their ministry. It is not to be denied that these experiences bear similarity to the initiation illness of the *mudang* in its external form. Moreover, the positive response by the Christian to this kind of leadership is not much different from that of shaman followers who "identify the spiritual power with shaman's initiation illness experience."[64]

Throughout the years, this pattern of charismatic leadership, by means of mysterious divine messages, has remained as a particular type of church leadership in Korea. Tong-Shik Ryu tries to see this phenomenon of divine message and charismatic leadership in relationship to traditional Shamanism.[65] Divine message or revelation should not be denied in the Christian Church as a part of biblical tradition. Yet, it is also an appropriate assertion that the charismatic leadership by means of divine messages in the Korean church is almost identical in its external form to that of this traditional religion. As was pointed out previously, the spiritual experience of the shaman and *gongsu* [the divine message] which build the charismatic leadership of the *mudang* and the initiation illness of the shaman can be easily compared to the diseases that were cured through ecstatic spiritual experiences and became the motif of the Christian ministry of many pastors today in Korea.

Shamanistic Prayer Service on the Mountain

One of the features of the contemporary Korean Protestant church is the prevalence of the mountain *kidowon* [a hall of prayer]. In recent years, there has been a tendency for *kidowons* in a mountain to become centers for faith healing. The purpose and importance of these mountain *kidowons* derives from the curative traditions of Korean shamanistic faith. Korean Christians go up to the mountain *kidowon* to pray. According to Jung, "a lot of people are actually confessing that they cannot maintain their life without going up to the mountain regularly."[66] Other theologians ask why Korean Christians like to go to the mountain to pray and conclude that the mountain location itself attaches a special significance to prayer.[67] The Korean church commonly practices early morning prayer meetings, all-night prayer meetings and fasting and praying for several days at a time at a prayer mountain. Every deep mountain valley has prayer houses where some men and women pray and fast for as many as forty days at one time.

In Korean shamanism, mountains have been considered to be as the place of divine revelation. As we see in the Korean myths, the mountain was the sacred place where the heavenly figures descended. It is the place of separation from secular life and the sacred space where rituals are to be performed.[68] Prayer at the prayer mountains, in their meanings and forms, could be strongly related to the tradition of the shamanistic rituals.[69] Many Korean Christians go to the mountain *kidowon* in hopes of receiving the Holy Spirit with mystical experience. These people who believe that prayer at the *kidowon* demands certain mannerisms and motions totally misunderstand the work of the Holy Spirit in Christian prayer. They may confuse emotional catharsis with the genuine work of the Holy Spirit. Psychological catharses, which are gained artificially, cannot reach deeply into one's spirit and thus offer only temporary benefits. Prayer must be repeated immediately and automatically in order to give a sustained feeling of well-being. Han Wan-sang criticizes this prayer mentality in the Korean church. "Korean Christians believe that the prayer ritual on the mountain itself can provide better opportunities to have divine experiences than praying in the church."[70] Thus, when they are present at the prayer services on the mountain, the atmosphere is usually more serious than in ordinary cases. Because of the fervent prayer life of Christians, several characteristics are evident in the Korean church. Korean Christianity emphasizes the experiential more than the intellectual side of faith. The real presence of God is experienced in prayer. Often the Korean church is accused of being influenced by its shamanistic cultural background. The zeal, dedication and enthusiasm of Korean Christians are very similar to extreme shamanistic practices.

However, local churches often criticize the prayer mountain experiences because of the shamanistic connection. Sometimes churches feel that they must protect themselves from the influence of a mountain prayer center. Local pastors recognize the existence of the *kidowons*, and some of them visit the mountain *kidowons*. They themselves are not influenced by negative factors of expecting material blessings as a natural outcome of faith when they go up to the mountain centers to pray. They are, however, concerned about the people in their congregations who, they feel, do not have the maturity to resist the shamanistic influences connected with prayer in the *kidowons*. Most Korean Christians have tried to understand the *kidowon* phenomenon by considering only the negative aspects and automatically attributing shamanistic influences to it. However, the numerical church growth in Korea has been strongly related to the development of faith-healing ministry on the mountain. The *kidowons* on the mountain are often used for faith-healing services. Large churches have their own *kidowons* on the mountain near the town or city. There are also independent *kidowons* which specialize in curative practices. Some of these are so large that they maintain pastors who specialize in particular diseases. According to Jin-hong Chung's study, fourteen percent of all visitors to the *Osanri kidowon* operated by the *Yoido* Full Gospel Church are the mentally or physically sick who seek a miraculous victory over the demons of illness.[71] This following sentence is not clear in meaning. Therefore, praying on the mountain with its shamanistic aspects and the attraction of it to people, has been one important element which has made the Korean people fertile soil for the seed of the Gospel.

SHAMANISTIC NEW CHRISTIAN RELIGIOUS MOVEMENTS

The development of New Christian Religious Movements in the modern century may be divided into three stages. The first stage would be the initial phase, beginning with the *Tonghak* Movement and encompassing the groups which grew out of or which were influenced by it. The second stage would be the emergence of syncretic religions during the Japanese period, while the third stage would be the development of those groups which trace their origin to, or which achieved their greatest success after, the Korean War. As we have discussed the phenomenon of *Tonghak* Movement earlier, we shall not say anything further about it here. The second stage is very interesting, as many of these religions came to establish themselves in or around *Kyeryongsan* mountain. This place is associated with a prophecy that a new dynastic capital would be build on this spot after the fall of the *Chosen* dynasty. The development of the New Christian Religious Movements in this stage must be seen against the background of the Japanese colonization of Korea and the expectations for national liberation. The third stage in the development of the New Christian Religious Movements began with the period following liberation from Japan up to the conclusion of the Korean War. This development is one measure of the importance of Christianity in modern Korean culture. In this section only some major New Christian Religious Movements originated from within will be traced to present what these particular movements believe and how they are related with shamanistic faith.

The Great Meditation Truth Movement

In the period of social upheaval in 1901, a new religious movement called *Taesun Jilrihoe*, which came to be known by various names including *Humchigyo, Chunsankyo* and *Pochunkyo,* was founded by Ilsun Kang (1871-1909).[72] In 1900, when he was 29, Kang, or *Chungsan* as he came to be known, entered into a nine-day period of intense meditation at *Taewonsa* temple near *Chungju.* He had a vision in which he was visited by five dragons who gave him the power to rid the world of the Four Evils, avarice, lust, anger, and stupidity. Kang also came to realize that he had the power to communicate with the spirit world, that he could predict the future, and that he had the power to understand the *Chunjiundo,* the divine plan of the movements of the universe. Following his experience at *Taewonsa* in 1900, Kang began to propagate his doctrines and to perform various 'miracles' which established his reputation as a sorcerer of great power. In 1902, he declared that he was the 'Lord of the Nine Heavens' who had descended to earth to order the public affairs of mankind. With the hopes that had been raised by the *Tonghaks* and through belief in the occult book of prophecy, the *chunggamrok*, many people came to feel that *Chungsan* might become a national savior and gathered around him.

According to legend, *Chunggamrok* is one of a number of books of prophecy handed down from ancient times. It combines prophecy and geomancy to speak specifically and apocalyptically about the southern part of Korea. *Chunggamrok* has received widespread popular attention and will likely continue in a position of significance on the Korean religious scene. Geomancy has thrived since the latter *Shilla* period (A.D. 503-935), and prophecy came into vogue in the *Yi* dynasty (A.D. 1392-1897). The *Chunggamrok*, published early in the *Yi* Period, contains a conversation between *Chunggamrok* and *Yi-son*, as well as more than 50 secrets, some credited to Priest *Toson* and *Muhak*. It is a hard book to understand. The main theme running through the *Chunggamrok* faith is *Chinin* [True Man], a new capital, good places, and South Korea. To explain it briefly, the faith in the True Man is the expectation of a new Messianic King like the Young Lord *Chung*, while the faith in a new capital is a hope for the emergence of a new dynasty to be founded in a new capital after the old dynasty perishes according to the dictate of Heaven. The faith in good places is intended to indicate havens that assure absolute safety in time of war. The faith in South Korea is grounded on the hope that a dreamlike paradise will be established in the southern part of Korea. Some Christians can easily identify with the *Chunggamrok* faith in the True Man, who, like Jesus Christ, is anxiously being awaited as a new messianic being.[73]

Twenty four persons came to be recognized as his principal disciples. After his death on 24 June 1909, various of his followers created movements which traced their origins to him and to his prophecies. In 1930 *Chunsankyo*, which was later renamed *Pochunkyo*, had a total of 557,700 followers, and its missionary organizations reached 260, 260.[74] To maintain such a large religious cult, some understanding had to be reached with the colonial authorities, so *Pochunkyo* created a pro-Japanese organization, *Taedonggyo*, and even sent goodwill missions to Japan. The influence of *Pochunkyo* declined with the death of its current leader, Kyungsok Cha, in 1936.

It is difficult to find any systematic thinking in Ilsun Kang's pronouncements, nor is there a definitive statement of his doctrines or beliefs. There are, however, some basic concepts which may be extracted from his statements. Kang's doctrines are of a highly polytheistic, shamanistic type. He believed that there were three eras, the past, the future, and the present era, in which the other two eras meet. Destiny is determined by the spirit world, especially by the Lord of Heaven who works in concert with mankind. Kang or *Chungsan* saw himself as the incarnation of the Lord of Heaven, also known as the Lord of the Nine Heavens, who had come to earth to reorder the public affairs of men. The incarnated Lord had three goals on earth: 1) to save mankind from the anxieties, troubles, and diseases of this life, 2) to re-establish the sovereignty of the Korean state, and 3) to redeem the people by purifying the religions of man of their endemic evils. *Chungsan* himself used and taught his disciples to use various incantations and talismans to cure the diseases of the people and help them achieve their wishes. In some cases amulets were carried with the believer for protection, and in order cases talismans were burned and the ashes eaten in order to cure or prevent disease.

The *Chungsan* tradition is essentially a shamanistic system. *Chungsan*'s birth is surrounded by various auspicious portents; *Chungsan*'s wife is seized by a spirit who speaks through her body; *Chungsan* claims both to cure disease and to be able to order the affairs of this world and of the spiritual universe; incantations and talismans are used.[75] Thus, while many of the elements of his doctrines reflect shamanistic or Taoist influences, *Chungsan*'s basic proclamation about himself is a reflection of an essential Christian doctrine, the incarnation of God Almighty. Christian belief concerns the incarnation of a monotheistic God, while *Chungsan*'s Lord of the Nine Heavens is the supreme ruler of a polytheistic universe. *Chungsan* claimed to be able to save people both physically and spiritually, while also being able to create a new world order. It was reported that there were over 36 places of worship and 1,193,632 members by the end of 1993.[76]

Church of the Heavenly God

Church of the Heavenly God, *Chongdokyo,* concentrates on the healing ministry and the proclamation of the second coming of Jesus Christ on Mt. *Kyeryong.* The land of Korea, particularly Mt. *Kyeryong,* is the center of God's theodicy, and the Koreans are called by God to be the chosen people for the salvation of the world. The nations of the world, therefore, should be united as one kingdom centering around Mt. *Kyeryong* for the construction of the kingdom of God.[77] Visions and the divine messages of the founder also played an important role in the establishment of this movement.[78] *Chongdokyo* was founded by Soon-wha Lee, a Christian woman, in 1917. Lee accepted the Christian faith at the age of forty for the purpose of ending a series of disasters in her family through her belief in God whom the Christians worship. After the Japanese invasion in 1911, she and her husband moved to *Bonchun*, Manchuria, and started this sectarian movement. According to Byung-duk Ryu, Lee received the gift of healing while she was praying in March, 1917, in Manchuria. She also received a divine message in which the name of *Chongdokyo* was given to her. She began to heal many people in Manchuria and spread *Chongdokyo* around *Bongchun* city. In 1925, Lee again received another divine message that asked her to move to Mt. *Kyeryong*, where the headquarters of *Chongdokyo* was located.[79] Soon-hwa Lee concentrated her ministry on healing. She cured many sicknesses of the people who visited her on Mt. *Kyeryong*. She also proclaimed the second coming of Jesus Christ on Mt. *Kyeryong*. This became her major message. Lee called herself *Daechunju*, the agent of the Heavenly God, and insisted that the second coming of Jesus Christ was already accomplished when she received the divine message in 1917 in Manchuria. Although the followers of *Chongdokyo* identify themselves as Christians, it was discovered that they worship the biblical God on the altar of *Tangun*, according to the procedure of traditional sacrifice. Yong-su Chu, the son of Lee, inherited her power after her death and now plays the role of messiah. Some of Lee's followers broke away from Chu and claim their orthodoxy by insisting that they inherited the divine books directly from Lee. One of the favorite prayers that has been cited by Lee's followers shows the mixture of Christianity and the shamanistic tradition.

> Mercy! Father and Mother! Mercy! Father and Mother! May Thy justification come on earth. Give thy heavenly kingdom on Kyeryong mountain. Forgive the sin of thy children... and keep thy children away from temptation... Thy children, the children of *Tangun*, shall be the saviors of the nations... Longevity, immortality, eternal blessing shall be in this heavenly kingdom.[80]

This prayer includes the Christian ideals shown in the Lord's Prayer and the shamanistic tradition of longevity, material blessing in this world and chosenness. As is true with other sects, *Chongdokyo* drew many followers from among those who had not been acculturated to the Western civilization that was brought to Korea with Christianity. It is a syncretistic sect that was founded on the grounds of a synthesis of Christianity and shamanism. There had been two revitalization movements which emphasized Korean religious culture in their beliefs and whose influence has been felt even in the remote parts of Korea. The two movements were the *"Tongilkyo"* and the *"Chundogwan."* Both of these movements were founded after the Korean War and became strong in South Korea in the 1960s and 70s.[81] It was reported that there were only 4 places of worship and 240 adherent members in 1991.[82]

Unification Church

Another large and active revitalization movement sprang up around the leadership of Sun-myung Moon (1920-) one year prior to that of Park Tae-sun. The *Tongilkyo* (The Unification Church) is called "The Holy Spirit Association for the Unification of World Christianity." Moon went to high school in Seoul, where he began to attend a Pentecostal church. Moon says that on Easter 1936, while deep in prayer on a Korean mountainside, he saw Jesus, who told him he had been chosen to finish the work Jesus had begun.[83] During World War II, Moon attended Waseda University in Tokyo, where he studied electrical engineering. In 1944, Moon went back to North Korea and succeeded in gathering some followers around him. Later, in 1946, Moon studied in a Christian monastery on a mountain for six months, formulating his own teachings, which were subsequently set forth in the *Divine Principle*. He then returned to his followers in Pyongyang, began preaching, and established the *Kwanghoe Kyohoe* (Broad Sea Church).[84] In 1954 Moon established his church in Seoul,[85] and in 1957 he published a book entitled *Divine Principle*, expressing the supposedly new revelation which he claimed to have received from God. This was revised in 1966 and published in English in the United States the same year. It was reissued again in 1973.[86]

The unification church movement is based on a belief system called *Divine Principle* which is claimed to be God's truth revealed by Sun-myung Moon. *Divine Principle*, for the Moonists, is a book of God's new truth, the Completed Testament, about the world, the destiny of man, and the role that the new messiah is to play. In the General Introduction, the *Divine Principle* says:

> With the fullness of time, God has sent His messenger to resolve the fundamental questions of life and the universe. His name is Sun Myung Moon... The Divine Principle revealed in this book is only part of the new

truth. We have recorded here what Sun Myung Moon's disciples have hitherto heard and witnessed. We believe with happy expectation that, as time goes on, deeper parts of the truth will be continually revealed.[87]

According to *Divine Principle*, in order for a man to be born again there must be a true mother and a true father. The true mother [*yin*] is the Holy Spirit. The true father [*yang*] is Jesus. Thus the Holy Spirit is the second Eve, the female principle, negativity, working in the earth. Jesus is the second Adam, the male principle, positively working in heaven.[88] Sa-hoon Shin, a well-known Christian scholar, dismissed the doctrine of Divine Principle as "a sort of sorcerer's story."[89] Moon had a doctrine of the unity of male and female in the God who created the earth and a doctrine of the fall. The founder, Moon, is believed to be superior to Jesus Christ.

As Sun-myung Moon, Dong-soo Sin, the founders of *Sinkwon Dohak* (the Way of Learning of Divine Authority), see Jesus as a failure, for he died on the cross before he could fulfill the purpose and plan of God. Sin claimed that God discovered him in Korea, the nation of the East, and God made him "the second Son of God" to complete the mission Jesus failed to fulfill. He claimed that he is the second coming of the Messiah, Savior and Judge. *Sinkwon Dohak* was founded in 1951, just after the Korea War, by Dong-Soo Sin, who graduated from the Salvation Army Seminary in Seoul and served as an evangelist of the Methodist Church. Since 1951, *Sinkwon Dohak* has grown to 10 churches of 2,000 members. Dong-Soo Sin claimed that he received revelation many times in his prayers. These included *A Letter of Great Truth*, his new name "*Baek Un*," Song of *Sinkown Dohak*, a Sign of *Sinwkon Dohak*, "*The Kingdom News,*" "*Fulfilled Testament,*" and 50,000 sacred songs. He also claimed that God gave him a mission to be "the second Son of God," and "the Judge of the Last Day." In common with many other cults, the followers of *Sinkwon Dohak* believe that the founder, Sin, is the second coming of the Messiah, Savior, Healer and Judge. They meet once a month on the third Sunday to worship. Their worship includes hymns, a sermon, declaration of the Angel's revelation, a song of *Sinkwon Dohak* and a prayer in tongues.[90]

He believes himself and the Unification Church to have taken the place of Jesus Christ in the Trinity.[91] The believers of the Unification Church take witches and fortune-tellers seriously, believing that even though these contain evil spirits, the witches and fortune-tellers may understand Moon better than established Christians do.[92] They also encourage believers to be proud of being Korean, for even though it is an undeveloped country, it is the highest honored country in the world because it produced "the lord of the second event," who is, of course, Moon Sun-myung.[93] One of the fundamental doctrines of the Unification Church is its acceptance of revelation outside of the Bible. The *Divine Principle* was accepted as a normative revelation for this generation. It denies not only the authority of the Bible but also denies Jesus Christ as Son of God and the only Savior.[94] It was reported that there are 5 religious institutes, 18 educational schools, 2 social centers, 8 cultural centers, and 150 business organizations in Korea.[95]

The Olive Tree Movement

The Olive Tree Movement, also known as Evangelistic Hall [*Chundokwan*], was organized in 1955 by Tae-sun Park (1916-1987), who spent his youth in Japan. He left Japan in 1944 for Seoul, where he established his permanent residence, opened a business and became active in the Presbyterian church. By 1955, having become increasingly disillusioned with the church and its leaders, he began to hold religious services himself, offering his own interpretation of the gospel. At these services, conducted much like revival meetings, Park was an immediate success, preaching and performing his own brand of faith healing. Park soon became nationwide and interdenominational. He attacked the existing churches, accusing them of their sins and failure, healing the sick, emphasizing and demonstrating the receiving of the Holy Spirit and prophesying that the end of the world was at hand. A great many Christians, lay and ordained, admired him and were attracted to him.

His revival movement may be the biggest one of its kind ever seen. He separated from the church and had enough followers to form a new branch. They were most enthusiastic and fervent, and most of them were very simple-minded believers. He soon developed a loyal following, and within a short time began to refer to himself as "the one and only Prophet and Interpreter of the True Law." He claimed that he was the Olive Tree mentioned in Revelation 11:4.[96] In 1956, he was expelled by the Presbyterian Churches of Korea but continued to profess Christianity. The Olive Tree Movement continued to flourish. By mid-1964, some 20,000 of his followers were congregated in their own community development near Seoul, called *Sinangchon* (the village of faith), and two other communities had been developed. By 1964 this movement had an estimated 800,000 to 1 million or more adherents.[97] However, this movement was accused by the Korean churches of being a form of syncretism, a blend of shamanism and Christianity, because of their belief and practice of shamanism.[98] In July 1955, the Korean National Church Council stated that Park's teaching was heretical.[99]

The doctrine of the Olive Tree Movement was very similar to the teaching of Unification Church in terms of their understanding of the theology of the Holy Spirit. As *Divine Principle* of the Unification Church, so *The Mysterious Principle of the Chundokwan* (Evangelistic Hall) sees "the rising of the sun" (Rev. 5:1; 6:1; 7:2-4) as referring to a country in the East. By Eastern nations, it always meant Korea, Japan, China. But Japan and China cannot be the nation which was chosen by God, for they are on the satanic side together. Therefore, the nation of the East, where the "Righteous Man" or "The Triumpher" will come to save people from sin and death, would be none other than Korea.[100]

In the creeds of the Evangelistic Hall, "The Olive Tree" was defined as the Holy Spirit who was sent by Jesus. Unless one receives the Holy Spirit in full measure, nobody can get eternal life. Only when "The Olive Tree" lays hands on anyone can one receive forgiveness of sin, living water, blessings and the Holy Spirit.[101] As in the Unification Church, the Evangelistic Hall makes its founder the giver of salvation. Salvation for both the Unification Church and the Evangelistic Hall means earth-bound blessing and physical salvation. It is a gospel of the present, not of the future. It had been said before he died that Park had totally denied the deity of Christ and the doctrine of the salvation in the Scripture, claiming that he himself was one of the Trinity and the mother of the spiritual world.[102]

Jehovah New Day Monastery

Jehovah *Saeil* Prayer Mountain or New Day Monastery Movement is located on Mt. *Kyeryong* in central Korea. It appears as a form of communal living with less than fifteen small houses in the valley of *Baekam*.[103] These houses are used for the healing services performed in this prayer mountain. The ministry of the center works through the power of prayer, deification of the founder and the expectation of the new millennial kingdom in which the *Saeil* Monastery will be the center and the founder will be the Lord. Reverend You-sung Lee was the founder of this monastery movement. He had been a Christian minister for ten years in the Korean Presbyterian Church before he started this movement.[104]

According to one resident of this monastery, Lee received a divine message that told him to found a monastery in Mt. *Kyeryong*. This took place on January 4, 1956, while he was at prayer at a small place in southern Korea. During this period, he also saw a heavenly vision in which he was able to see the door of heaven located at the present site of this monastery. In 1965, Lee moved to the present site and changed his name from You-sung Lee to Noe-ja Kee, the Son of Thunder. It was insisted by his followers that Lee received the secret of the last days of the world through the thunder while he was praying on this mountain. In his vision, two dragons threatened to kill him, and he was able to defeat them. At that moment, he received electric power through the thunder and was given the secret of the last days. He drew heavy crowds from all over the country for several years until he died in the summer of 1972 of a heart attack. His followers, because of his healing and his claim of the Lordship, believed him to be the Lord of the second coming. After his death, his body was placed in a room at this monastery for five days, with the expectation of his resurrection, which he had claimed while he was alive. His followers waited in vain and finally left the monastery, beginning the decline of the once-flourishing *Saeil* Prayer Monastery.

According to *Secret Principles of the Last Days* written by Lee, Mt. *Kyeryong* is the center of the salvation of the world. Korea has been chosen for this honor, and the last judgment is imminent. This age is full of signs of the last days, such as the contemporary political atmosphere in the world, the formation of the United Nations and the rise of Communism. The secret of the last days, therefore, is to save the people by letting them know of the heavenly kingdom of *Kyeryong* Mountain, where they can enter without experiencing death.[105] According to Myung-whan Tak, the *Saeil* Prayer Monastery Movement was inherited by Lee's eight disciples. In-yong Kim founded the Church of the Pure Gold Light House and claimed orthodox succession from *Saeil* Prayer Monastery. Kim insisted on the direct revelation of Lee to him. This implies the centrality of his church. Jin-mo Song, Jae-man Lee, Daw-kwang Chung and several others also founded Jehovah *Saeil* Churches in several cities of Korea.[106] They insisted that there were 80 churches with 1800 dedicated members.[107] This movement was grounded on the divine message, deification of the founder, and the idea of chosenness at the time of socio-cultural transformation.

One Family World Movement Church of the Heavenly God

Sakey Ilka Kongwhe [One Family World Movement], was founded by Do-chun Yang, the former minister of the Holiness church in Korea. He was one of the leading revivalists of the Korean Church before he came to Mt. *Kyeryong* in 1964.[108] Yang started his church after he received a divine message during a fasting prayer for forty days at a small island in the South Sea of Korea. The divine message ordered him to come to Mt. *Kyeryong* and to start the church of One Family World. The ultimate purpose of Yang's movement is the reformation of religion, education, and even politics through spiritual revolution to build a unified and peaceful world.[109] The followers of this movement firmly believe that the *Kyeryong* mountain in Korea will be the center of the New Israel, the headquarters of the unified world. Yang identified *Kyeryong* mountain with Zion, and he claimed that God's reign will be realized from that mountain.[110] In common with many other cults, this movement has an extra-Scriptural source of authority. *Yongyak* [The Eternal Testament], a catechism, is its source of authority. In short, the ideology of *The Eternal Testament* is a combination of Biblical millenarianism, which asserts the unified and peaceful world (Unification Church calls it the United family) as the fundamental structure of the new age of the Eternal (or complete) Covenant; and the messianic authority of Do-ryung Jung which was prophesied in *chunggamrok* and Korean ethnocentrism.[111]

On December 22, 1979, he conducted his own marriage and explained it as the wedding of Christ the little Lamb. According to the scholars, Yang started his movement by convincing himself that he was the messiah during the last days of the world. He called himself messiah or Little Lamb Jesus Christ and called Korea the land of chosen people. In the past, according to his idea, God elected Israel as his people. The prophets of the history of Israel were merely the introducers of God. In the present time, God has chosen Koreans as his newly elected people and has come to Korea to rule the world in peace.[112] Yang drew from the teachings of traditional religion, such as fearing God and loving men, as the basic idea of his movement and combined Christianity with them. It is reported that there were a few places of worship and 80 members in 1993.[113]

CONCLUSION

It has been said that the gospel spreads rapidly and large numbers of Christian people have been won in societies and countries where shamanistic faith is prevalent. Christianity had a comparatively easy entrance to Korea because of the syncretistic nature of Korean shamanism. Syncretistic Korean shamanism did not oppose the coming of Christianity at all. Christianity was regarded in the same way as Buddhism and Confucianism. The early missionaries may not have understood the prevalence of shamanism as a very important part of the religious culture of Korean people.[114] The religio-cultural factors, particularly shamanistic faith, were the most influential keys to the rapid growth of the church in Korea. For instance, Korean shamanistic faith through its belief in a higher being, *Hananim*, made it easy for Koreans to understand the God of Christianity. The problem is that many Christians in Korea still believe and practice shamanistic faith in their everyday life. Kwang-Sun Suh pointed out that the "style of the religious life of the Christians in Korea is not different from that of the believers in *mukyo*."[115]

Many Korean Christians understand and practice Christian faith from the perspective of the shamanistic consciousness of earthly blessings, physical healing, exorcism, and spiritual experience and power. Many Christians consult with the *mudang* According to the Korean folklore scholars, today 49 percent of the Koreans have traditional beliefs in shamanism, such as *Kosa*, the sacrifice to the spirit-gods; *Kut*, the rituals; *Jum*, divination.(1,411 respondants) accept the validity of *kwansang*, physiognomy, *susang*, palm reading, *saju*, fortune telling and *palja*, astrological interpretation of fate.[116]

The author believes that the presence of shamanistic faith in Korea has played an important role in bringing about the present numerical growth of the Korean churches. As discussed in this chapter, some shamanistic elements are very effectively used by the Christian churches, mostly without fully realizing their origin, in order to attract more people. There are certain similarities common to most of the churches and the shamanistic new Christian religious movements in Korea. The term "new Christian religious movement" itself has been the subject of much discussion by Korean theologians. In the strict sense of the word, the content of the new religions cannot be called "new." It is an extension of the old shamanistic faith. In their basic doctrines one finds a popularization of shamanistic faith teaching: the advent of a future world, paradise on earth, faith in a savior, the notion of a chosen people on the basis of the teaching from the Scripture, and the faith in *Chunggamrok*.[117]

In a survey of a brief history of these new religious movements, the author has spent more effort on the founders of these movements. That is because in many respects, those individual molded and defined the religious doctrine and shamanistic practices of their movements. That factor is one reason these new religious movements are often termed "sects." It has been observed that "sects" manifested specific needs in the lives of their founders. Out of these needs, the founders construct a their own theology which then bring them out of their lethargy. These movements deny essential tenets of orthodox Protestant theology. The founders of these movements are conceived as a prophet and demands obedience. They place some other authority as equal to or higher than the Bible. And they claim that only they have truth, all others are lost. In a survey of some new religious movements in Korea, the author sees aspects of this observation. More than this, the author sees a consistent pattern of role of a *mudang* of shamanism in the lives of the founders of these movements. In case of the *Great Meditation Truth Movement*, Ilsun Kang proclaimed that he had a power to communicate with the spirit of the world and to understand the divine plan of the universe. The founder of *Church of the Heavenly God* concentrated in healing ministry as the Second Coming of Christ. Sun-Myung Moon and his followers of *Unification Church* believe shamanistic fortune-tellers and witches. The founder of *Olive Tree Movement* emphasized earth-bound and physical blessing and claimed to be a mother of spiritual world. In the case of *Jehovah Newday Monastery Movement* and *One family World Movement Church of the Heavenly God*, the founders of these movements focused on the shamanistic faith in *Chunggamrok* and Mt. *Kyeryung* where is believed to be a center of new salvation of the world. Most of these shamanistic new religious movements in Korea died out rather rapidly. However, some other shamanistic new Christian religious movements in Korea have been increasing in numbers, and their influence has been expanding in recent years. According to a recent report there are 76 independent new Christian sects of indigenous origin in Korea including *Mankyo Tongwhakyo* (Church of All Church, 1980), *Hananim-eui Jayekyo* (Children of God, 1981), *Chil Sadokyo* (Church of Seven Apostles, 1983).[118]

NOTES

[1]Cf. Kim Yong-choon, *Oriental Thought* (Totowa, NJ: Littlefield, Adams and Company, 1973), p. 66.

[2]Yeul-gyu Kim, *Hankuk Shinwha-wa Musok Yungu* [*Korean Mythology and Study of Shamanism*] (Seoul, Korea: Iljokak, 1977), p. 184.

[3]Sung-bum Yun, *Hankuk Shinhak* [*Korean Theology*] (Seoul, Korea: Sunmyung Moonwha Sa, 1972), p. 202.

[4]J. Stewart, *Nestorian Missionary Enterprise* (Edinburgh, UK: T.& T. Clark, 1928), p. 87.

[5]Cf. Ihl-sik Hong, *Yooktang Yunku* [*A Study on Nam Sun Choi*] (Seoul, Korea: Ihlshinsa, 1959), pp. 146ff. See Nam-sun Choi, *Asi Chosun* [*Ancient Korea*] (Seoul, Korea: Tongyang Suwon, 1927); Yong-man Cho, *Yoontang Choi Nam-sun* [*Nam-sun Choi*] (Seoul, Korea: Samchoong Tang, 1964); Joo-tong Yang, *Koka Yunku* [*A Study on Ancient Songs*] (Seoul, Korea: Ilchokak,1965); Che-hong Ahn, *Chosun Sanggo Sagam* [*A History of Ancient Korea*] (Seoul, Korea: Minwoo Sa, 1947).

[6]Ross, *History of Korea*, p. 356.

[7]Palmer, *Korea and Christianity*, p. 91.

[8]Hurbert, *op.cit.*, pp. 404-405.

[9]*Ibid.*, p. 404.

[10]Eui-whan Kim, *Bokeum-kwa Yeuksa* [*Gospel and History*] (Seoul, Korea: Christian Literature Crusade, 1975), pp. 13-18.

[11]Richardson, *Eternity in Their Hearts*, pp. 64-71.

[12]Suck-woo Choi, "Modern Korean Society and Roman Catholic Christianity," *Song Chun Journal* 5, (1974), p. 429, in Myung-hyuk Kim, "Historical Analysis of Ancestor Worship in the Korean Church," ed., Bong Rin Ro, *Christian Alternatives to Ancestor Practices*, p. 166.

[13]William Blair, Bruce Hunt, *The Korean Pentecost and the Suffering which Followed* (Edinburgh, Banner of Truth Trust, 1977), p. 34.

[14]Clark, *Religion of Korea*, p. 114.

[15]Too-jin Kim, *Chosen Kajok Chedo Yungu* [*A Study of Korean Family System*], pp.700-701.

[16]Daniel L. Gifford, *Everyday Life in Korea* (New York, NY: Fleming H. Revell Co., 1898), p. 98.

[17]Harry Genet, "Big Trouble at the World's Largest Church," *Christianity Today* 26 (January 22, 1982), p. 39.

[18]Jones, *Korea, the Land, People and Custom*, p. 58.

[19]Cf. Changbok Chung, "Indigenization of Worship: The Holy Dinner," *The Northeast Asia Journal of Theology* 18/19 (March-September, 1977), p. 50.

[20]Genet, "Big Trouble at the World's Largest Church," *Christianity Today* *26*, p. 39.

[21]*The Christian Weekly Press* [a weekly paper published in Seoul, Korea], 1015 (No. 7, 1981), pp. 4f.

[22]*Ibid.*

[23]Sun-whan Pyun, *Dong-A Daily News Paper*, December 24, 1983.

[24]Youn-hee Kang, "*Hyundae Hankuk Sahoe Kitokyo-wa Josang Sungbae-eui Munje*" [The Problem of Ancestor Worship in Christianity in Modern Korean Society], *Samock* 37 (Seoul, Korea: Hankuk Chujukyo Press, 1975), pp. 100ff.

[25]Cf. Sebastian Bullough, *Roman Catholicism* (Harmondworth, NY: Penguin Books, 1963), p. 141.

[26]Jae-young Choo, *Chunju-eui Yukyo-jek Gaenyeum-kwa Josang Sungbae* [*Confucian Concept of the Heavenly Lord and Ancestor Worship*] (Seoul, Korea: Kyunghyang Press, 1958), p. 202.

[27]Allen C. Covell, *Ecstasy, Korean Shamanism* (Seoul, Korea: Hallym Publisher, 1983), p. 57.

[28]Tae-gon Kim, *Korean Shamanim*, p. 431.

[29]Jin-hong Chung, "*Daehyung Kyohoe Sungjang-eui Yunku*" [A Study of the Gigantic Churches of Korea], Wan-sang Han, et.al. *A Study on the Pentecostal Movement in Korea* (Seoul, Korea: Christian Academy, 1981), p. 137.

[30]Annual great visitation program of a church.

[31]Tack-jin Im, in a lecture during a *koinonia*-meeting in the Third World Church Leadership Center in Seoul on October 21, 1987.

[32]Byong Suh Kim, *International Review of Mission*, Vol. LXXIV, No. 293, (Jan. 1985), p. 70.

[33]Young-bock Kim, *Messiah and Minjung*, p. 120-121.

[34]Paul Y. Cho, *More Than Numbers* (Waco, TX: Word Books, 1984), pp. 15-30.

[35]Grayson, *Korea: A Religious History*, p. 205.

[36]This term was first used by James S. Tinny at Howard University in his dissertation "The Prosperity Doctrine: An Accretion to Black Pentecostalism."

[37]Bong-ho Son, "Some Dangers of Rapid Growth," Ro and Nelson, *op.cit.*, p. 338.

[38]Jin-Hong Jung, "*Kupsungjang Taehyung Kyohae-eui Hyunsang-kwa Kujo*"[The Phenomena and Structure of Fast Growing and Large Size Church] *Hankuk Kyohae Sungryong Undong-eui Hyunsang-kwa Kujo* [*A Study on the Pentecostal Movement in Korea*] (Seoul, Korea: Dae Wha Publishing Co, 1982). p. 129.

[39]Kwang-iel Kim,"*Kut-kwa Jungshin Chiryo*," [*Kut and Mental Therapy*],

Hankuk Musok-eui Shimri-jek Jayoo [*Psychological Therapy in Folklore of Korean II*] (Seoul, Korea: Korean Cultural Anthropology Association, 1979), p. 41.

[40]Bu-yong Lee,"*Hankuk Musok-eui Shimrihak-jek Gochal*" [*Psychological Study of the Korean Shamanism*], In-hoe Kim, *Hankuk Musok-eui Chonghap-jek Kochal* [*A Comprehensive Study of Korean Shamanism*] (Seoul, Korea: Koryu University Press, 1982), p. 156.

[41]*Ibid.*, p. 169.

[42]Kwang-iel Kim, *Psychological Therapy in Folklore of Korean II*, p. 42.

[43]*Ibid.*

[44]Covell, *Ecstasy: Shamanism in Korea*, p. 101.

[45]Jin-hong Chung, *A Study on the Pentecostal Movement in Korea*, p. 120.

[46]*Byungma* is a traditional expression of the illness in Korean Shamanism and now is used by the Korean Christians.

[47]*Unsaja* or *Unheja* are the charismatic Christians who claim that they received special spiritual powers and gifts directly from God for their healing ministry.

[48]M. F. Scranton, "Days Schools and Bible," *The Korea Mission Field*, Vol. III No. 4 (April, 1907). p. 53.

[49]Sister Isabel, "A *Mudang*'s Conversion," *The Korea Mission Field*, Vol. III. No. 6 (June, 1907), p. 86f.

[50]Gin Hur, *Hankuk Kyuhoe-eui Buhoong Wundong-ae daehan Kochal* [*A Study on the Revival Movement*] (Seoul, Korea: Theological Fund Conference, 1980), p. 190.

[51]Kyung-bae Min, "*Hankuk Kyohoe-wa Shinbi-jueui,*" [The Korean Church and Mysticism], *Kitokkyo Sasang* [*Christian Thoughts*] (Seoul, Korea: Christian Literature Society, 1971), p. 170.

[52]Yeul-gyu Kim, "*Hankuk Musok Shinang-kwa Minsok,*" [Korean Shamanism and Folklore], In-hoe Kim, et.al., *A Comprehensive Study of Korean Shamanism*, p. 60.

[53]Kyong-ho Lee, *A Study on the Belief Structure of Korean Ministers*, Unpublished Master's thesis (Seoul, Korea: Methodist Theological Seminary, 1983), p. 15.

[54]*Ibid.*

[55]Jae-yong Choo, "*Hankuk Kyohoe Buhoong Undong-eui Yeksa-jek Yunku,*" [A Historical Criticism of the Revival Movements of the Korean Church] *Kitokkyo Sasang*_[*Christian Thoughts*] (Seoul, Korea: Korean Christian Literature Society, 1978), p. 63.

[56]Tae-gon Kim, *Korean Shamanism*, p. 194.

[57]Mircea Eliade, *Shamanism; Archaic Techniques of Ecstasy* (New York, NY: Pantheon Books, 1964), p. 31.

[58]Kwang-Sun Suh, "*Hankuk Kristo-In-eui Sago*" [Korean Christian's Way

of Thinking], *Theological Thoughts of Korea*, p. 118.

[59]*Ibid.*

[60]Jong-il Kim, *Mukyo and Its Implications to the Christian Church in Korea* (Pasadena, CA: Ph.D. Dissertation, Fuller Theological Seminary, 1985), pp. 116-118.

[61]Yong-do Lee, "Yong-do Lee, the Reformer of the Korean Church," *Theology and The World*, p. 127.

[62]Ja-shil Choi, *Na-nun Halleluja Ajuma-yekda* [*I Was A Hallelujah Woman*] (Seoul, Korea: Yongsan Press, 1977), p. 143; See also Duk-hwan Kim, *Cho Yonggi, Keu-nun Kwayun Nugu-inga* [*Yonggi Cho, Who Is He?*] (Seoul, Korea: Kwang-go Kaebalwon Press, 1981).

[63]Kwang-sun Suh, "*Hankuk Kyohoe Sungryung Undong-kwa Buheung Undongeui Shinhak-jok Yiehae,*" [A Theological Analysis of the Spiritual Movement and Revivalism of the Korean Church], Kwang-sun Suh, et.al. *Hankuk Kyohoe Sungryng Undong-eui Hyunsang-kwa Kujo* [*A Study on the Pentecostal Movement in Korea*] (Seoul, Korea: Dae Hwa Publishing Co.,1982), p. 57.

[64]Tae-gon Kim, *Korean Shamanism*, p. 243.

[65]Ryu, "The Way of Refinement and Christianity," *Modern Theology and Creative Ministry*, p. 119.

[66]Jin-hong Jung, "*Kupsungjang Taehyung Kyuhae-eui Hyunsang-kwa Kujo*" [The Phenomena and Structure of Fast Growing and Large Size Church], Kwang-sun Suh, et.al. *Hankuk Kyuhoe Sungryung Undong-eui Hyunsang-kwa Kujo* [*A Study on the Pentecostal Movement in Korea*] (Seoul, Korea: Dae Hwa Publishing Co.,1982), p. 132.

[67]See Jong-il Kim, *Mukyo and Its Implications to the Christian Church in Korea,* pp. 29-33.

[68]Tae-gon Kim, *Korean Shamanism*, p. 286.

[69]In-keun Bang, *Kyohoe Aneui Mukyo-wa Dokyo* [*Mudang Religion and Taoism in the Korean Church*] (Seoul, Korea: Peulbit-Mokhoe Press, 1982), p. 57-63.

[70]Wan-sang Han,"*Euaddeohan Yaebae-ryul Deuril-geoinga?*" [How Can We Worship?], *Kitokkyo Sasang* [*Christian Thoughts*], Vol.II (Seoul, Korea: Christian Thought Co., 1979), p. 28.

[71]Jin-hong Chung, *A Study on the Pentecostal Movement in Korea*, p. 128.

[72]See Duk-whang Kim, *A History of Religions in Korea* (Seoul, Korea: Daeji Moonhwa-sa, 1988), pp. 444- 446.

[73]Cf. Sang-hee Mun, "The Phenomenon of the New Religion," *Yunsei Chunchu Weekly* (Yonsei University Press, 19 June, 1982), p.24.

[74]Byung-kil Chang, *Religions in Korea*, p.30.

[75]Tong-shik Ryu, *History and Structure of Korean Shamanism*, pp. 234-235.

[76]Yusachongkyo Yungu Wionhoe, ed. *Edan mik Bukgeunjun Jipdan* [*Heresy and Occult Sects in Korea*], (Seoul, Korea: Chonghoe Publishing Department, 1994), p. 89.

[77]See Byung-duk Ryu, *History of New Religions of Korea*, p. 248.

[78]See Jong-il Kim, *Mukyo and Its Implications to Christian Church in Korea*, pp. 232-233.

[79]Byung-duk Ryu, *History of New Religions of Korea*, p. 246.

[80]Tak, *A Report of the New Religious Movements in Korea*, p. 97.

[81]Tong-shik Ryu, *History and the Structure of Korean Shamanism*, p. 234.

[82]Myung-whan Tak, *Hankuk Sinheung Chongkyo* [*The New Religions in Korea*] Vol. 3, (Seoul, Korea: International Religious Reseach Center, 1992), p. 309.

[83]Wi-jo Kang, "The Influence of the Unification Church in United States of America," *Missiology: An International Review*, July, 1975, Vol.III. No.3.

[84]Synduck Choi, *Shinheoung Jongkyo Jipdan-ui Kwanhan Bikyo Yungu* [*A Comparative Study on the New Religions in Korea*] (Seoul, Korea: Chambicsha, 1965), p. 10.

[85]Everet N. Hunt, Jr. "Mun Sun Myung and Tong-Il" David J. Husselgraver, *Dynamic Religious Movements* (Grand Rapids, MI: Baker Publishing Co., 1978), p. 105.

[86]Ronald Enroth, et al, *A Guide to Cults and New Religions* (Downers Grove, IL: InterVarsity Press, 1983), p. 153.

[87]H.S.A.U.W.C. *Divine Principle* (Washington, DC: Holy Spirit Association for the Unification of World Christianity Press, 1977), p. 16.

[88]Young-kwan Park, *The Unification Church* (Seoul, Korea: Christian Literature Crusade, 1980), p. 77.

[89]Sa-hoon Shin, *Paganism and Present Day-Criticism, and Our Life Direction* (Seoul, Korea: Kodokyo Munwhasa, 1957), p.121.

[90]See Tak, *The New Religions in Korea*, Vol.I. p.167.

[91]Shin D. Choi, *Korea's Tongil Movement* (Seoul, Korea: Royal Asiatic Society, 1967), p. 175.

[92]*Ibid.*, p. 179.

[93]*Ibid.*

[94]Yong-jo Song, *The Holy Spirit and Mission: Toward a Biblical Understanding of the Holy Spirit in Relation to the Mission of the Church with Special Reference to Contemporary Religious Movements in Korea* (Pasadena, CA: D.Miss. dissertation, Fuller Theological Seminary, 1981), p. 389.

[95]Tak, *op.cit*, p. 180.

[96]Young-kwan Park, *The Two and Four Major Cults*, pp. 150-152.

[97]A. D. Clark, ed., *Area Handbook for the Republic of Korea*, p. 160.

[98]"A Public Statement on Tae-Sun Park" by the National Church Council of Chunju, June 17, 1956, in: Park, *The Two and Four Major Cults*, pp. 176-179.

[99]Tak, *New Religion in Korea*, Vol.1 (Seoul, Korea, Sungchunsa, 1972), p. 109.

[100]H.S.A.-U.W.A. *Divine Principle*, p. 539; Park Yong-Kwan, *The Two and Four Major Cults* (Seoul, Korea: Christian Literature Crusade, 1977), p. 148.

[101]Tak, *New Religion in Korea*, p. 115; Constitution of Evangelical Hall, *Creeds,* Chapter 4-7.

[102]*Ibid.,* pp. 173-175.

[103]See Jong-il Kim, *Mukyo and Implications to the Christian Church in Korea*, pp. 231-231.

[104]*Ibid.,* pp. 230.

[105]Byung-duk Ryu, *Hankuk Sinheung Jongkyosa* [*History of New Religions of Korea*] (Seoul, Korea: Wonkwang University Press, 1974), p. 256.

[106]Tak, *Sinheong Jongkyo Siltae Bogosea* [*A Report of New Religious Movements in Korea*] (Seoul, International Religious Study Institute, 1980), p. 93.

[107]Tak, *A Report of the New Religious Movements in Korea*, p. 155.

[108]Tak, *The New Religions in Korea, Vol. I*, pp. 221-222.

[109]See Jong-il Kim, *Mukyo and Its Implications to Christian Church in Korea*, pp. 234-235.

[110]*Ibid.,* pp.38-40.

[111]Song, *The Holy Spirit and Mission*, p. 396.

[112]Tak, *A Report of the New Religious Movements in Korea*, p. 97.

[113]Yusa Chongkyo Yungu Wiwonhoe, *op.cit.*, p. 134.

[114]Underwood, *The Call of Korea*, pp. 90-91.

[115]Suh, "Soteriology of the Korean Christian," [*Hankuk-eui Shinhank Sasang*], *Theological Thoughts of Korea* [*Hankuk eui Shinhak Sasang*] (Seoul, Korea: Christian Literature Society, 1977), p. 268.

[116]Suh, "Korean Christian's Way of Thinking," *Theological Thoughts of Korea*, p. 247.

[117]Sang-hee Moon, "Fundamental Doctrines of the New Religions in Korea," *Korean Christian Academy* (Seoul, Korea: Korean Christian Academy Publishers, Nov. 20, 1971), p. 14.

[118]*Hankuk Daily Newspaper*, February 23, 1994. p. 20; data concerning nuumbers of adherents is not available.

———————— Chapter Seven ————————

CONTEXTUALIZATION IN KOREA AND MISSIOLOGICAL IMPERATIVES

INTRODUCTION

In this chapter, the author will first explain the way in which from the beginning of Christianity in Korea the church was open to indigenization and what today is called contextualization. Next, in order to clarify the author's position in regard to contextualization, the debates on this matter that were conducted in Korea during the past few decades will be discussed. Then we will deal briefly with *Minjung* theology, which focuses on one of the indispensable aspects of contextualization, namely, the relation of the gospel to the sociopolitical situation. Finally, the author will evaluate the foregoing and state his views regarding the kind of contextualization the Korean church should strive after with an eye to continued growth in the future.

THE SHAPE OF HISTORICAL CONTEXTUALIZATION

Thus far in previous chapters, the author has analyzed the contributing factors for Korean church growth. First, native Korean evangelistic work and mission efforts, such as national evangelistic work, foreign mission work by Korean Christians, emphasis on Bible study, family evangelism, nationwide mass revival meetings and communication, and the army Christian movement, caused the Korean church to grow. Secondly, the sociopolitical context and missionary polices and methods brought about church growth in Korea. Sociopolitical factors for church growth were the attraction of modernization

(1885-1910), the search for national independence (1910-1950), anti-communism (1950-1970) and the economic boom (after 1970). Foreign missionary methods and policies such as the Nevius method, Bible translation and literature work, modern educational work, humanitarian social and welfare service contributed to church growth. Thirdly, shamanistic faith was very effectively used by the Christian churches in order to attract more people; an excessive emphasis was placed on the believer's earthly blessings and physical healings. The Christian ministry in Korea has taken a shamanistic form in that a major part of the ministry takes place in homes, praying for blessing upon the home and business, and praying for healing when there is sickness. The promise of this kind of blessing may be seen as preparation for the Christian gospel.

Another apparent feature of shamanistic faith which contributed to church growth is the fact that Korean shamanism has a world view and a view of God which are similar to Christian ideas. The shamanistic world is populated with many spirits, good and evil, and one chief God. This is similar to the New Testament view of the world and of spirits. The term for God is part of the living language in Korea. Korean faith in *Hananim* has been an integral part of Korean thought and mental and spiritual life from primitive times. All of these factors contributed to and influenced the growth of the Christian church in Korea. It has been shown that a church has to be related to its own sociopolitical context to be the church of Jesus Christ. Therefore, if it is to remain responsible and maintain its growth in the near future, the Korean church must take careful account of the sociopolitical as well as the cultural and religious context.

Many Korean Christian theologians and pastors have been misled into thinking that shamanism died out with the coming of Christianity and Western civilization into Korean society. Shamanistic faith in Korea is neither a religion of the ancient past nor a primitive practice. It has survived down through the cultural history of Korea and today, despite the presence of the traditions of the great world religions, it still has an important function as a system of folk religion. There has never been any great change in the deeper level of the people's general beliefs or in their way of thinking. There are many Christians who also embrace the shaman traditions in their religious practice, particularly during times of personal and family crisis. With regard to the Christian leaders, therefore, it is crucially important that they correctly understand this traditional religion, neither simply rejecting it nor syncretistically mixing it with Christianity. In order to achieve effective communication of the gospel and ensure sound future growth of the church, they must not treat this deeper level of shamanistic belief lightly.

Since the 1961 New Delhi Assembly of the WCC, those involved in mission activity throughout the world found themselves confronted by the issue of "indigenous theology." Not that this issue had not been previously discussed, but it now took on the major dimensions of an official mandate. This ferment did not escape the Korean church.[1] From 1962 onward, the Korean church has been caught up in the indigenization debate. In the year 1963 the Korean Church was very seriously concerned with the problem of the development of self-awareness and indigenization of the gospel in its own cultural context. The task of contextualization of theology and gospel was not only that of theologians, but of all workers who preached the gospel. Theologians as well as church leaders in Korea have considered seriously the importance of the contextualization of theology and gospel.

During the 1960s, Korea became increasingly aware of her own history and culture. The Korean people were everywhere using such terms as "nationalism," "national consciousness," and "national selfhood." Long-forgotten or ignored Korean tradition and culture gained new appreciation.[2] Similarly, within the church, the resurgence of national consciousness stirred the latent self-consciousness that was already developing strongly in the discussion on the life and mission of the church. At the same time the Korean church became alert to the importance of the tradition and culture within which it lived its life.

Under the influence of ecumenical theology, many Korean theologians, especially among the theologically liberal churches, have sought to establish what is termed "Korean theology." This activity of defining "Korean theology" has involved them in much criticism of the attitudes and work of Western missionaries. A number of Korean theologians have assumed that the early missionaries did not take into consideration the traditions and values of Korean religious culture. Amid all this, and with its Western origin, the Korean church began a new self-examination aimed at seeking its own identity as a body fully Korean and fully Christian. The central issue in the Korean theological debate has been the distinction between indigenization and syncretism.[3] In the next section we will examine the debates on indigenization and contextualization, which for some people meant a syncretization of the gospel.

DEBATES ON INDIGENIZATION AND CONTEXTUALIZATION IN KOREA

As already indicated in the 1960's there were unending debates and discussion among Korean theologians about the problems of indigenization in the Korean church.[4] Concerning indigenization and contextualization the primary issue is the problem of contact and encounter between national identity and Christian identity, or between Korean culture and Christianity. The question was put: How can the church maintain its true identity and at the same time become genuinely Korean in order that it may continue to grow in the future? In 1962, D.T. Niles of Ceylon visited the Korean church and spoke on indigenization at the Christian Literature Society in Seoul. This greatly stimulated the debate on indigenization in Korea. In his lecture, Niles stressed the necessity of a Korean theology. He used the following simile:

> First, the gospel is seed, the Church is a flower grown from the seed. But the flowers that come from the seed differ according to the soil in which they are grown. Likewise, each church has its own distinctiveness according to its national culture... Second, the gospel is theology. There is German theology in Germany, English theology in England, Indian theology in India; likewise the Korean church should have its own Korean theology.[5]

At this time the Korean church became increasingly concerned with the problem of indigenization and discussion on the issue commenced in all seriousness among the church leaders and theologians. The question of the self-identity of the Korean church was first raised in October 1962 by Tong-shik Ryu, professor of the Methodist Theological Seminary, Seoul, as a problem of indigenization and self-understanding of the gospel relating to the church's dynamic missionary outreach.[6]

Ryu developed the thesis that the meaning of mission and the mode of indigenization are to be found in the manner of the gospel's divine appearance on earth. God, in the Incarnation, disclosed himself in man and in the process restored his fellowship with mankind.[7] According to Ryu, the Incarnation means that God, himself becoming human, shares humankind's destiny unto death and enables people to share his life and glory in Christ (Phil 2:7). In other words, to restore his fellowship with humanity, God became "indigenized" in the world. In this sense, "incarnation" and "indigenization"are synonyms. The incarnation was no speculative, abstract conception but a concrete historical event expressed through Jewish life and reality in the unique Jewish national culture.[8] The method of the Incarnation was God's self-emptying, self-denial and self-sacrifice. Ryu carefully distinguished these terms from self-deprivation, self-surrender and self-relinquishment, for all of the latter lead to syncretism. Indigenization and syncretism are two different and incompatible concepts. Indigenization presupposes the selfhood of the event, but syncretism requires the negation of selfhood.[9] Ryu projects that task of indigenization on three levels: 1) the development of a Korean Christian theology in which the gospel is appropriated and crystallized into a cradle formula framed appropriately within the context of the Korean ethos and culture; 2) the expression of a Korean Christian lifestyle which confesses the faith and witnesses to Christ in such fashion that a new Korean culture is formed; and 3) the reformation of the church with a life and structure appropriate to the Korean reality in which the cultus is manifested.[10]

In response to Ryu's principal question: Can Christian culture be indigenized? Kyung-yun Jun, professor of theology at the Seoul Methodist Seminary, wrote a critical analysis of the problem of theological indigenization in the Korean church.[11] In viewing indigenization negatively and examining it from the standpoint of the "Theology of the Word," Jun asserted that the Christian faith does not start from cultural phenomena but from man's response to the revelation of God in Christ. He maintained that Christianity could not be transmitted to a non-Christian country in the form of culture. Faith and culture must be separated. Christianity is an historical and world-wide religion. It is an historical fact that Christianity was brought to Western soil, where it lived for nearly two thousand years, and later came to Korea in a certain form. It is wrong to ignore this fact as if there were no such tradition behind Korean Christianity. The plan to create a Korean Christianity is non-Christian thinking, for it represents only a cultural concern with Christianity. Such a creation cannot be accomplished by a purposeful plan; in the course of history, the Christian gospel will naturally form a tradition and something will emerge from that tradition. Christians have no spare time to plan such sentiment.[12] He says,

> ...the expression of Christian faith should be primarily theological. It should not be contradictory to the tradition of primitive Christianity and should be made clear from the beginning. Unless Christian faith is thus adequately expressed, the Christian must translate and take into consideration the expression and form of Western culture, which theologically expresses the content of faith. In the expression of Christian faith, the adjectives, Korean, German and any other national name, cannot come first, but the true expression of the mercy of Christ must come to the front...The problem of the indigenization of Christian faith is not how to make alive the form of the indigenous religion, or the inherent artistic tra-

dition of the people, but to let these indigenous materials be burnt by the fire of the gospel and to find out what is the new sprout arising from the ashes.[13]

However, Tong-shik Ryu, sharply distinguishing between the gospel and Christian religion, attempted to discover those elements in the traditional religions of Korea that reflect the truth of the gospel and through a process of de-Westernization to indigenize the gospel in Korea.[14] Ryu clarifies this by saying:

> Indigenization does not propose to change the essence of the gospel. "Indigenization" is only a name for the methodology which tries to find how the transcendent truth can live and how the life-power of that truth can work in a particular and concrete historical reality. The way in which the gospel transcends the nation and yet saves it is the problem of missionary methodology... Therefore, the problem of the indigenization of Christianity arises from recognition of the fact that historical Christianity has been acculturated in a particular cultural environment and from the necessity of making that Christianity appropriate to another cultural environment.[15]

Jun replied to Ryu's argument by producing "A Return to the Primitive, or Indigenization?"[16] "Indigenization," Jun wrote, means "a particularization of universal truth." Therefore, the issue of indigenization turns on the method by which the universal truth of the gospel can be proclaimed and confessed in the particular situation of Korea. He felt that Ryu was more interested in finding a Korean type of Christianity over against that of the West, and criticized that approach.

> Although he [Ryu] vigorously describes the theory of indigenization, having forgotten that Christianity is a historical and world-wide religion, he only repeats his leading idea... He is wrong to think of Korean Christianity as a type of Christianity which can only be found in Korea... It reminds us that during the Pacific War, the Japanese tried to create a Japanese Christianity and to develop a Japanese theology. Christianity is a historical religion. But Ryu's curiosity is caught up with what Christianity would have been like if the gospel had been formulated first on Korean soil. That is unrealistic thinking. It is a historical fact that Christianity was implanted on Western soil where it lived for nearly two thousand years fighting against various heresies. Then it came to Korea in a certain refined and established form. It is wrong to ignore this fact and to speculate as if there were no such tradition. And it is equally wrong to attempt to create a Korean Christianity, for this is only a cultural concern about Christianity... Moreover, such a creation cannot be accomplished by a purposeful plan. In the course of history Christianity will naturally form a tradition and a great thing will surely come out of that tradition.[17]

Thus Jun rejected what he judged to be Ryu's position: the absurdity of conceiving of Christianity as if it had no history, the harmful attempt to

Koreanize Christianity, and the dangerous eclecticism which chose only certain elements from both Christianity and Korean traditions. Jun further condemned all attempts to find "Korean-ness," because he believed that all such attempts are generated by nationalism or by man's self-assertion. Jun resolutely said "No" to Ryu on indigenization.

According to Jun, the expression of Christian faith is primarily theological and must be in accord with its past tradition. The task of the Korean Christian, therefore, lies in translating the content of faith which has already been adequately expressed in the form of Western theology. Because there is no point of contact between Christianity and Korean culture and because Western culture is the true manifestation of the content of Christian faith, Jun holds that the de-Westernization and indigenization of Christianity are unreasonable and improper. In the expression of Christian faith, adjectival identification, e.g., Korean, Japanese, German or any other national or cultural designation, must not come to the fore; any attempt to develop Christianity or theology on the basis of indigenous culture is destined to fail and to betray the truth of Christianity. If there can be any indigenization of Christianity, it can be only through renewing the inherited confession of faith and only on the basis of the Christian tradition developed in the West.[18]

The Ryu-Jun exchange produced results. Suddenly a debate on indigenization swept over the entire Korean church, and many theologians who favored indigenization participated in the discussion. From 1963 onward, articles and essays on indigenization increasingly appeared.[19] Sung-bum Yun, also of Seoul Methodist Seminary, was the first contemporary Korean scholar to advocate Korean theology. His book *Christianity and Korean Thought* was a significant treatise on indigenization.[20] He defines indigenization in terms of the pre-understanding of self, or self-identity, prior to receiving the gospel. Yun's study of indigenization begins with the *Tangun* myth, which is a traditional legend concerning the foundation of ancient Korea. Yun regarded the myth to be a treasure of the Korean people[21] and a *vestigium trinitatis*.[22] In this myth, according to Yun, one comes upon interesting similarities with the concept of the trinity in Scripture. In fact, in his opinion, the three gods of the *Tangun* legend are analogous to the triune God of the Bible.[23] This debate has been forcing evangelical churches in Korea to deal more specifically with the complex issue of how to relate the gospel to the context, that is, to the needs of the whole person and society.[24]

According to this myth, in the beginning there was a heavenly emperor, *Whan-in*, whose son was called *Whan-ung*. The father gave his son three royal seals to rule the world. The son descended into the world near *Taeback* Mountain in the central part of Korea by a divine tree with his 3,000 tribesmen to erect a divine city. He married a female bear who bore a son called *Tangun Whan-gum*. He established the first Korean dynasty, *Tangun Chosen*. The Supreme God, *Whan-in*, God's Son, *Wan-ung*, and the female bear, a terrestrial goddess, were united to produce a human being. Yun says:

> It is my interpretation that the *Tangun* mythology may be an indigenized form of the Christian doctrine of the Trinity which was spread to northeast Siberia through the Eastern Orthodox Church and finally reached Korean soil...[25]

In his "Pre-Understanding as Requirement for the Indigenization of the Gospel,"[26] Yun utilized an epistemological perspective to examine indigenization. His thesis was that unless one knows who he is when he receives the gospel, he is incapable of knowing what the gospel is. If the task of indigenization is to discover how to appropriate the gospel without altering, distorting or perverting its essence in the minds and thought of Korean people, its accomplishment requires a pre-understanding of Koreans. Since people are constituted by their history and culture, these must be studied so that particular people may be understood. Yun cautions, however, that "pre-understanding is not the ground of being but the ground of knowing for faith." Therefore, the Korean church arrives at consciousness through the process of pre-understanding.[27] Yun viewed indigenization as "a problem of the theological way of thinking." As an academic discipline, theology can be developed only with reference to its philosophical background. By the same token, Korean Christian theology can be developed only with knowledge of the philosophical background of the Korean people. Yun suggests that the *Tangun* myth is a part of the philosophical background which provides the Korean's pre-understanding for the Christian doctrine of God.[28]

Yun follows this with a study of *sung* (sincerity). He begins with an exploration of the meaning of *sung*. He then goes on to relate it to revelation in much the same way that *Tangun* is related to the triune God. According to him, the literal meaning of *sung* is "the accomplished word." This concept is derived from Jesus' saying on the Cross: "It is finished." *sung* then can be regarded as the "authentic word." He asserted:

> Is it unjustifiable interpretation to identify the oriental concept of *Sung* with the Word of God? According to Genesis, God created the world by the

Word. Jesus also rebuked the temptations of the devil in the wilderness. The Word is not an abstract, empty language but a power which makes events out of nothing. When Jesus spoke to the sick person, the latter was immediately healed by his powerful Word. The Word of God is the word of power...Thus, the Fourth gospel starts as follows: "In the beginning was the Word and the Word was with God and the Word was God."[29]

He insisted that *sung* as understood by Yul-gok Yi, a great scholar in the *Yi* dynasty, greatly contributes to the understanding of the gospel. Yul-gok Yi 's philosophy can be defined as the theology of *sung*. In other words, according to Yun's understanding, sincerity is the equivalent of revelation and sincere thinking or the sincere doing is the equivalent of faith. Thus, Yun concluded that the Confucian *sung* is God himself, and the one who practices *sung* is the believer.

Tong-shik Ryu continued the indigenization debate in 1965 with his book *The Christian Faith Encounters the Religions of Korea*, in which he likewise insisted on the formation of a Korean theology.

> We must meet Christ through the Holy Spirit. This is the task of indigenization. We must not remain indefinitely enslaved to Western traditions. To this end we must discover anew the cosmic Christ and the universality of his gospel. The God of the gospel, who created heaven and earth, who is the Lord of history and has redeemed all persons, cannot remain for us an unrelated Western God. If he is the Lord of the Western church, then he must be also be the Lord of Korean culture and history. He is not a "foreign God" who followed Western missionaries into this country only a few years ago. He has always been present in Korea, working as the Lord of creation within our culture and history. Our task, then, is to follow the traces of his Handiwork and to participate with him in his work of creation. It is for this reason that we have a renewed interest in the origins and development of Korean culture. The task of indigenization is not to clothe God in Korean attire, but to render songs of praise and worship to the God who in his providence created all that is true and beautiful in Korean experience. We must give praise to God not only for Luther and Calvin, but also for *Ui Sang* and *Won Hyo* [Buddhist priests of the ancient *Shilla* dynasty], and to *Toe Gye* and *Yul Gok* [renowned Korean Confucian scholars].[30]

Ryu argued that the gospel and historical Christianity are two distinctive realities. The gospel is the seed or essence of Christianity. The historical Christianity that was planted into Korea from the West is the plant which originally grew and flowered in Western soil. Therefore, indigenization and mission in Korea require: 1) a determination of the nature of the gospel and its de-Westernization, or separation from the non-essential Western elements encasing it in Korea; and 2) an apprehension of Korean history and culture in which the gospel seed is to be planted. The latter includes a careful examination of folk religions, Confucianism, Buddhism, and *Chundokyo,* all of which are constitutive elements of Korean tradition and culture.[31] Ryu defines the truth of the gospel in terms of "the restoration of humanity" and "human liberation." With that definition, he examines all of Korea's traditional religions.[32] Ryu makes short shrift of shamanism. He acknowledges that the emphasis upon spirits may help some Koreans to understand the existence of a spiritual realm, and this indirectly may help some to appropriate the gospel, but fundamentally it "distorts the essence of the gospel and makes it meaningless." He elaborates his points in this manner:

> Generally speaking, its spell of incantation does not accompany ethical determination for a responsible human existence or possess any element that contributes to the formation of historical reality, and the liberation of man cannot be expected from Shamanism. It only brings about antisocial and non-creative total stagnation by promoting conservatism and fatalism. The concepts of justice and love, which are absolutely indispensable for social relationships and constitute one of the important points of contact with the gospel, are non-existent in shamanism. Viewed in the light of the gospel, shamanism has no value.[33]

Ryu is also critical of Korean Confucianism. It brought into Korea the social-class system, rejected human rights and imposed upon Korea its submission to the Chinese way of life. Thus, Confucianism is seen to have obstructed humanization and to have bred anti-gospel elements in Korea. Most of all, family-centered selfishness and self-assertion arising from the Confucian notion of family and human duty have caused a tragic factionalism directly contradictory to the message of the gospel. In its proclamation of a new man and a new society to be realized in self-denial and sacrifice made possible through the reconciling power of God, Christianity must overcome Confucianism as another major obstacle in Korea. Yet in Korean Buddhism and *Chundokyo* (The Heavenly Way Religion), Ryu finds positive elements. In assessing the first, he says:

> In Korean Buddhism, and especially in the *Mahayana* Buddhism of the *Shilla* Dynasty, we find many noble characters. It may not be wrong to say that *Wonhyo,* the representative figure of *Shilla* Buddhism, was a Christian before Christ had been introduced into Korea. Regardless of what he thought of Buddhism itself, his teaching that every human being has the Buddha's nature in himself is a claim for human dignity. Surely, therefore, he preached the liberation of man and the restoration of humanity which are the core of the gospel. He also lived his life transcending both the secular and the sacred boundaries. He was a man truly liberated from all laws and regulations. He taught the truth of reconciliation in his treatises on

"singleness of mind." These elements clearly indicate that he reflected the essence of the gospel in his life and teaching. Although he taught the truth in the context of Buddhism, in reality his teaching was that of the gospel which pierces through both the secular and the sacred boundaries. In *Wonhyo* I find a Christian image occurring before Christ.[34]

Ryu, however, is critical of later Buddhism in Korea. In it he discerns the perverted elements which emerged from the syncretism that occurred when Buddhism encountered shamanism and Confucianism. Therefore, later Buddhism, bewitched by shamanism, degenerated into superstition or, overpowered by Confucian legalism, succumbed to formalism. To fulfill its task, Korean Buddhism has to be liberated from the alien elements of shamanism and Confucianism that corrupt it and be restored to its original nature. Ryu also sees creative elements in *Chundokyo*. In spite of the fact that in its formative stage *Chundokyo* took a strong anti-Christian stance, its teaching and practice reflect much of the truth of the gospel. "The doctrines of *Sichunchu* [service to the Lord of the heaven], and *Innaechun* [heaven's presence in man]," Ryu observes, "are no less than a Korean expression of the truth of the gospel." These doctrines of *Chundokyo* point to ultimate human dignity and selfhood in the same way the gospel does and, as in the case of the *Tonghak* Revolution of 1894, encourage humans to strive for a free and creative world.[35] No religion in itself possesses redeeming power. Only in the gospel of Jesus Christ does redemptive power exist.

Thus, Ryu asserts, religions have true meaning and value only when they express the gospel in their teaching and practice. If any traditional religion in Korea has contributed toward the redemption of man, it has done so only by reflecting the gospel in its doctrine and life. Such an assertion does not nullify the contribution made by *Shilla* Buddhism and *Chundokyo*, for they are "satellites." In the same way that a satellite reflects the light of the sun, their function has been to reflect the gospel of Christ. Yet, no longer do Koreans need to be satellites, reflecting the gospel over Korea; that is past and the morning has come. The light of the gospel's truth, like the morning sun, "is shining upon us," and "we are, therefore, stirred by the sunlight of the gospel to become new persons and to build a bright world appropriate to this new day."[36]

Tong-shik Ryu expresses the conviction that the task of religions in Korea is to renew deprived humanity, to restore the primal nature of humanity that has been perverted, and to reform the national community that has been destroyed by shamanism and Confucianism. Here also he enumerates those elements in the Korean character that were produced by shamanism and Confucianism: 1) lack of autonomous selfhood and dependence upon others, 2) stagnated conservatism, 3) family-centered factionalism, 4) bureaucratism—the deplorable custom of making much of officials and little of the people, and 5) pleasure-seeking life.[37] To accomplish this task, Buddhism, *Chundokyo* and Christianity first need to be freed from the destructive elements of shamanism and Confucianism that saturate them. Then they need to be unified. With this large program in mind, Ryu would call for a general mobilization of all the religions in Korea to renew the Korean nature, to restore humanity and to reform the national community.

The first step in that mobilization would be an inter-religious dialogue among all, and it would be conducted on the principle of the equality of all religions but under the guidance and judgment of Christ.[38] Such a proposal naturally evoked comment. In 1965, a panel discussion was held on Ryu's views. One of the participants, Myungkwan Chi, responded favorably to Ryu, likening his work to the great achievement of Christians in the early centuries. Another panel member, Yong-ok Kim, expressed doubt about the general mobilization plan, however, simply because no religion except Christianity would accept the validity of Christ as a norm. Nevertheless, Kim gave high credit to Ryu's work as a missionary methodology and strategy.[39]

Ryu argued that Christian faith is the subjective response to the grace of God's salvation.[40] He defines indigenization as the self-adjustment or self-transformation of transcendental truth into the historical situation. As the word "self-adjustment" implies, Ryu's discussion of indigenization tends to emphasize the need of the gospel to be adjusted to the cultural situation rather than the need of the native culture to be transformed by the gospel. Thus he compares indigenization to the Incarnation of the truth in Jesus Christ, but here again he emphasized the downward movement of Incarnation. His idea on indigenization is seemingly somewhat different from Yun's because he claimed that "indigenization of Christianity is neither syncretistic nor compromising."[41] However, like Yun, he claimed that the traditional religions of Korea made the Korean people's understanding of the gospel easy. Thus, whereas he strongly rejects Yun's syncretistic approach, he does assume the "fulfillment" hypothesis and seeks to uncover the gospel in these religions.

> As a religion, Christianity has only a relative position. Christianity could never become a religious *a priori* to judge the other religions... Jesus Christ is only one revelation, but he has universal meaning. The religions do not all have equal value. Insofar as they reflect the gospel manifested in Jesus

Christ, they have religious meaning and truth. Thus we should judge other religions in the light of the gospel of Christ. In other words, other religions have their own meanings insofar as they contain and reflect gospel truth in their forms and functions... The traditional Korean religions likewise have their own meaning, not because they have their own values, but because they reflect the truth of the gospel. On the contrary, if they fail to reflect the truth of the gospel, their existence is meaningless.[42]

The indigenization theses of Yun and Ryu aroused immediate responses within the Korean Church. In *Kitokkyo Sasang Kangjowa [Lectures on Christian Thought]*, ten articles on the issue were collected, which originally appeared mainly in a monthly, *Kitokkyo Sasang [Christian Thought]*, and some in *Sasangge [World of Thought]*, a leading popular monthly for ministers and church leaders in Korea.[43] It is very interesting to see that the Korean church's response has been surprisingly to concern itself with the issue. Lee Chang-shik joined the debate with his article, "The Indigenization of Christianity Is an Historical Task."[44] Viewing Christian history through the twin motifs of indigenization and mission, he sought to shift the discussion from the theoretical or ideological to a missiological and historical perspective.

Lee opposed the position taken by Kyung-yun Jun, which we described earlier, by arguing that indigenization in Korea is an essential task because Christianity is an historical religion and had previously been inseparably bound with Western culture, shaping and being shaped by it. To become what it must be as an historical religion in Korea, it needs to be de-Westernized and adapted. Both processes require Korean Christianity's independence from external control and a "re-formation of Christianity" appropriate to the Korean scene. The indigenization of Christianity in Korea involves the localization of the unique and universal gospel into the natural life of Korea.[45] Kyung-yun Jun, still skeptical about the problems of indigenization, reacted again and argued that between the Christian doctrine of God and the *Tangun* myth there is neither similarity nor connection. He suspected Sung-bum Yun's motive for advocating indigenization and warned of its consequences:

The intention of Dr. Yun's emphasis on the *Tangun* myth as a sage is to recognize the existence of the Korean nation as a power and to promote the power of national culture with which he attempts to confront Christian tradition. This clearly indicates that he wants to place the self-asserting national culture over against the redemptive history of God found in biblical faith... Recent history reminds us that this kind of force which collaborates with the political self-claim of a nation easily becomes either anti-Semitic or anti-Christian.[46]

He goes on to say that those who seek Christian faith on the basis of national selfhood override the selfhood of Christian faith. Consequently, they abandon the Christian selfhood which they claim to seek. He says, "I repeat that the identity of the gospel is the Holy Spirit, and he always takes the way of self-denial."[47] Believing that Yun was substituting "pre-understanding" for theological form, Jun said,

> One should be reminded again that Paul, Luther, and Calvin found their theological form only in the Scriptures...No one can develop true Christian theology apart from this principle. Doing theology on the basis of the Scripture is the only way to restore Christian selfhood.[48]

The discussion of indigenization, carried on largely in written form, was heated and often tended to confuse the issues. Among those who tried to clarify them was Harold Hong. In his "The Possible and Impossible Elements of Indigenization," he tried to distinguish between and separate the changeable from the unchangeable elements of Christianity. "Christian tradition, e.g., theological method and cultural developments, are proper subjects for indigenization."[49] Following Hong's principle, Lee Jong-Sung also insisted that Christianity can be indigenized, but that the gospel cannot be. True indigenization occurs when Korean Christians discard Christianity's Western garb and seek to express the gospel in Korean forms. He believed that this principle of indigenization could be found in and could be founded on the principles of *sola fide* and *sola Scriptura*.[50] Meanwhile, Chung-choon Kim agreed on the validity of forming an indigenous theology, insofar as it helps to establish the national church. He stated that:

> When Christianity is indigenized in a country the actual and the concrete fact of indigenization is related to problems of the national church. In other words, the church should be indigenized; the church should be an indigenous church.[51]

Concerning the method of indigenization, Kim drew attention to leadership, evangelism and worship. Concerning evangelism, he said that we must always keep in mind that it is Korean people we are seeking to reach with the gospel. That is, we must ponder their historical and cultural background. Indigenization is an expression of the subjective consciousness of people in the mission of the Church and it is not simply cultural creativeness for its own sake at the expense of that mission. Concerning worship, Kim insisted that all national expressions of faith must be carefully considered; in other words, all Bible translations, hymns, church music and church building should be indigenous expressions of Korea culture.[52] Kim wrote strongly in support of indigenization but, to avoid some of the errors easily committed in that process, suggested certain guiding principles:

1. The indigenous Church should be rooted in God through Jesus Christ and be an integral part of the church universal. It must be theologically sound.

2. A national Church should conserve the heritage of the Apostolic Church. It must be historically sound.

3. In its interpretation of Christ, its expression in worship and service, in customs, and in art and architecture, the church should be indigenized. It must be culturally relevant to the people of the land.

4. The Church should be an organ through which the Spirit of Christ permeates and influences all phases of the life of the people for the purpose of creating and building up a Christian culture.

5. The Church should be alert to the problems of the times and be morally responsible for the changing society.[53]

Chung-choon Kim argued the need for indigenization on two grounds. First, "wherever it goes the church must be identified with the people who receive the gospel," for the very nature of the gospel shown forth in the Incarnation of Christ requires this identification. Second, the effectiveness of the mission of the church requires it.[54] Making a separation like that of Harold Hong, Kim then distinguished between those elements appropriate for indigenization and those which are not. The essence of the gospel, the event of Jesus Christ, is the universal truth and transcends all historical and local realities. But "its interpretation, expression, application, and communication need to take on contemporary, national, and local color so that it may take root in the soil where it is planted by preaching." Both "the functioning of the church and the expression of the faith" require indigenization.[55] Kim noted that "strong nationalism often has taken advantage of the attempt to indigenize Christianity. But nationalism must not be lord over the Christian faith." He then focused on the central issue.

At the heart of the problem of indigenization, it seems, lies the difficult and paradoxical matter of how to blend the local and the universal element of the church of Jesus Christ, so that it may be both a part of the people of one nation and a part of all nations.[56]

Kim's theology of indigenization can be summarized as follows: First, when the gospel is brought to a nation by foreign missionaries, it must be carefully examined whether it comes in Western thought forms and whether it remains in this indigenous clothing. For instance, denomi-nationalism, or authoritarianism or all forms of imperialism, are by all means to be avoided in the formulating of indigenous theology; sec-ond, the Christian gospel must also be carefully examined as to whether or not some of the national content or thought patterns do not cover the fundamentals of the gospel; third, special efforts should be made to formulate a theology that is relevant to the people.[57] As indi-cated above, Kim desires to add to the gospel the flavor of nationalism, even though he agrees that "nationalism must be criticized and purified by the Word of God and in the light of the gospel."[58]

Bong-rang Park, alert to broader contacts and new nationalism, was another contributor to the emerging indigenization issue. In 1969 he wrote:

> First of all, there was contact with the churches of Southeast Asia. Secondly, there was a growing sense of autonomous "I" consciousness, as Korean existence in the Christian proclamation, since the heritage of the missionary church in the past was too orthodox, heteronomous, and exclu-sive to meet the Korea of today, changed culturally and economically. The church of Korea found it responsible and even inevitable to re-evaluate the Korean cultural traditions (including religion and culture) if she wished to be the religion for this people today. Thirdly, another and more direct ele-ment was the political climate of that time. Korea was experiencing a polit-ical revolution through military power. With this revolutionary change something new was in waiting. The key word of the new government was "national renewal," with a strong emphasis on "nationality," or "national subjectivity," which has a dominating voice among the younger genera-tion. With this tendency the spirit of the nation called for the rediscovery of national traditions.[59]

One readily notes that the tension between Korean consciousness and Christian consciousness led to the indigenization discussion. For example, the special conference on "The New Generation Diagnoses the Korean Church," held under the auspices of the Korean Student Christian Movement in 1962, pointed to the lack of national identity in the Korean Church. In it the primary issue has been the problem of contact and encounter between national identity and Christian identi-ty or between Korean culture and Christianity. Because Christianity in Korea was transplanted from the West, indigenization requires de-Westernization and the independence of the Korean church from the West. Naturally, this involves the effort to eliminate from Korean Christianity the Western, foreign, heteronomous elements which have been brought into Korea by Western missionaries, but also to elimi-nate certain forms of religious expression relating to the ever-growing consciousness of national identity. At this relatively early stage of the discussion, some theologians have attempted to develop a Korean theology. Chai-choon Kim, the late professor of *Hankuk* Theological Seminary, wrote:

> Indigenization is another urgent task which the Korean church is facing. Since indigenization is to take up the indigenous culture for communicating Christian faith without changing its essence, great care is necessary in the enterprise. We must first of all abandon the kind of attitude which tries to identify Occidental culture with Christianity. At the same time, we must discard the idea that there is not and cannot be any relevancy between Oriental culture and Christianity...The tasks which the church in Korea faces are 1) to understand more deeply the heart, faith, and work of Jesus Christ, instead of swallowing Western Christianity, which was contaminated by the Greco-Roman culture and power politics, and 2) to reformulate the pattern of the Christian church and its life, according to the heart and life of Christ, absorbing and fulfilling Korea's own indigenous culture... There is a further task which the church in Korea must not ignore. That is to contribute in creating a common universal culture.[60]

Concerning the transformational approach, Bong-bae Park defined a position influenced by H. R. Niebuhr. He maintained that neither exclusivism nor relativism contains any element of transformation. Exclusivism tries to change the recipient of the gospel more radically than transformationism, and relativism also assumes gradual progress and movement toward the ultimate of one true religion in the end. He said,

> I am deeply influenced by Niebuhr's transformationism in constructing my theological scheme of indigenization. It provides a better answer to the synthesis between Christianity and traditional culture. It offers room for a positive appreciation of native culture and religion through retaining whatever is found to be good and exemplary.[61]

Park tries to find in traditional culture and ethics a potentiality which could be developed into a workable maturity through the impact of the transforming power of the gospel. Thus, Park attempted an approach that used the transformation theory as one means of obtaining a viable synthesis between Christianity and traditional culture. According to him, traditional culture and ethics need not be condemned as pagan. Rather, they should be regarded as positive elements of interaction with the Christian gospel. This would entail the transformation of an individual and his culture by developing his potential as a bearer of traditional culture. This could be achieved through the illuminating power of the gospel. He stated his approach to transformation theory as follows:

In transformation theology, the Christian gospel has two important functions to play. One is to liberate traditional man and culture from the negative elements of the past and tradition. Here the gospel is the power of liberation. The other is to reorient traditional man and culture through which true humanization becomes possible. Thus, indigenization means that the Light of the gospel shines upon man and society in non-Christian culture. The salt of Christianity permeates into the minds of people and into the center of their traditional value system, and the leaven of the Christian message spreads in the hearts of individuals and in the ethos of the traditional community.[62]

Byung-mu Ahn, professor of *Hankuk* Theological Seminary, argued that the message of the Bible must be boldly related to heathen thought if true indigenization is to be achieved. He contended that the Apostle Paul sought for points of contact with heathen philosophy in presenting his gospel. This led Ahn to seek an answer to the question of indigenization in terms of hermeneutics. Ahn's hermeneutic is based on the methods of form-criticism; he was very critical of the Korean words for "gospel," "Cross," "God," etc., and said that these translations should be reexamined because they separated these biblical concepts from Korean thought.[63] Furthermore, he insisted on a reformulation of systematic theology on the grounds that the present concepts of the doctrine of God within systematic theology were formed in the West and were planted in Western metaphysical soil. The doctrine of the church was, in his judgment, also established on the basis of Western political situations. Accordingly, these terms in their Western form are not hermeneutically appropriate in Korea. However, Ahn did not provide any concrete method of indigenization, nor did he define its limits.

Chul-ha Han, professor at Asia Theological Seminary, realized the necessity for the independence of Korean Christian theology from that of the West. Yet he expressed much doubt about the approaches of Yun and Ryu and pointed to some of the difficulties involved in their positions. About the former he wrote:

Dr. Yun gives a very positive evaluation to the *Tangun* myth as material, and Yul-kok's philosophy as methodology for Korean Christian theology, but he appraises very negatively the idea of history found in *Chunggamrok* [Sang-he Mun, The Phenomenon of the New Religion," *Yonsei Chunchu Weekly* (Yonsei University Press, 19, June, 1982), p. 24]... If this is the case, the theological style created on the basis of that found in *Chunggamrok* [which Dr. Yun believes to be the conclusion of Korean theology] is inadequate. Should we not give it up from the outset and return to a unique Christian theology? Are not the Korean idea of God, Yul-kok's thought, and the historical concept of *Chunggamrok* simply materials for Korean theology? In any case, Dr. Yun's enterprise appears to be still premature. Although he wants to read Christian ideas in traditional Korean thought, he disregards completely the different structure of meaning in Christian thought and in Korean traditional thought and seeks to find and compare similarities of theoretical forms.[64]

Han also questioned Ryu's approach to indigenization and was critical of his understanding of other religions. "How can Ryu claim that Buddhism and *Chundokyo* have reflected the gospel while they do not recognize the event of Christ which is the heart of the gospel?"[65] Chul-ha Han also felt that Ryu, like Yun, neglected the differences between Christianity and other religions. He questioned Ryu's call for a general mobilization of all Korea's religions because of its inconsistencies. Further, Han asked whether it is possible, as Ryu believed, to draw a sharp difference between an historical religion and the gospel. Any attempt to differentiate between an historical manifestation of the gospel and the gospel itself could easily overlook the inner dynamic relation that exists between the two and might involve the error of reductionism.

Finally, Eui-whan Kim, professor at the General Assembly Theological Seminary, likewise criticized Yun's Korean theology and regarded it as a dangerous form of syncretism. To many in the Korean church, syncretism represents the attempt to integrate Korean traditional religious elements into the Christian religious tradition which conflict with the original content of Christianity.[66] Arguing that Yun's Korean theology was both anti-Christian and anti-missionary in its thrust, Kim contended that Christian truth has an absoluteness and unchangeableness regardless of place or time. He said:

> The forming of "indigenization theology" seems to be fitted to the spirit of this age, because Korea [is] attempting to establish Korean democracy. Korean democracy could be possible, but there is no possibility of pure Korean theology. Christian truth, we believe, is not a relativistic, political theory or a philosophy but it is absolutely unchangeable; therefore, we cannot conceive of any Korean gospel truth which was only true according to the Korean situation. Seeds containing life never produce different fruits according to different soil.[67]

MINJUNG THEOLOGY

Minjung theology represents an attempt to relate the gospel to the Korean context. There is no agreement among Korean *Minjung* theologians regarding the precise definition of the word *minjung*. The term is dynamic. But most would agree that Wan-sang Han's definition is useful. Young-hak Hyun interprets him as saying that "the *minjung* are those who are oppressed politically, exploited economically, alienated sociologically, and kept uneducated in cultural and intellectual matters."[68] Yong-bock Kim says,

> "*Minjung*" is not a concept or object which can be easily explained or defined. "*Minjung*" signifies a living reality which is dynamic. This living reality defines its own experiences, and generates new acts and dramas in history; and it refuses in principle to be defined conceptually.[69]

Minjung is a Korean combination of two Chinese characters, "*min*" meaning "people," and "*jung*" meaning "the mass." Therefore, "*minjung*" means "the mass of the people, or the masses, or just the people." But when we try to translate it into English, "mass" is not adequate for our theological purpose; and "the people" is politically dangerous in anti-Communist South Korea because it has become a Communist word. Although "the people of God" may seem to be the most safe and a neutral expression both in Korean and English, theologically and politically "*minjung*" cannot be translated in this way. Kwang-sun Suh gave a definition of *minjung* theology as follows:

> Theology of *Minjung* or *Minjung* theology is an accumulation and articulation of theological reflection on the political experiences of Christian students, laborers, the press, professors, farmers, writers and intellectuals as well as theologians in Korea in the 1970's. It is a theology of the oppressed in the Korean political situation, a theocentric response to the oppressors, and it is the response of the oppressed to the Korean church and its mission.[70]

Byung-mu Ahn's "Jesus and the *Minjung* in the Gospel of Mark" makes a sharper presentation of the notion of *minjung* in terms of Mark's use of the word "*ochlos*" [crowd] as opposed to the word "*laos*".[71] For him, the *minjung* is definitely "*ochlos*" rather than "*laos.*" His conclusion is that Mark does not define *ochlos* in a deterministic way but rather uses the term in connection with a social historical context.[72] According to Ahn, the characteristics of *ochlos* are as follows.[73] First, wherever Jesus went, there were always people who gathered around him. They are called the *ochlos* (2:4, 13; 3:9, 20, 32; 4:1; 5:21, 24, 31; 8:1; 10:1). These people were the so-called sinners, who stood condemned in their society. Especially at the beginning of his gospel, Mark applies the term *ochlos* in a typical way to the tax collectors and sinners. Under the category of the so-called sinners, the sick, the poor and hungry, the widows are also included, because they cannot fulfill the requirements of the law on account of their illness and poverty. In a word, the *ochlos* are the despised, condemned, alienated people socially, economically, religiously and politically in their community (2:13-17). Second, the *ochlos* are differentiated from the disciples (8:34; 9:14; 10:46). In some instances Jesus teaches only the disciples (4:36; 6:46; 7:17, 33). Thus it seems that Jesus placed the disciples above the *ochlos*. However, we must note that Jesus often fiercely criticized the disciples. Jesus mainly rebukes their ignorance, for example, their misunderstanding of the parables (4:13; 7:18), their unbelief during the storm (4:35-41; 6:51f.) and their lack of understanding of Jesus' suffering (8:32ff; 9:32; 10:32, etc.).The *ochlos* are never rebuked by Jesus but always welcomed and accepted as they are without any condition such as repentance of their sins. Third, the *ochlos* are contrasted with the ruling class from Jerusalem who attack and criticize Jesus as their enemy. The *ochlos* take an anti-Jerusalem position; they are the *minjung* of Galilee.[74] Geographically, Galilee symbolizes the *ochlos*. Mark sets forth Galilee as the background to show the position of the victims of society at that time (2:4-6; 3:2-21; 4:1; 11:18, 27, 32). Fourth, because the *ochlos* were against the rulers, the rulers were afraid of them and tried not to arouse their anger (11:18, 32; 12:12; 15:8,15). To get the *ochlos* on their side, the rulers had to bribe them. For instance, when Jesus was arrested the rulers are said to have given money to mobilize the *ochlos* - a fact which indicates the strength of the *ochlos*. The fact that they were mobilized in such a way does not mean that they were necessarily anti-Jesus but that they could be manipulated.

It is noteworthy that Kwang-sun Suh, one of the representative *minjung* theologians, points out in his research that the majority of the Korean *minjung-ochlos* are charmed by the Pentecostal-charismatic movement.[75] He says, "I have found the other side of *minjung* in the churches which have fast-growing non-denominational congregations."[76] If the majority of Korean *minjung-ochlos* draw their consolation, encouragement, aspiration and strength of hope from the charismatic fellowship of the Rev. Yonggi Cho's Full Gospel Central Church in Seoul and, as usually happens, escape from sickness and poverty, and manage to climb the social ladder with the help of the Pentecostal-charismatic ministry, he asks, how can *Minjung* theology help the Pentecostal *minjung* with the proper guidelines, and how can they dialogue with each other?[77]

Ahn's characterization of *minjung* is generally accepted and supported by other Korean *minjung* theologians. But Hee-suk Moon defines the *minjung* as "the have-nots, the victims of social injustice," namely, the exploited laborers.[78] Ha-eun Jung views the *minjung* as the alienated crowd who have been robbed of human rights, those oppressed by structural evil, and social revolutionaries, particularly the imprisoned social revolutionaries of today.[79] Nam-dong Suh defines the *minjung* as "the people full of *han* who experience *han* politically, socially, economically, and religiously." *Han* is a deep feeling that rises out of the unjust, suppressed, amassed and condensed experience of oppression caused by mischief or misfortune so that it forms a kind of "lump" in one's spirit. "Just indignation yearning for justice to be done" may be a close translation of *han*.[80] According to Dae-jung Kim, the goal of *minjung* theology is the establishment of a democratic regime, which guarantees individual basic human rights and the social welfare of the people and which opposes any monopolistic possession of riches.[81] *Minjung* theology emphasizes the restoration of human rights and the new social order in which the alienated and despised can be treated as human.[82] In sum, the *minjung* are the politically oppressed, economically exploited, culturally alienated productive laborers and social revolutionaries as the subjects of history.

Minjung theology was a sociopolitical biography of Korean Christianity in the 1970s, a sociopolitical interpretation of the Korean Christian experience so to speak.[83] This theology arose against the background of the political oppression of the dictatorial Chung-hee Park regime[84] and the economic deprivation of city workers and rural peasants. In this situation, a group of theologians and church ministers issued a manifesto in 1972 entitled *A Declaration of Korean Christians*, in which they affirmed their resolve to follow Jesus in his fight for the poor and the oppressed *minjung*. It was soon followed by a statement on human rights by the Korean National Council of Churches on November 24, 1973. The 1972 manifesto declared:

> ...We believe that God is the one who necessarily protects with His justice the oppressed, poor, and weak from the evil forces and judges those forces in history. We believe that Jesus the Messiah and the Kingdom of the Messiah are coming and that this messianic kingdom should be the haven of the poor, oppressed, and despised... Therefore, we Christians, at the time of historical crisis, confess our faith as follows:
>
> 1. We believe that we are commanded, in the presence of God, the Master and Judge of history, to pray for the oppressed who are suffering at the hands of their fellow human beings.
>
> 2. We believe that we have to stand and fall together with the oppressed,

poor, and despised just as Jesus did...

3. We believe that the Holy Spirit reforms our character and demands us
    to take part in creating a new society and history. This Spirit of the
    Messianic Kingdom commands us to struggle for the cause of social
    and political renovation in this world. [85]

And the 1973 Human Rights Statement declared in the same vein:

> We believe that God is the ultimate vindicator of the oppressed, weak, and
> poor; he judges the evil forces in history. We believe that Jesus the Messiah
> proclaimed the coming of the Messianic kingdom, to be subversive to the
> evil powers, and that his Messianic kingdom will be the haven of the dis-
> possessed, rejected, and downtrodden... We resolve that we will follow the
> footsteps of our Lord, living among our oppressed and poor people, stand-
> ing against political oppression, and participating in the transformation of
> history, for this is the only way to the messianic kingdom. [86]

But until 1979, Korean *Minjung* theology was just an underground
movement. In 1979, some significant historic events for *Minjung* theology broke out. One was the slaying of Miss Gyung-sook Kim of the
Y. H. Company. On August 9, 1979, 200 women workers of that company went to the New Democratic Party office building to appeal to the
government party to work out a fair solution to an employment problem. After three days, during a forced dispersal of the workers by the
police force, Miss Gyung-sook Kim was killed. It was reported that a
few leaders of the Korean civil rights movement and Urban Industrial
Mission intervened just before the workers went to the New
Democratic Party building.[87]

Another case concerned a Mr. Won-choon Oh and the Catholic
Farmer's Association [CFA]. Mr. Oh was a board member of the
Andong Diocese Federation of the CFA.[88] He was active in the farmers' rights movement and the campaign for the refund of damages to
sweet potato farmers. He was kidnapped by a certain authority (Korean
CIA) from May, 5, to May 26, 1979 and was beaten severely. This case
provided the impetus for the church leaders to organize special prayer
meetings and stimulated the Catholic Farmer's Association and all the
Catholic churches in Korea, the Urban Industrial Mission, the rural
activities of the Korea Christian Academy, and the National Council of
Churches Human Rights Committee to react against the government
authority. Several theologians working for the Institute for Mission
Education had been involved in these two events and had written theological reflections on these cases. About a dozen Korean theologians
and about an equal number of writers, sociologists, historians, etc.,

were engaged in this discussion of *Minjung* theology. It did not take long, however, before the movement was noticed by the churches outside Korea and by the World Council of Churches. In October 1979 the Christian Conference of Asia held a conference on *Minjung* theology in Seoul, Korea, and the papers presented were published in English and German as well as in Korean.[89] Thus *Minjung* theology has come to be discussed in many parts of the world as a genuine Korean contribution to theology.

MISSIOLOGICAL IMPERATIVES

Early in 1972, Shoki Coe and Aharon Sapsezian, directors of the Theological Education Fund, introduced into our vocabulary the term, "contextualization,"[90] which in the TEF report *Ministry and Context* was described as follows:

> Contextualization is not simply a fad or catch-word but a theological necessity by the incarnational nature of the Word. What does the term imply? It means all that is implied in the familiar term "indigenization" and yet seeks to press beyond. Contextualization has to do with how we assess the peculiarity of Third World contexts. Indigenization tends to be used in the sense of responding to the gospel in terms of a traditional culture. Contextualization, while not ignoring this, takes into account the process of secularity, technology, and struggle for human justice, which characterize the historical movement of nations in the Third World.[91]

On the basis of the foregoing we may argue that an authentic contextual theology should contain two interrelated elements: inculturation and liberation. In this dissertation the author has considered the sociopolitical, cultural and religious conditions of the nation and the activities of the churches and the unique characteristics of the Korean Christians throughout Korean church history to find various factors which helped the Protestant Christian mission to be successful and which caused rapid church growth in Korea. From the beginning of Protestant missions, many foreign missionaries struggled to discover the reasons for the rapid growth of the Korean church. The foreign missionaries and their methods had been believed to be the primary cause for the growth of the early church in Korea. Indeed, church growth in Korea owes much to the foreign missionaries who first introduced Nevius' methods and policies of self-propagation, self-government and self-support. The missionaries engaged in much welfare work and cared for abandoned children, orphans and children from desperately poor families. All these projects were funded by early missionaries.

However, one of the most important human factors influencing the spread of the gospel was the witnessing activity of Korean Christians. In the early church in Korea, new Christians never shared the gospel merely as a system of beliefs to be accepted, but presented it as a way of life to be followed. They preached the gospel by uniting words and deeds. The gospel was offered and communicated in love and demonstrated by Christian compassion for the physical needs of the people. This is one of the primary reasons why the Korean church has grown to be a healthy and mature church regardless of a long series of severe trials, persecutions and sufferings. The Korean church bears witness to the truth that holistic evangelism in preaching the gospel of sovereign grace and implementing it by practice has as its fruit genuine church growth in quality as well as quantity. Harvie Conn, a former missionary in Korea, wrote about his new understanding of the importance of holistic evangelism contributing to the rapid growth of the church in Korea.

> I remember visiting a church in rural Korea some years ago. A small congregation for years, it had doubled in the last five years. I went there with a seminary student to find out why. We met one evening with the elders and deacons of the fellowship. I asked, "How do you explain this rapid growth?" There was a long silence. Then an elder said, "I don't really know. Maybe you should ask deaconess Kim." Again I asked, "What are you doing now that may be different from your former ministry?" One replied, "I don't know." I met Mrs. Kim and found my answer. She had moved into the area five years before with her husband. A dynamo of enthusiasm for the gospel, she shared herself and her faith with her neighbors. When a woman was sick, Mrs. Kim cooked the meals for the family and gossiped about Jesus. When one of the men in the village needed help, Mrs. Kim's husband was there to offer it. I had found my opinion leader in that church. She couldn't even attend lay leader meetings.[92]

Christian mission and church growth in Korea began as the witness to the gospel among the people of shamanistic faith and practice, and the church faced the question of how to define its relationship to shamanism. Korean theology emerged as an effort to define this relationship. Its significance can never be over-emphasized, considering its crucial role in interpreting the gospel in relation to the dominant folk religion.

According to the author's investigation, there are some aspects that can be used for Christian mission and theological indigenization though many elements of shamanism are in conflict with Christian teaching and must therefore be reinterpreted if used in the Christian church. Particularly, shamanist zealousness in prayer, fear of evil spirits and methods of communication are suitable for Christian adaptation in Korea. On the other hand, magical techniques and objects, ritual as the magical power of transformation, the concepts of gods and human beings, and the aspect of this-worldliness of human religion are in conflict with the Christian understanding. Particularly, the kingdom of God, the sinfulness of human nature, and salvation through Christ are not communicable in the framework of shamanistic faith.

The problem of syncretism arises when the gospel is not communicated at the worldview level, especially with regard to shamanism, which is polytheistic in nature. Worldview is the basic idea and values shared by the members of a particular society. These concepts provide a way by which the people normally order their life experiences. The Christian God easily becomes one more addition to the numerous deities already within the shamanistic pantheon when the deeper level of the people's belief is not touched. Although Korean Christians hold firmly to the idea that there is only one God, the conception of Godhead for some shamanistic Christians was significantly altered in certain aspects by spiritual understanding derived from elements of Korean shamanistic faith. It is very important to emphasize the reality of spirits for the people of shamanism for the communication of the gospel. By a careful reinterpretation of the nature of spirit-gods and evil spirits, the people's fear of the latter and their everyday experiences with the spirit-gods can be transformed into a stepping stone for the communication of the gospel. The spirit-experiences of the Christian Church resulted in a syncretistic mixture of both religions among the Korean Christians who were not provided with a functional substitute.

Careless adaptation, however, prevented new Christians from making a clear break with the old shamanistic beliefs and turning to the new faith-allegiance. Many of the problems within the Korean Church arise from a misunderstanding of conversion. Conversion is understood as a change of the religions or religious behavior by many Korean Christians. For many Christians in Korea, Christianity is another form of religious practice with which they replaced the traditional shamanistic faith. A Christian mission for the people under the influence of traditional shamanism means bringing them into a relationship with Christ. The Church must provide the proper teaching to meet the varied needs of the individuals who are in the process of growth toward a mature Christian life. It is very important for Christian pastors and evangelists, therefore, to examine the shamanism in depth and learn to communicate at the level of its worldview. Therefore, there is a need for the rapid development of an indigenous church and theology for church growth in Korea. Indigenization can be applied in the methodology of presenting the gospel in Korea. For example, the Christian message must be expressed in national and cultural patterns, liturgical settings, church music and church architecture. Contextualization is also applied by various theologians in dealing with the content of the gospel. Some theologies are characterized by syncretistic contamination of the gospel with incompatible shamanistic beliefs, but others represent systematized interpretations relevant to the Korean situation. Korean theology can be categorized in three ways.

First, there is syncretistic theology in Korea. Certain Christian theologians and other religious thinkers have syncretized Christianity with a national religion in an attempt to contextualize theology into the national situation in Korea. As discussed earlier, while the Korean Church itself was not yet prepared to engage in the inculturation of Christian theology, various founders of shamanistic Christian movements in Korea attempted to intermix the Christian heritage with the metaphysics of the *yin-yang* relationship, shamanism, animism and certain forms of Oriental mysticism. In a sense they have met the felt-need of Korean religious people for the indigenous expression of Christianity, but, unfortunately, they altered the gospel through unacceptable contextualization of shamanistic religions. This syncretistic theology is also illustrated in Sung-bum Yun's theology, which relates the doctrine of the Trinity to the Korean conception of creation. As indicated, Yun's study of contextualization begins with the *Tangun* myth, which he identified with the Trinitarian God. Yun follows this with a study of the significance of the Confucian concept of *sung* [sincerity]. He related *sung* with "the accomplished word," which derived from Jesus' saying on the Cross: "It is finished." According to Yun, *sung* is God himself, and the one who practices *sung* is the believer. He sought for linkages between Christianity and traditional Korean thought, but made a great mistake in attempting to synthesize native culture and biblical Christianity. Yun made certain basic errors in the way he attempted to establish a Korean theology. Assuming that it was possible to separate culture and religion, he tried to interpret the gospel of Scripture in the light of Confucian concept of *sung*. He attempted to establish a Yellow theology and illicitly to extend the meaning and significance of the notion of *sung*. He understood *sung* as a person, whereas in Confucianism *sung* is connected to moral training and in no way carries a salvific meaning in the sense of "the accomplished word." Theological syncretism begins when the interpreter uses the cultural context as the final authority in determining the extent and limits of contextualization.

There are many new Christian religious movements which originated in Christianity, but whose beliefs and practices are a syncretistic mix of shamanism and Christianity. Whatever their differences, the new Christian religious movements all share certain common features. First, they are syncretistic religious movements which have mixed together Buddhist, Taoist, Confucian and Christian beliefs to create a new system of belief. Second, these religions are based largely on shamanistic concepts and practices to which other elements have been added. Third, the new religious movements may be divided into various traditions, primarily Buddhist, Christian, Confucian or shamanistic. Fourth, in varying degrees, these new religions evince a strong element of nationalism in their doctrine and methods of propagation. Finally, the new Christian religious movements look towards a utopian condition in this world, or in some manner offer hope to their members of a better life.

The Korean shamanistic new Christian movements seek to be authentically Christian and at the same time genuine expressions of the people and culture in which they have taken root. These new religions must not be regarded as authentic Christian movements, however, but rather as oriental mystical movements featuring doctrines which are a mixture of yin-yang philosophy, shamanistic mysticism and certain peculiar interpretations of Scripture. For instance, the relation between the doctrines of the Unification Church and the Bible are clearly spelled out by this church. The *Divine Principle* emphasizes that truth is unique, eternal, unchangeable and absolute. However, the "Bible is not the truth itself, but a textbook teaching the truth."[93] Though the New Testament was adequate for teaching the truth to people two thousand years ago - "people whose spiritual and intellectual standard was very low"- it is not sufficient to meet the needs of modern people.[94] In the early days of Christianity, truth could be expressed in parables and symbols. Today truth must be expressed "with a higher standard and with a scientific method of expression" in order to speak to human beings in the present.[95]

Definitely influenced by oriental philosophical and shamanistic religious concepts, Moon's teachings are mathematically inclined and present an impersonal, technical view of man's predicament and the ultimate solution. There are frequent passages which, while not explicitly which, naming Moon, quite obviously refer to his central role in the final restoration of mankind.[96] In the *Divine Principle*, Moon says that Jesus failed in his purpose in coming to earth, which was to establish the Kingdom of Heaven on earth; his death on the cross was not an essential part of God's plan for redeeming sinners. Moon says that there must be a true father and a true mother in order for a person to be born again. According to Moon, the true mother is the Holy Spirit, and the true father is Jesus. Thus the Holy Spirit is the second Eve, the female principle, negativity, working in the earth. Jesus is the second Adam, the male principle, positivity, working in heaven. When we have a special rebirth, it is through the love of the spiritual true parents emanating from the give-and-take action between Jesus, the spiritual true father, and the Holy Spirit, the spiritual true mother. The *Divine Principle* not only denies the divine inspiration and the authority of the canon of the Holy Scriptures, but it also makes the Bible an auxiliary textbook for the *Divine Principle*.[97]

The fundamental error of the shamanistic new Christian religious movements is their acceptance of revelation outside of the Bible. We cannot describe the Korean church without recognizing the influence of this shamanistic faith. Shamanistic belief has played a major role in formulating faith within Korean Christianity. Nevertheless, the Korean church should be very discreet in the practice of shamanistic faith; sacrifices in the form of offerings, encouragement of the state of ecstasy, mystical experience, exercise of spiritual power, and particularly sermons oriented to worldly and material blessings as rewards of faith, including wealth, health, power and honor, and curses including disease, poverty, failure in business, and the use of special spiritual techniques. Prayer with fasting, speaking in tongues, prayer services on the mountain, exorcism and faith healing should not be excessively stressed in the Korean churches. Biblical contextualization requires that the interpreter be willing to take risks, but also to avoid syncretism by not losing sight of the goal of evangelism, working toward the establishment of a truly Christian culture, developing sound hermeneutical principles, and seeking to recover the central themes of dogmatic theology.

Second, there is situational theology in Korea. *Minjung* theology is a typical illustration. The main thrust of ecumenical theology today in Korea is the liberation of people from social injustice, economic exploitation, political oppression, and racial discrimination. *Minjung* theology is a Korean version of liberation theology and teaches Jesus Christ as the liberator of the oppressed. Latin American liberation theology starts from the evil situational structure of bondage, oppression and exploitation resulting from dehumanization, selfishness and the negation of brotherly love, and seeks to overcome this situation by way of revolutionary participation in the class struggle of the poor and oppressed, the special elect people of God. While Latin American liberation theology focuses on the economic aspect of the poor and oppressed, Korean *Minjung* theology tries to develop the concept of the poor and oppressed in broader terms. *Minjung* theology deals comprehensively with the various aspects of the condition of the poor: social, political, cultural, religious as well as economic. Considering these above-mentioned theological backgrounds, it is impossible to deny that Korean *Minjung* theology and Latin American liberation theology have exactly the same theological origins and therefore have many common points.[98]

Some *Minjung* theologians, however, understand the *minjung* simply in socioeconomic and political terms, without regard for the spiritual relationship with God.[99] A second problem is that *Minjung* theology limits the data of *ochlos* to the gospel according to Mark and its usage to "the Galilean masses contrasted with the Jerusalem authorities," and thereby glorifies the *minjung*.[100] Third, the kingdom of God of *Minjung* theology is not biblical in nature and character. It is surely biblical to try to achieve a society with a better living standard. Liberation from oppression and the creation of a new and better society are definitely God's good will for humankind. God is greatly concerned for both our bodies and our society. *Minjung* theology in Korea emphasizes the kingdom of God as actually present, operative and authentically realized, but discards the otherworldliness of the kingdom as unbiblical.[101] The notion of transcendence and otherworldliness is understood only as symbolic of an open future in which the *minjung* may participate as the subjects of history.[102]

Third, there is biblically oriented theology in Korea. The West had dominated theological education in Korea with Western theological thought and the influence of Western missionaries. Western theologies such as Calvinism, Arminianism, and the Death of God theology have been derived from their own cultural and historical background. Yet in Korea Christians face different circumstances than in the West. Some of the issues there today are poverty, overpopulation, hunger, war, demon possession, idolatry, secularism, resurgent shamanism and

Buddhism, and the rise of new religions. Remembering the differences between East and West, the Korean church desperately needs to formulate Korean theologies which are relevant to Koreans yet based on biblical teaching.

How should the Korean Christian deal with primal religions and traditional culture? The primal worldview remains deeply imbedded in the religious mind of the Korean people. The Korean Christian must choose between two extremes in the contextualization of the Korean church. On the one hand, it is possible to reject all aspects of primal religion and traditional culture, as did many of the former missionaries. As we have already stated, to do this only causes a cultural vacuum that needs to be filled. Western forms of Christianity fail to replace that which is lost and often lead to a foreign church which stands out with a great incongruity within the community. In the Korean church there is still a great disjuncture between peoples' lives as Christians and as Koreans. Korean church buildings are constructed to Western designs, and the music that is sung and played is European. The forms of service, dress of pastors, and patterns of worship in Korean churches are almost all from a Western tradition. James Grayson illustrates a few examples of this apparent disjuncture with Korean tradition from his missionary experiences in Korea:

> During the meeting held to decide on the plans for the new church building, I made the suggestion that the church should be a Korean-style building...The unanimous reactions of the church elders, however, was that to build a church in such a style was impossible because to do so would make the church look like a Buddhist temple. A church to be a church had to be built in either a Victorian pseudo-Gothic style, or in a pseudo-Gregorian style.... The handful of hymns composed by Koreans was rarely sung, even by young people, whom I would have expected to be less traditional in their religious outlook.[103]

On the other hand, it is also possible to view all the rituals and customs of primal society uncritically as meaningful and significant. This approach appears to answer many of the questions involved in contextualization by making Christianity seem relevant to the Korean people. For instance, the *Donghak* movement of the peasants in 1892 is regarded by *minjung* theologians to be the most outstanding revolution of the *minjung*.[104] However, the Korean *Donghaks* never confessed the true Christian faith. The Korean *Donghak* religious faith is syncretistic, mixing Confucianism, Buddhism and Roman Catholicism. It can never be equated with true Christianity. It must be noted that it is one thing for the Christian church to be concerned with the poor and oppressed *minjung*, but it is another for theologians to equate the shamanistic and syncretistic *Donghak* movement with Christianity. The key issue in the whole argument of contextual theology is whether the biblical and historical doctrines of the Christian Church can be preserved without compromise in the process of contextualization. At the heart of the problem of indigenization and contextualization, it seems, lies the difficult and paradoxical matter of how to blend the local and the universal elements of the church of Jesus Christ, so that it may be both a part of the people of one nation and a part of all nations. Since indigenization and contextualization are to make use of indigenous culture for communicating the Christian faith without changing the latter's essence, great care is necessary in this enterprise. We must first of all abandon the kind of attitude which tries to identify Korean culture directly with Christianity. At the same time, we must discard the idea that there is not or cannot be any relevancy of Korean culture for Christianity.

We have observed various theological attempts to contextualize the Christian gospel in Korea as well as political attempts to de-Westernize and nationalize the Christian tradition there. But much more has yet to be undertaken. The Korean church needs to take risks for Christ and the gospel's sake, to become all things to all people that some may be saved. It must be willing to accept the sacrifice of being misunderstood. Korean Christians should not be so fearful of syncretism that they fail to attempt the task of contextualization in the cross-cultural communication of the gospel. For instance, shamanistic ancestor worship has been one of the most important traditional practices and a continuing obstacle to Christian evangelism and missions in Korea. The problem of ancestor worship is a vastly complex matter involving religious, social and other elements. It is a problem to which Christians have no easy solutions. And yet, in the interest of contextualization for the sake of church growth the Korean church might well adopt certain elements of this ancient religious practice, while at the same time remaining fully faithful to the teachings of Scripture.

As indicated in an earlier chapter, a serious attempt should be made by the Korean Church to transform the traditional meaning of ancestor worship into a form of Christian ancestor respect,[105] to develop a theology that deals meaningfully with ancestral rites and honoring the dead. An understanding of ancestor worship in many African societies is very similar to the one in Korea: 1) The dead are almost always honored in some way according to the funeral ceremonies. 2) A grave is where the presence of the invisible is concentrated. 3) Burial places where the ancestors lie are sacred spots where they can be approached with offering and consulted in times of the crisis. 4) Death of the ancestor is not the annihilation of a being. Absence of sons is the worst of curses for Korean people. Koreans fear dying without someone behind who will remember them. Some Korean churches are in fact trying to produce a form of a memorial for the dead that would not be considered unorthodox. Christians should have some way of showing to their non-Christian neighbors that they do not dishonor the dead in Korea. Scriptural support for this position could be found in the Ten Commandments, where God directs believers to honor their fathers and mothers. Christians in Korea should work out a Christian ritual which would remember, honor and exalt the ancestors even more impressively than non-Christians bowing before the ancestor table. As stated earlier, *Chudo Yebae* in the Korean church is a Christian memorial ritual offered on behalf of deceased parents or other near relatives, normally up to two or three ascending generations. The family gathers with a minister of the church for a service of thanksgiving for the life of the deceased, singing hymns and reading the Scripture. Afterward, the family and minister eat a communal meal together. Another way of honoring ancestors is for Korean Christians to have a book telling of the good and great deeds of ancestors. However, there seem to be two primary elements involved: worship of one's ancestors and fellowship with the spirits. The Christian reserves his worship for God alone. One's ancestors may not presume on the divine prerogative of worship, nor would it be coveted by the Christian forebear.[106] Korean Christians should examine the honoring of ancestors not only in terms of the second commandment, but also in terms of the fifth.

The Korean church needs to recognize the lordship of Christ over culture. What is the relationship between God, Christianity, and context, between the revealed gospel and human cultures? This was the question posed by H. Richard Niebuhr in his classic, *Christ and Culture* (1951). Niebuhr identified five basic positions: 1) Christ *against* culture, 2) Christ *in* culture, 3) Christ *above* culture, 4) Christ and culture *in paradox*, and 5) Christ the *transformer* of culture.[107] From the argumentation of Niebuhr's book, it is clear that he favors the fifth position, Christ *transforming* culture. For those who assume a more affirmative stance toward culture,

> History is the story of God's mighty deeds and of man's response to them...
> Eternal life is a quality of existence in the here and now. Hence the con-

versionist is less concerned with the conservation of what has been given in creation, less with preparation for what will be given in a final redemption, than with the divine possibility of a present renewal... The conversionist... does not live so much in expectation of a final ending of the world of creation and culture as in the awareness of the power of the Lord to transform all things by lifting them up to himself.[108]

Anton Wessels summarized the three theological aspects of this position. First, humanity lives by the power of the word of creation, and for that reason God's creative goodness can be found in human culture. Second, people turn the goodness inherent in creation around by their perverse rebellion against God. The culture may be sinful, but no apocalyptic revision is demanded — no new creation —only a radical conversion. Third, history becomes an open, dynamic interaction between humanity and God.[109] Charles Kraft underlines the *transcendence of God* with respect to culture.

> God, being completely unbound by any culture (except as he chooses to operate within or in terms of culture) is "*supra*cultural" (i.e., above and outside culture). Likewise, any absolute principles or functions proceeding from God's nature, attributes or activities may be labeled "*supra*cultural." For they, too, transcend and are not bound by any specific culture, except when they are expressed within a culture. [110]

It is the task of the Korean church to work towards the development of a truly Christian culture which manifests both the universality of the gospel and the fruits of the Holy Spirit and at the same time reflects the particularity of the national culture refined by the Word of God. This book has been written to meet the urgent need for a greater knowledge of shamanism and its relation to church growth in Korea. However, some areas are not covered in this limited study. For the future study of shamanism by theologians, it is suggested that more field research be included, particularly on the practical phenomenon of syncretism between Christianity and shamanism among lay Christians in Korea. It is also suggested that there be more extensive field research on the present-day practice of shamanism. Concerning the issue of contextualization of the Korean church, the writer recommends the gathering of sufficient data on shamanism without simplifying its nature. Koreans need to understand their own culture to bring about church growth. Oversimplification results in the inconsiderate rejection of anything connected with traditional culture or in a naive identification of Christian faith with shamanism, which leads to syncretism. Contextualization of the gospel in Korea will be possible only when the church comes to understand the nature of traditional culture more fully. Effective communication of the gospel depends upon the church's ability to discern both the positive and negative elements of that culture. It is incumbent upon the Korean church to listen to, evaluate and maintain an open mind toward different theological views of contextualization, and yet without compromise to be faithful to the gospel and proclaim it in love.

NOTES

[1]See Ha-eun Chung, *"Shinhak-eui Tochakhwa-eui Gijeom"* [A Basis of Indigenization of Theology in Korea], *Kitokkyo Sasang* [*The Christian Thought*] (July, 1963), p. 22.

[2]Cf. Boo-woong Yoo, *Korean Pentecostalism: Its History and Theology* (Frankfurt am Main: Verlag Peter Lang GmbH, 1988), pp. 166, 169, 189-190.

[3]Il-sub Shim, *"Hankuk Shinhak Hyungsungsa Seasul"* [An Introduction to the Formation of Korean Theology], *Hankuk-eui Shinhak Sasang* [*Theological Thought of Korea*], eds., Theological Thought Editorial Committee (Seoul, Korea: The Christian Literature Society, 1966), pp. 194-202.

[4]See Sung-bum Yun, *Kitohyo-wa Hankuk Sasang* [*Christianity and Korean Thought*] (Seoul, Korea: The Christian Literature Society, 1964); Yun, *A Korean Theology: The Hermeneutic of Sung - A Yellow Theology* (Seoul, Korea: Sun Myung Whasa,1972); Tong-shik Ryu, *Hankuk Jongkyo-wa Kitokkyo* [*The Christian Faith Encounters the Religions of Korea*] (Seoul, Korea: The Christian Literature Society, 1965), pp. 246-258; So-young Kim, ed., *Hankuk-eui Shinhak Sasang* [*Theological Thought of Korea*] (Seoul, Korea: The Christian Literature Society, 1983), pp. 137-304; Kwang-sun Suh, *Hankuk Kitokkyo-eui Sae Euishik* [*New Consciousness of Korean Christianity*] (Seoul, Korea: The Christian Literature Society, 1985), pp. 209-216; Gil-sop Song, *Hankuk Shinhak Sasangsa* [*History of Theological Thought in Korea*] (Seoul, Korea: The Christian Literature Society, 1987), pp. 330-343.

[5]D. T. Niles, *"Sungseo Yungu-wa Tochakhwa Munjae"* [A Study of the Bible and the Problem of Indigenization], *Kitokkyo Sasang Kangjowa* [*Lectures on Christian Thought*].Vol. 3, p. 279. *Kitokkyo Sasang Kangjowa* constitutes a series consisting of volumes of collected articles on a given subject which originally appeared in the monthly journal *Kitokkyo Sasang*; *Kitokkyo Sasang Kangjowa* is not to be confused with another series, *Kitokkyo Sasang-eui Yungu* [Studies on Christian Thought] to which we also refer in this study.

[6]Tong-shik Ryu, *"Bokeum-eui Tochkhwa-wa Hankuk-ese-eui Sunkyo-jek Kwajae,"* [The Indigenization of the Gospel and the Missionary Task in Korea] *Gamrikyo Shinhakbo* [*Methodist Theological Bulletin*], Vol. 14, (Seoul, Korea: Methodist Theological Seminary Press, 1962), pp. 43-58.

[7]*Ibid.,* pp. 43-50.

[8]*Ibid.,* pp. 43-44.

[9]*Ibid,* p. 44.

[10]Ryu, "The Indigenization of the Gospel and the Missionary Task in Korea", *Theological Bulletin,* (Seoul, Korea: Methodist Theological Seminary, 1962), pp. 43-58.

[11]Kyung-yun Jun, *"Gristokyo Munwha-nun Tochakhwa Halsu Inknunga?"* [Can Christian Culture Be Indigenized?] *Kitokkyo Sasang Kangjowa* [*Lectures on Christian Thought*], Vol. 5, (Seoul, Korea: The Christian Literature Society,

1963), pp. 207-208; Song kil-sub, *Hankuk Shinhak Sasangsa* [*A History of Theological Thought in Korea*], (Seoul, Korea: Christian Literature Society, 1987), pp. 331-342.

[12]Jun, "*Gristokyo Munwha-nun Tochakwa halsu Inknunga?*" [Can Christian Culture be Indigenized?], *Lectures on Christian Thought*. p. 213.

[13]*Ibid.*, pp. 211-212.

[14]Ryu, "*Gristokyo Tochakwha-ye Daehan Yhae*" [An Understanding of the Indigenization of Christianity] , *Christian Thought* (April, 1963), p.48.

[15]*Ibid.*, p. 50.

[16]Kyung Y. Jun, *Tochakhwa-nya Wonshihwa-nya?* [A Return to the Primitive, or Indigenization?], *Lectures on Christian Thought*, 1963, Vol. III, pp. 220ff.

[17]*Ibid.*, Vol. III. pp. 221-222.

[18]*Ibid.*

[19]Sung-bum Yun, "*Hyundae Shikhak-eui Kwaje, Tochakhwa Munje,*" [The Task of Contemporary Theology and Indigenization Problem], *Christian Thought*, August, September, 1962, pp.4-12; Cf. Tong-shik Ryu, "*Kitokkyo-eui Tochakhwa-ye Deahan Yhae,*" [An Understanding of the Indigenization of Christianity], *Lectures on Christian Thought* (April, 1963); Sung-bum Yun, "*Hwan-In, Hwan-Ung, Hwan-Gum-eun gok Hananimida,*" [*Hwan-in, Hwan-Ung, Hwan-Gum* is God the Trinity], *Sasanggye* [*World of Thought*], May, 1963; Kyung-yun Jun, "*Yeksa-ryul Mushihan Tochakhwa Yiron-eun wonshih-wa-ryul Euimi.*" [Theory of Indigenization Which Ignores History Leads to Primitivism], *Christian Thought*, May, 1963; Bong-rang Park, "*Kitokkyo Tochakhwa-wa Tangun Shinhwa,*" [Christian Indigenization and *Tangun* Myth], *Sasanggye* [*World of Thought*], July 1963; Ha-eun Chung, "*Shinhak-eui Tochakhwa-eui Gijeom,*" [A Beginning Point of Indigenization of Theology] *Christian Thought*, July,1963; Hyun-sul Hong, "*Tochakhwa-eui Kanung-myun-kwa Bulkanung-myun*" [Possibility and Impossibity of Indigenization] *Christian Thought*, August-September 1963; Chul-ha Han, "*Tochakhwa Munje-ryl Dulreosan Sasang-jek Je-honran,*" [An Ideological Confusion around the Problem of Indigenization], *Shikhak Jinam* [*Theological Journal*], September,1963; Sung-bum Yun, "*Dangun Shinhwa-wa Shamwi Ilche,*"[*Tangun* Myth as *Vestigium Trinitatis*], *Christian Thought*, October 1963; Bong-rang Park, *Sungseo nun Kitokkyo Gyeshi-eui Yuil-han Sos*, [The Bible Is the Unique Source of Christian Revelation], *World of Thought*, October, 1963; Kyu-ho Lee, *Tochakhwa-ron-eui Chulhak-jek Keungeo*, [Philosophical Foundation of Indigenization], *Christian Thought*, October, 1963; Kyung-yun Jun, *Gristokyo Munhwa-nun Tochakhwa Halsu Iknunga?* [Can Christian Culture Be Indigenized?], *Christian Thought*, November,1963; Kyung-yun Jun, *Tochakhwa-nya Wonshihwa-nya?* [Indigenization or a Return to the Primitive], *Lectures on Christian Thought*, November, 1963; Tong-shik Ryu, *Kittokyo Tochakhwa-ye Daehan Yhae* [An Understanding of the Indigenization of Christianity], *Lectures on Christian Thought*, November, 1963; Chang-shik, Lee, *Kitokkyo-eui Tochakhwa-nun Yeksa-jek Kwaup* [The Indigenization of Christianity Is an Historical Task], *Lectures on Christian*

Thought, November, 1963; Kyung-yun Jun, *Hankuk Kyohoe-wa Sunkyo* [Korean Church and Mission], *Lectures on Christian Thought,* November 1963; Jong-sung Lee, *Kitokkyo Tochakhwa Yiron-ey Daehan Shinha-jek Gochal* [A Theological Study of the Theory of Indigenization], *Christian Thought,* November 1963.

[20]Sung-bum Yun, *Kitokkyo-wa Hankuk Sasang* [*Christianity and Korean Thought*] (Seoul, Korea: The Christian Literature Society Press, 1964).

[21]Yun, *World of Thought,* pp. 258ff.

[22]Yun, "The *Tangun* Myth as *Vestigium Trinitatis,*" *Christian Thoughts,* October 1963, p. 68.

[23]Yun, *World of Thought,* pp. 258ff.

[24]Kyung J. Kim, "Theological and Historical Meaning of Debates on Indigenization in the 1960's," *Hankuk-eui Shinhak Sasang* [*Theological Thought of Korea*], p. 306.

[25]Yun, "*Dangun Shinhwa-wa Shamwi Ilche,*"[The *Tangun* Myth as *Vestigium Trinitatis*], *Christian Thought,* October 1963. p. 16.

[26]Yun, *Bokeum-eui Jun-yhae-wa Daeuhas Junyie* [Pre-Understanding as Requirement for the Indigenization of the Gospel], *Ibid.,* Vol. III. pp. 235-240.

[27]*Ibid.*

[28]*Ibid.,* pp. 240-242.

[29]Yun, "*Chunggamrok Yeaeun-sokeui Yeuksa-eui Sago*" [The Idea of History in the *Chunggamrok* Prophecy], *Christian Thought,* Vol. 14, No.1, January, 1970, p. 73.

[30]Ryu, *Hankuk Jongkyo-wa Kitokkyo* [*The Christian Faith Encounters the Religions of Korea*], (Seoul, Korea: The Christian Literature Society, 1965), p. 176.

[31]*Ibid.,* p. 51.

[32]*Ibid.,* p. 178.

[33]*Ibid.,* p. 181.

[34]*Ibid.,* p. 182.

[35]*Ibid.,* pp. 183-184.

[36]*Ibid.,* p. 184.

[37]*Ibid.,* p. 196.

[38]*Ibid.,* pp. 197-212

[39]Panel Discussion, "The Korean Religions and Christianity," *Christian Thought,* Vol. 9, No. 10, November, 1965, pp. 78-84.

[40]Ryu, "Korean Religion and Christianity," *Christian Thought,* p. 246.

[41]*Ibid.,* p. 248.

[42]Ryu, *Hankuk Jongkyo-wa Kitokkyo* [*The Christian Faith Encounters the Religions of Korea*], p. 176-178.

[43]*Studies on Christian Thought*, Vol.3 (Seoul, Korea: Christian Literature Society, 1964), pp. 207-287.

[44]Chang-shik Lee, *"Kitokkyo Tochakhwa-nun Yeksa-jek kwaup"* [The Indigenization of Christianity Is an Historical Task], *Christian Thought* (Seoul, Korea: Christian Literature Society, 1963), pp. 226-234.

[45]*Ibid.*

[46]Kyung-yun Jun, *"Sonwi June-ihae-wa Dangun Shinhwa"* [The So-Called Pre-Understanding and the Tangun Myth], *Christian Thought*, Vol. 7, No. 8 (August and September, 1963), pp. 23-24.

[47]*Ibid.*

[48]*Ibid.*, pp. 27-29.

[49]Harold S. Hong, *"Tochakhwa-eui Ganeung-myun-kwa Bulkanung-myun"* [The Possible and Impossible Elements of Indigenization], *Christian Thought*, Vol.7, No.8 (August and September, 1963), p. 260-264.

[50]Jong-sung Lee, *"Tochkhwa Yron-eui Shinhak-jek Pyungga"* [A Theological Evaluation of the Indigenization Theory], *Christian Thought*, Vol. 7. No. 10 (November, 1963), pp. 22-31.

[51]Chung-choon Kim, *Yisrael Shinang-kwa Shinhak* [*Faith of Israel and Theology*], (Seoul, Korea: Sungmoon Haksa, 1966), p. 105.

[52]*Ibid.*, pp. 109-110.

[53]Chung-choon Kim, "The Church and the Problem of Indigenization," Harold S. Hong, Won-yong Ji, and Chung-Choon Kim, eds. *Korea Struggles for Christ*, pp. 105-106.

[54]*Ibid.*, p. 108.

[55]*Ibid.*

[56]*Ibid.*, pp. 110-112.

[57]*Ibid.*, pp. 110-111.

[58]*Ibid.*

[59]Bong-rang Park, "A Theological Approach to the Understanding of the Indigenization of Christianity," *The North East Asia Journal of Theology*, September, 1969, pp.107-108.

[60]Chai-choon Kim, "The Present Situation and Future Prospect of the Korean Church," Harold S. Hong, Won-yong Ji, and Chung-choon Kim, eds. *Korea Struggles for Christ*, pp. 35-36.

[61]Bong-bae Park, *"Kitokkyo-wa Tochakhwa"* [Christianity and Indigenization], [*Christian Thought*], 1971. Vol.IV., p. 72; Cf. H. R. Niebuhr, *Christ and Culture*, (New York, NY: Harper & Row, 1951), pp. 191-194.

[62]*Ibid.*, p. 296.

[63]Myung-mu Ahn, *"Kitokkyo-wa Seoguhwa"* [Christianization and Westernization] *Christian Thought*, December 1965, p. 63.

[64]Chul-ha Han, *"Hankuk Shinahk-eui Gaeyeum"* [The Trend of Korean

Theology], *Kyohoe-wa Shinkhak* [*Church and Theology*] (Seoul, Korea: The Presbyterian Seminary Press, 1970), p. 58; for information on *Chunggamrok* cf. footnote 75 on p. 227.

[65]*Ibid.*, pp. 59, 60-62

[66]*The Christian Message in a Non-Christian World* (London, Edinburgh, UK, 1938), p. 210; Cf. Andre Droogers, "Syncretism: The Problem of Definition, the Definition of the Problem," Dirk C. Mulder, "Dialogue and Syncretism: Some Concluding Observations," Jerald Gort, Hendrik Vroom, Rein Fernhout, and Anton Wessels, eds. *Dialogue and Syncretism* (Grand Rapids, MI: William B. Eerdmans Publishing Co., 1989), pp. 7-22, 203-206.

[67]Eui-whan Kim, *Bokeum-kwa Yeksa* [*Gospel and History*], (Seoul, Korea: Christian Literature Crusade Press, 1975), p. 24.

[68]According to Hyun, Wan-sang Han's definition appeared in his book, *Minjung and Society*. Han is a sociologist and formerly taught at Seoul National University. Cf. The Commission on Theological Concerns of the Christian Conference of Asia. See Yong-bock Kim, ed. *Minjung Theology* (Maryknoll, NY: Orbis Books, 1981).

[69]Yong-bock Kim, *op.cit.*, p. 183.

[70]Kwang-sun Suh, "*Minjung* and Theology in Korea: A Biographical Sketch of an Asian Theological Consultation," Yong-bock Kim, *op.cit.*, p. 13.

[71]Ahn, "Jesus and the *Minjung* in the Gospel of Mark," *Minjung Theology*, (New York, NY: Orbis Books, 1983), pp. 138-154.

[72]Byung-mu Ahn is famous for his study of the notion *ochlos* in the gospel according to Mark. In addition to the chapter in his book, *Minjung Theology*, just referred to above, he has contributed articles to *Hyunjon* [*Present Reality*], 106 (Nov., 1979), *Minjung* (1981), *Shinhak Sasang* [*Theological Thought*] 34 (Sept., 1981), *Minjung-kwa Hankuk Shinkhak* [*Minjung and Korean Theology*] (1982), and *Gyohoe Yunhap Shinbo* [*Church United News Report*] (July 11, 1982).

[73]Ahn, "Jesus and the *Minjung* in the Gospel of Mark," *Minjung Theology*, pp. 138-154.

[74]The first to contrast Galilee with Jerusalem were Ernest Lohmeyer, *Galilaa und Jerusalem, 1936*, and W. Marxen, *Der Evangelist Markus*, 1969. Both simply note the contrasting characteristics of the two words in the light of the history of the church, but do not investigate the use of these words in terms of the socio-economic context. Cf. Byung-mu Ahn, *op.cit.*, p. 152.

[75]Kwang-sun Suh, "*Hankuk Kyohoe Sungryung Undong-kwa Shinkhak-jek Yhae*" [The Korean Pentecostal Movement and Its Theological Understanding] *Hakuk Kyohoe-eui Sae Inshik* [*A New Understanding of the Korean Church*] (Seoul, Korea: Korea Christian Academy, 1982, pp.23-100; idem,"*Minjung-kwa Sungryung*" [*Minjung* and Holy Spirit], *Minjung and Korean Theology* (Seoul, Korea: Korea Theological Study Institute, 1985), p. 303.

[76]*Ibid.*

[77]*Ibid.*, p. 304.

[78]Hee-suk Moon "An Old Testament Understanding of *Minjung,"* *Minjung Theology*, pp. 130-131.

[79]Ha-eun Jung, "Doctrine of *Minjung* of Korean-Japanese Theological Field in 1970s," *The Theological Thought*, 25 (June, 1979), pp. 185-187.

[80]Nam-dong Suh, "Toward a Theology of *Han,"* *Minjung Theology*, p. 65.

[81]*Hankuk Bokeun Shinmoon* [*The Korea Gospel Weekly*], January 9, 1983; Cf. *The Joong-ang Daily News*, March 8, 1983.

[82]Kyung-jae Kim, *"Minjung Kyoyuk Bangbumron Yunku"* [A Study on Educational Methodology of *Minjung*], *Minjung and Korean Theology*, pp. 410-411.

[83]Kwang-sun Suh, *A New Understanding of Korean Christianity* (Seoul, Korea: Korean Christian Press, 1985), p. 190.

[84]His presidency was for eighteen years, 1961-1979. For a detailed study of his dictatorship, see Eric O Hansen, *South Korea: Cry of the People*, American Society of Missiology series. No. 2. (New York, NY: Orbis Books, 1980), pp. 98-111; Cf. Chi-ha Kim, *Cry of the People and Other Poems* (Tokyo, Japan: Autumn Press, 1974).

[85]Cited in Nam-dong Suh, *"Yesu, Kyohoesa, Hakuk Kyohoe"* [Jesus, Church History, and the Korean Church], *Christian Thought* (Seoul, Korea: February, 1975), p. 62ff.

[86]Human Rights Statement, quoted in Ho-jn Jun, *A Critique of Ecumenical Mission And Its Influence on the Korean Church,* (Pasadena, CA: from D.Miss. Dissertation, Fuller Theological Seminary, 1978), p. 299.

[87]Cf. Nam-dong Suh, "Towards a Theology of *Han*," *Minjung Theology*, p. 32.

[88]*Andong* CFA is famous as a strategic base for the *minjung* movement in Korea.

[89]"The People of God and the Mission of the Church." That was the general theme of the first theological consultation organized by the Theological Commission of the National Council of Churches in Korea. A CTC-CCA (Commission on Theological Concerns of the Christian Conference of Asia) consultation was held in Seoul, October 22-24, 1979; seventeen Asians whose countries ranged from India to Japan came to participate in this gathering. Cf. Yong-bock Kim, ed. *Minjung Theology-People as the Subjects of History*, CCT-CCA (New York, NY: Orbis Books), 1981.

[90]For a theological analysis of what contextualization means in this thesis, consult H.M.Conn, "Contextualization: Where Do We Begin?" *Evangelicals and Liberation*, ed. Carl E. Armerding (Nutley, NJ: Presbyterian and Reformed Publishing, 1977), 90-119.

[91]Theological Education Fund, *Ministry in Context: The Third Mandate Program of the Theological Education Fund 1970-1977* (Bromley, England: TEF,1972), pp. 19-20.

[92]Harvie M. Conn, *Evangelism: Doing Justice and Preaching Grace* (Grand Rapids, MI: Zondervan Publishing House, 1982), pp. 104-105.

[93]General Introduction of *Divine Principle*, p. 9.

[94]*Ibid.*, p. 131.

[95]*Ibid.*, p.132.

[96]Everett, N. Hunt, Jr. "Sun Myung Mun and Tong-Il" *Dynamic Religious Movements.* Ed. David J. Hesselgrave (Grand Rapids, MI: Baker Book House, 1978), pp. 106-107.

[97]Cf. *Divine Principle*, pp.145, 148; Cf. Wi-jo Kang, "The Influence of the Unification Church in the United States of America" *Missiology: An International Review*, July, 1975, Vol.III. No.3. p. 77.

[98]See Yong-hwa Na, *Special Lecture Notes: Minjung Theology*, (Grand Rapids, MI: Calvin Theological Seminary, 1983), pp. 51- 57.

[99]Cf. Isa.3:13-15; 10:1-2.61:1; Luk.4:18,19; Isa. 66:2; Matt.5:3; Rev.2:8-11.3:14-21.

[100]Cf. Jn. 6:2,22,24; 7:11ff; Lk.6:19; Jn.6:2, 26; Mk.3:9,5:50ff; Mk.2:4ff; Mt.20:31; Lk.19:3ff; Jn. 6:15,66.

[101]Byung-mu Ahn, *The Liberator Jesus*, p. 134.

[102]Symposium, *Theological Thought* 24, 1979, pp. 212ff.

[103]Grayson, "Elements of Protestant Accommodation to Korean Religious Culture: A Personal Ethnographic Perspective." *Missiology: An International Review,* Vol. XXIII, No.1, January 1995, pp. 47-48.

[104]Ahn, *"Minjok Minjung Kyohoe"* [Nation, *Minjung*, and Church], *Minjung-kwa Hankuk Shinhak* [*Minjung and Korean Theology*], pp. 20-21; Nam-dong Suh, "Confluences of Two Stories," *Minjung and Korean Theology,* pp. 259-262.

[105]Cf. Jean-Marc Ela, *My Faith as An African*, John Pairman Brown and Susan Perry, trans. (Maryknoll, NY: Orbis Books, 1988), pp. 13-22.

[106]Morris A. Inch, *Doing Theology: Across Cultures* (Grand Rapids, MI: Baker Book House, 1982), p. 87.

[107]H. Richard Niebuhr, *Christ and Culture* (New York, NY: Harper & Row, 1951), pp. 76ff., 102-108, 148, 152, 159, 191ff.

[108]*Ibid.*, pp. 190, 194, 195.

[109]Anton Wessels, *Images of Jesus* (Grand Rapids, MI: William B. Eerdman Publishing Co., 1986), p. 162.

[110]Cf. Charles Kraft, *Christianity in Culture* (Maryknoll, NY: Orbis Books, 1979), p. 120ff.

NEDERLANDSE SAMENVATTING

Dit proefschrift bedoelt een dieper inzicht te geven in godsdienstige en kulturele krachten in de Koreaanse samenleving en ook in de boodschap en methoden van zending en evangelisatie in de Koreaanse kerk die allen de opbouw van het Protestantisme beïnvloeden. De schrijver poogt die aspekten van deze samenleving en haar kerkgeschiedenis te ontleden die bijgedragen hebben aan het succes en de onvoorstelbare snelle groei van christelijke kerken in dit land met zijn unieke geschiedenis, politiek en menselijke karaktertrekken. Protestantse zendelingen hebben van begin af aan getracht de verscheidene redenen voor deze snelle groei van kerken in Korea te ontdekken. In eerste instantie meende men dat de buitenlandse zendelingen en hun methoden primair verantwoordelijk waren. Het is waar, zij hebben een enorme invloed uitgeoefend: het inbrengen van de methoden en gedragslijnen van Nevius, het indragen van christelijke begrippen en instellingen, en het aandringen op een demokratische werkwijze waardoor de leden zelf de leiding van de kerk in handen namen.

Omstreeks de laatste eeuwwisseling hebben de Presbyterianen, destijds het grootste zendingsgezelschap, een programma van zelfvoortplanting, zelf-regering en zelf-ondersteuning ingesteld. Dit bracht gloednieuwe sociale en opvoedkundige mogelijkheden waardoor men — zowel vrouw als man — vooruit kon komen door deelname aan het leven van de kerk. Deze zendelingen accepteerden de kinderen van "gewone mensen" in de scholen en gaven hen les in westerse manieren van doen zowel als in de bijbel. Zij hebben veel bijgedragen — met inzet en financiële steun — aan het werk onder de armen, verlaten kinderen en wezen. Aan het begin van deze eeuw heeft het christendom in Korea een zeer belangrijke rol gespeeld als een duidelijk alternatieve stroming in de maatschappij. Koreanen zagen de kerk namelijk als een veilige haven waar ze bescherming zochten tegen de Japanse onderdrukking. De snelle groei van de kerk en de populariteit van haar instellingen vindt zijn verklaring vooral in het feit dat het christendom de Koreaanse gelovige in staat stelde zichzelf zowel vaderlandslievend als modern te ervaren.

Toch is de primaire godsdienstige en kulturele reden voor de snelle groei van Koreaanse kerken hiermee nog niet gegeven. Deze is met name de sjamanistische achtergrond van de Koreaanse kultuur. Het sjamanisme, met zijn vat op natuur-aanbiddende Koreanen (bijgeloof,

mystieke praktijken), heeft in de eerste fase van het Protestantse zendingswerk weliswaar de vooruitgang van het evangelie in de weg ges-
taan. En al is het misschien wel onmogelijk om aan te duiden hoe de
strijd tussen het christendom en het animistische sjamanisme verloopt,
toch gelooft de schrijver dat de aanwezigheid van dit geloof bijgedragen heeft in de snelle groei van kerken. Bepaalde sjamanistische elementen worden doeltreffend door christelijke kerken gebruikt om meer
mensen aan te trekken, vaak zonder een goed inzicht in de oorsprong
van die elementen. Het sjamanisme heeft dus een duidelijke invloed op
de mentaliteit en het leven van de Koreaanse christen.

Het meest voor de hand liggende kenmerk van het sjamanisme
waardoor de christelijke godsdienst betrekkelijk vlot aanvaard kon
worden in Korea is een vertrouwen op de sjamaanse gebeden voor
gezondheid en materiele belangen — een vertrouwen dat nu gericht
werd op de christelijke pastor. Zo was er in de christelijke kerken een
duidelijke nadruk op de aardse zegeningen en lichamelijke genezingen
en wat men een sjamanistische vormgeving aan christelijke zielzorg
zou kunnen noemen. Die zielzorg vindt namelijk grotendeels plaats
van huis tot huis. Het vooruitzicht op deze zegeningen baande de weg
voor het evangelie. Wat, ten tweede, ook voor de hand ligt is dat het
sjamanisme en het christendom een soortgelijke *Weltanschauung* en
godsbegrip delen. De sjamanistische wereld telt veel geesten, zowel
goede als boze, en ook een goddelijk opperwezen, zoals ook het
Nieuwe Testament de wereld en geesten beschouwt.

De Koreaanse godsaanduiding *Hananim* heeft van primitieve tijden
af aan een bestaan gevonden in de taal, het denken en het geestelijk
leven in dit land. Mede daarom is de schrijver overtuigt dat deze elementen in Koreaans-sjamanistische godsdienstige en kulturele kracht-
en bijgedragen hebben aan de opbouw van de christelijke kerk in
Korea. Veel christelijke theologen en predikanten in Korea zijn misleid
door de gedachte dat met de komst van het christendom en de westerse
kultuur het sjamanisme uitgestorven zou zijn. Maar het shamanistisch
geloof is in Korea noch allen maar iets uit het verleden noch allen maar
een primitieve praktijk. Het blijft bestaan in de Koreaanse kultu-
urgeschiedenis tot vandaag de dag toe. Zelfs in de schaduw van belan-
grijker wereld-godsdiensten blijft het functioneren als een inheems
volksreligieus systeem. Grote veranderingen in denken en geloven zijn
er in Korea nooit geweest. Er zijn veel christenen die zowel christelijke
als sjamanistische tradities omhelzen, vooral in tijden van crisis in
eigen of gezinsleven. Christelijke leiders moeten daarom deze tradi-

tionele godsdienst goed begrijpen. Zij moeten het niet zonder meer afwijzen, ook niet eenvoudigweg syncretistisch vermengen met het christendom. Wanneer men het evangelie op een effectieve wijze wil overbrengen en de opbouw van de kerk wil garanderen, dan zal men ernst moeten maken met de diepste kern van het sjamanistisch geloof. Wat houdt dit theologisch en missiologisch in? De christelijke zending en de opbouw van de christelijke kerk is begonnen als een getuigenis van het evangelie aan een sjamanistisch volk. De kerk moest dus haar houding bepalen ten opzichte van deze godsdienst en haar praktijken. Koreaanse theologie is tot stand gekomen als een poging deze verhouding te bepalen. Haar betekenis mag men niet onderschatten, gezien haar cruciale rol in het uitleggen van het evangelie in relatie tot het shamanisme. Het is niet mogelijk enige godsdienst gronding in kort bestek te onderzoeken en volgens maatstaven die in een ander godsdienst is ontwikkeld to beoordelen. Het is echter niet onmogelijk enkele van de belangrijke aspecten van beide godsdiensten te vergelijken.

Het resultaat is dat sommige aspekten van het sjamanisme bruikbaar zijn in het christelijke zendingswerk en de inheemse theologie, terwijl juist andere aspekten inderdaad de christelijke leer tegenstaan. Bepaalde rituele en ideologische vormen zijn niet verenigbaar en moeten dus opnieuw geïnterpreteerd worden als ze in de christelijke kerk opgenomen worden. Bruikbaar zijn vooral gebedsijver, vrees voor boze geesten en zekere communicatiemethoden. Maar de meeste aspekten van het sjamanisme moeten toch afgewezen worden. De techniek en voorwerpen van de magie, het ritueel als magische kracht tot transformatie, gods- en mensbegrippen, en het aspekt van *dieseitigkeit* in deze menselijke godsdienst zijn allen in strijd met christelijke opvattingen. Vooral begrippen zoals het koninkrijk Gods, de zonde in de mensheid en verlossing door Christus zijn in het kader van de sjamanistische godsdienst niet mededeelbaar. Het probleem van het syncretisme komt vooral in zicht wanneer het evangelie niet verkondigd wordt op het niveau van *Weltanschauung*, juist omdat het sjamanisme polytheïstisch is. Waar de diepste laag van het geloof niet geraakt wordt, wordt de christelijke God al gauw een bijvoegsel in een sjamanistisch Pantheon. Het is bv. zeer belangrijk de werkelijkheid van de geest te benadrukken. Een zorgvuldige herinterpretatie van de geest-goden — waarmee men dagelijks omgaat — en van de boze geesten die men vreest kan de communicatie van het evangelie ten dienste zijn. De geestelijke ervaringen van de christelijke kerk leidden tot een syncretistische vermenging van beide godsdiensten voor Koreaanse christenen die geen functionele vervanger aangeboden kregen. Onbezonnen adaptatie heeft trouwens weinig geholpen in het streven naar een duidelijke ommekeer van het sjamanisme naar het christelijk geloof. Veel problemen binnen de Koreaanse kerk hebben te maken met een misverstand omtrent bekering. Het christendom is voor velen in Korea een andere vorm van godsdienstige praktijken waarmee men het traditionele sjamanisme verruilt. Maar een christelijke zending betekent juist een leiden tot een persoonlijke verhouding met Christus. De kerk moet mensen voorzien van de juiste leer. Persoonlijke behoeften moeten gerespekteerd worden, vooral bij hen die zich blijven ontwikkelen in het christelijk geloof. Predikanten en evangelisten moeten dus de diepste kern van het sjamanisme onderzoeken en ook leren om op het niveau van *Weltanschauung* te communiceren.

Wij moeten de gevolgen van het sjamaniseren van de Koreaanse kerk duidelijk trekken. Wanneer het evangelie intree doet in een zekere maatschappij is het onvermijdelijk dat het traditionele godsdiensten en kulturen aantreft. Het is dus zeer belangrijk dat zendelingen dit goed begrijpen: het evangelie komt niet in een godsdienstig ledige ruimte terecht, maar in een specifieke historische context, een zeer bepaalde kultuur met eigen grenzen. Mensen in deze samenleving zijn sterk beinvloed door een dominante kultuur die hun taal, manier van doen en denken, leermethodes, emotionele reakties, waarden en doeleinden veelal bepaald heeft. Het evangelie bereikt hen alleen door de kultuur; zo niet, dan wordt het afgewezen of misverstaan. Het evangelie moet dus geincarneerd worden in een maatschappij met eigen kulturele eigenschappen. Dit proefschrift wil tegemoet komen aan de dringende noodzaak het sjamanisme en zijn verband met de opbouw van de kerk in Korea beter te verstaan om zodoende het evangelie meer effectief over te brengen. Uiteraard kan deze begrensde studie niet alle aspekten belichten. Theologen die geinteresseerd zijn in het sjamanisme zouden ten eerste meer praktisch onderzoek moeten doen, vooral naar het verschijnsel van syncretisme van het christendom en het sjamanisme bij Koreaanse kerkleden. Ook zou de hedendaagse sjamanistische praktijk aan de orde moeten komen. In verband met de contextualisering van de Koreaanse kerk ziet de schrijver de noodzaak voldoende data te verzamelen zonder de aard van het sjamanisme te vereenvoudigen. Wij moeten onze eigen kultuur kennen om de groei van de kerk te bevorderen. Teveel vereenvoudiging loopt uit op een onbezonnen afwijzing van de traditionale kultuur en ook op een naieve vereenzelviging van het christelijk geloof met het sjamanisme die tot een syncretisme leidt. De contextualisering van het evangelie is alleen mogelijk wanneer wij de traditionele kultuur beter begrijpen en in staat worden gesteld zowel positieve als negatieve elementen te onderscheiden. Dit bevordert een meer doeltreffende evangelieverkondiging.

Eindelijk moet nog gekonstateerd worden dat de Koreaanse kerk bewezen heeft hoe het sterk evangeliseren — het evangelie van soevereine genade verkondigen — en het invoeren van het evangelie in de praktijk echte kerkelijke groei teweeg kan brengen, zowel in kwaliteit als in kwantiteit. Korea heeft een lange nationale en godsdienstige geschiedenis, maar de meeste traditionele religies hebben hun invloed op het grootste deel van de bevolking verloren. Politieke, sociologische, kulturele en vooral sjamanistische omstandigheden bleken gunstig voor het verspreiden van het christelijk geloof in Korea. De protestantse zending met zijn honderd en tien-jarige geschiedenis in Korea heeft het meeste succes bereikt in het binnenbrengen van bekeerlingen en de groei van kerken te bevorderen. De Geest van God heeft deze aangelegenheden gekombineerd met het onvermoeide werk van zendelingen en de geestdrift van vele christenen. De belangrijkste factor in dit lopend vuur van het evangelie is ongetwijfeld het verlossende werk van de Geest van God. Wij moeten toegeven dat die Geest al bezig was voordat het christendom in Korea ingang vond. God schonk de Koreanen een open hart en een ontvankelijkheid. Hij heeft een groot aantal Koreanen doen geloven en het goede nieuws van het christendom doen herkennen. In zijn voorzienigheid was dit het juiste nieuws op de juiste *kairos*. Zodoende werd er bijna direkt gehoor gegeven aan het evangelie. "We found that God by his spirit had been at work throughout the length and breadth of this land before we reached here," schreef Underwood, een van de eerste zendelingen in zijn boek *Call of Korea* (p. 91). Hij had gelijk. De Geest van God werkte om het evangelie de overhand te laten hebben en grote vooruitgang in Korea te doen geven. Dit heeft de groei van kerken beinvloed.Evangelisatie en groei in de Koreaanse kerk is begonnen met de kracht van de Geest van God om te overtuigen, te zuiveren, te bezielen en te leven in een liefde die gestalte vindt in een christelijk geloof en levenswandel die tegemoet komt aan de geestelijkse en lichamelijke behoeften. Wij moeten erkennen dat reveil door de kracht van de Heilige Geest het allerbelangrijkste is in het totstandkomen en de groei van de Koreaanse kerk. De Geest heeft onvoorstelbare kerkopbouw teweeg gebracht door alle menselijke, socio-politische, kulturele en godsdienstige aspekten.

Meer dan vijftig jaar geleden gaf Moffett een antwoord dat weinigen hebben verbeterd: "For years we have simply held before these people the word of God, and the Holy Spirit has done the rest" ("What Makes the Korean Church Grow?," *Christianity Today* 18 [Nov. 23, 1973], p. 11). Maar in plaats van opgeblazen te zijn met een hoogmoed in wat de kerk heeft kunnen presteren, zou elke Koreaanse christen zichzelf opnieuw moeten toewijden aan Christus, aan het kerstenen van Korea en aan het evangeliseren van de wereld.

MAP OF KOREA

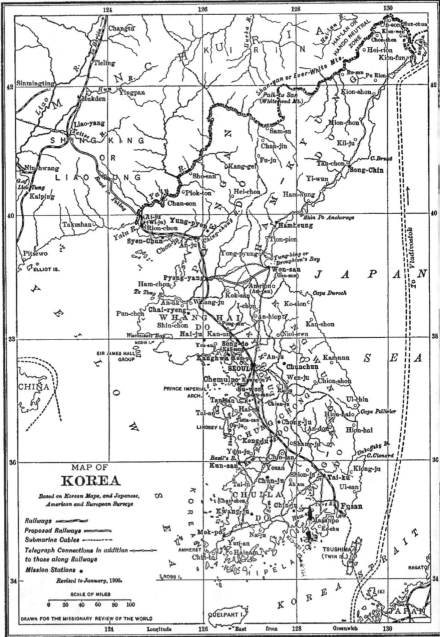

MAP OF
KOREA
Based on Korean Maps, and Japanese,
American and European Surveys

Railways
Proposed Railways
Submarine Cables
Telegraph Connections in addition
to those along Railways
Mission Stations •

Revised to January, 1906.

SCALE OF MILES
0 20 40 60 80 100

DRAWN FOR THE MISSIONARY REVIEW OF THE WORLD

Longitude   East   from   Greenwich

L.L. POATES ENG'G CO., N.Y.

CHRONOLOGY

2333 - 108 B.C.	**THE OLD *CHOSEN* PERIOD**
2333 B.C.	The traditional date of the founding of the Kingdom of *Chosen* by *Tangun*.
1122 B.C.	The establishment of *Kija* Chosen.
57B.C- 935 A.D.	**THE THREE KINGDOM PERIOD**
37B.C- 668 A.D.	*Koguryo* Kingdom
18B.C- 660 A.D.	*Paekche* Kingdom
372 A.D.	Official adoption of Buddhism and the establishment of a school for Confucian studies in *Koguryo*.
384	Official adoption of Buddhism in *Paekche*.
527	Official adoption of Buddhism in *Shilla*.
668 - 935	United Korea of *Shilla*
682	The establishment of a school for Confucian learning.
935 -1392	**THE *KORYO* PERIOD**
993	Invasion of the Khitans.
1011	Publication of the *Tripitaka* with wooden blocks began.
1018	Scond invasion of the Khitans.
1231	The first Mongol invasion.
1251	Production of new printing blocks: publication of the *Tripitaka Koreana*.
1259	Establishment of the peace with the Mongols; and acceptance of Mongol domination.
1392 -1910	**THE *YI* DYNASTY (*CHOSEN*) PERIOD**
1394	*Hanyang* (now Seoul) became the capital of Korea.
1446	Promulgation of the new Korean script (*Hangul*).

1592	Invasion of the Japanese.
1594	Fr. Gregorio de Cespedes came to Korean with the Japanese army.
1610	Introduction of Catholicism.
1628	The crew of a ship-wrecked Dutch vessel rescued off.
1650	Beginning of *Shirhak* Movement.
1653	Another Dutch ship, the *Sparrow Hawk*, wrecked off *Cheju* Island; its crew taken to Seoul.
1784	Lee Sung-hun baptized in Peking
1785	First anti-Catholic persecution; Lee and others organized and underground church at *Myungdong*, where now stands the Seoul Cathedral.
1831	Establishment of Korean Catholic diocese; arrival of French Catholic priests.
1832	German Protestant missionary A.C. Gutzlaff visited the coast of Korea.
1845	Kim Tae-kun, the first Korean priest, ordained in Shanghai.
1866	Beginning of a large-scale anti-Catholic persecution; August, the destruction of an American merchant ship, the *General Sherman*. Thomas of Scotland Bible Society martyred.
1871	Invasion of American troops; proclamation of policy of isolation.
1876	McIntyre and Ross baptize Korean Protestant in Manchuria.
1882	Suh, Sang-yun, a Protestant covert, translated the Gospels according to Mark and Luke into Korean and published them. The signing of the *Chemulpo* treaty with the United States; The signing of the *Chemulpo* treaty with Japan.
1883	The signing of Korean-British and Korean-German treaties.
1884	The signing of the Korea-Russian treaty; Arrival of first Protestant missionary, Dr. Horace N. Allen; Lee, Soo-jung translated the Gospel

	according to John, and published it.
1885	The signing of the Korean-Japanese agreement; Ordained missionaries Appenzeller, Methodist, and Underwood, Presbyterian arrive.
1887	Wide missionary itineration begins.
1889	Australian Presbyterian Mission opens.
1890	Presbyterian Church in Korea adopts the Nevius Method;Church of England Mission opens.
1892	Southern Presbyterian Mission opens.
1894	March, the beginning of the *Tonghak* uprising; July 25, the outbreak of the Sino-Japanese War.
1895	Explosion of growth in churches occurs.
1897	Taehan Empire Proclaimed.
1900	The whole New Testament translation completed.
1903	October, founding of the YMCA in Seoul and Seoul Medical School
1904	February 8, the outbreak of the Russo-Japanese War; February 23, the signing of the Korean-Japanese agreement protocol.
1907	Great Revival in *Pyongyang*; Methodist Theological Seminary founded; First graduation at Presbyterian Theological Seminary.
1909	The Methodist church sent a missionary to Manchuria; The Presbyterian church sent a missionary to Tokyo
1910	Million Soul for Christian Movement begins. The signing of the Treaty of Annexation, and the end of the *Yi* dynasty, and Korean independence
1910-1945	**JAPANESE COLONIAL RULE**
1912	General Assembly of Presbyterian Church organized; Conspiracy Case.
1915	The governor-general issued the Revised Regulation for Private Schools, by which religious education in mission schools was threatened.
1919	Beginning of the March First Movement.

1920	Most churches begin to grow rapidly
1924	National Council of Churches organized.
1935	The *Shinto* Shrine trial starts.
1937	Northern and Southern Presbyterian Missions close schools.
1938	Church membership begins to decline.
1942	All denominations amalgamated into one organization.
1945	Churches and denominations forced to unite to form *Kyodan*. End of theWorld War II; Korean lliberated to Russia in North and USA in south; Liberation of Korea.
1945-1948	The Allied occupation period
1948	Inauguration of the Republic and its government; Refugees move into South.
1950	North Korean invasion of the South; The beginning of the Korean War.
1951	First Presbyterian church schism.
1953	Armistices agreement completed; Churches again grow rapidly.
1954	Reconstruction and relief finds pour into Korean churches.
1959	Jesus Presbyterian church divided into two sections: *Hadong* and *Tonghap*
1960	Several major trends develops in the Korean church. Spectacular growth rate. The complete devolution of control of church institutions from foreign to Korean hands; Student uprising in Seoul.
1961	The military revolution and the fall of the Second Republic.
1963	The emergence of the Third Republic.
1965	The Evangelization of the Whole nation movement starts.
1972	The emergence of the Fourth Republic.
1973	Billy Graham Crusade held in Seoul.
1974	Explore '74 Evangelistic Crusade.

1981	The Fifth Republic.
1984	The bicentennial of Catholicism and the centennial of Protestantism. John Paul II visits.
1988	The Sixth Republic.
1993	The Seventh Republic.

GLOSSARY OF TERMS

Korean Pronunciation Key

a like [a] in f*a*ther,

i like [i] in p*i*n,

u, oo like [oo, a] in b*oo*t and *a*go,

yo like [yaw] in *yaw*,

j like [j] in *J*esus,

o like [o, a] in s*o*ng and *a*go,

e like [e] in p*e*n,

ai, ae, ei like [a] in N*a*ncy,

yu, yo like [you] in *you*ng,

ch like [ch, j] in *ch*urch and *J*esus,

wh like [hw] in the *Hwang Hai* (theYellow Sea)

Ancestors	Spiritual beings, ghosts, who are in some ways supposed to be related to the living family, and so concerned about their well-being.
Adherents	The total number of baptized, children, inquires, catechumens, and communicant members. Same as "community."
An-dong	Town in North *Kyungsang* Province, also Northern Presbyterian Missions station.
Animism	A term used by E.B. Taylor to describe belief in spirits and the supernatural.
Anthropology	The study of the culture and way of life of the peoples of the world.
Bae-jae Hak-dang	Literally " Learning hall for rearing useful men."
Byung-ma	Demon of illness.
Catechumen	Person who promises to lead a Christian life, regularly attending worship services and studying prescribed Biblical material in order to be examined for church membership six months after being admitted to the catechumenate. Same as "probationer."
Chaesu-kut	A ritual of welfare and blessings.

Chai[e]-ryung	Town in *Whanghai* Province of northwest Korea, also Northern Presbyterian Mission Station.
Chang-yun	Town in *Kyungsang Namdo.*
Che-dang	An altar.
Che-ju	Large Island off southland coast of Korea, now a separate province.
Che-mul-po	Same as *"Inchun."*
Che-wang-ung-gi	Songs of Emperors and Kings during the Three kingdom period.
Chik-sin	The lavatory god.
Chin-chang	Officer Spirits under the *Obangchanggun.*
Chin-kut	A ritual to appease angry spirits of the dead ancestors.
Cho-gye-jong	A conservative sect of unmarried monks.
Chong-kyo	Religion.
Chon-shin Kut	Shamanistic ritual of welfare and blessings of the home and individual. Same as *"Chaesu Kut."*
Choong-chung	Province in west central Korea, divided into North and South *Choongchung* in 1896.
Cho-sang-sin	Spirits of ancestors transformed into gods.
Cho-sen(Chosun)	Land of Morning Calm.
Cho-sen dynasty	1392 -1910 A.D. in Korea. See, *"Yi* dynasty."
Cho-wang-sin	God of housewives; also called the god of the kitchen and sacred fire.
Chun-do Pu-in	Bible woman.
Chun-do-kyo	Literally, "the Religion of Heavenly Way." Korean religion which has borrowed much from Christianity but is based mainly on patriotic motivation.

Chudo-yebae	Christian memorial service for the deceased.
Chung-gam-rok	Religious Books were written during the later period of *Yi* dynasty. Their teachings are the advent of a future world, paradise on earth, faith in the Savior and the notion of a chosen people.
Chun-gun	The masters of rituals to the heavenly spirits. Literally, "Heaven Prince."
Chun-ji-un-do	The divine plan of the movement of the universe.
Chung-san-kyo	A name of the church of the great meditation truth movement.
Chun-min class	The class of humble people as the slaves during *Yi* dynasty.
Chun-sin	The gods who are the tutelary divinities presiding over villages located in a plain.
Church Growth	Church growth as a movement came into being in the fall of 1972. It took root in the mind and ministry of Donald McGavran while he was serving over a period of thirty years in India. His first attempts to put his ideas into writing date back to 1936. Church growth is a science which investigates the planting, multiplication, function and health of Christian churches as they relate specifically to the effective implementation of God's commission to "make disciples of all nations."
Colporteur	Traveling Bible salesmen.
Comity agreement	A territorial agreement of the mission societies as to how to divide the Korean mission field.
Communicant member	Person who after being a catechumen for six months or more is accepted after examination of his faith and practice into full membership of the church, either through baptism or, if previously baptized in infancy, confirmed.

Conspiracy Case	In 1912,105 Koreans were convinced of conspiracy against the Japanese government. All but six judgments were reversed by a higher court.
Cult	A term widely used in anthropology for a collection of religious ideas and practices which are associated with a given divinity, ancestor or social group.
Dae-shim-bang	Annual great visitation program of a church.
Divination	The art of reaching a judgment concerning the cause and solution of some event which may be past, present or future. It is usually fairly standardized in each culture, and is believed to depend upon revelation by spiritual beings.
Ecstasy,	A short rapturous trance during which the person feels an intense sense of well-being and a dissociation from his surroundings.
Exorcism	The expelling of spirits of ghosts from persons or places, usually by means of rituals of incarnations.
Eui-ju	Town on the China-Korea border in North *Pyongan* Province.
E[I]-wha Hak-dang	Literally "Learning Hall for Pear blossom"
Folk religion	A general term used for popular religious practices and superstitions within a major world religion.
Ghosts	Supernatural beings who were once human or animal; the souls of dead people.
Gods	Spiritual beings of non-human origin who are regarded as being in command of a particular domain, or area of human life.
Gu-byung-je	A shamanistic ritual for healing the sick.
Ha-na-nim	The most ancient and the most indigenous term for god in Korea. The highest deity used for shamanists, Confucians and

	Buddhists and Christians adopted the same word to designated their God.
Han-gul	A phonetic alphabet, originally called "*Hun-min-jung-oom,*" literally, "the sounds to teach the people," was invented about 143 A.D. by King *Sejong*.
Hai-ju	Town in *Whanghai* Province, also a Northern Methodist Mission Station.
Hap-tong	An anti-WCC conservative Presbyterian Church group in Korea.
I(1)-Chin	The sexagenary cycle of a day.
In-chon	Port city twenty miles west of Seoul in *Kyunggi* Province, also a Northern Methodist Mission Station.
Independence Movement	Peaceful attempt in 1919 by the Korean people to free themselves from Japan's yoke by demonstrations. Many Koreans were shot and killed in the demonstration and the leaders were imprisoned.
Indigenous	Religious or native, pertaining to the original inhabitants of a religion.
Inquirer	Person who gives up former religious practices and attends church regularly.
In-nae-chun	Heaven's presence in man.
Jae-am	Town in *Kyunggi* province, where the church was set fire while the Christians were in it during Japanese occupation.
Jum	Divination.
Jum-jaeng-i	Diviner.
Kae-sung (Song-do)	Ancient capital of Korea in *Whanghai* Province, also a Southern Methodist Mission Station.
Kang-kei	Town in the far north of North *Pyongan* Province, also a Northern Presbyterian Mission Station.
Kang-nung	Town in the far east of Eastern central

	Kangwon Province.
Kang-won	Eastern province of Central Korea.
Kang-wha	Island located near Seoul, in which *Tangun* performed shamanistic rituals to heavenly God on the great altar on *Mani* mountain.
Ki-bok-je	A shamanistic ritual for praying for material blessings.
Kibok Sinang	Shamanistic beliefs in material blessings.
Kidowon	A hall of prayer in a mountain.
Ko-ryo Kingdom	935-1395 A.D. in Korea.
Ko-sa	A celebrative shamanistic sacrifice to the spirits for opening of business and initiation or completion of construction.
Kyung-gi	Province in west central Korea containing Seoul.
Kyung-kyo	The Nestorian sect came during *Shilla* kingdom, literally means, "Religion of Light."
Kyung-sang	Province in southeast Korea divided into North and South *Kyungsang* in 1896.
Kyung-shin-hoe	An organization comprised of *mudang* and fortune-tellers.
Kut	A shamanistic ritual.
Kwan-sang	Physiognomy.
Kwi-sin	Ghosts.
Magic	The performance of certain rituals which are believed to compel the supernatural powers to act in particular way.
Man-sin	A shaman who serves ten thousands spirits.
Min-jung	The mass of the people.
Monotheism	The belief in or worship of a single god.
Moon-sin	God who guards the house from the invasion of evil spirits and accidents and misfortune.

Mu-chon	A dance performed to worship heaven in ancient Korea.
Mu-dang	A shaman, one who acts as mediators between the world of the supernatural and the world of man, and attempts control of animistic spirits, especially in the sick, by dancing and chanting.
Mu-geo[o]k	Male shaman. Same as " *Paksu.*"
Mu-gu	Shamanistic tools for rituals.
Mu-kyo	Religion of Shamanism.
Mu-sok-mun-wha	Shamanistic faith culture.
Mystic	A person claiming that through trance, or spiritual exercises, they are able to enter into a unity with deity.
New religious Movement	A new religion resulting from the interaction of two cultures and religions, and although having features in common with both, it is in itself new and different.
Nevius Method	Policy of mission work advocated by John L. Nevius, missionary to China, for the planting and developing of younger Churches, adopted by the Northern Presbyterian Mission in Korea. The Policy's goal was a strong, indigenous Church with particular emphasis on Bible training for all Christians as in the annual Bible classes held in each area, wide itineration by the missionaries to care for the needs of the new churches, and the three "self": 1) Self-support required the Korean Christians to build their own churches and pay their own pastors. 2) Self-government early placed the Korean Christians in charge of their own affairs. 3) Self-propagation stressed the responsibility of each Christian to win those around him to Christ.
O-bang-chang-gun	The gods of general who are the spirits of the Eastern, Southern, Western, Northern, and Zenith heavens.

Pak-su	Male shaman. Same as *"Mugeok."*
Pal-ja	Astrological interpretation of fate.
Pal-kwan-hoe	A national shamanistic ceremony worshipping the heavenly spirit, mountain spirit and dragon spirit during *Koryo* kingdom.
Pantheism	The teaching that god is all and all is god.
Po-chun-kyo	A sect of *Chung-san-kyo* founded by Cha, Kyungsuk.
Possession	The temporary or permanent domination of a person by a supernatural being.
Prayer	A verbal petition made to any object, but usually to a supernatural being, often associated with sacrifice.
Priest	In primal societire, a priest is a person who acts as an intermediary between human beings and gods; a religious expert.
Primal religion	The word primal denotes something basic, fundamental, and coming before. Primal religions are the non-universal religions of pre-literate people, existing before the influence brought by the major world religions.
Probationer	Same as "catechumen."
Prophet	A person claiming to speak on behalf of a particular deity, and who usually becomes the central figure of a new religious cult.
Pu-san	Large port city on southeast coast of Korea, also Australian Presbyterian Mission Station.
Pyong-an	Province of northwest Korea divided into North and South Pyongan in 1896.
Pyong-yang	Capital city of North Korea located in the central section of *Pyongan* Province, also Northern Methodist and Presbyterian Mission Station.
Reincarnation	The condition of being reborn in another body.

Religion	The shared beliefs and practices of a people which relate to their understanding of the supranational.
Rituals	An established ceremonial procedure, with religious meaning.
Russo-Japanese War	1904 war in which Japan defeated Russia partly on Korea soil, giving Japan a clear path to take Korea into the Japanese Empire.
Sacrifice	The propitiatory offering of plant, animal or object to some supernatural being.
Sa-dang	A Shrine.
Sa-jik Shrine	Confucian shrine located in a city park of Seoul.
Sa-ju	Fortune telling.
Sa-kyung-hoe	Literally, "Search the Scripture Conference.
Sa-kwi	Unclean or Tramp Spirit.
Sam-kuk-sa-gi	History of Three kingdoms, *Koguryo, Baikje, Shilla.*
Sam-kuk-yu-sa	Memorabilia of the Three kingdoms, *Koguyo, Baikje, Shilla.*
Sang-min	The class of commoners as the farmer and merchants during *Yi* dynasty.
San-sin	Mountain gods and fertility gods.
Sa-ryung-je	Ritual for the dead.
Seong-sook-cheong	An organization of official shamans who foretold the kingdom's future and misfortune during *Yi* dynasty.
Seoul	The capital city of Korea located in the west central section.
Shaman	A healer who seeks to cure people by means of supernatural powers. See, "*mudang.*"
Shil-la kingdom	57.B.C.-935 A.D. in Korea

Shin-dang	A divine hall for shamanistic rituals.
Shin-hung Jong-kyo	New religions influenced by Shamanistic faith and Christianity.
Shin-kyo	Religion of Spirit.
Shinto	State religion of Japan.
Shrine issue	Beginning in 1930, the Japanese occupation government forced all Korean students and teachers to bow in obeisance before the state Shinto shrines. This, according to the government, was not a religious act. Some Korean Christians and missionaries believed bowing to the shrine was a religious act. Churches were later required to bow at the shrines.
Sino-Japanese War	1894 war between China and Japan, fought partly on Korean soil.
So-do	A sacred place dedicated to the Heavenly God in ancient Korea. Someone who had committed a crime and who sought asylum in this place could not be arrested, and could stay as long as he wished.
So-rai	Village in *Whanghai* Province where the majority of the population rapidly became Christian.
Sorcerer	An antisocial practitioner who causes evil by manipulating material objects and performing rituals.
Soul	The integral part of a human being, or, in some cases, an animal.
Spirit	Supernatural beings who are lower in prestige than gods, but closer to the people; they may be helpful, mischievous, or evil in nature.
Sung-cho-sin	God who protects the master of the house.
Sun-chun	Town in North *Pyongan* Province, also Northern Presbyterian Mission Station.
Sung	Literally "The accomplished Word." It is

	"authentic word" in Yun's theology of *Sung*.
Sung-whang-dang	The altar where local deities reside and where they are worshiped.
Superstition	Beliefs and practices resulting from ignorance, fear of the unknown, trust in magic and chance.
Supreme Being	The transcendent, all-powerful creator god who exists above all the other gods and spirits.
Su-sang	Palm reading.
Syncretism	The fusion of two distinct systems of belief and practice.
Tae-chong-kyo	The oldest Korean shaman religion.
Tae-gu(e)	Capital city of North *Kyungsang* Province, also a Northern Presbyterian Mission Station.
Tae-jong	A liberal sect of married monks.
Tae-sun jilri-hoe	The great meditation truth movement.
Tang-kut	A communal ritual performed by the professional shamanesses.
Tan-gun	Mythical originator of the Korean race and nation of four thousand years B.C. The incarnated son of *Whan Ung* in *Tangun* mythology.
Taoism	A philosophy of nature concerned with the transcentend and the technique of acquiring the power of command over the life force of the cosmos.
*Tien-chu shil-eui**	The True Doctrine of the Lord of Heaven", written by a Catholic Missionary Matteo Riucci, introduced in 1631 in Korea.
To-chu	God of the house site.
Tondang-kut	A community ritual held biennially.
To-ge-bi	Ghosts.

To-jong	The Book of fortune-telling.
Tong-hak	Literally "Eastern Learning." A reaction against the Western learning of the Catholics in 1850's which occurred as a revolt in 1894 against the corrupt government.
Tong-hap	A pro WCC ecumenical Presbyterian Church group in Korea.
Tong-il-kyo	Unification Church.
Tong-maeng	An ancestor worship ritual in *Koguryo* kingdom.
Tongseo-whal-in-seo	A place treatment of patients by official shamans during *Yi* dynasty.
Trance	An altered state of consciousness which may result in visions and ecstasy.
Tribe	A group of people who share a common language, culture and territory, and see themselves as an autonomous unit.
Un-sa-ja	The specially gifted person of the spiritual power of exorcism.
Up	The god of luck.
Whang-hai	Province in northwest Korea.
Whan-In	The supreme god.
Whan-Ung	The prince of the Heavenly King in *Tangun* Myth.
Wha-rang-do	An order of knighthood which resulted from the merging of the indigenous and foreign religions, such as Buddhism and Confucianism during *Silla* kingdom.
Witch	An antisocial person who is believed to be able to harm others by means of an innate spiritual power.
Won-kwi	Evil spirits causing diseases in shamanism.
Won-san	Port city in *Hamkyung* province, also a Sourthern Methodist Mission Station.

Worldview	The basic ideas and values shared by the members of a particular society. These concepts provide a way by which the people normally order their life experience. Because of the widespread acceptance of these concepts within the society, the ideas are usually regarded as being non-negotiable and beyond dispute.
Yang-ban	Landed gentry who were considered in the upper class. The *yangban*'s position was hereditary, and manual labor was beneath his dignity.
Yi(Lee) Dynasty	1392-1910 in Korea.
*Yin-Yang**	A division of two opposite elements or principles in Korean philosophy of One Totality.
Yo-jun-do-sa	The evangelistic Bible woman.
Yon-dung-hoe	One of the largest national Buddhist festivals in *Shilla* and *Koryo* kingdoms.
Yong	Dragon.
Yong-go	A shamanistic ceremony of invoking spirit in ancient Korea.
Young-byun	Ancient Buddhist center and town in North *Pyongan* province, also a Northern Methodist Mission Station.

* indicates Chinese pronunciation. [ ] indicates more correct spelling.

BIBLIOGRAPHY

Korean Language Publications
Books

Ahn, Che-hong, *A History of Ancient Korea*, Seoul, Korea: Minwoosa, 1947.

Ahn, Ho-sang, *Religion, Philosophy, and History of Korea*, Seoul: Omungak, 1959.

An Overview of Korean Religion, Seoul, Korea: Sunghwasha, 1973.

Bak, Si-in, *A Study of Altaic Civilization: History of Korea.* Seoul, Korea: Tamgudang Publishing Company, 1973.

Bang, In-keun, *Mudang Religion and Taoism in the Korean Church*, Seoul, Korea: Puelbit Mokhoe Press, 1982.

Cha, Joo-whan, *A Taoistic Thought in Korea*, Seoul, Korea: Dongwha Publishing Company, 1984.

Chang, Byung-il, *A Typological Approach to Christianity and Shamanism*, Seoul, Korea: Kitokkyo Moonhak, 1971.

Chang, Do-bin, *History of the Last Year of Korea*, 3 Vols. Seoul, Korea: Tokyung Sulim, 1935.

Chang, Sung-sik, *A Retrospect and Prospect of Korean Church*, Seoul, Korea: Sungkwang Moonwhasa, 1977.

Cho, Ji-hoon, *The Modern Institute*, Seoul, Korea: Pakmoonsa, 1962.

Cho, Jin-ho, *The History of Korean National Movement*, Seoul: National History Completion society, 1964.

Cho, Yonggi, *Church Growth III*, Seoul, Korea: Yongsan Publishing, 1983.

Cho, Yong-man, *Nam Sun Choi*, Seoul, Korea: Samchoong Tang, 1964.

Choi, Che-woo, *Great Canon of the East*, trans. Man-sung Nam, Seoul, Korea: Eulyoo Moonwhasa, 1973.

Choi, Duk-shin, *A Comparative Study on the New Religions in Korea*, Seoul, Korea: Chambicsha, 1965.

Choi, Ja-shil, *I Was A Hallelujah*, Seoul, Korea: Yongsan Press, 1977.

Choi, Ki-bock, *A Study of the Confucian Ceremony of Mouring*,

Seoul: Sungkyunkwan University Press, 1979.

Choi, Nam-sun, *History of the Korean People*, Seoul, Korea: Dong Myung Co., 1946.

Choi, Tong-Hee, *Modern Translation of the Scripture of the Eastern Learning*, Seoul, Korea: Kowoo Publishing Company, 1961.

Choi, Jae-young, *Confucian Concept of the Heavenly Lord and Ancestor Worship*, Seoul: Kyunghyang Press, 1958.

Chundokyo, *Scripture of Chundokyo*, Seoul, Korea: Chundokyo, 1969.

____. The Scriptures of Chundokyo with Notes, Seoul, Korea: Chundokyo Choongang Chongpoo, 1956.

____. *A History of Chundokyo*, Seoul, Korea: Chundokyo, 1964.

Chung, Chin-hong, ed., *The Study on the Korean Church Growth and Its Characteristics*, Seoul, Korea: Hyundae Sawhhee Younguso, 1982.

Chung, Chung-han, *History of Ehwa 80 Years*, Seoul: Ewha Women's University Press, 1967.

Chun, Taikpoo, *The History of the Church Development in Korea*, Seoul: The Christian Literature Society, 1985.

Daechongkyo Chongbonsa, *Three Days Philosophy*, Seoul, Korea: Daechong Chongbonsa, Korea.1949.

Ha, Tae-sung, *Folk Customs and Family Life*, Seoul, Korea:Yonsei University Press, 1958.

Hakwonsa, *Korea, its Land, People and Culture of All Ages*. Seoul, Korea: Hakwonsa Ltd, 1968.

____. *Korea, its People and Culture*. Seoul, Korea: Hakwonsa Ltd. 1970.

____. *Dictionary of Philosophy*, rev. ed., Seoul, Korea: Hakwonsa, 1974.

Handbook of Religion, Seoul, Korea: Ministry of Culture and Information, 1969.

Han, U-keun, *The National History*, Seoul, Korea: Suhomyongsa, 1955.

____. *A Comprehensive History of Korea*, Seoul, Korea: Eulyoo Moohwhasa, 1970.

Han, Wan-sang, et.al. *A Study of the Pentecostal Movement in Korea,* Seoul: Christian Academy, 1981.

Han, Young-Je, *The Church Growth of One Hundred Years in Korea,*

Seoul: The Christian Literature Society, 1986.

History of Korea, Seoul, Korea: Chindanhak Co., 1961.

Hong, Ihl-shik, *A Study on Nam Sun Choi*, Seoul, Korea: Ihlshinsa, 1959.

Hur, Gin, *A Study on the Revivalistic Movement*, Seoul, Korea: Theological Fund Conference, 1980.

Hyun, Sang-yun, *History of Confucianism in Korea*, Seoul, Korea: Minjungseakwan, 1949.

Hyun, Yong-jun, *Chejudo Folklore Dictionary*, Seoul, Korea: Singu Munwhasa, 1980.

Ilyon, *The Events of the Three Kingdoms*, trans. Ha Tae-sung, Grafteon, K.Mintes, Seoul, Korea: Yunsei University Press, 1972.

Im, Tong-kwon, *A Study of Korean Folklore*, Seoul: Sorwhadang, 1971.

Inmoon Yungusil, *A Social Change and Religions in Korea*, Seoul: Hankuk Junsin Moonwha Yunguwon, 1987.

Kil, Jin-kyung, *Spiritual Valley, Kil Sun-zu*, Seoul: Jong-ro Seajek, 1980.

Kim, C. G., ed., *An Empirical Study of Korean Church Growth and Faith*, Seoul: Institute of Modern Society, 1982.

Kim, Choon Bae, *History of Korean Church Growth*, Seoul: Korean Christian Literature Society, 1966.

_____. *Historical Story of Persecution in Korean Church*, Seoul: Sungmoon Haksa, 1969.

Kim, Deuk-whang, *History of Korean Thought*, Seoul: Nam San-dang, 1958.

_____. *History of Religion in Korea*, Seoul: Hai Moon-Sa, 1963.

Kim, Doo-jin, *A Study on the Korean Family System*, Seoul: Jimmundang, 1974.

Kim, Duk-whan, *Yonggi Cho, Who is He?*, Seoul: Kwanggo Kaebalwon Press, 1981.

Kim, Eui-whan, *Gospel and History*, Seoul: Christian Literature Crusade, 1975.

Kim, Gyu-tae, *Korean Mythology and Consciousness of Origin*, Seoul: Ewoo Publishing Co., 1980.

Kim, In-hoe, et.al. *A Synthetic Study of Korean Shamanism*, Seoul:

Institute of National Culture of Korea University, 1982.

Kim, Jae-won, *Recent Studies in the Myth of Tangun*, Seoul: Chungeumsa, 1947.

Kim, Joonggi, et, al., *The Study on the Korean Church Growth and Its Characteristics*, Seoul: Hyundae Sawhee Younguso, 1982.

Kim, K. Syuk, *Korean Research Report of Korean Mission One Hundred years*, Seoul: Christian Institute for the Study of Justice and Development, 1982.

Kim, Ki-tae, *A Study of the Theory and Practice of the Army Mission*, Seoul: Voice Publishing Co., 1985.

Kim, Kwang-il, *Consciousness of Healing in the Christian New Religious Cults*, Seoul: Christian Academy House, 1976.

_____. *A Study on the Pentecostal Movement in Korea* , Seoul: Christian Academy House, 1981.

Kim, Kwang-soo, *Korean Church Yesterday and Today*, Seoul: Sejong Moonwhasa, 1971.

_____. *A History of the Introduction of Christianity in Korea*, Seoul: Christian Literature Company, 1974.

_____. *A History of the Growth of Christianity in Korea*, Seoul: Christian Literature Company, 1976.

Kim, L. S., *Korean Church Martyrs and Their Sermons*, Seoul: Kimunsa, 1968.

Kim, Seung-tae, *A Historical Reflection on Korean Christianity*, Seoul: Dasan Keulbang, 1994.

Kim, So-young, ed. *Theological Thought of Korea*, Seoul: The Christian Literature Society, 1983.

Kim, Tae-gon, *A Study of Korean Folklore*, Seoul: Chimmundang, 1981.

Kim, Yeul-kyu, *Korean Mythology and Study of Shamanism*, Seoul: Iljokak, 1977.

Kim, Yong-choon, *The Concept of Man in Chundokyo*, Temple University, 1969.

Kim, Yang-sun, *Korean Christianity and the Korean War*, Seoul: Yehsookyo Changhohkyo Book, 1956.

_____. *History of the Korean Church*, Seoul: Christian Literature Company, 1971.

Kim, Yung-Jae, *A History of the Korean Church*, Seoul: The Korea Society for Reformed Faith and Action, 1992.

Kinda Hakhoe Pyun, *History of Korea*, Seoul: The Eluoo Moonwhasa, 1964.

Kwak, Ahn-jun. *History of the Korean Church*, Seoul: Korean Christian Literature Society, 1970.

Lee, Byung-gil, *Yesterday and Today of Mission in China*, Seoul: Shinhang Heybhoe Press, 1987.

Lee, Choon-bang, *Shamanism and Korean Mentality*, Seoul: Kunkuk University Press, 1978.

Lee, Ho-oon, *History of the Early Korean Church*, Seoul: Korean Christian Literature Society, 1970.

Lee, Jang-sik, *Today and Yesterday of the Christian Church in Korea*, Seoul: Christian Literature Society Press, 1977.

____. *The Centennial History of the Christian Literature Society of Korea*, Seoul: The Christian Literature Society Press, 1984.

Lee, Jin-ho, *Gutzlaff who ministered to the Orient*, Seoul: Department of Methodist Church in Korea, 1988.

Lee, Jong-yoon, Ho-jin Jun, Nelso, *Theories of the Church Growth*. Seoul: Emmaus Publishing House, 1983.

Lee, Ki-baik, and Min, Hyun-ku, *Cultural History of Korea*. Seoul: Iljisa, 1984.

Lee, Kyung-ho, *A Study on the Belief Structue of Korean Ministers*, Unpublished Master's Thesis, Seoul: Methodist Theological Seminary, 1983.

Lee, Neung-hwa, *History of Christianity and Foreign Relations of Korea*, Seoul: Chosen Kitokyo Changmunsa, 1925.

____. *A History of Korean Buddhism*, Seoul: 1918.

____. *A History of Taoism in Korea*, Seoul: 1910.

Lee, Sun-kun, *Korean Thought*, Seoul: Hanguk Sasang, Vol. 4, 1967.

____. *History of Korea: Modern History*, Seoul: Jindan Hakhoe, 1951.

Lee, Un-bong, *A Study of the Korean Ancient Religion*, Seoul: Chimmundang, 1974.

Lee, Won-soon, *History of the Catholic Church in Korea*, Seoul: Tamgoodang, 1971.

Lee, Won-sun, Huh In, *Letters of the Priest Kim Tae-gon*, Seoul: Jungmunsa, 1975.

Lee, Yung-hun, *The History of Korean Church*, Seoul: Concordia Press, 1978.

Minjung and Korean Theology, Seoul: Korea Theological Study Institute, 1985.

Min, Kyung-bae, *History of Korean Christianity*, Seoul: Korean Christian Literature Society, 1972.

____. *The Korean Church and People*, Seoul: Korean Christian Literature Society, 1981.

Na, Kyum-il, *Church Growth and Early Morning Prayer*, Inchon: Chamkeulsa, 1989.

New Korean Dictionary, Seoul: Tong-A Publishing Co., 1958.

Oh, Yun-tae, *History of Korean Christianity : Nestorianism*, Seoul: Haesun Moonwhasa, 1973.

Outlines of Six Main Philosophies of Religion in Korean Culture, Seoul: Minjok Moonwha Yungoosah, 1970.

Paik, Lak-joon, *The History of Protestant Missions in Korea : 1832-1910*, Seoul: Yunsei University Press, 1973.

Paik, Se-myung, *The Thought of the Eastern Learning and the Heavenly Way Religion*, Seoul: Tonghak Company, 1956.

____. *Commentary on the Scripture of the Eastern Learning*, Seoul: Illshin Publishing Company, 1963.

Park, Jong-koo, *An Analytical Study of Contemporary Movement of the World Mission of the Korean Church and a Projection to AD 2000*, Seoul, Shin-Mang-Ae Press, 1994.

Park, Young-kwan, *The Unification Church*, Seoul: Christian Literature Crusade, 1980.

Pyun, Chong-ho, *Biography of Minister Yi Yong-do*, Seoul: Simyuwon, 1958.

____. ed. *A Collection of Minister Yi Yong-do*, Seoul: Sinsaengkwn, 1966.

____. ed. *Diary of Minister Yi Yong-do's Letters*, Seoul: Simyuwon, 1953.

____. *A Comparative Study of Religions and Its Conclusion*, Seoul: Simwoowon, 1959.

Ryu, Byung-duk, *History of the Religions of Korea*, Seoul: Wonkwang University Press, 1974.

Ryu, Tong-shik, *Christianity and Korean Religions*, Seoul: Korean Christian Literature Society, 1967.

____. *History and Structure of Korean Shamanism*, Seoul: Yunsei University Press, 1975.

Sin, Sha-hoon, *Criticism on Both Heresies and Modern Age and Our Living Road*, Seoul: Christian Culture Press, 1957.

So, Tae-sok, *A Study of Songs of Korean Shamans*, Seoul: Munhak Sasangsa Chulpanpu,1980.

Son, Chin-tae, *A Study of Korean People's Culture*, Seoul: Eulyoo Moonwhasa, 1948.

Song, Kil-sub, *A History of Theological Thought in Korea*, Seoul: Christian Literature Society, 1987.

Suh, Kuk-sung, *The Identity of the Korean People: A History of Legitimacy on the Korean Peninsular*, Seoul: National Unification Board, 1983.

Suh, Kwang-sun, et.al. *A Study on the Pentecost Movement in Korea*, Seoul: Korean Christian Academy Press, 1982.

_____. *A New Understanding of Korean Christianity*, Seoul: Korean Christian Press, 1985.

_____. *Minjung and Korean Theology*, Seoul: Korea Theological Study Institute, 1985.

Suh, Nam-dong, *A Study on Minjung Theology*, Seoul: Han Kilsa, 1983.

_____. *Christ's Presence*, Seoul: Yunsei University, n.d.

Taichongkyo Chongpansa, *Sixty Years History of Recreation on Taichongkkyo*, Seoul: Taechongkkyo Chongpansa, 1971.

Tak, Myung-whan, *The New Religions Near Seoul*, Seoul: International Religious Research Center, 1981.

The Institute of Korean Church History Studies, *A History of Korea Church* Vol.I (7ct.-1918), Seoul: The Christian Literature Press, 1989.

_____. *A History of Korea Church* Vol.II (1919-1945), Seoul: The Christian Literature Press, 1990.

Yang, Joo-dong, *A Study on Ancient Songs*, Seoul: Ilchokak, 1965.

Yang, Ju-sam, *30 Year Memorial History of the Korean Southern Methodist Church*, Seoul: Korean Southern Methodist Church, 1926.

Yi, Byung-do, *History of Korea*, Seoul: Eulyoo Munwhasa, 1961.

Yi, Ki-baik, *A New History of Korea*, Seoul: Ilchokak, 1967.

Yi, Kwang-su, *Yi Kwang-su's Complete Works*, Seoul: Oolyu Moonwhasa, 1965.

Yi, Man-yeul, et.al. *Christianity and National Movement in Korea*,

Seoul: Bosung press, 1986.

Yi, Pyung-do, *An Outline History of Korea*, Seoul: Tonghisa, 1949.

Yi, Su-kwang, *Collected Essay of Chibong*, Kyungin Moonwhasa, Seoul: Korea. 1970.

Yim, Seok-che, *A Study of Korean Shamanism*, n.p.

Yu, Heung-yul, *History of the Catholic Church in Korea*, Seoul: Catholic Publishing House, 1962.

_____. *Studies on Catholic Persecutions During King Ko-Jong's Reign* (1863-1907), Seoul: Pungmunsa, 1975.

_____. *Korean Catholicism*, Seoul Sejongdaewang Kiyeumsahoe, 1976.

Yun, Sung-bum, *Christianity and Korean Thought*, Seoul: Korean Christian Literature Society, 1964.

_____. Theology of Fidelity, Seoul: Seoul Moonwhasa, 1976.

_____. *A Korean Theology: The Hermenuetic of Sung-A Yellow Theology*, Seoul: Sun Myung Whasa, 1972.

Yun, Tai-rim, *Korean People*, Seoul: Hyunamsa, 1979.

Reports, Minutes, and Year Books

Cheilhoe Kotokkyo Chosun Kmalihoe Chonghoelog: December 2-12, 1930 (Minutes of the First General Conference of the Korean Methodist Church: December 2-12, 1930), Seoul: Korean Methodist Church, 1930.

Hankuk Kitokkyo Changhohoe Che 50hoe Hoeeilong (Minutes, the 50th General Assembly, The Presbyterian Church, R.O.K., September 24-29, 1969), Seoul: The Presbyterian Church in the Republic of Korea, 1969.

Hong, Harold Song, *Samchunman Bokkumhwa Wundong* (Win Thirty Million to Christ, Report on the Nation-wide Evangelistic Campaign of 1965), Seoul: Chunkuk Kokumwha Weiwonhoe, 1965.

Jaryo: Haksaeng Wondong Sununmoon, 1960: 4.19 Eehoo (Source Collection of Student Movement Resolution Movement: 1965-1966), n.p.

Kim, Helen, *Chunkuk Rokumhwa Undong Bogoseu*: 1965-1966 (Report on the National Evangelization Movement: 1965-1966), Seoul: Chunkuk Bokukwha Weiwonhoe, 1966.

Kitokkyo Yeunkam (Christian Year Book), Seoul: Korean National Church Council, 1957, 1970, 1972.

Kukuk Sunumoon (Declaration for Saving the Nation), issued by the Committee to Save the Nation, n.p., July 1, 1965.

Kyohoeei Hyuksinkwa Sunkyo: Chilhoe Chunkuk Kutokchungneun Taehoe Bogoseu (The Renewal and Mission of the Church: Report of the First Korean Youth Ecumenical Conference), Seoul: Korean National Church Council, 1907.

Taehan Kitokkyo Changhohoe Che 44hoe Chonghoe Hoeeilog (Minutes of the 44th General Assembly, 1959), Seoul: The Presbyterian Church in the Republic of Korea, 1959.

Taechan Yesukyo Changnohoe Conghoe Hoeeilog, 1952-1960 (Minutes of the General Assembly of the Presbyterian Chruch of Korea, 1952-1960), Seoul: Publication Committee, The Presbyterian Church of Korea, 1961.

Tong-A Nyungam, 1983.

Chonsun Ilpo [Chosen Daily], 1922 ff.

Christian Shinmoon [The Christian Press], July, 1981.

Ecumenical [Ecumenical Review], 1961-1966.

Hankuk Ilbo [Korean Daily News], April, 1972.

Hankuk Mokeum Shinmoon [The Korea Gospel Weekly], January, 1983.

Hynjon [Present Reality], Vol. 106, Nov. 1979.

Hyundae-wa Sinhak [Theology and Modern Times], 1964 ff.

Jungang Ilbo [Central Daily News], March, 1983.

Kamshin Hakbo [Theological Bulletin], 1957 ff.

Kitokkyo Sasang [Christian Thought], 1957 ff.

Kitokkyo Sasang Kangjowa [Lectures on Christian Thought], 1963 ff.

Kitokkyo Sasang Yungu [Studies on Christian Thought], 1966 ff.

Kitokk Shinbo [Christian Weekly Press], 1015, Nov. 1981.

Kyemyong [The Morning Star], 1927, Vol. 19.

Minjung [People], 1981.

Minjung-kwa Hankuk Sasang [*Minjung* and Korean Theology], 1982.

SinangSaenghwal [Believing Life], Vols. 1-9 (December, 1931-August, 1938) Vols. 10-15 (1951-1956).

Sinhak Jinam [Theological Review], Vols. 1-40 (1978-1985)

Shinhak-kwa Sasang [Theology and Thought], 1968 ff.

Sinhak Sasang [Theological Thought], 1966 ff.

Sinhak Saeke [Theological World], Vol.14, No. 3-Vol. 24, No. (1929-1939).

Tong-A Ilbo [Tonga Daily News], 1922 ff. December 24, 1983.

Yeung-kwa Chinli [The Spirit and Truth], 1934-1937.

Yunsei Chunchu [*Yunsei* Spring-Fall Weekly], Vol. 19, June, 1972.

Articles

Ahn, Byung-mu, "The Image of Jesus in Korea Since 100 Years," *The Theological Thought* Vol, 19, Winter, 1977, p. 738-39.

_____. "Nation, People, Church," Kim, So-yong, ed. *The Theological Thought of Korea*, p.342-348, 1983.

_____. "The People and Church," *Church United News Report*, July 11, 1982.

Chai, Pil-keun, "Religion and the Orient," *Christian Youth*, Vol. 18, No.3 (August, 1938), pp.3-5.

Chang, Byung-il, "A Typological Approach to Christianity and Shamanism," *Studies on Christian Thought*, Seoul: Kitokkyo Moonhak, 1971. pp. 174-179.

Chi, Tong-shik, "The Poems, Critical Essays, and Theology of Chai Tae-Yong," *Theology and Modern Times*, Vol. VI, pp. 125-136.

Cho, Hyang-rok, "Things for which Christ Presbyterian should Repent," *Christian Thought*, Vol.4, No. 10 (November, 1960), pp. 52-55.

Choi, Suck-woo, "Modern Korean Society and Roman Catholic Christianity," *Song Chun Journal*, 5, 1974, p. 429.

Choo, Jae-yong, "A Historical Criticism of the Revival Movements of the Korean Church," *Christian Thought*, Seoul, Korean Christian Literature Society, 1978. p. 63.

Chung, Ha-eun, "*Minjung* of Korean-Japanese Theological Field in 1970's." *Theological Thought*, Vol. 25, June, 1979, p. 184.

_____. "Doctrine of *Minjung* of Korean-Japanese Theological Field in 1970s," *The Theological Thought*, 25 (June, 1979), pp. 185-189.

Chung, Kyung-yeun, "A Return to the Primitive or Indegenization?"*Lectures on Christian Thought*, Vol. III. 1963.

_____. "Can Christian Culture be Indigenized?" *Lectures on Christian Thought*, Vol. III. 43-59.

_____. "The So-called Pre-understanding and the *Tangun* Myth" *Christian Thought*, Vol. 7, No. 8 (August and September, 1963, Combined issue), pp. 22-29.

Chun, Ho-jin, "Korean Church Growth and Its Causes," Jong Y. Lee, Marlin Nelson, eds. *Theories of Church Growth*, Emmaus Publishing House, 1983. P. 261.

Han, Chul-ha, "A Secular Interpretation of the Gospel," *Christian Thought*,Vol.11, No. 9 October, 1967), pp.67 ff.

_____. "The Trend of Korean Theology," Christian Year Book, 1970.

Han, Wan-sang, "How Can Worship?," *Christian Thought*, Seoul: Christian Thought Co., 1979, p. 28.

Hong, Harold Song, "The Possible and Impossible Elements of Indigenization," *Lectures on Christian Thought*, Vol. III, 1963.

_____. "Lessons from April 19," Christian Thought, Vol. 4, No. 6 (June, 1960), pp. 23-25.

_____. "An Outline of the National Evangelization Movement," *Christian Thought*, Vol. 9, No. 2 (February, 1965), pp. 57-63.

Hong, I-seop, "General Remarks on Korean Thought," *Korea: Its Land, People and Culture of All Ages*, Seoul: Hakwonsa, 1960.

Im, Cok-che, "An Introduction to the Korean Folklore," *A Study of Asia Women*, Seoul: Sungmyung Yoja Taehakkyo, 1971.

Im, Tong-kwon, *"Mudang," Korean Encyclopedia*, Seoul: Dong-A Publishing Co., 1962, p. 921.

Jung, Jin-hong, "A Study of the Gigantic Churches on Korea," Wan-sang Han, et.al. *A Study on the Pentecostal Movement in Korea*, Seoul: Christian Academy, 1981.

Jun, Kyung-yun, "Can Christian Culture Be Indigenized?" *Lectures on Christian Thought*. Vol. 5, Seoul: The Christian Literature Society, 1963, pp. 207-208.

Kim, Che-choon, "Beware of the Misleading Sects," Kyung Rai Kim, ed. *A Social Evil and Heretical Movements*, Seoul: Kimoonsa, 1958. p. 104.

Kim, Chung-choon, "The Church and the Problem of Indigenization," Harold Hong, et.al. *Korea Struggle for Christ*, pp. 105-106.

Kim, Ha-tae, "Korean Church in Cultural Upheaval," *Lectures on Christian Thought*, Seoul: Korean Christian Literature Society, 1963.

Kim, Hyung-suk, *"Chundokyo," Korean Encyclopedia*, Vol. 5. Seoul: Hakwonsa, 1962. p. 569.

Kim, In-seu, "Reverend Yi Yong-do and My Relationship with Him," *Believing Life*, Vol. 2, No.11-12 (November-December, 1933), pp. 39-42.

Kim, Kwang-il, *"Kut* and Mental Therapy,*" Psychological Therapy in Folklore of Korean II*, Seoul: Korean Cultural Anthropology Association, 1979, p. 41.

Kim, Kyung-jae, "Theological and Historical Meaning of Debates on Indigenization in 1960's," *Theological Thought of Korea*, Seoul: Christian Literature Society, 1973. p. 306.

Kim, Sung-whan, "A Survey of Mission Work in Korean Church and Recommendation, *Chongshin Daebo*, September 25, 1990.

Kim, Whal-ran, "Putting a Corner Stone of National Evangelization Movement," *Report of National Evangelization Movement Center Committee*, Seoul: 1965, p. 325.

Kim, Yeul-gyu, "Korean Shamanism and Folklore," Kim, In-hoe, et, al, *A Compresentive Study of Korean Shamanism*, Seoul: Koryo University Press, p. 60.

Lee, Bu-yong, "Psychological Study of the Korean Shamanism," Kim, In-hoe, *A Comprehensive Study of Korean Shamanism*, Seoul: Koryo University Press, 1982, p. 156.

Lee, Jang-shik, "The Indigenization of Christianity is a Historical Task," *Lectures on Christian Thought*, Vol. III, 1963, pp. 226-234.

Lee, Jong-sung, "A Theological Evaluation of the Indigenization Theory," *Christian Thought*. Vol. 7 (Nov. 1963), pp. 22-31.

Lee, Hyo-Jae, "The One Hundred Year History of Christian Women in Korea," *Women Be Awakend*, Seoul: Korean Christian Publishing Co., 1985. Pp. 23-26.

Lee, Neung-wha, "A Study on Korean Shamanism," *The Morning Star*, Vol. 19, p. 13."Mass Baptismal Ceremony," *Hankuk Ilbo*, April 26, 1972, p. 6.

Min, Kyung-bae, "A Study in Yi Yong-do's Mysticism," *Theology and Modern Times*, Vol. V, May, 1969, pp. 128-129.

Moon, Sang-hee, "The Phenomenon of the New Religion," *Yunsei Chunchu Weekly*, Seoul: Yonsei University Press, 19, June, 1972. p. 12.

Niles, D. T. "A Study on the Bible and the Problem of

Indigenization," *Lectures on Christian Thought*, Vol.3, Seoul: The Christian Literature Society, 1961. Pp. P. 279.

"Panel Discussion: "The Korean Religions and Christianity," *Christian Thought*, Vol. 9, No. 10, November, 1965, pp. 78-84.

"Panel Discussion: "Self-Criticism after a Political change in Korea," *Christian Thought*, Vol. 4. No. 6 (June, 1960), pp. 48-57.

Park, Bong-bae, "Christianity and Ancestor Worship," Harold Hong, et.al. eds.*Church and Mission in Korea*, Seoul: The Christian Literature Society, 1963, pp. 20ff.

Park, Bong-rang, "A Theological Approach to the Understanding of the Indigenization of Christianity, *The North East Asia Journal of Theology*, September, 1969, pp. 107-108.

Park, Hung-nong, "The Christology of Gnosticism," *Theological Review*, Vol. 15, No.5, pp. 18-25.

Park, Hyu-seung, "History of Christian Medical Work in Korea," Young-je Han, *The Church Growth of One Hundred Year in Korea*, 1986, pp. 101-102.

Park, Paul U. U., "A Study on the Relation of Shamanism to Other Religion," *Korean Religions*, Vol. II,1, Jan. 1970.

Pyun, Sun-whan, "Ancestor Worship in Korean Church," *Tong-A Daily Newspaper*, Dec. 24, 1983.

Rhee, Jong-sung, "Why Are the Presbyterians Divided," *Christian Thought of Korea*, Nov., 1960.

Ross, J., "The Christian Dawn in Korea," *A History of Korean Church*, Vol.I., Seoul: The Christian Literature Press, 1978, p. 155.

Ryu, Tong-shik, "Indigenization of the Gospel and the Missionary Task in Korea," *Theological Bulletin*, October, 1962. "An Understanding of the Indigenization of Christianity," *Lectures on Christian Thought*, Vol. III, 1963.

____. "*Chundokyo*: Korea's Only Indigenous Religion," *Japanese Religions*, 5, No. 1(July 1967), pp. 59, 63-64.

____. "The Way of Refinement and Christianity," *Modern Theology and Creative Ministry*, Seoul: Younsei University Press, 1984. p. 124.

Shim, Il-sub, "Theological Debates on Indigenization," *Theological Thought of Korea*, Seoul: Christian Literature Society, pp. 194-202.

Song, Kil-sup, "Understanding the Holy Spirit by Church of Korea,"

The Theological Thought, Vol. 31, No. 4, 1980.

____. "Yong Do Lee, the Reformer of the Korean Church," *Theology and the World*, Seoul: Methodist Theological Seminary Press, 1978. p. 127.

Suh, Kwang-sun, "Soteriology of the Korean Christian," *Theological Thought of Korea*, Seoul: Christian Literature Society, 1977.

____. "Korean Christian's Way of Thinking," *Theology and Thought*, Seoul: Korean Theological Study Institute, Summer, 1993, p. 286.

____. "A Theological Analysis of the Spiritual Movement," Han, Wan-sang, et.al., *A Study on the Pentecostal Movement in Korea,* Seoul: Christian Academy, 1981, p. 57.

Suh, Nam-dong, "Jesus, Church History, and Korean Church," *Christian Thought*, Seoul: Christian Thought Press, February, 1975, pp. 62ff. "Symposium," *Theological Thought*, Vol. 24, Spring, 1979, p. 116.

Taechongkyo, "Scripture of Assembling Three," *Philosophy of Three-one: Commentary on the Scripture*, Seoul: Taechongkyo Chongpansa, 1949.

Tak, Myung-whan, "The Devil's Feast," *Consecration*, Seungbyul, 1978. "Theology of *Minjung* Theology," *The Christian Press*, July, 11, 1981, p. 2.

Yi, Duk-ju, "A Study on Translation of the Korean Bible," Yi, Man-yeul, et.al., *Korean Christianity and National Movement in Korea*, Seoul: Bosung, 1986.

Yun, Kyung-ro, "The Foundation and the Process of Association of New Nation, *Christianity and National Culture*, Seoul: Kitokkyomunsa, 1987, pp. 233-234.

Yun, Sung-bum, "Pre-understanding and the Indigenization of the Gospel,*"Lectures on Christian Thought*, Vol. III, 1963.

____. "Formation of the Concept of God in Korea," *Christian Thought*, Vol. 13, No. 6 (June, 1969), pp. 104-125.

____. "Karl Barth's Understanding of the Spirit and the Problem of Technology," *Christian Thought* Vol, 13. No. 10 (October 1969), pp. 145-159.

____. "The Idea of History in *Chunggamrok* Prophecy," *Christian Thought*, Vol. 14, No. 1 (January, 1970), pp. 102-115.

____. "The *Tangun* Myth is the *Vestigium Trinitiatis*," *Christian Thought*, Vol, 13, No, 16, June. pp. 104-125.

____. "Pre-Understanding with regard to the Indigenization of the Gospel, *Christian Thought*, Vol. III, pp. 235-240.

English Language Publications
II.1 Books

Ahn, Ho Sang. *The Ancient History of the Korean-Dong-I Race.* Institute of Baedal Culture, Seoul, Korea. 1974.

Albrecht. Marck C. eds. *God in Asia Contexts.* Asia Theological Association, Taiching, Taiwan, 1988.

Alexander, W. Menzie. *Demonic Possession in the New Testament.* Baker Book House, Grand Rapids, MI. 1980.

Allen, Carter C., *Ecstasy: Shamanism in Korea*, Royal Asiatic Society, Seoul, Korea. 1981.

Allen, Horace N. *Things Korea.* Fleming H. Revell Company, New York, NY. 1908.

Allen, Roland. *Missionary Methods: St. Paul's or Ours.* WilliamB. Eerdmans Publishing Company, Grand Rapids, MI. 1962.

Alston, William P. *Religious Belief and Philosophical Thought.* Harcourt, Brace and World Inc. New York, NY. 1963.

Anderson, Gerald H., ed. *Mission Trends No.1.* William B. Eerdmans Publishing Company, Grand Rapids, MI. 1974.

____. *Mssion Trends No.2. Evangelization.* William B.Eerdmans Publishing Company, Grand Rapids, MI. 1975.

____. *Mission Trends No.3. Third World Theologies.* William B. Eerdmans Publishing Company, Grand Rapids, MI. 1976.

____.*Mission Trends No.4. Liberation Theologies.* Williams B. Eerdmans Publishing Company, Grand Rapids, MI. 1979.

____. *Mission Trends No.5. Faith Meets Faith.* William B. Eerdmans Publishing Company,Grand Rapids, MI.1981.

____. *Asian Voices in Christian Theology*, Orbis Book, New York, NY. 1976.

Anderson, James N., ed. *The World Religions.* William B. Eerdmans Publishing Company, Grand Rapids, MI. 1953.

____.*Christianity and Comparative Religion.* InterVarsity Press, Downers Grove, IL. 1971.

Anderson, Sir Norman. *The World's Religions.* William B. Eerdmans

Publishing Company, Grand Rapids, MI. 1976.

Annan, Nelson. *More People : Is Church Growth Worth It.* Harold Shaw Publishers, Wheaton, IL. 1987.

Autrey, C. E. *Basic Evangelism.* Zondervan Publishing Company, Grand Rapids, MI. 1959.

Baker, Donald Leslie. *Confucians Confront Catholicism in Eighteenth-Century Korea.* Ph.D. Dissertation, University of Washington, University Microfilms International, Ann Arbor, MI. 1983.

Bapat, P. V., ed. *2500 Years of Buddha.* The Publishing Division, Ministry of Information and Broadcasting, New Delhi, India. 1959.

Barclay, William. *A New Testament Word Book*, Harper and Brothers, New York, NY. 1957.

Barth, Karl. *Church Dogmatic IV*, Trans. G. W. Bromley, William Eerdman Publishing Co., Grand Rapids, MI. 1959.

Barret, David B. ed, *The World Christian Encyclopedia: A Comparative Survey of Churches and Religions in the Modern World, A.D. 1900- 2,000,* Oxford University Press, Kenya, Nairobi. 1982.

Bassham, Rodger C. *Mission Theology: 1948-1975 Years of Worldwide Creative Tension Ecumenical, Evangelical and Roman Catholic.* William Carey Library, Pasadena, CA. 1979.

Bauer, Paul. *Christianity and Superstition.* Marshall Morgen and Scott, London, England. 1966.

Bavinck, J. Hendrick. *The Church Between Temple and Mosque.* William B. Eerdmans Publishing Comapny, Grand Rapids, MI. 1981.

. *An introduction to the Science of Mission.* David H. Freeman, trans. Baker Book House, Grand Rapids, MI. 1960.

Beals, Paul A. *A People For His Name.* Baker Book House, Grand Rapids, MI. 1985.

Beyerhaus. Peter. *Missions: Which Way?,* Zondervan Publishing House, Grand Rapids, MI.1971.

_____. *Shaken Foundation.* Zondervan Publishing House, Grand Rapids, MI. 1972.

Bishop, Isabella Bird. *Korea and Her Neighbor,* London, 1898, reprinted, Yunsei University Press, Seoul, Korea. 1970.

Blair, William N, and Bruce F. Hunt. *Korea Pentecost: The Suffering*

Which Followed, Banner of Truth Trust, Edinburgh, UK. 1977.

____. *Gold in Korea*, The Presbyterian Church in the U.S.A., New York, NY. 1957.

Blauw, Johannes. *The Missionary Nature of the Church : A Survey of the Biblical Theology of Mission*, McGraw-Hill, New York, NY. 1962.

Blinkely, F., *A History of the Japanese People*, The Encyclopedia Press, London, UK. 1915.

Boa, Kenneth. *Cults, World Religions, and You*. Victor Book, Wheaton, IL. 1977.

Boer, Harry R., *Pentecost and Missions*. William B. Eerdmans Publishing Company, Grand Rapids, MI. 1961.

Bonino, Jose Miguez. *Doing Theology in a Revolutionary Situation*. Fortress Press, Philadelphia, PA. 1975.

Bonwick, G. F. E. William, eds., *The Korea Missions Year Book*, The Christian Literature Society of Korea, Seoul, Korea. 1928.

Bosch, David J. *Witness to the World: The Christian Mission in Theological Perspective*, John Knox, Atlanta, GA. 1980.

Botterwrck, Johanners, Helmer Ringgren, eds., trans. John T. Willis, *Theological Dictionary of the Old Testament*, William B. Eerdman Publishing Co., Grand Rapids, MI. 1975.

Bradley, David G. *A Guide to the World's Religions*. Prentice Hall, Inc. Englewood, Cliffs, NJ. 1963.

Breunig, Jerome. *Have You had Your Rice Today*, Loyola University Press, Chicago, IL. 1964.

Bridge, Donald, and David Phyphers. *Spiritual Gifts and the Church*, Leicester, NY. InterVarsity Press, 1973.

Bright, Bill. *Come, Help Change Our World*. Campus CrusadeInternational, San Bernandino, CA. 1979.

Brown, A. J. *The Mastery of the Far East*, Scribners, New York, NY. 1919.

____. *Toward a United Church*, Jerusalem Conference Publishing Committee, New York, NY. 1946

Brown, Collin, ed. *The International Dictionary of New Testament Theology*, Vol.2, Zondervan Publishing House, Grand Rapids, MI. 1967.

Brown, George T. *Mission to Korea*. Board Missions, Presbyterian Church. U.S.A. New York, NY. 1962.

Bullough, Sebastian. *Roman Catholicism*, Penguin Book, Harmondworth, NY. 1963.

Burnett, David, *God's Mission: Healing the Nations*, MARC Europe, Bromley, England. 1986.

Bush, Richard C. *Religion in China*. William B. Eerdmans Publishing Company, Grand Rapids. MI. 1968.

Calvin, John, *Commentary on the Epistles of Paul the Apostle to the Philippians, Colossians, and Thessalonians*, trans. ed., John Pringle, William B. Eerdmans Publishing Co., Grand Rapids, MI. 1948.

Campbell, Arch. *The Christ of the Korean Heart*, Falco Publishing Co., Columbus, Ohio, 1954.

Capps, Walter H., ed. *Ways of Understanding Religion*. The MacMillan Company, New York, NY. 1972.

Carus, Paul. *Gospel of Buddha*. Omen Communication Inc. Tuscon, AZ. 1972.

Cary, Otis. *A History of Christianity in Japan*, Fleming H. Revell, New York, NY: 1909.

Chaffer, Lewis Sperry. *True Evangelism*, Zondervan Publishing House, Grand Rapids, MI. 1919.

Chan, Wing-Tsit. *The Great Asian Religions: An Anthropology*. The MacMillan Company, London, England. 1969.

Chaney, Charles L. *The Birth of Missions in America*. William Carey Library, Pasadena, CA. 1976.

Chang, Byung-Kil. *Religions in Korea*. Korea Overseas Information Service, Seoul, Korea. 1984.

Chantry, Walter J. *Today's Gospel authentic or Synthetic*. The Banner of Truth Trust, Edinburgh, 1976.

Ch'en, Kenneth K. S. *Buddhism in the Light of Asia*. Omen Communication Inc. Tuscon, AZ. 1976.

Cho, David, J. Ed. *New Forces in Mission*, East-West Center Mission Research and Development, Seoul, Korea, 1975.

Cho, Paul Yonggi. *More Than Numbers*. Word Books Publisher, Waco, TX. 1984.

Choi, Jashil. *Korean Miracles*. Youngsan Publishing Company. Seoul, Korea. 1978.

Choi, Min-Hong. *A Modern History of Korean Philosophy*. Seong Moon Sa. Seoul, Korea. 1980.

Choi, Shin, D. *Korea's Unification Movement*, Royal Asiatic Society, Seoul, Korea. 1967.

Chun, Shin-Yong. ed. *Customs and Manners in Korea*. International Cultural Foundation, Seoul, Korea. 1980.

_____. ed. *Buddhist Culture in Korea*. International Cultural Foundation, Seoul, Korea. 1974.

_____. ed. *Korean Thoughts*. International Cultural Foundation, Seoul, Korea. 1979.

_____. ed. *Folk Culture in Korea*. International Cultural Foundation, Seoul, Korea. 1974.

Chun, Sung C. *Shism and Unity in the Protestant Church of Korea*, The Christian Literature Society, Seoul, Korea. 1979.

Chung, Kyung-cho. *Korea Tomorrow: Land of the Morning Calm*. The Macmillan Company, New York, NY. 1961.

Clark, Allen D. *History of the Korean Church*, The Christian Literature Society, Seoul, Korea, 1916.

Clark, Charles Allen. *Religions of Old Korea*. The Christian Literature Society of Korea, Seoul, Korea, 1961.

_____. *Digest of the Presbyterian Church of Korea(Chosen)*. Korean Religious Book & Tract Society, Seoul, Korea, 1918.

_____. *Korean Church and Nevius Methods*, Fleming H. Revell Co., 1885, New York, NY. 1885.

Clark, N. Donald. *Christianity in Modern Korea*. University Press of America, Lanham, MD. 1986.

Cocoris, C. Michael. *Evangelism: A Biblical Approach*. Moody Press, Chicago, IL. 1984.

Coleman, Robert E. ed. *Evangelism on the Cutting Edge*. Fleming H. Revell Company, Old Tapan, NJ. 1986.

_____. *Evangelism in Perspective*. Christian Publication, Inc. Harrisburg, PA. 1975.

_____. *The Master Plan of Evangelism*. Fleming H. Revell, Company, Old Tapan, NJ. 1963.

Conn, Harvie M. *Eternal Word and Changing World*. Academic Books Grand Rapids, MI. 1984.

_____. *Evangelism: Doing Justice and Preaching Grace*. Zondervan Publishing House, Grand Rapids, MI. 1982.

_____. *Contemporary World Theology*. Presbyterian and Reformed Publishing Company, Nutley, NJ. 1973.

_____. ed. *Theological Perspective on Church Growth*, Presbyterian and Reformed Publishing Company, Nutely, NJ. 1976.

Costas, Orlando. *The Church and Its Mission*, Tyndale House, Wheaton, IL. 1974.

Coze, Edward. *Buddhism, the Essence and Development*. Harper & Row Publishing Company, New York, NY. 1951.

Cook, Harold R. *An Introduction to Christian Missions*. Moody Press, Chicago, IL. 1978.

Covell, Alan Carter. *Shamanistic Folk Paintings: Korea's Eternal Spirits*. Hollym International Corp, Seoul, Korea. 1984.

_____. *Ecstasy: Shamanism in Korea*. Hollym International Corp, Seoul, Korea. 1983.

Crim, Keith. ed. *Abingdon Dictionary of Living Religions*. Abingdon Press, Nashville, TN. 1981.

Dale, Kenneth J. *Circle of Harmony*. William Carey Library, South Pasadena, CA. 1975.

Danker, William. *Two Worlds or None*, Concordia Publishing House, St. Louis, MO. 1964.

Davis, George T. *Korea For Christ*. Christian Workers' Depot, London, UK. 1910.

Dayton, Edward R. *The Future of World Evangelization*. MARC.Monrovia, CA. 1984.

_____.*Planning Strategies for World Evangelization*.William B. Eerdmans Publishing Company, MI. 1980.

De Ridder, Richard R. *Discipling the Nations*. Baker Book House, Grand Rapid, MI. 1975.

De Rubruck, William. *The Journey of William Rebruck to the Eastern Part of the World,* 1253-1255, trans. W.W. Rockhill, The Hakluyt Society, London, UK. 1900.

Dix, Mortimer Griffin. *The East Asian Country of Propriety: Confucianism in a Korean Village*. Ph.D. Dissertation University of California, San Diego, University Microfilms International, Ann Arbor, MI. 1985.

Dixon, Roland B. *The Racial History of Man*. Scribner's, New York, NY. 1923.

Douglas, J. D. *Let the Earth Hear His Voice*. International Congress on World evangelization, Lausanne, Switzerland. Worldwide Publication, Minneapolis, MN. 1975.

Draper, Edyther. *The Almanac of the Christian World*, Tyndale House Publishers, Wheaton, IL. 1990.

Drummond, Lewis A. *Evangelism: The Encounter Revolution*.Marchall, Morgan and Scott, Blundell House, London, England. 1972

Drumond, Ricahrd Henry. *Gautama The Buddha*. William B. Eerdmans Publishing Company, Grand Rapids, MI. 1974.

Dubose, Francis M. ed. *Classics of Christian Missions*. Broadman Press, Nashville, TN. 1979.

Dumezil, George. *Gods of the Ancient Northmen*. University of California Press, Berkeley, CA. 1973.

Eddy, Sherwood, *The New Era in Asia*, Missionary Education Movement of the United States and Canada, New York, NY. 1913.

Eerdman's Handbook of the World Religions. William B. Eerdmans Publishing Company, Grand Rapids. MI. 1982.

Emile, Durkheim. *The Elementary Forms of the Religious Life*. trans., Joseph Ward Swain, The Free Press, New York, NY. 1966.

Engel, James F., Norton, H. Wilbert. *What's Gone Wrong with the Harvest?*.Zondervan Publishing Company House, Grand Rapids, MI. 1975.

Engstrom, Ted W. *What in the World is God Doing?*. Word Books, Publisher, Waco. TX. 1978.

Enroth, Ronald. et.al. *A Guide to Cults and New Religions*. InterVarsity Press, Downers Grove, IL. 1983.

Eliade, Mircea. *Shamanism: Archaic Techniques of Ecstasy*. Bollingen Foundation, New York. NY. 1964.

____. *Myth and Reality*. Harvill Press, London, England. 1958.

____. *Rites and Symbols of Initiation*. Shead and Ward. New York, NY. 1958.

Elliot, Ralph H. *Church Growth that Counts*. Jodson Press, Valley Forge, PA. 1982.

Elwood Douglas J. ed. *What Asian Christians Are Thinking*. New Day Publishers of the Christian Literature Society of the Philippines, Quezon City, Philippine, 1976.

Era, Jean-Marc, *My Faith as an African*. John Pairman Brown and Susan Perry, trans. Orbis Books, Maryknoll, NY. 1988.

Facts About Korea 1988. Korean Overseas Information Service,

Seoul, Korea. 1988.

Fernando, Antony. *Buddhism Made Plain*. Orbis Books, Maryknoll, NY. 1985.

Fenwick, Malcom, C. *The Church of Christ in Corea*. Hodder and Stoughton-Doran, New York, NY. 1911.

Fisher, James Earnest. *Democracy and Mission Education in Korea*. Reprinted by Yonsei University Press, Seoul, Korea. 1970.

____. *Pioneers of Modern Korea*. The Christian Literature Society of Korea, Seoul, Korea. 1977.

Fry, C. George. and others. *Great Asian Religions*. Baker Book House, Grand Rapids, MI. 1984.

Fulton, C. Darby. *Star in the East.*, Presbyterian Committee of Publication, Richmond, VA. 1938.

Fung, Yu-lan, *A History of Chinese Philosophy*, Princeton University Press, Princeton, NJ. 1952.

Gale, James S. *Korean Sketches*. Fleming H. Revell, New York, NY. 1898.

____.*Korea in Transition*. Young People's Missionary Movement of the United States and Canada, New York. NY. 1909.

____. *The Vanguard : A Tale Of Korea*. Fleming H. Revell Company, New York. NY. 1904.

Gard, Richard Abbot. ed. *Buddhism*. George Braziller, New York. NY. 1961.

Gibbs, Eddi. *I Believe in Church Growth*. William B. Eerdmans Publishing Company, Grand Rapids, MI. 1981.

Gifford, D. L., *Everyday Life in Korea*. Fleming H. Revell Company, New York, NY. 1898.

Gilliland, Dean S. *Pauline Theology and Mission Practice*. Baker Book House Company, Grand Rapdis, MI. 1983.

Glasser, Arthur F., McGavran, Donald A. *Contemporary Theology of Mission*. Baker Book House Company, Grand Rapids, MI.1983.

Glover, Robert Hall. *The Progress of Worldwide Missions*. Harper and Row Publishers, New York, NY. 1960.

____. *The Biblical Basis of Mission*. Moody Press, Chicago, IL. 1946.

Goden, Alfred S. *Studies in the Religions of the East*. Charles H. Kelley, London, England. 1913.

Goforth, Jonathan. *When the Spirit's Fir Swept Korea*, Zondervan

Publishing House, Grand Rapids, MI. 1942.

Gort, Jerald D. et al., eds., *Dialogue and Syncretism: An Interdisciplinary Approach*, Rodopi, Amsterdam, Netherlands, 1989.

_____. *On Sharing Religious Experience: Possibilities of Interfaith Mutuality*, Rodopi, Amsterdam, Netherlands. 1992.

Grayson, James Huntly. *Early Buddhism and Christianity in Korea.* E. J. Brill, Leiden, Netherlands. 1985.

_____. *Korea: A Religious History,* Clarendon Press, Oxford, UK. 1989.

Green, Bryan. *The Practice of Evangelism*, Charles Scriber's Sons, New York, NY. 1951.

Green, Michael. *Evangelism Now and Then.* InterVarsity Press,Downers Grove, IL. 1979.

_____. *Evangelism in the Early Church.* William B. Eerdmans Publishing Company, Grand Rapids, MI. 1970.

Greenway, Roger S. ed. *A World to Win: Preaching World Missions Today.* Baker Book House, Grand Rapids, MI. 1975.

_____. *Lengthened Cords.* Baker Book House Company, Grand Rapids, MI. 1975.

Griffins, William E. *Corea the Hermit Nation.* Charles Scribner's Sons, New York, NY. 1882.

_____. *Henry G. Appenzeller: A Modern Pioneer in Korea*, Fleming H. Revell Co., New York, NY. 1912.

_____. *A Modern Pioneer in Korea, the Life Study of Whney G. Appenzeller,* Fleming H. Revell Co., New York, NY. 1912.

Griffiths, Michael. *The Church and world Mission.* Zondervan Publishing House, Grand Rapids, MI. 1982.

Guisso, Richard W. I., Chai-shin Yu. *Shamanism: The Spirit World of Korea*, Asian Humanities Press, Berkeley, CA. 1988.

Gutzlaff, Charles K., *Journal of Three Voyages Along the Coast of China,* Frederick Westley and A.H. Davis Second Edition, London, UK. 1834.

Hamel, Hendrick. *Narrative of an Unlucky Voyage and Imprisonment in Korea 1653-1677*, trans. Pyong-do Yi, Iljikak, Seoul, Korea. 1954.

Hansen, Eric O. *South Korea: Cry of the People.* Orbis Books, Maryknoll, NY. 1980.

Han, Woo-Keun. *The History of Korea.* trans. Lee, Kyung-Shik. The Eul-Yoo Publishing Company, Seoul, Korea. 1970.

Hedlund, Roger E. *Roots of the Great Debate in Mission.* Evangelical Literature Service, Madras, India. 1981.

Henry, Matthew. *The Matthew Henry Commentary,* Zondervan Publishing House, Grand Rapids, MI. 1961.

Hesselgrave, David J. *Planting Churches Cross-Culturally.* Baker Book House Company, Grand Rapids, MI. 1980.

_____. ed. *Dynamic Religious Movements.* Baker Book House, Company, Grand Rapids, MI. 1978.

Hiebert, Paul G. *Cultural Anthropology.* Baker Book House Company, Grand Rapids, MI. 1976.

_____. *Anthropological Insights for Missionaries.* Baker Book House, Grand Rapids, MI. 1985.

Hocking, William Erness. *Living Religions and A World Faith,* The MacMilliam Company, New York, NY. 1940.

Hoekstra, Harvey T. *The World Council of Churches and the Demise of Evangelism.* Tyndale House Publishers Inc. Wheaton, IL. 1979.

Hoke, Donald, ed. *The Church in Korea*, The Moody Press, Chicago, IL. 1975.

Holton, D. C. *The National Faith of Japan: A Study in Modern Shinto*, E. P. Dutton, New York, NY. 1938.

Hong, Harold S., Won Yong Ji., Chung Choon Kim. eds. *Korea Struggle for Christ.* Christian Literature Society of Korea, Seoul. Korea. 1966.

_____. *Church and Mission in Korea*, Christian Literature Society, Seoul, Korea. 1963.

Horner, Norman A. ed. *Protestant Crosscurrents.* Abingdon Press, Nashville, TN. 1968.

H.S.A.U.W.C., *Divine Principle*, Holy Spirit Association for the Unification of World Christianity Press, 1977, Washington D.C.

Humn, Halla Pai. *Kut : Korean Shamanist Rituals.* Hollym International Corp. Seoul, Korea. 1980.

Hulbert, H. B., *The Passing of Korea.* Yonsei University Press, Seoul, Korea. 1969.

Hume, David. *The Natural History of Religion.* Standford University Press, Standford, CA. 1957.

Hunt, Everett N. Jr. *Protestant Pioneers In Korea.* Orbis Books, Maryknoll, New York, NY. 1980.

Huntley, Martha. *To Start a Work: The Foundation of Protestant Mission in Korea (1884-1919),* Mokyangsa, Seoul, Korea. 1987.

Ilyon. *Samguk Yusa.* trans. Ha, Tae-Hung. Yonsei University Press, Seoul, Korea. 1972.

Inch, Morris, A. *Doing Theology: A Cross Cultures.* Baker Book House, Grand Rapids, MI. 1982.

Ireland, Alleyne. *The New Korea.* E.P. Dutton and Company, New York, NY. 1926.

Janelli, Roeger L., Dawnhee Yim. *Ancestor Worship and Korean Society.* Standford University Press, Standford, CA. 1982.

Jaspers, Karl.,Rudolf Bultman. *Myth and Christianity.* The Noonday Press, New York, NY. 1958.

Jenson, Ron., Jin Stevens. *Dynamic of Church Growth.* Baker Book House, Grand Rapids, MI. 1981.

Joe, Wanne J. *Traditional Korea : A Cultural History.* Chung'ang University Press, Seoul, Korea. 1972.

Johnson, Ben Campbell. *Rethinking Evangelism: A Theological Approach.* The Westminster Press, Philadelphia, PA. 1987.

Johnson, Arthur P. *World Evangelism and the Word of God.* Bethany Fellowship. Inc. Minneapolis, MN. 1974.

_____. *The Battle for World Evangelism.* Tyndale House Publishers, Inc. Wheaton, IL. 1978.

Johnstone, Partick, *Operation World*, Zondervan Publishing House, Grand Rapids, MI. 1993.

Jones, G. Herbert. *Korea: the Land, People, the Custom.* Easton and Mains, New York, NY. 1895.

_____. *Royal Asiatic Society Record*, Transactions of the Korean Branch, Seoul, Korea. 1900.

Jones G. H. and J. Flowler Wiling, *The Lure of Korea*, Fleming H. Revell Co., New York, NY. 1905

Jun, Ho-jin. *A Critique of Ecumenical Mission and Its Influence on the Korean Church*, D. Miss. Dissertation, Fuller Theological Seminary, Pasadena, CA. 1978.

Kane, J. Herbert. *Christian Missions in Biblical Perspective.* Baker Book House, Grand Rapids, MI. 1976.

_____. *A Global View of Christian Missions from Pentecost to the*

Present. Baker Book House, Grand Rapids. MI.1975.

____. *A Concise History of the Christian World Mission*. Baker Book House, Grand Rapids, MI. 1978.

____. *Wanted: World Christians*. Baker Book House Company, Grand Rapids, MI. 1986.

Kang, Hugh, W. ed. *The Traditional Culture and Society of Korea: Thought and Institution*. Center for Korean Studies, University of Hawaii, Honolulu, HI. 1975.

Keel, Hee-Sung. *Chinul: The Founder of the Korean Son Tradition*. Berkeley Buddhist Studies Series, Berkeley, CA. and Bo Chin Chai LTD, Seoul, Korea. 1984.

Keesing, Felix M. *Cultural Anthropology: The Science of Custom*. Rinehart & Co., Inc., New York, NY. 1960.

Keyes, Lawrence E., *The Last Age of Mission*, William Carey Library, Pasadena, CA. 1983,

Kim, Byung-suh. *A History of the Growth of Christianity in Korea*, Christian Literature Society, Seoul, Korea. 1971.

Kim, Chang-Seok Thaddeus. *Lives of 103 Martyr Saints of Korea*. Catholic Publishing House, Seoul, Korea.1984.

Kim, Chi-ha. *Cry of the People and Other Poem*, Autumn Press, Tokyo, Japan, 1974.

Kim, Duk-whang. *A History of Religions in Korea*, Seoul, Korea: Daeji Moonwhasa, 1988.

Kim, Jang-moon. *Catholic Korea, Yesterday and Today*, Catholic Korean Press, Seoul, Korea. 1964.

Kim, John Yohn-Taek. *Korean Evangelism and Church Growth in Confrontation with the Powers: A Historical and Biblical Evaluation*. Th.M. Thesis. Calvin Theological Seminary, Grand Rapids, MI. 1984.

Kim, Jong-Il. *Mukyo and Its Implications to the Christian Church in Korea,* Ph.D. Dissertation, Fuller Theological Seminary, Pasadena, CA.1985.

Kim, Paul Taek-Yong. *Church Growth Development of the Korean Churches in America*. Word of Life Press, Seoul, Korea. 1985.

Kim, Tae-whan. *A Empirical Study of the Factors Contributing to Rapid Church Growth in Korea,* Eastern Baptist Theological Seminary, Philadelphia, PA. 1984.

Kim, Young-bock. Ed. *Minjung Theology*. Orbis Books, Maryknoll, NY. 1981.

Kim, Yong-choon. *Oriental Thought*. Littlefield, Adams and Company, Totowa, NJ. 1973.

Kim, Yung-Chung. ed. *Women of Korea: History from Ancient Times to 1945*, Ewha Women University Press, Seoul, Korea. 1976.

Kittle, G., ed. *Theological Dictionary of the New Testament*, Vol.4., William B. Eerdmans Publishing Co., Grand Rapids, MI. 1975.

Ko, Tae-Woo. *Religions in North Korea*, Seoul, Korea: Institute of Korean Religions, 1988.

Kong, Jong-Won. *Faith without Heaven: How Religion was Extinguished in North Korea*. Kwangmyung Publishing Company, Seoul, Korea. 1974.

Kraemer, Hendrik. *The Christian Message in a Non-Christian World*. The Edinburgh House Press, London, England. 1938.

_____. *Religion and the Christian Faith*. Lutterworth Press, London, England. 1938.

Kraft, Charles. *Christianity in Culture*, Orbis Books, Maryknoll, NY. 1979.

_____. H., Tom N. Wisley. eds. *Readings in Dynamic Indigeneity*. William Carey Library, Pasadena, CA. 1979.

Kromminga, Carl G. *Bringing God's News to Neighbors*. Presbyterian and Reformed Publishing Company, Nutley, NJ. 1977.

Kuiper, R. B. *God Centered Evangelism*, The Banner of Truth Trust, Edinburgh, Scotland. 1961.

Kusan. *The Way of Korean Zen*. trans. Martin Foges. John Weatherhill Inc. New York, NY. 1985.

Ladd, George E. *The Presence of the Future*, William Eerdman Publishing Co., Grand Rapids, MI. 1974.

_____. *A Theology of the New Testament*, Erdman Publishing, Grand Rapids, MI. 1974.

Latourette, Kenneth Scot. *A History of the Expansion of Christianity Vol.6. The Great Century: North Africa and Asia.1800-1914.A.D.* Zondervan Publishing House, Grand Rapids, MI. 1970.

Ledyard, Gari. *The Dutch Come to Korea*, Royal Asiatic Society, Seoul, Korea. 1971.

Lee, Dong-Choon. ed. *The Way of Korea*. International Toegyehak Society, Seoul. Korea. non date.

Lee, Honggoo, Seungdoo Yang, Byongie Jon, Chaibong Hahm, eds. *Korean Jurisprudence, Policies and Culture*, Yonsei University

Press, Seoul, Korea. 1986.

Lee, Jung Young. *Korean Shamanistic Rituals.* Mouton Publishers, The Hague, The Netherlands, 1981.

_____. *The Theology of Change.* Orbis Books, New York. NY. 1979. ed. *Ancestor Worship and Christianity in Korea,* The Edwin Mellen Press, Lewiston, NY. 1988.

Lee, Kun-sam *The Christian Confrontation with Shinto Nationalism,* The Presbyterian and Reformed Press, Philadelphia, PA. 1966.

Lee, Ki-Baik. *A New History of Korea.* trans. Edward W. Wagner with Edward J. Shultz. Ilchikak Publishers, Seoul, Korea. 1984.

Lee, Kyung-ho. *A Study on the Belief Structure of Korean Ministries,* Methodist Theological Seminary, Unpublished Master's Thesis, Seoul, Korea. 1983.

Lenski, R. C. H., *The Interpretation of the Acts of the Apostle,* Augusburg Press, Minneapolis, MN. 1934.

Lindsell, Harold. ed. *The Church's Worldwide Mission.* Wheaton Congress on Mission. Word Books, Waco, TX. 1966.

Lowell, Percival. *Chosen the Land of the Morning Calm.* Tichnor and Company, Boston, MA. 1886.

Lueras, Leonard, Nedra Chung. eds. *Korea.* Apa Productions, LTD. Hong Kong. 1981.

Luzbetak, Louis J. *The Church and Cultures.* William Carey Library, South Pasadena. 1977.

Maddocks, Morris. *The Christian Healing Ministry.* London SPCK, Holy Trinity Church, England. 1981.

Mahan, Brian, L. Dale Richesin. eds. *The Challenge of Liberation Theology: A First World Response.* Orbis Books, Maryknoll, New York, NY. 1981.

Mason, Alfred Dewitt. *Outlines of Missionary History.* Hodder Stoughton, New York, NY. 1912.

Mayers, Marvins K. *Christianity Confronts Culture.* Zondervan Publishing House, Grand Rapids, MI. 1974.

McCune, George M. *Korea Today.* Harvard University Press, NewYork, NY. 1950.

McCune, Shannon. *Views of the Geography of Korea.* The Korean Research Center, Seoul, Korea. 1980.

_____. *Korea's Heritage: A Regional and Social Geography.* Charles Tuttle, 1956, Rutland, VT. 1956.

McGavran, Donald A. *How Churches Grow*. Friendship Press, New York, NY. 1959.

____. *Understanding Church Growth*. William B. Eerdmans Publishing Company, Grand Rapids, MI.1970.

____. *The Bridges of God: A Study in the Strategy of Mission*. Friendship Press, New York, NY.1955.

____. Winfield C. Arn. *Ten Steps for Church Growth,* Harper & Row Publishers, San Francisco, CA. 1977.

McGavran Donald, George G. Hunter III. *Church Growth Strategies the Work*. Abingdon Press, Nashville, TN. 1980.

Meskill, John. trans. *Ch'oe Pu's Diary: A Record of Drifting Across the Sea*. The University of Arizona Press, Tucson, AZ. 1965.

Milan, Louise J. *Quaint Korea*, Osgood, McIlvaine & Company, London, UK. 1895.

Miller, Frederick S. *Korean Young Folks*, Fleming H. Revell Co., New York, NY. 1963.

Min, Tai-Hyung. *Korean Statistical Yearbook 1992,* National Statistical Office, Seoul, Korea. 1992.

Moffet, Samuel. *The Christian in Korea*. Friendship Press, New York, NY. 1962.

Mooneyham, Stanley. ed. *Christ Seeks Asia*. Official Reference Volume, Asia-South Pacific Congress on Evangelism, Singapore, 1968. The Rock House Publishing, Hong Kong. 1969.

Moose, J. Robert. *Village Life in Korea*, Publishing House of the Methodist Episcopal Church South, Smith and Lamar, Agent, Nashville, TN. 1911.

Montgomery, John W. ed. *Demon Possession*. Bethany House Publisher, Minneapolis, MN. 1976.

Montgomery, James H., Donald A. McGavran. *the Discipling a Nation*. Global Church Growth, Milpitas, CA. 1980.

Morris, M. F. *The Million Soul Man*. Christ For the World Publishers, Orlando, Florida, 1980.

Murray, John, *Collected Writings of John Murray*, Vol.2, The Banner of Truth Trust, Edinburgh, Scotland, 1975.

Nakil, Emerito P., Douglas J, Elwood. eds. *The Human and the Holy*. Asian Perspectives in Christian Theology. New Day Publishers, Quezon City, Philippines. 1978.

Nahm, Andrew C. *Korea: Tradition and Transformation*. A History of the Korean people. Hollym International Corp. Seoul, Korea. 1988.

_____. *Introduction to Korean History and Culture*, Seoul, Korea, 1994.

Na, Yong-hwa. *Special Lecture Notes: Minjung Theology*. Grand Rapids, MI. 1983

Neill, Stephen, *A History of Christian Mission*. Penguin Books, New Yotk, NY. 1964.

Nelson, Marlin L. ed. *Readings in Third World Missionary*. William Carey Library, South Pasadena, CA. 1976.

Nevius, John L. *The Planting and Development of missionary Churches*. Student Volunteer Movement for Foreign Missions, New York, NY. 1899.

Nevis, H. S. C., *The Life of John Livingston Nevius*, Fleming H. Revell Co., New York, NY. 1895.

Newport, John P. *Demons, Demons, Demons*. Broadman Press, Nashville, TN. 1972.

Niebur, H. Richard. *Christ and Culture*. Harper & Row, New York, NY. 1951.

Nicholson, E. ed. *Shamanism*. Quest, Wheaton, IL. 1987.

Nida, Eugene. William A Smalley. *Introducing Animism*. Friendship Press, New York, NY. 1959.

_____. *Customs and Cultures*. William Carey Library, South Pasadena, CA. 1975.

_____. *Message and Mission*. William Carey Library, Pasadena, CA. 1960.

_____. *Religion Across Cultures*. The William Carey Library Pasadena, CA. 1968.

Ogle, George E. *Liberty to the Captives*. John Knox Press, Atlanta, GA. 1977.

One, Sokyo. *Shinto: The Kami Way*, Tuttle, Rutland, VA. 1962.

Oosterom, Leo. *Contemporary Missionary Thought in the Republic of Korea*. Rijksuniversiteit, Utrecht. 1988.

Oosterm-Flier, Christien. *Church Growth in the Republic of Korea: A Survey and Evaluation of its Explanations*. University of Utrecht. Faculty of Theology, Utrecht, 1988.

Osgood, Cornelius. *The Koreans and Their Culture*. The Ronald Press, New York, NY, 1951.

Packer, J. I. *Evangelism and the Sovereignty of God*. Inter Varsity Press, Downers Grove, IL. 1961.

Paik, George L. *The History of Protestant Missions in Korea, 1832-1910*. Union Christian Press, Pyongyang, Korea. 1929.

Palmer, Spencer J. *Korea and Christianity*. Holly Corporation Publishers, Seoul, Korea. 1967.

_____. *Confucian Rituals in Korea*. Asian Humanities Press, Berkely, Ca. and Po Chin Chai Ltd. Seoul, Korea. non dated.

_____. *Korean and Christianity: The Problem of Identification with Tradition*, Hollym Cooperation, Seoul, Korea. 1967.

Papers on Philosophy, Religion and Ethic. The 1st International Conference on Korean Studies. The Academy of Korean Studies, Seoul, Korea. 1979.

Park, Choong-chul, ed. *Korean Church and Other Third World Churches*, Presbyterian Seminary, Seoul, Korea. 1984.

Park, H.N. ed. *The Standard Bible Commentary*, Pyengyang Theological Seminary, Seoul, Korea. 1937.

_____. *Proverbs, Ecclesiastics, Song of Solomon*, Pyongyang Theological Seminary, Seoul, Korea. 1937.

Parrinder, Geoffery. *Mysticism in the World's Religions*. Oxford University Press, New York, NY. 1976.

Pattison, Peter. *Crisis Unawareness*, Overseas Missionary Fellowship Press, Robersonia, PA. 1981.

Peters, George W. *Saturation Evangelism*. Zondervan Publishing House, Grand Rapids, MI. 1970.

_____. *Theology of Church Growth*. Zondervan Publishing House, Grand Rapids, MI. 1981.

Phillips, Earl H. Euip-young Yu, eds. *Religions in Korea: Beliefs and Cultural Values*, California State University, Los Angeles, CA. 1982.

Piediscalzi, Nicholas, Robert G. Thobaben. eds. *From Hope to Liberation Toward: A New Marxist Christian Dialogue*. Fortress Press, Philadelphia, PA. 1974.

Pomerville, Paul A. *The Third Force in Missions*. Hendrickson Publishers, Peabody, MASS. 1985.

Prive, L. Shirley. *Confucius and Christ*, Philosophical Library, New York, NY. 1951.

Ray, Benjamin C. *African Religions*. Prentice-Hall, Inc. Engle-Wood,

Cliffs, NJ. 1976.

Reid, Gavin. *The Gagging of God*, Hodder and Stoughton, London, England. 1969.

Reisinger, Ernest C. *Today's Evangelism*. Craig Press, Phillipsburg, NJ. 1982.

Religion in Korea. Seoul, Korea: Korea Overseas Information Service, 1993

Rha, Young-Bok. *An Analysis of the Terms used for God in Korea*, Th.D. Dissertation. Boston University, School of Theology. Boston. MASS. 1977.

Rhi, Ki-Yong. *Buddhism and National Culture in Korea*. First International Conference on Buddhism and National Cultures. New Delhi, India. non dated.

Rhodes, Harry A, and Campell. *A History of the Korean Missions, Presbyterian Church in the U.S.A.1935-1959.Vol.II*. Commission on Ecumenical Mission and Relations, the United Presbyterian Church in the U.S.A. New York, NY. 1964.

Richardson, Don. *Eternity in Their Hearts*. Regal Books, Ventura. CA. 1981.

Ridderbos, Herman. *The Coming of the Kingdom*, The Presbyterian and Reformed Publishing Company, Philadelphia, PA. 1974.

Ripinsky-Naxon, Michel, *The Nature of Shamanism*, State University of New York Press, Albany, NY. 1993.

Robinson, C. H. *History of Christian Missions*, T. & T. Clark, Edinburgh, UK. 1915.

Ro, Bong Rin. ed. *Christian Alternatives to Ancestor Practices*. Asia Theological Association, Taiching, Taiwan. 1985.

_____. Marlin L. Nelson. eds. *Korean Church Growth Explosion*. Word of Life Press, Seoul, Korea. 1983.

Ross, John. *Mission Methods in Manchuria*. Fleming H. Revell Company, New York. NY. 1903.

Rutt, Richard. *James Scarth and His History of the Korean People*. The Royal Asiatic Society, Seoul, Korea. 1972.

Sangster, W. E. *Let Me Command*, Abingdon Press, Nashville, TN. 1948.

Schaff, Phillip. *History of the Christian Church III*, William Eerdmans Publishing Company, Grand Rapids, MI. 1953.

Schaller, Lyle. *Growing Pain*, Abingdon Press, Nashville, TN, 1983.

Schuller, Robert H. *Your Church Has Real Possibilites*. Regal Books, Ventura, CA. 1975.

Scott, Waldron. *Bring Forth Justice*. William B. Eerdmans Publishing Company, Grand Rapids, MI. 1980.

Seo, Kyung-Bo. *A Study of Korean Zen Buddhism Approached through The Chondanjip*. Temple University, Ph.D. 1969. University Microfilms, Inc. Ann Arbor. MI. 1969.

Sharpe, Eric J. *Comparative Religion : A History*. Charles Scribner's Sons, New York, NY. 1975.

Shearer, Roy E. *Wildfire: Church Growth in Korea*. William B. Eerdmans Publishing Company, Grand Rapids, MI. 1966.

Shenk, Wilbert R. ed. *The Challenge of Church Growth*. Herald Press, Scottdale, PA. 1973.

_____. *Exploring Church Growth*. William B. Eerdmans Publishing Company, Grand Rapdis, MI. 1983.

Shin, Sa-hoon. *Paganism and Present-Day Criticism of Our Life Direction*, Kodokyo Munwhasa, Seoul, Korea. 1957.

Shon, Pow-Key, Kim Chol-Choon, Hong Yi-Sup. *The History of Korea*. Korean National Commission for UNESCO, Seoul, Korea. 1970.

_____. *The History of Korea*. Korean National Commission for UNESCO, Seoul, Korea. 1970.

Smalley, William A. ed. *Readings in Missionary Anthropology II*. William Carey Library, South, Pasadena, CA. 1978.

Smith, Eugene L. *God's Mission and Ours*. Abingdon Press, New York, NY. 1961.

Solberg, S. E. *The Land and People of Korea*. J. B. Lippincott Company, Philadelphia and New York. 1966.

Soltau, T. Stanley. *Korea: The Hermit Nation and Its Response to Christianity*. World Dominion Press, London, 1932.

Sookhdeo, Patrick. *New Frontiers in Mission*. Baker Book House, Grand Rapids, MI. 1987.

Song, Yong-jo. *The Holy Spirit and Mission*. D. Miss. Dissertation, Fuller Theological Seminary, Pasadena, CA. 1981.

Soper, Edmund Davision. *The Religions of Mankind*. Abingdon-Cokesbury Press, New York, NY. 1921.

Stewart, J. *Nestorian Missionary Enterprise*. T.T. Clark, Endinburgh, UK. 1928.

Stoke, Chares D. *History of Methodist Missions in Korea: 1885-1930*, Yale University Doctoral Thesis, New Haven, CT. 1947.

Stott, John R. W. *Christian Mission in the Modern World.* InterVarsity Press, Downers Grove, IL. 1977.

Stroup, Herbert. *Founders of Living Religions.* The Westminster Press, Philadelphia. 1974.

Suh, Cheong-Soo, Park Chun-kin. *Aspects of Korean Culture.* Soodo Women's Teacher's College Press, Seoul, Korea. 1974.

Suh, Kuk-Sung, and others. eds. *The Identity of the Korean People.* Research Center for Peace and Unification, Seoul, Korea. 1983.

Sweazey, George E. S. *Effective Evangelism.* Harper and Row Publishers, New York.NY. 1953.

Synna, Vinson. *The Holiness-Pentecostal Movement in the United States.*William B. Eerdmans Publishing Company, Grand Rapids, MI. 1971.

The Commission on Theological Concerns of the Christian Conference of Asia. *Minjung Theology.* Orbis Books, Maryknoll, New York. 1981.

The Continuation Committee Conference in Asia 1912-1923. Published by the Chairman of the Continuation Committee. New York. 1913.

The Humans Rights Situation in North Korea. Seoul, Korea: The Korea Herald Inc., 1992

The Korean National Commission for UNSCO. *Main Current of Korea Thought.* The Isayongosa Publishers, Inc. Seoul, Korea. 1983.

_____. *Korean Folklore.* The Sisayungusa Publishers, Inc, Seoul, Korea. 1983.

The Korean Repository, Vol.II. Jan.-Dec. The Trilingual Press, Seoul, Korea. 1895.

The Korean Repository, Vol.III. Jan.-Dec. 1896. The Trilingual Press, Seoul, Korea. 1896.

Theological Education Fund. *Ministry in Context: The Third Mandate Program of the Theological Education Fund 1970-1977,* T.E.F., Bromley, England. 1972.

Thompason, Lawrence G. *Chinese Religion; An Introduction.* Dickinson Publishing Company, Inc. Belmont, CA. 1969.

Thomas, T. K. ed. *Christianity in Asia.* Published by Christian Conference of Asia, Toa Payoh, Singapore. 1979.

Tillich, Paul, *Christianity and the Encounter of the World Religions*, Columbia University Press, New York, NY. 1963.

Toynbee, Anold. G. *Christianity Among the Religions of the World*, Charles E. Tuttle Company, London, England. 1961.

Underwood, Horace G. *The Call of Korea.* Young People's Missionary Movement of the United States and Canada, New York. Fleming H. Revell Company, New York, NY. 1908.

_____. *Letter to the Board of Foreign Missions of the Presbyterian Church U.S.A.,* The Presbyterian Press, New York, NY. 1887.

_____. *Tragedy and Faith*, Friendship Press, New York, NY. 1951.

_____. *Letters of the Presbyterian Church in the United States of America,* The Presbyterian Historical Society, Philadelphia, PA. 1912.

_____. *The Religions of Eastern Asia*, The Macmillan Co., New York, NY. 1910.

Underwood, L. H. *Fifteen Years among the Top-Knots or Life in Korea.* American Tract Society, New York, NY. 1904.

_____. *Underwood of Korea.* Reprinted by Yonsei University Press, Seoul, Korea. 1983.

Unger, Merrill F. *Demon in the World Today.* Tyndale House Publishers, Wheaton, IL. 1971.

Van Engen, Charles, *The Growth of the True Church.* Rodopi, Amsterdam, The Netherlands. 1981

_____. *God's Missionary People.* Baker Book House, Grand Rapids, MI. 1991.

Vaughan, John N. *The World's 20 Largest Churches.* Baker Book House. Grand Rapids, MI. 1984.

Verkuyl, J. *Contemporary Missiology.* trans. Dale Cooper. William B. Eerdmans Publishing Company, Grand Rapids, MI. 1978.

_____. *The Message of Liberation in Our Age.* trans. Dale Cooper. William B. Eerdmans Publishing Company, Grand Rapids. MI. 1970.

Vicedom, George, *The Mission of God*, Concordia Press, St. Louis, MO. 1965.

Visser't Hooft. W. A. *No Other Name.* SCM Press, London, England. 1963.

Voelkel, Jack. *Student Evangelism in A World of Revolution.* Zondervan Publishing House, Grand Rapids, MI. 1974.

Voskuil, Dennis. *Mountains into Gold Mines*. William B. Eerdmans Publishing Company, Grand Rapids, MI. 1983.

Wagner, Peter. *Your Church Can Grow*. Regal Books, Glendale, CA. 1976.

____. *Church Growth and the Whole Gospel*. Harper and Row, Publishers, San Francisco, CA. 1981.

____. *Leading Your Church to Growth*. Regal Books, Ventura, CA. 1984.

____. *On the Crest of the Wave*. Regal Books, Ventura, CA. 1983.

____. *Your Spiritual Gifts can Help Your Church Growth*. Regal Books, Ventura, CA. 1979.

Walker, Alan. *The New Evangelism*, The Abingdon Press, Nashville, TN. 1975.

Wallace, Anthony F. C. *Religion: An Anthropological View,* Random House Press, New York, NY. 1966.

Walravern, B. Christiaan Alexander. *Muga : The Songs of Korean Shamanism*, Doctoral thesis, Leiden University, unpublished, Leiden, Netherlands. 1985.

Walsh, Roger N. *The Spirit of Shamanism*, Jeremy P. Tarcher, Inc., Los Angeles, CA. 1990.

Warren, Max. *I Believe in the Great Commission*. William B.Eerdmans Publishing Company, Grand Rapids, MI. 1976.

Wasson, Alfred W. *Church Growth in Korea*. International Missionary Council, New York, 1934. Rumford Press, Concord, NH. 1934.

Watson, David. *I Believe in Evangelism*. William B. Eerdmans Publishing Company. Grand Rapids, MI. 1976.

Watts, Allan Willison. *The Ways of Zen*. Vintage Book A Division of Random House. New York, NY. 1957.

Weiss, C. Christian. *The Heart of Missionary Theology*. Moody Press, Chicago, IL. 1976.

Wells, Donald A. *God, Man, and the Thinker*. Random House Inc. New York, NY. 1962.

Wessels, Anton, *Images of Jesus*, tran. John Vriend, William B.Eerdmans Publishing Co., Grand Rapids, MI. 1986.

Williams, F.E.C., Bonwick G. Eds. *The Korean Missions Year Book*. The Christian Literature Society of Korea, Seoul, Korea. 1928.

Wirt, Sherwood Eliot. ed. *Evangelism, the Next Ten Years*. Word

Books Publishers, Waco, TX. 1978.

Wood, A. Skevington. *Evangelism,Its Theology and Practices*, Zondervan Publishing Co., Grand Rapids, MI. 1966.

Yamamoto, J. Isamu. *Beyond Buddhism*. Inter Varsity Press, DownersGrove, IL. 1982.

Yim, Janelli Dawnhee. *Logical Contradictions in Korea Learned Fortunetelling*. Ph.D. Dissertation, University of Pennsylvania. 1977.

Yoo, Boo-Woong. *Korean Pentecostalism : Its His History and Theology*, Verlag Peter Land GmbH, Frankfrut am Main, Germany. 1988.

Young, Babara Elizabeth. *Spirit and other Signs:* Ph.D. University of Washington, Microfilms International, Ann Arbor, MI.1980.

Yun Chi-Ho's Diary: 1903-1906 Vol.6. National History Compilation Committee, Seoul, Korea. 1976.

Minutes, Reports, and Year Books

A Handbook of Korea. Office of Public Information, Seoul, Korea, 1955.

A Handbook of Korea. Korean Overseas Information Service, Seoul, Korea, 1978.

A Handbook of Korea. Korean Overseas Information Service, Seoul, Korea, 1982.

A Handbook of Korea. Korean Overseas Information Service, Seoul, Korea, 1990.

A Handbook of Korea. Korean Overseas Information Service, Seoul, Korea, 1993.

Annual Meetings of the General Council of Protestant EvangelicalMissions in Korea. October, 1909, Seoul, Korea.

Annual Reports of the American Bible Society, 1896-1920, New York. NY.*Annual Reports of Board of Foreign Missions, Methodist Episcopal Church,* New York, NY.

Annual Reports of Board of Foreign Missions, Presbyterian Church in the U.S.A., New York, NY.

Annual Reports of the British and Foreign Bible Society, 1896-1929, The Bible House, London.

Annual Reports on Reforms and Progress in Korea, 1907-1910,

Compiled by H.I.J.M.'s Residency General, Seoul, Korea.

Annual Reports on Reforms and Progress in Chosen, 1910-1922, Compiled by Government-General of Chosen.

Board of Mission of the Netherlands Reformed Church. ed. *Report of the First Consultation of Representative of the Presbyterian Church of Korea(PCK), the Netherlands Reformed Church (NRC) and the Reformed Church in the Netherlands(RCN)*: August 27-30, 1988. Woudschoten, Zeist, Netherlands. Oegstgeest, Netherlands, 1988.

Facts about Korea 1988, Korea Overseas Information Service, Seoul, Korea.

Facts about Korea 1993, Korea Overseas Information Service, Seoul, Korea

International Missionary Council 1938, Madras, India.

Jubilee Paper, Vol. 16, 1934.

Journal of the Korean Conference of the Methodist Episcopal Church, South, 1910-1930, New York, NY.

Korea Annual 1993, Yonhap News Agency, Seoul, Korea.

Methodist Episcopal North Report, 1888, New York, NY.

New Forms of Christian Service and Participation in Korea. The Report of the Consultation held April 13-16, 1962. in *Onyang,* Korea. The committee on Inter-Church Aid and on Church and Society of the East Asia Christian Conference.

Outline of Administrative Reforms in Chosen (Reprinted from "Seoul Press"), Seoul: Seoul Press office, August, 1920.

Report of a Visitation of Korea Mission 1898, New York, NY.

Report of the Conference of Representative Christian Leaders Korea, Seoul, Korea, December 28-29, 1925.

Republic of Korea, Insight Guides, Singapore, 1986.

The Continuation Committee Conference in Asia 1912-1913, New York, NY. The Chairman of the Continuation Committee, 1913.

The Edinburgh Review, Vol. 136, 1872.

The Korea Magazine, 1917-1919, Seoul, Korea.

The Korea Mission Field, 1905-1930, a Monthly Journal issued by the Federal Council of Evangelical Missions in Korea, Seoul, Korea.

The Korea Mission Field, July 1923- September 1927. n.p. Chapter 8.

Yearbook, Board of Missions, Methodist Episcopal Church, South, Nashville, TN: Board of Missions, 1903-1930.

Journals

Acts Theological Journals, Vols. 1-2, 1985-1986.

Asia Theological News, January-March 1982 ff.

Asian Perspective, Vol. 17. n.d.

Christianity Today, Vol. 16, 1972; Vol. XVIII. October, 1973; Vol. 18, November, 1973; Vol. 18, August 1974; Vol. 26, January 1982; Vol. 24, September, 1980.

Church at Home and Abroad, February, 1894.

Church Growth Bulletin, 8, March, 1972. Vol.XIII, No.1. 1976.

CTC Bulletin, Vols. 1-7.

Far Eastern Economic Review, April, 1984 ff.

Gospel in All Lands, April, 1893, September 1894.

Gospel Light, February-March 1983.

International Bulletin, Vols. 1-12.

Korea Journal, Dec. 1972, Vol. II.

Korea Review III (June, 1903).

London Times, 1907.

Moody Monthly, Vol. 74, June, 1974; Vol. 84, Sep. 1983.

National Christian Council Review, Vol. 75, December, 1955.

North East Asia Journal of Theology, 1968 ff.

Presbyterian Survey, Vol. 38, August 1926 ff.

Student World, Vols. 1062, 1908-1969.

The Banner, April 18, 1983.

The Christian Century, Vols. 17 ff, 1900 ff.

The Foreign Missionary, June, 1883., Sep. 1886.

The International Review of Missions, 1912 ff.

The Korea Mission Field, Vols. 2 ff, 1906 ff.

The Korean Repository, Vo. 3, October, 1896 ff.

The Missionary Voice, Vols. 1-21, 1911-1931.

The Missionary Review, May 1885.

The Missionary Review of the World, Vol. 2, No. 4.

Theology Today, Vols. X ff.

The Other Side, Vol. 14, December, 1978.

The United Presbyterian Missionary Record, Oct. 1885. June 1890.

The Westminster Theological Journal, Vols. 24 ff, 1963 ff.

Times, May .1982.

World and Mission, June, 1972- March, 1973.

World Vision, Vol. 12, March 1968.

Articles

Ahn, Byung-mu, "Jesus and the *Minjung* in the Gospel of Mark," *Minjung Theology*, New York, NY: Orbis Books, 1983, pp. 138-155.

____. "The Korean Church's Understanding of Jesus," *International Review of Mission*, Vol. LXXIV. No. 293, January 1985, pp. 82-92.

Allen, H.N. and J.W. Heron, "First Annual Report of the Korean Government Hospital, Seoul," *Journal of Social Science and Humanities*, Dec, 42, The Korea Research Center, Seoul, Korea: 1975, pp. 105-129.

Baird, W. M., "An Address to the Presbyterian Mission on the Million Movement," *The Korean Mission Field*, Vol. 7, No. 11 November 1911.

Barret, David, "The World Religions," *Times,* May, 1982. p. 67.

Barth, Karl, "No Christian Marshall Plan," *Christian Century* Vol.65, no. 49, Dec. 8, 1948. p. 1332.

Bernheisel, C.F. *Letter to the Christian endeavors of Chicago Presbytery*, December 19, 1991.

Blair, H. E., "Fifty Years of Development of the Korean Church," *Jubilee Paper*, Vol. 16, 1934. p. 84.

Bonwick, G. "The Birth of the Korean Religious Tract Society," *The Korea Mission Field*, Vol. 10, No.1, January, 1914.

____. "The Korean Religious Tract Society," *The Korean Repository*, Vol. 3, October, 1896, pp. 413-414.

Brown, A. J., "The Rev. Horace Grant Underwood, D.D.,LL.D.," *The Korea Mission Field*, Vol. 13, No.2, February, 1917. p. 34.

Buruma, Ian, "Phenomenon of the Cross: Confucianist South Korea
    Rapidly Converts to Christianity," *Far Eastern Economic
    Review*, April 19, 1984, p. 54.

Chang, Sue-keun, "*Musok*, the Shaman Culture in Korea," *Folk
    Culture in Korea*, Seoul, International Cultural Foundation, 1974.
    p. 60.

____. "Introduction to Korean Shamanism," Richard W.I.
    Guisso,Chai-shinYu, *Shamanism: The Spirit World of Korea*,
    Berkeley, CA: Asian Humanities Press, 1988, p. 35.

Chang, Yun-shik, "Shamanism as Folk Existentialism," Earl H.
    Phillips, Eui-Young Yu, eds. *Religions in Korea: Beliefs and
    Cultural Values*, California State University, Los Angels, CA. pp.
    27-29.

Cho, David J. "The Growth of Korean Mission and Its Contribution
    to World Evangelization," *Korean Church Growth Explosion
    1884-1984*, Seoul: Word of Life Press, 1983, pp. 103-126.

Cho, Yonggi, "Ministry Through Home Cell Units," *Korean Church
    Growth Explosion 1884-1984*, Ro and Nelson, eds. Seoul: Word
    of Life Press, 1983, pp. 270-289.

Choan Seng-song, "Building a Theological Culture of People," *CTC
    Bulletin*, Vol. 5 No. 3- Vol. 6 No. 1, pp. 16-25.

Choo, Jae-yong, "A Brief Sketch of Korean Christian History from
    the *Minjung* Perspective," *Minjung Theology*, New York, Orbis
    Books, 1983, pp. 73-39.

Chung, Changbok, "Indigenization of Worship: the Holy Dinner,"
    The Northeast Asia Journal of Theology, 18/19 (March-
    September, 1977), p. 50.

Chu, Sun-ae, "Korean Church Growth and Christian Education," Ro
    and Nelson, eds., *Korean Church Growth Explosion*, p. 312.

Chi, Myung-kwan, "Theological Development in Korea,"
    International Review of Mission, Vol. LXXIV. No.293, pp. 75-
    81.

Clowney, Edmund P., "The Missionary Flame of Reformed Theology,
    "*Theological Perspective on Church Growth*, ed., Havie M.
    Conn, The Presbyterian and Reformed Publishing Co., 1976.
    p.141.

Coit, R. T., "What is the Good of a Hospital in Korea?," *Presbyterian
    Survey*, Vol. 38, August 1926, pp. 458-486.

Conn, Havie M., "Studies in the Theology of the Korean Presbyterian
    Church (Part I)," *The Westminster Theological Journal*, Vol.

XXIX, No.1. Nov. 1966, p. 26.

_____."Contextualization: Where Do We Begin?" *Evangelical and Liberation*, ed. Carl E.Armerding, Presbyterian and Reformed Publishing Co., 1977.

_____. "The Exploding Korean Church," *Moody Monthly* 74, June, 1974, p. 24.

Cory, Ralph M. "Korea's First European Visitor," *Some Notes on Father Gregorio Cespedes*, Royal Asiatic Society, Vol. XXVII, 1937, pp. 1-55.

Drooger, Andre, "Syncretism: The Problem of Definition, the Definition of the Problem," Jerald Gort, Hendrik Vroom, Rein Fernhout, and Anton Wessels, eds. *Dialogue and Syncretism*, Grand Rapids, MI: William B. Eerdmans Publishing Co, 1989, pp. 7-22.

Ellinwood, F. F., "Rev. John L. Nevius, D. D.," *Church at Home and Abroad*, February, 1894, pp. 110-112.

Fitch, Geraldine Townsend, "What Happened to the Korean Church," *The Christian Century*, Vol. LXII. No. 39, September 26, 1945. p.16.

Furuyama, Andrew, "Area Report: Japan," David J. Cho, ed., *New Forces in Missions*, Seoul: The East-West Center for MissionResearch and Development, 1976, p. 115.

Gale, James S. "A History of Korea," *The Korean Mission Field*, Vol. 22, No. 9 (Sept. 1926), p. 191; No.8. (Aug. 1926), p. 163. No.10, (Oct. 1926). p. 191.

Genet, Harry, "Big Trouble at the World's Largest Church, *Christianity Today*, Vol. 26, January 22,1982, p. 39.

Graham, Lee, "How the Spirit Came to *Pyongyang*," *The Korean Missions Field* 3, March 1907, pp. 33-37.

Grayson, James H. "Elements of Protestant Accommodation to Korean Religious Culture: A Personal Ethnographic Perspective," *Missiology,* January 1995, pp. 43-59.

Hahm, Pyong-choon, "Shamanism: Foundation of the Korean World-View," Honggoo Lee, SeoungdooYang, Byongie Jon, Chaibong Hahm, eds. *Korean Jurisprudence, policies and Culture*, Seoul, Korea: Yonsei University Press, 1986. p. 333.

Han, Chul-ha, "Involvement of the Korean Church in the Evangelization of Asia," *Korean Church Growth Explosion*, Seoul: Word of Life Press, 1983, pp. 51-68.

Han, Kyung-chik, "The Present and Future of the Korean Church," Ro and Nelson, eds. *Korean Church Growth Explosion*, Seoul: Word of Life Press, 1983, p. 349.

Hanson, Eric O., "South Korea: Cry of the People," *Catholic Politicians in China and Korea*, New York, NY: Orbis Books, 1980, pp. 98-111.

Hollenweger Walter J. "After Twenty Years' Research onPentecostalism, " *International Review of Mission*, Vol. LXXV No. 297, pp.3-12.

_____."Intercultural Theology," *Theology Today*, Vol. XLIII, 1, April 1986.

Hong, Harold S. "General Picture of the Korean Church: Yesterday and Today," *Korean Struggle for Christ*, Seoul: Korean Christian Literature Society, 1973, pp. 13-26.

_____."Social, Political and Psychological Aspects of Church," *Korean Church Growth Explosion*, Seoul: Word of Life Press,1983, pp. 171-185.

Hong, I-seop, "General Remarks on Korean Thought," *Korea: Its Land, People and Culture of All Ages*, Hakwonsa, Seoul, Korea:1960, pp. 316-322.

Humbert, Homer B., "The Korean *Mudang* and *Pansu*," *The Korea Mission Review*, Vol.3., No. 4-9, Grand Rapids, MI. Baker Publishing Co., 1978.

Hunt, Jr. Everett, N. "Mun Sun Myung and Tong-Il" *Dynamic Religious Movements*. Ed. David J. Hesselgraver, Grand Rapdis, MI.Baker Book House, p. 106-107.

Hyun, Young Hak, "Theology as Rumormongering," *CTC Bulletin*, Vol. 5. No.3 -Vol. 6 No.1, pp. 40-48.

_____. "A Theological Look at the Mask Dance in Korea," *Minjung Theology*, New York, Orbis Books, 1983, pp. 47-54.

_____. "Theology of Sweat, Tears, and Laughter," *CTC Bulletin*, Vol. 4, No. 1, 1983, pp. 18-25.

Isabel, S., "A *Mudang*'s Conversion," *The Korea Mission Field*, Vol. III, No. 6, June, 1907, p.86f.

Ji, Won-yong, "Christian Church and Sects," *Korea Struggle for Christ*, Seoul: Korean Christian Literature Society, 1973, pp. 113-132.

Jones, George H., "The Spirit Worship of the Korean," *Transactions of the Korean Branch of the Royal Asiatic Society*, Vol. II, Part 1.

1910. pp. 38-39.

_____. "Mission Work on the *Chemulpo* District," *Gospel in All Lands*, September, 1894.

_____. "The Spirit Worship in Korea," *Royal Asiatic Society*, Vol. II, Seoul, Korea, 1901. pp. 42-43.

Jung, Chang-bok, "Indigenization of Worship: the Holy Dinner," *The Northeast Asia Journal of Theology*, Vol. 18, March-September, 1977.

Kang, Wi-jo, "The Influence of the Unification Church in United States of America," *Missiology*, An International Review, July, 1975, Vol. III. No. 3.

_____. "Conference on North Korea," *Missiology: An International Review*, Vol. 10, October, 1982, pp. 487-88.

Kennedym, Neil L., "Troubled South Koreans Manage a Very Big Bash for Missions," *Christianity Today*, Vol. 24, September 19, 1980, p. 44.

Kim, Byung-suh, "The Explosive Growth of the Korean Church Today: A Sociological Analysis," *International Review of Mission*, Vol. LXXIV, No. 293, Jan, 1985, pp. 61-74.

_____. "Phenomenon of the Cross: Confucianist South Korea Rapidly to Christianity," *Far Eastern Economic Review*, April 19, 1984.

Kim, Chai-chon, "The present Situation and Future Prospect of the Korean Church," *Korea Struggle for Christ*, Seoul: Korean Christian Literature Society, 1973, pp. 27-37.

Kim Chung-chon, "The Church and the Problem of Indigenization," *Korea Struggle for Christ*, Seoul: Korean Christian Literature Society, 1973, pp.101-112.

Kim, Jay-kwon, "The Impact of Mass Communications," Ro and Nelson, eds., *Korean Church Growth Explosion*, p. 143.

Kim, Jong-il, "*Kuts*, the Rituals of *Mudang* An Anthropological Point of View," *ACT Theological Journal*, Vol. 2. pp. 240-274.

Kim, Joon-gon, "Korea's Total Evangelization Movement," *Korea Church Growth Explosion*, Seoul: Word of Life Press, 1983, pp. 17-50.

_____."Six New Churches Everyday: Korean Church Growth," *Asian Perspective*,Vol.17, n.d., pp.1-2.

_____. "How to Spark a Spiritual Explosion," *Asian Theological News* Vol. 9, April-June, 1983, p.17.

Kim, Kwang-il, "*Kut* and the Treatment of Mental Disorder," Richard

Guisso, Chai-shin Yu, eds., *Shamanism:The Spirit World of Korea*, Asian Humanities Press, Berkeley, CA. 1988, p. 132-33.

Kim, Samuel, "Area Report in Korea," David Cho, ed. *New Forces in Missions,* East-West Center for Mission Research and Development, Seoul, Korea: 1976, p. 123.

Kim, Se-yoon, "Christianity and Culture in Korea: Nationalism, Dialogue, Indigenization and Contextualization," *ACT Theological Journal*, Vol. 2, pp. 32-63.

Kim, Sun-do, "Church Growth in Korea, David Cho, ed. *The Third Force,"* East-West Center for Mission Research and Development, Seoul, Korea: 1986, p. 183.

Kim, Yong-bock, "Korea Christianity as a Messianic Movement of the People," *Minjung Theology*, New York: Orbis Books, 1983, pp. 80-122.

____."Theology and the Social Bibliography of the *Minjung*," *CTC Bulletin*, Vol. 5 No. 3 -Vol. 6 No.1, pp. 66-78.

Knox, G. W., "Affairs in Corea," *The Foreign Missionary*, June 1883, p. 17.

Koh, W. Y., "The Missionary Vision of the Korean Church," *Church Growth Bulletin*, Vol. 8, March, 1972.

"Korea: GIs and Jesus," *Christianity Today* Vol. 18, November 9, 1973, p. 60.

Krass, Alfred, "Church Growth and the Methodology of the Kingdom: Reflection on My Personal Search for Direction," *The Other Side*, Vol. 14, no. 12, December 1978, p. 62.

Lash, William, "Reflection on Indigenization," *National Christian Council Review*, Vol 75, No. 12, December, 1955, p. 472.

Lee, Graham, "How the Spirit came to Pyongyang," *The Korean Mission Field*, Vol. 3, No.3, 1907, pp. 33-37.

Lee, Ki-yong, "Background of Sects," *New World*, February, 1964.

Lee, Won-sul, "Korean Church in Historical Perspective," *Gospel Light*, February-March 1983, p. 9.

Lee, Youn-ok, "The Role of Women in Korean Church," Ron and Nelson, eds. *Korean Church Growth Explosion*, Word of Life Press, Seoul, 1983.

"Local Churches win University Students," *Asian Theological News*, Vol. 8, Jan-March, 1982, p. 16.

Loomis, H., "The First Korean Protestant in Japan," *The Korea Mission Field*, July, 1937, pp. 139-41.

Maclay, R. S., "Commencement of the Korean Methodist Episcopal Mission," *The Gospel in All Lands*, August, 1885, p. 328.

Min, Kyung-bae, "The Korean Church and Mysticism," *Christian Thoughts*, Seoul, Korea: Christian Literature Society, 1971, p. 170.

Moffet, Samuel H., "What Makes the Korean Church Grow?," *Christianity Today*, Vol. 18, November 23, 1973, p. 11.

Moon, Hee-suk, "An Old Testament understanding of *Minjung*," *Minjung Theology*, New York: Orbis Books, 1983, pp.123-137.

Moon, Sang-hee, "Shamanism and the Mental Structure of Koreans," *Aspects of Korean Culture*, Seoul: Soods Women's Teaching College Press, 1974, p. 183.

_____. "Shamanism in Korea," *Korean Thoughts*, Seoul: International Cultural Foundation, 1979. p. 27.

_____."Fundamental Doctrines of the New Religions in Korea," *Korean Christian Academy*, Seoul: Korean Christian Academy Publishers, 20, Nov., 1971, p. 14.

Moore, S. F. "An Epock- Making Conference in Korea," *The Mission Review of World,* Vol. 18, No. 9, September, 1905, pp. 689-692.

Moosem J. R. "A Great Awakening," *The Korean Mission Field*, Vol. 2, No. 3, 1907, pp. 51-58.

Morris, C. D., "Division of the Territory between the Presbyterian and Methodist Missions, *The Korean Mission Field*, Vol. 19, No.1, Jan. 1914, p. 18-19.

_____. "Agreement on Division of Territory, "*Annual Meetings of the General Council of Protestant Evangelical Missions in Korea*, Oct., 1909, pp. 32-34.

Mulder, Dirk C., "Dialogue and Syncretism: Some Concluding Observations," Jerald Gort, Hendirk Vroom, Rein Fernhout, and Anton Wessels, eds. *Dialogue and Syncretism*, William B. Eerdmans Publishing Co.,Grand Rapids, MI: 1989, pp. 203-206.

Mun, Dong-whan, "Liberation Theology and Christian Education," *World and Mission*, June,1972 - March, 1973, pp. 24-33.

"Native Bible Women," *The Korean Mission Field*, Vol, VII. No.5, June, 1910, pp. 119ff.

Nelson, Marilin L. "Some Strategies for the Evangelization of Asia," *ACTS Theological Journal*, Vol. 2, pp. 212-239.

_____. "Korea Church Mission Growth," Ro and Nelson, eds. *Korean Church Growth Explosion*, Seoul: Word of Life Press, 1983, pp. 88-102.

_____. "Foreigner's View of the Korean Church," Ro and Nelson, eds. *Korean Church Growth Explosion*, Seoul: Word of Life Press, 1973. p. 192.

Oh, M. W., Two Visits of the Rev, R.J. Thomas to Korea, " *A Transaction of the Royal Asiatic Society*, Korean Branch, Vol. XXI. p.104.

Oh, Pyeng-seh, "Keeping the Faith Pure," Ro and Nelson, eds. *Korean Church Growth Explosion*, Seoul: Word of Life Press, 1973, p. 220.

_____. "Theological Education and Rapid Church Growth in Korea," *Asian Theological News*, Vol. 7 July-September 1981, p. 12.

Okmoto, R., "Japan," *Look*, September 10, 1963,

_____."Fanning the Fire of a Fervent Faith," *The Asia Magazine*, October, 18, 1964,

Orr, J., "The Gospel in Corea," *The United Presbyterian Missionary Record*, June 2, 1890, p. 188.

Oswalt, John N., "Bishall," R. Laid Harries, et, al., *Theological Wordbook of the Old Testament*, Vol.I., The Moody Bible Institute, Chicago, IL. 1980, p. 135.

Packer, J. I., "What is Evangelism,?" Harvie M. Conn, *Theological Perspective on Church Growth*, The Presbyterian and Reformed Publishing Co., Nutley, NJ, 1976. pp. 94-97.

Palau, Louis, "City-wide Crusade Evangelization," J. D. Douglas, ed., *Let The Earth Hear His Voice*, Worldwide Publications, Minneapolis, MN. 1975, p. 602.

Park, Bong-bae, "Christianity and Ancestor Worship," Harold Hong, et.al. eds. *Church and Mission in Korea*, Seoul: Christian Literature Society, pp. 201.

Park, Bong-rang, "A Theological Approach to the Understanding of the Indigenization of Christianity," *The North East Asia Journal of Theology*, September, 1969, pp. 107-108.

Park, Hyung-kyu, "The Search for self-identity and Liberation," *International Review of Mission*, Vol.LXXIV, No, 293, pp. 38-50.

Park, Keun-won, Evangelism and Mission in Korea: A Reflection from an Ecumenical Perspective," *International Review of Mission*, Vol. LXXIV, No. 293, pp. 51-60.

Park, U. U. Paul, "A Study on the Relation of Shamanism to other Religion," *Korean Religions*, Vol. II. Jan. 1970. p. 1.

Recker, Robert. "The Redemptive Focus of the Kingdom of God," *Calvin Theological Journal* 14, 1979. pp. 154-186.

"Religion in Transit," *Christianity Today*, Vol. 18, November, 9, 1973. p. 40.

"Revival in Indochina: Action in the Far East," *Christianity Today*, Vol. 16, May, 1972, pp. 32-33.

Reynold, W. D, "The Native Ministry," *The Korean Repository*, Vol. III, May, 1896, p. 201.

_____. "Fifty Years of Bible Translation and Revision," *The Korean Mission Field*, Vol. 35, No. 6, June, 1936, p. 172.

_____. "The Board of Bible Translators," *The Korean Mission Field*, Vol. 2, No.6, April, 1906, p. 101.

Rhee, Song-nei, "Church Growth in Confucian Stronghold," *Church Growth Bulletin*, Vol. 10, May, 1974, p. 419.

Ro,Bong-rin, "Do Theological School Help Local Churches?," *Asia Theological News*, January-March, 1982. p. 4.

Ross, J., "A Bright Light in Northern Korea, *Foreign Missionary*, September 1886, pp. 151-152.

_____. "Corean Converts," *The Missionary Review*, May 1885, p. 207-209.

Ryu, Tong-shik, "The Religions of Korea and the personality of Koreans," *Korea Struggle for Christ*, Seoul: Korean Christian Literature Society, 1973, pp. 133-147.

_____. "Shamanism: the Dominant Folk Religion in Asia, "the inter-religious Conference held at Ecumenical Center in Hong Kong, September, 13-17, 1983.

_____. "Rough Road to Theological Maturity," Gerald H. Anderson, ed., *Asian Voices in Christian Theology*, New York, NY: Orbis Book, 1976, p. 173.

Schrotenboer, Paul, and Bernice, "Growth Dangers in Korean Church," *The Banner*, Vol. 118, April, 18, 1983, p. 6.

Scranton, M. F., "Days Schools and Bible," *The Korea Mission Field*, Vol. III., No. 4, April 1907, p. 53.

Sharp, C.E. "Motives for Seeking Christ," *The Korea Mission Field*, Vol. 2, No. 10, 1906, pp. 357-364.

Sharp Nigel, "Palau and Graham Rekindle Flame of Revival in England," *Christianity Today*, Vol. 28, February 17, 1984, p. 35.

Smith, Harold B., Myung-hyuk Kim, "Will Success Spoil the South

Korean Church," *Christianity Today,* Nov. 20, 1987, p. 34.

Smith, John C., "Policy Lessons from Korea," *The International Review of Missions,* Vol. 50. July 1961, p. 320-323.

Son, Bong-ho, "Some danger of Rapid Growth, " *Korean Church Growth Explosion,* Seoul: Word of Life Press, 1983, pp. 333-347.

Song, Kon-ho, "A History of the Christian Movement in Korea," *International Review of Mission,* Vol. LXXIV, No. 293, pp. 20-37.

Suh, Kwang-sun, "A Biographical Sketch of an Asian Theological Consultation," *Minjung* Theology, New York: Orbis Books, 1983, pp. 6-19.

____. "American Missionaries and a Hundred Years of Korean Protestantism," *International Review of Mission,* Vol. LXXIV. No. 293, pp. 6-19

____. "Called to Witness to the Gospel Today: The Priesthood of *Han,*" *CTC Bulletin,* Vol. 5 No. 3 -Vol. 6 No.1, pp. 57-65.

____. "Korean Theological Development in the 1970s, "*Minjung Theology,* New York: Orbis Books, 1983, pp. 38-46.

____. "*Minjung* Theology and Theology in Korea: A Biographical Sketch of an Asian Theological Consultation," Kim, Yong-bock, ed. *Minjung Theology,* Singapore: The Christian Conference of Asia, 1981, p. 13.

Suh, Nam-dong, "Cultural Theology, Political Theology and *Minjung* Theology," *CTC Bulletin,* Vol. 5, No. 3 -Vol. 6 No. 1, pp. 12-14.

____. "Theology as Story-telling: A Counter-theology," *CTC Bulletin,* Vol. 5 No. 3 -Vol. 6 No. 1, pp. 4-11.

____. "Towards a Theology of *Han,*" *Minjung Theology,* New York: Orbis Books, 1983, pp. 55-72

Swallen, W. L., "God's Work of Grace continued in Pyongyang Korea," *The Korean Mission Field,* Vol. 3, No. 5, May 1907, pp. 2-11.

Sweazey, George E., "Evangelization Among the Secondary School Students," J. D. Douglas, ed., *Let the Earth Hear His Voice,* Worldwide Publication, Minneapolis, MN. 1975. p. 759.

Sweeting, George, "Land of the Morning Calm," *Moody Monthly* Vol.,84, September 1984, p. 91.

Synder, H. A., "Misunderstanding Spiritual Gifts," *Christianity Today,* XVIII:1, October 12, 1973, pp.15-18.

Tabor, Charles R., "Missiology and the Bible," *Missiology* II, April,

1983, p. 235.

Tippett, Alan R. "The Evangelization of Animists," J.D. Douglas, ed. *Let the Earth Hear His Voice*, Worldwide Publications, Minneapolis, MN. 1975, p. 848.

Town, Elmer, "The Largest Little Church in the World," *Church Growth Bulletin*, Vol.XIII, No.1, 1976, p. 83.

Underwood, G. Horace, "Korean Missionaries Incoming and Outgoing," *Letters of the Presbyterian Church in the United States of America,* February 8, 1888, p. 128.

____. "Mr. Underwood's Letter from Seoul, Dec. 23, 1883," *The Missionary Review of the World*, New York, NY: Northern Presbyterian Church, Vol.w, No. 4, April, 1889, pp. 288-289.

____. "Division of the Field," *The Korean Mission Field*, Vol.5, No. 12, Dec.1909, p. 211.

Van Halsema, Dick L. "Korea Impression," *Missionary Monthly*, Nov. 1983, p. 2.

Young, John M. L., "The Place and Importance of Numerical Church Growth," Harvie Conn,ed., *Theological Perspective on Church Growth*, Presbyterian and Reformed Publishing Co., Philadelphia, PA. 1976. pp. 57-73.

Ward, Larry, "Dr. Han Kyungjik, Korea's Quiet Dynamo," *World Vision*, 12. March, 1968, pp. 16-19.

Webster, J., "Journey to the *Corean* Valley," *The United Presbyterian Mission Record*, Oct.1885, p. 321-326.

Wimber, John, "Signs and Wonders in the Growth of the Church," C. Peter Wagner, *Church Growth, State of Art*, Wheaton, IL: Tyndale House Publishing Co., 1986, p. 216.

Winter, Ralph D. "Quality or Quantity," *Crucial Issues in Missions Tomorrow*, ed. Donald McGavran, Chicago, IL. Moody Press, 1974, p. 235-238.

"World Scene," *Christianity Today*, Vol. 18, August 30, 1974. p. 44.

Yi, Pu-yong, "A Psychological Study on the New Religion," *Korea Journal*, Dec. 1972, Vol II, No. 12, p. 24. 1972.

Yim, Dawnhee J., "Faith, Fortunetelling, and Social Failure," Earl H. Phillips, Eui-Young Yu, eds., *Religions in Korea: Beliefs and Cultural Values*, California State University, Los Angeles, CA. 1982, p. 71-62.

INDEX OF AUTHORS